The Peasant Rebellions of the Late Ming Dynasty

MONOGRAPHS AND PAPERS OF THE ASSOCIATION FOR ASIAN STUDIES

I. *Money Economy in Medieval Japan,* by Delmer M. Brown, Locust Valley, New York: J. J. Augustin, 1951. $2.50
II. *China's Management of the American Barbarians,* by Earl Swisher. J. J. Augustin, 1951. $7.50
III. *Leadership and Power in the Chinese Community of Thailand,* by G. William Skinner. Cornell University Press, 1958. $6.50
IV. *Siam Under Rama III,* 1824-1851, by Walter F. Vella. J. J. Augustin, 1957. $5.00
V. *The Rise of the Merchant Class in Tokugawa Japan:* 1600-1868, by Charles David Sheldon. J. J. Augustin, 1958. $5.00
VI. *Chinese Secret Societies in Malaya,* by L. F. Comber. J. J. Augustin, 1959. $6.50
VII. *The Traditional Chinese Clan Rules,* by Hui-chen Wang Liu. J. J. Augustin, 1959. $5.50
VIII. *A Comparative Analysis of the Jajmani System,* by Thomas O. Beidelman. J. J. Augustin, 1959. $2.50
IX. *Colonial Labour Policy and Administration,* by J. Norman Parmer. J. J. Augustin, 1959. $6.00
X. *Bankguad—A Community Study in Thailand,* by Howard Keva Kaufman. J. J. Augustin: 1959. $5.50
XI. *Agricultural Involution: The Processes of Ecological Change in Indonesia,* by Clifford Geertz. The University of California Press. 1963. $4.00
XII. *Maharashta Purana,* by Edward C. Dimock, Jr., and Pratul Chandra. Honolulu: The East-West Center Press, 1964. $5.00
XIII. *Conciliation in Japanese Legal Practice,* by Dan Fenno Henderson. The University of Washington Press, 1964.
XIV. *The Malayan Tin Industry to 1914,* by Wong Lin Ken. The University of Arizona Press, 1965. $6.50
XV. *Reform, Rebellion, and the Heavenly Way,* by Benjamin F. Weems. The University of Arizona Press, 1964. $3.75
XVI. *Korean Literature: Topics and Themes,* by Peter H. Lee. The University of Arizona Press, 1965. $3.75
XVII. *Ch'oe Pu's Diary: A Record of Drifting Across the Sea,* by John Meskill. The University of Arizona Press, 1965. $4.50
XVIII. *The British in Malaya: The First Forty Years,* by K. G. Tregonning. The University of Arizona Press, 1965. $4.50
XIX. *Chiaraijima Village: Land Tenure, Taxation, and Local Trade,* by William Chambliss. The University of Arizona Press, 1965. $5.00
XX. *Shinran's Gospel of Pure Grace,* by Alfred Bloom. The University of Arizona Press, 1965. $5.00
XXI. *Before Aggression: Europeans Prepare the Japanese Army,* by Ernst L. Presseisen. The University of Arizona Press, 1965. $5.00
XXII. *A Documentary Chronicle of Sino-Western Relations:* 1644-1820, by Lo-shu Fu. The University of Arizona Press, 1966. xviii + 792 pp. $14.50
XXIII. *K'ang Yu-Wei: A Biography and a Symposium,* edited by Lo Jung-pang. The University of Arizona Press, 1967. 541 pp. $14.50
XXIV. *The Restoration of Thailand Under Rama I:* 1782-1809, by Klaus Wenk. The University of Arizona Press, 1968. 150 pp. $7.50
XXV. *Political Centers and Cultural Regions in Early Bengal,* by Barrie M. Morrison. The University of Arizona Press, 1969. $7.50
XXVI. *The Peasant Rebellions of the Late Ming Dynasty,* by James Bunyan Parsons. The University of Arizona Press, 1969. $7.50

The Association for Asian Studies: Monographs and Papers, No. XXVI
Paul Wheatley, Editor

THE PEASANT REBELLIONS
OF
THE LATE MING DYNASTY

by JAMES BUNYAN PARSONS

Published for the Association for Asian Studies by

THE UNIVERSITY OF ARIZONA PRESS
TUSCON   ARIZONA

About the Author...

JAMES BUNYAN PARSONS' research on peasant rebellions of the Ming period has been pursued both in the United States and the Far East. Parsons began graduate work in Chinese history at the University of California, then held a Fulbright fellowship to China for study at the College of Chinese Studies in Peking, followed by a year of special studies at Yenching University. In 1957-58, he did further research at the Institute of Humanistic Sciences in Kyoto on a Social Science Research Council grant, and again in 1960-61 at the Academica Sinica in Taiwan. Parsons received his Ph.D. at Berkeley in 1954 and joined the faculty at the University of California, Riverside, a base from which he has frequently traveled for research in the Far East and visiting professorships in the U.S. He has been a member of several conferences and panels in the United States, Canada, and England on Chinese historiography and the government of the Ming dynasty.

Publication of this volume has been
made possible by a generous grant to
the Association for Asian Studies
by the Ford Foundation

THE UNIVERSITY OF ARIZONA PRESS

Copyright © 1970
The Arizona Board of Regents
All Rights Reserved
Manufactured in the U.S.A.

S. B. N. 8165-0155-6
L. C. No. 68-9341

To P.W.O. in spite of whom this book was written, and to F.M. who will find what follows quite irrelevant

Acknowledgments

I wish to recognize with gratitude the valuable advice given during the initial period of my research on the late Ming peasant rebellions by Professors Woodbridge Bingham, Wolfram Eberhard, and Joseph Levenson of the University of California and by the late Professor Teng Chih-ch'eng of Yenching University. I am also grateful for the research assistance supplied by Mr. Ch'i Hsia and Mr. Edward Hsin-tsu Ch'ien. Finally, I express my appreciation for the pre-publication financial support provided by the Academic Senate of the University of California, Riverside, the Haynes Foundation, and the Fulbright program, and to The Association for Asian Studies through which publication has been effected.

Contents

Introduction xiii
- I: The Background and Beginning Years of the Late Ming Peasant Rebellions (1627-31) 1
  - Background of the Rebellions. 1
  - Launching of the Rebellions 4
  - Yang Ho and the Policy of Peaceful Settlement . 8
  - The Pre-rebel Lives of Chang Hsien-chung and Li Tzu-ch'eng and the Launching of their Rebel Careers. 16
  - Review of the 1627-31 Period of the Rebellions . . 20
- II: The Disorganized Raiding Phase of the Rebellions, Part I: The Expansion and Initial Climax of the Peasant Uprisings (1631-36) 22
  - Appointment of Hung Ch'eng-ch'ou to Head the Rebel-suppression Campaign 22
  - Eastward Shift of the Rebellions 26
  - The Focal Area of the Rebellions Shifts to the South and West 32
  - The Jung-yang Conclave and the Attempt at Rebel Unity 36
  - The Rebels Return to Disunity 40
  - Li Tzu-ch'eng in Shensi. 43
  - General Assessment of the 1631-36 Period of the Rebellions. 46
- III: The Disorganized Raiding Phase of the Rebellions, Part II: The Temporary Decline of the Rebellions, their Resurgence, and the Failure of the Government's Last Chance for Suppression (1636-41). . . 53
  - Rise of Yang Ssu-ch'ang to Power 53
  - Rebel Operations during 1637. 57
  - Defeat and Surrender of Chang Hsien-chung. . . 60
  - Activities of Other Rebel Groups during 1638 . . 64

CONTENTS

The Nadir of the Rebellions and the Increase of Manchu Pressure. 66
Revival of the Rebellions and Yang Ssu-ch'ang's Assumption of the Field Command against the Rebels 68
The Anti-rebel Campaign of Yang Ssu-ch'ang . . 71
Li Tzu-ch'eng Moves into Honan 81
Death of Yang Ssu-ch'ang 82
General Assessment of the 1636-41 Period of the Rebellions. 83

IV: The Dynastic Ambitions Phase of the Rebellions: Li Tzu-ch'eng's Drive to Peking and Chang Hsien-chung's Power Centers in Hukuang and Szechwan (1641-44) 90
Li Tzu-ch'eng in Honan (1641) 90
Li Tzu-ch'eng Moves toward Enhanced Power in Honan (1642) 96
Li Tzu-ch'eng in Hukuang (1643) 106
Peking's Last Attempts to Organize Resistance to Li Tzu-ch'eng. 113
The Struggle between Li Tzu-ch'eng and Sun Ch'üan-t'ing for Mastery of Honan 117
Li Tzu-ch'eng Seizes Control of Shensi 120
Li Tzu-ch'eng's Drive to Peking 123
Li Tzu-ch'eng in Peking 132
The Activities of Chang Hsien-chung and Minor Rebel Groups in 1641 142
Chang Hsien-chung in Nan-chihli (1642) . . . 145
Chang Hsien-chung's Power Center in Hukuang . 149
Transfer of Chang Hsien-chung's Power Center to Szechwan 156

V: The Collapse of the Rebellions (1644-46) . . . 161
Retreat of Li Tzu-ch'eng from Peking to Sian . . 161
Final Months of Li Tzu-ch'eng 164
Chang Hsien-chung and the Establishment of the Rebel Regime at Chengtu 167
Expansion of Chang's Area of Control in Szechwan 171
Development of Opposition to Chang in Szechwan 173
Adoption of Terroristic Policies by Chang's Chengtu Regime 176

	Abandonment of Chengtu by Chang Hsien-chung and His Eventual Fate	179
VI:	Specialized Aspects of the Rebellions	186
	The Problem of Statistics	186
	Elements of Religion and Superstition in the Late Ming Rebellions	189
	The Concept of Patriotism as Expressed by Opponents of the Rebels	200
	Rebel Leadership and Relations with the Gentry	206
	Relations between the Rebels and the General Populace	216
	Rebel Organization	222
	Military Aspects of the Rebellions	228
	The Rebellions and the Northern Frontier	245
	A Summary Assessment of Li Tzu-ch'eng and Chang Hsien-chung	247
	Varying Interpretations of the Rebellions	252
Conclusion		256
Appendixes		261
1.	Rebel nicknames (with translations)	261
2.	Names of persons	266
3.	Names of places	268
4.	Miscellaneous entries	270
Notes to Chapters		273
Bibliography		279
Index		283

Maps

1.	Locations of Peasant Rebel Activity in 1628	3
2.	Locations of Peasant Rebel Activity in 1629	7
3.	Locations of Peasant Rebel Activity in 1630	9
4.	Locations of Peasant Rebel Activity in 1631	13
5.	Locations of Peasant Rebel Activity in 1632	25
6.	Locations of Peasant Rebel Activity in 1633	27
7.	Locations of Peasant Rebel Activity in 1634	31
8.	Locations of Peasant Rebel Activity in 1635	37
9.	Locations of Peasant Rebel Activity in 1636	45
10.	Locations of Peasant Rebel Activity in 1637	59

11. Locations of Peasant Rebel Activity in 1638 61
12. Locations of Peasant Rebel Activity in 1639 67
13. Locations of Peasant Rebel Activity in 1640 73
14. Locations of Peasant Rebel Activity in 1641 79
15. Locations of Peasant Rebel Activity in 1642 84
16. The Late Ming Peasant Rebellions, 1628-36 86
17. The Late Ming Peasant Rebellions, 1636-41 87
18. Li Tzu-ch'eng, 1641-45 91
19. Chang Hsien-chung, 1642-44 143
20. Chang Hsien-chung in Szechwan, 1644-47. 155

Introduction

Particularly difficult problems began accumulating for the Ming dynasty during the late sixteenth century, making their presence especially apparent during the last three decades of the reign of the corpulent and eccentric Wan-li Emperor (1572-1620). One of the problems was the decline in the stability and efficiency of the Wan-li bureaucracy, particularly at the level of the central government. The decline is attributable most immediately to the actions of the Emperor who, by the 1590's, had adopted an almost Taoistic non-action attitude toward the processes of government. He secluded himself within the palace for years and refused to hold audiences with the officials or perform any of the numerous ceremonial duties connected with the imperial position. During these long periods of seclusion, the functioning of the administration proceeded in a decidedly haphazard and chaotic fashion. The Emperor would meet individual officials upon rare occasions for discussions of state problems, but, for the most part, communication between the Emperor and the officials was conducted via eunuch messengers. Such an indirect means of contact functioned so ineffectively that decisions on even important matters were delayed for extended periods and high offices were allowed to remain vacant indefinitely.

Financial problems also became increasingly serious during the Wan-li period, due in part to extravagant imperial expenditures in constructing palaces, in providing lavish support for the Emperor's sons who were appointed district princes, and in observing elaborate ceremonies in honor of various members of the imperial family. A more important source of the financial difficulty was the crisis on the northeastern frontier which produced a combination of military, economic, and political problems.

The northeastern frontier crisis developed gradually during the last two decades of the 1500's and the first decade and a half of the 1600's. It was produced by the successes achieved by ·Nuerhaci in consolidating the tribal groups on the eastern border of the Chinese enclave into an effective federation which was eventually to adopt for itself the name "Manchu." Nuerhaci's encroachment on the Chinese sphere in Manchuria began in 1618 when the city of Fu-shun fell to his forces which, in the following year, captured K'ai-yüan as well. In attempting to recoup these losses, the Chinese commander suffered a disastrous defeat and the drain of Ming resources to the northeast began.

The need of supporting vastly intensified military activity in Manchuria necessitated increasing the land tax rate three years in succession (1618, 1619, and 1620). These increases were destined to be the first in an unfortunate series, subsequent ones occurring in 1630, 1632, 1634, and 1636. The total effect of all the increases between 1618 and 1636 was to double the tax rate. How much additional revenue the increases actually produced is highly questionable. Certainly the revenue never remotely approached being doubled.

The death of the Wan-li Emperor in the late summer of 1620 brought to the throne the dissolute Heir Apparent who reigned for less than two months as the T'ai-ch'ang Emperor. His chief contribution to the dynasty was the intensification of political in-fighting caused by the manner of his death. He died after having taken a type of medicine of which the efficacy was in dispute, and the suspicion arose that he might have been poisoned.

The unfortunately low quality of Ming imperial leadership persisted following the death of the T'ai-ch'ang Emperor and the accession of his teenage son who reigned as the T'ien-ch'i Emperor and was destined to become the most pathetic of all the Ming rulers. The new Emperor was not vicious and depraved, a Chinese Nero, but was simply limited mentally. Thus, it was obviously necessary for someone to arise and exercise the power which the Emperor was incapable of wielding personally.

The contest for control of the imperial power was dominated by two groups: the Tung-lin faction among the regular bureaucracy and an inner palace faction headed by a eunuch, Wei Chung-hsien, and the Emperor's nurse, Mme. K'o. The Tung-lin faction had some two decades of political experience behind it and regarded itself as a reform movement with a basis in Confucian-oriented morality. Faced now with the possibility of real influence and power, it proved incapable of consolidating its position and of formulating an effective program. Gradually the advantage slipped to Wei Chung-hsien who first assured his dominance within the palace by eliminating the eunuch, Wang An, who had formerly exercised the controlling influence. Wang's moderate position would have made possible an alliance with the Tung-lin in a joint wielding of power. Following the death of Wang, Wei displayed a masterful sense of political timing while undermining the political foundations of the Tung-lin. Realizing that an attempt at a rapid overthrow of the Tung-lin probably would have produced a reaction sufficiently strong to destroy him, Wei proceeded slowly and cautiously. Initially he took action against only minor figures associated with the Tung-lin and not until 1625 did he arrest and execute the principal leaders, eliminating Tung-lin influence completely.

After the Tung-lin collapse, Wei Chung-hsien attained a virtually unchallenged position which he maintained for two years and became the most powerful of the four eunuch strongmen who dominated the government at various times during the Ming dynasty. He packed offices with his favorites, accumulated a vast fortune through graft, piled honors and rewards on members of his family, encouraged sycophants to render him the most extravagant adulation, squandered the resources of the government, and generally demoralized the bureaucracy.

The drastic deterioration in the Ming position in Manchuria during the first two years of the T'ien-ch'i period (1621-22) affords the most striking evidence of the paralysis, irresponsibility, and incompetence which had descended upon the administration in Peking. It was during these years that the Manchus erased Ming control from the region east of the Liao River with the exception of Lu-shun-k'ou which held out until 1625. Also, the Manchus began the seizure of the area west of the Liao, Kuang-ning falling to them in 1622. These losses suffered by the Ming were destined to be permanent and Wei Chung-hsien accomplished substantially nothing to better the Ming cause in Manchuria following his final breakthrough to power in 1625.

When the Ch'ung-chen Emperor came to the throne in the summer of 1627, he found himself faced with a situation sufficiently dire to make one almost willing to accept the portents of doom. Most immediately pressing was the question of the fate of Wei Chung-hsien, an issue which was rather quickly resolved, though initially the path toward the resolution took a somewhat indirect course in accordance with the rhythm of many events in traditional Chinese politics. Wei was retained in the palace for some three months following the new Emperor's enthronement and was then exiled to Feng-yang. Realizing that exile was merely the first step toward his complete ruin, Wei committed suicide enroute to Feng-yang. Mme. K'o was executed shortly thereafter.

The elimination of Wei Chung-hsien in itself obviously could not solve the more basic problem of bureaucratic demoralization and loss of effectiveness. Thus, though Wei's downfall rid the government of a positive evil, no substitute was destined to be found who could provide the central administration with an adequate reform program and vigorous leadership. The crisis on the northeastern frontier remained and the new reign almost immediately witnessed the initial phases of another equally serious threat which began to confront the dynasty internally: peasant rebellion. The history of that peasant rebellion will be considered in the following chapters.

Chapter I

The Background and Beginning Years of the Late Ming Peasant Rebellions (1627-31)

Background of the Rebellions

Northern Shensi has played a key role upon several occasions in crucial Chinese historical developments. Most recently, in the 1930's and 1940's, it was the base area for the Chinese Communists. Its part in the downfall of the Ming three centuries earlier was almost as significant, northern Shensi being the region where the peasant movements began and gained the momentum which the Ming authorities never succeeded in halting completely.

The peasant uprisings originated in northern Shensi for a variety of reasons. Perhaps most immediately basic of all were the limitations of geography: uncertain rainfall, difficult communications, and a limited amount of arable land. The resulting socio-economic conditions meant that the area was a backwater, touched only indirectly, if at all, by the significant developments taking place in more favored sections of China. It experienced nothing of the prosperity of the lower Yangtze Valley where there was a growth of agricultural techniques, increasingly sophisticated handicraft production, and the expansion of a money economy. The northern Shensi area did possess an economic advantage in having one of the several horse markets which the central government consented to open as part of the peace settlement made with the Mongol prince, Anda, in 1571.[1] However, it is doubtful that the area benefitted very directly from the operation of the market. Probably outside interests reaped most of the profits, and in fact the region generally seems to have been economically subservient to outside interests with Shansi merchants apparently being the single most important group. Livelihood in the region approached the bare subsistence level and it lacked the surplus stores of grain which wealthy areas hoarded during years of plentiful harvests and used when less favorable times occurred. As a consequence, it was particularly vulnerable to natural calamities and the resulting famines.

Political and military conditions exaggerated potential troubles inherent in the geographical milieu and economic situation. There is virtual unanimity in the sources attesting to the fact that northern Shensi was misruled and "underruled" during the 1620's. The Grand Coordinator* for the special district in northern Shensi during the T'ien-ch'i period, Chu T'ung-meng, together with the Grand Coordinator for the rest of the province, Ch'iao Ying-chia, had been particularly closely identified with the notorious eunuch strongman, Wei Chung-hsien. They had been extremely lax about maintaining an effective administration and a proper state of preparedness in the armed forces, being far more interested in flattering their master in Peking by sending him funds to promote his program of palace construction even if this meant cutting down on military supplies.[2]

Much more important than these individual examples of rather transitory misrule at the top was the continuing situation at the prefectural, subprefectural, and county levels of administration. There is evidence to suggest that many offices at the subprefectural and county levels remained unoccupied, due probably to the inefficiency of the Ministry of Personnel and to the dislike which potential officials had for service in a remote and backward area. A modern scholar has estimated that as many as one-half of such offices were unfilled, seriously hampering the effectiveness of crucial administrative units.[3] To compound the local political instability, there was a decline in the quality of local officials, particularly at the prefectural level.** For example, nine officials served as Magistrate of Yenan Prefecture in crucial northern Shensi during the T'ien-ch'i (1621-27) and Ch'ung-chen (1628-44) periods, and only two of them held the *chin-shih* degree. Six were *chü-jen* and one held a lower degree. This compares very unfavorably with earlier periods: in the Chia-ching (1522-66) and Lung-ch'ing (1567-72) eras, all sixteen occupants of the office were *chin-shih;* and in Wan-li (1573-1620), ten were *chin-shih* and three were *chü-jen.* Given the great prestige attending the holding of a *chin-shih* degree, it would be logical to assume that holders of lower degrees would be hampered in their effectiveness while serving

---

* Translations of official titles generally follow Charles O. Hucker, "Governmental Organization of the Ming Dynasty," *HJAS* XXI (1958).

** James B. Parsons, "The Ming Dynasty Bureaucracy: Aspects of Background Forces," *Monumenta Serica* XXII (1963), 393-394. A survey of the magistrates in 136 of the 159 Ming prefectures reveals that only forty-five percent of them during the Ch'ung-chen reign period (1628-44) were holders of the *chin-shih* degree. This is the lowest percentage for the entire dynasty.

MING DYNASTY PEASANT REBELLIONS

1 LOCATIONS OF PEASANT REBEL ACTIVITY IN 1628

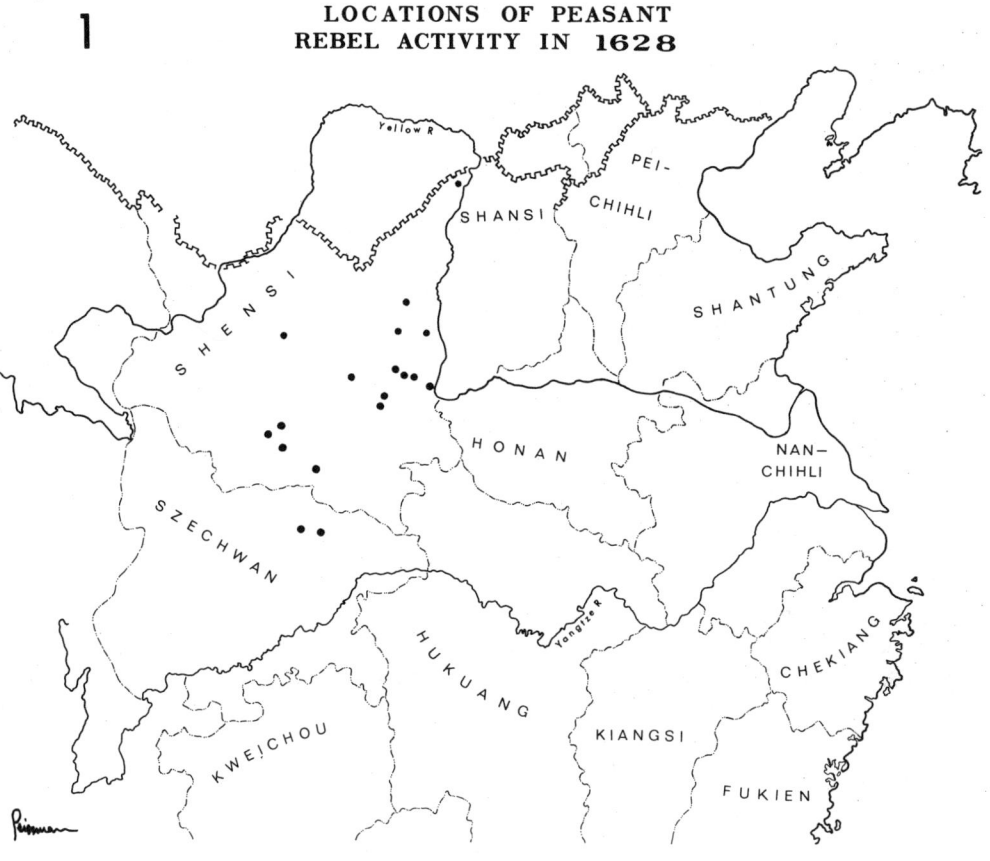

as prefectural magistrates at the very time when the greatest political adroitness and administrative wisdom were needed. For it was beginning in the 1620's that heavier taxes had to be collected and even weightier problems were impending.

In the more strictly military sphere, the strategic position occupied by northern Shensi was its one claim to national attention and its single asset which could be used to attract grain surpluses from outside to compensate for its own food deficits. Though less important than border areas farther east where Peking was more directly threatened, the area still faced the crucial northern frontier and accordingly profited from the set policy of the central government to maintain a line of defense along the Great Wall and to expend there a considerable percentage of the national budget. By the 1620's, however, the benefit accruing to Shensi for possessing a share of the frontier had suffered a considerable decline and the Great Wall military posture was largely a hollow pretense. The sources speak with one voice in describing unpaid and mutinous soldiers, troop rosters padded with fake names, undermanned garrisons, financial deficits, and food shortages. Undoubtedly this dire picture is, in some measure, an overstatement by bureaucrats anxious to put their cases for being granted additional support in the strongest possible terms. Still, it is probably essentially correct. Northern Shensi's military position could hardly have failed to have been adversely affected by the incompetence and corruption prevalent in Peking during the T'ien-ch'i period. More important, the military defenses in the area had been neglected and financially starved as a result of the situation in Manchuria where real disasters for the dynasty were occurring and the most pressing threat was posed. The western border had been relatively peaceful for more than half a century, since the 1571 settlement with Prince Anda, and there was some justification for its being neglected. Unfortunately, this neglect exceeded the margin of safety.

Launching of the Rebellions

In 1628 the event occurred which served to galvanize the diverse possibilities for serious trouble in northern Shensi into actuality. A severe drought, beginning in the spring, settled upon most of the region and by early winter the resulting famine had reached such proportions that it triggered widespread popular disorders. The horrors of the famine conditions are presented in lurid colors in a famous memorial by an official named Liu Mao, a native of Shensi who had actually witnessed the famine's progress.[4] Liu began by stating that he had never seen suffering of such magnitude, though his official duties had carried him all the way from Kweichow to Liaotung and had included being present at a Manchu massacre of a Chinese force in Manchuria. He then continued by citing specific horrors: wives sold by husbands; abandoned children; people forced to eat such items as grass, bark, and earth; mass burials of famine victims; outbreaks of lawlessness; and instances of cannibalism.

One might be justified in suspecting Liu of a certain amount of exaggeration for the benefit of his native province, yet the general seriousness of the famine can hardly be denied. Virtually all the sources mention it, even though they vary somewhat in citing its specific manifestations and duration. However, there is no reason to believe that the disaster was unprecedented. No real claims that it was so are advanced. On the contrary, some of the sources contain comments which go to considerable lengths to point out that the famine would have been relatively unimportant had the government taken effective measures to control it quickly. Thus, the famine can be branded a catalyst rather than a dominant causative factor in its own right.

The uprisings evoked by the famine were launched by two major groups: ordinary peasants and soldiers who had deserted or mutinied. Some of these deserters and mutineers had escaped to northern Shensi from as far away as Manchuria where Chinese forces had been suffering disasters for a decade. The peasants were largely reacting automatically to starvation, though they also might have been influenced to some extent by a decade of increasingly heavy taxation. The soldiers had somewhat more complicated motives: demoralization, specific grievances against their officers,* and resentment against not having received their rations and pay.

In addition to the two major components forming the rebel groups, other elements were of decidedly secondary importance: old established bandit gangs and Mongol tribesmen from beyond the border. The Mongols played a very fleeting role in the uprisings. They are known to have aided individual Chinese rebel groups for very limited periods in attacking towns inside the border.** Such incidents were largely confined to the late 1620's and the total Mongol role in the late Ming rebellions was insignificant.

---

* One of the most colorful, but unfortunately less reliable, of the sources, the *MCPL* 4/11a-b, recounts in some detail an incident which it claims marked the very beginning of the rebellions in Shensi. The incident involved four soldiers and an oppressive moneylender, appropriately named Ch'ien (money). The moneylender bribed the commander of the garrison to join him in a plot to force the soldiers to repay much more money than they had actually borrowed. This piece of chicanery prompted the soldiers to mutiny and organize local famine victims to ally with them in rebellion. Perhaps some such incident as this did occur, though the contention that it marked the very start of the Shensi troubles is undoubtedly an exaggeration.
** For example, in the *HLLK* 4/4a it is recorded that a rebel leader was joined by 1,000 Mongol horsemen in attacking Pao-an, Shensi.

The peasant and military groups intermingled to some extent, though there was also a definite tendency for them to maintain a degree of separateness. The soldiers were the dominant element in the uprisings in the area north of Yenan* while the peasants predominated to the south. Of the two groups, the soldiers were more powerful and dangerous, possessing the obvious advantages of greater practical military experience and martial attitudes. Throughout the entire literature dealing with the late Ming rebellions run testimonials to the hardiness and warlike qualities of the Shensi troops.

In geographical spread, the main area covered by the beginning uprisings was roughly the northern half of Shensi. There were sporadic incidents in the Wei River Valley and even further south, spilling over in a few cases into northern Szechwan,** but these incidents were relatively isolated and unimportant.

As for the military potential of both groups of rebels, in absolute terms it was certainly not formidable. None of the bands was very large, numbering no more than a few thousand at most, and the peasants were generally armed with nothing but simple farming tools. The author of one of the sources states that the rebels would flee at the approach of an official force of only a hundred men. He continues in a classic Confucian vein by suggesting that the whole affair would have been quickly settled had a few good officials been on hand to deal with it. However, despite all the rebel deficiencies in the absolute, they had considerable potential for trouble-making in the specific Shensi context where the authorities took a decidedly lackadaisical attitude toward the task of suppressing them. The Grand Coordinator was well known for his dislike of even hearing of uprisings and the local officials sometimes suppressed such unwelcome news. For this indirect aid, the rebels, in a display of ironic humor, dubbed the Grand Coordinator "our good host at the provincial capital."

When one comes to analyzing details of the uprising—precisely what rebel groups were operating, their movements, and their leadership—considerable confusion must be faced in the sources. Obviously the situation was so chaotic that the bureaucrats, charged with keeping the records, could not present a picture of great clarity. It does seem possible to say, though, that five leaders were especially important. In the extreme north were Wang Chia-yün and Shen-i-yüan, both of whom

---

* See Map 16 for the location of places mentioned in this chapter.
** See Maps 1 through 15 for the locations of the initial rebel outbreaks and their subsequent spread.

MING DYNASTY PEASANT REBELLIONS

2 LOCATIONS OF PEASANT REBEL ACTIVITY IN 1629

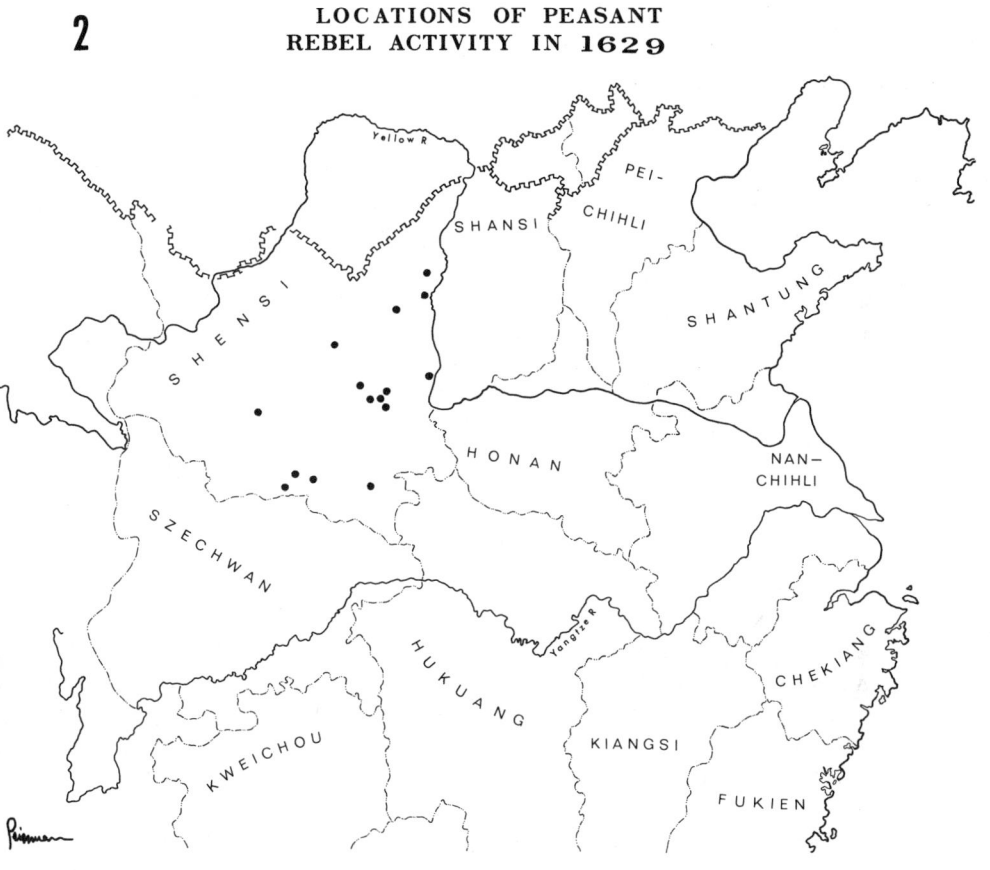

were army deserters. Their center was around Fu-ku. South of Yenan in the central part of Shensi, the chief leaders were Wang Tso-kua, Miao Mei, and Chao Sheng. Nothing definite is known of the backgrounds of Wang and Miao, though they were probably either old established leaders of bandit gangs or peasants. Chao seems to have been somewhat unique in that he apparently belonged to at least the fringes of the gentry. He is described as having been an assiduous student and adopted Tien-teng-tzu ("Lighted Lamp") as his rebel nickname, signifying the diligence with which he had pursued his studies far into the night. He is said to have joined the uprisings only after false rumors had arisen that he was plotting rebellion.

There were many secondary rebel leaders, most of them known only by the nicknames which they adopted in accordance with long-established rebel tradition and in some cases because they wanted to conceal their identities so as to avoid implicating their families. Some of these nicknames of early rebels are highly colorful or amusing: "Unmuddied" (Pu-chan-ni), "Heaven-disturbing Monkey" (Hun-t'ien-hou), "Lone-going Wolf" (Tu-hsing-lang), and—the one which perhaps most appeals to our twentieth century sense of humor—"Friend of the Red Army" (Hung-chün-yu).

Among these secondary leaders was one who was destined to play a major role. This was Kao Ying-hsiang, nicknamed "Dashing King" (Ch'uang-wang). He was a subordinate of Wang Chia-yün and, like Wang, was probably an army deserter.

Yang Ho and the Policy of Peaceful Settlement

The central government could not help but react to half a province slipping into disorder even though it had such other pressing problems as the Manchu threat and internal political stresses accompanying the coming to the throne of a new emperor. A decision was reached in Peking relatively quickly and in the early spring of 1629, Yang Ho was appointed Supreme Commander of northern Shensi with the specific task of pacifying the rebellions.

Yang was a native of Wu-ling, Hukuang* in the lush central Yangtze Valley. He had had a relatively distinguished official career and enjoyed a good reputation. He was not tarnished by shady connections with the eunuch clique dominant during the T'ien-ch'i period, having ridden out this political bad weather in retirement. However, he possessed no special qualities to make him an obvious choice for the important

---

* In Ming times the two modern provinces of Hupeh and Hunan were united and had the name Hukuang.

MING DYNASTY PEASANT REBELLIONS

3   LOCATIONS OF PEASANT
REBEL ACTIVITY IN **1630**

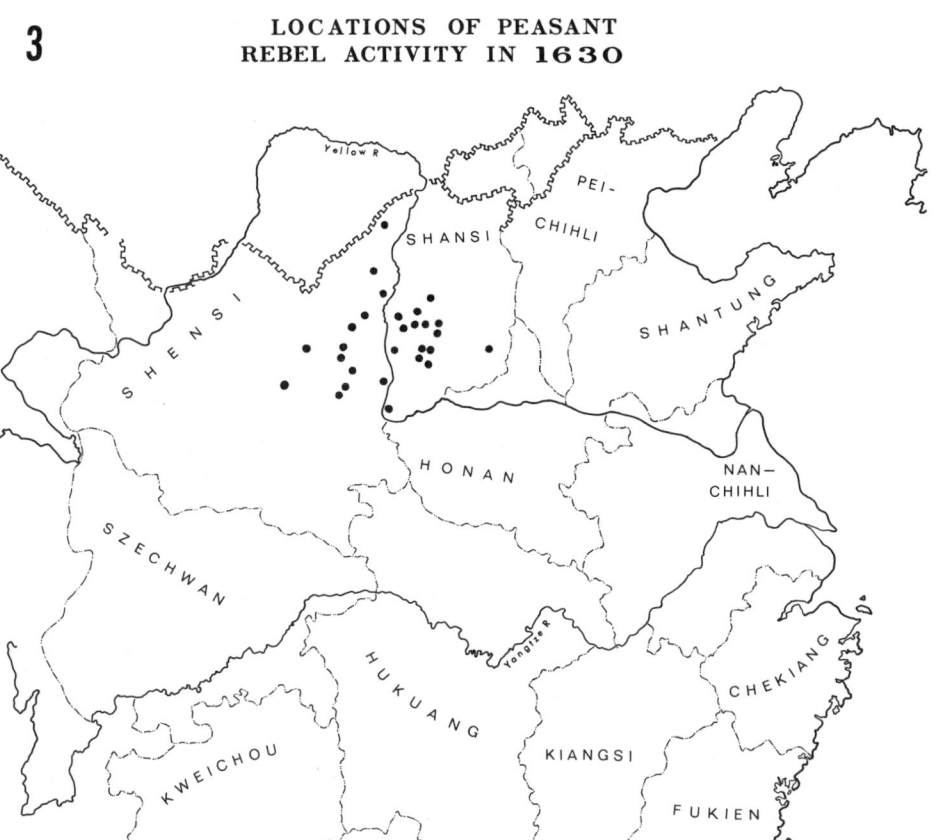

assignment in Shensi and undoubtedly in accepting it his major motivation was a genuine desire for service in an area where it was desperately needed.

Yang brought with him to Shensi a sincere commitment to the Confucian abhorrence of a strictly military approach to state problems, and in carrying out his official assignment, he instituted a policy which emphasized encouraging the rebels to surrender. Following such surrender, the ex-rebels should be issued certificates to serve as protection against being attacked by government troops. Subsequently, they should be allowed to return to their regular occupations or absorbed into the official armed forces.

Yang ably defended his policy of peaceful settlement against critics in both Shensi and Peking.[5] He argued principally that there were few genuine rebels in the area. The so-called rebels were mainly starving peasants who would return to their homes once the natural calamities were over and it was possible for agricultural production to return to normal. In the meantime, the peasants who had rebelled under the stress of circumstances should not be slaughtered without mercy. Furthermore, Yang pointed out the formidable task of achieving a strictly military solution to the problem, given the extensive area affected by the disorders and the large number of people involved in the uprisings.

Yang was not, however, such a complete Confucian idealist that he ruled out all resort to military force. Though he was willing to threaten the Shensi local authorities with punishment, even including the death penalty, if they killed rebels who had surrendered, he admitted that stern action had to be taken against rebels who refused to surrender. Also, he was particularly interested in strengthening local forces so that any future outbreak could be taken care of at that level.

Yang's policy achieved some initial success, reaching something of a climax with the surrender of Shen-i-k'uei, a major rebel figure who had succeeded to the leadership of his brother's (Shen-i-yüan) group following his death at the hands of government forces. Yang instituted negotiations with Shen by inviting a relative to visit his headquarters and, when he arrived, paid him the honor of allowing him to sleep in his own room as a demonstration of confidence. Subsequently, Shen returned the compliment by sending an emissary to hand over a county magistrate whom he had been holding captive. Following the completion of these preliminary formalities, Shen himself arrived at Yang's headquarters, together with his band of some 5,000 cavalrymen. Yang received them and displayed a picture of a dragon, the symbol of the emperor, from the tower of one of the town gates.* The rebels were required to kowtow

---

* *HLLK* 4/5b-6a. The ceremony occurred at Ning-chou, Shensi.

and shout *wan sui*. Next, Yang took a group of rebels to a local temple dedicated to the God of War, Kuan Yü, where they swore allegiance to the Emperor and were given certificates guaranteeing their protection against arrest and attack. Finally, Yang received Shen in a more private audience, read aloud his ten crimes, together with the imperial order pardoning him, and bestowed upon him the military rank of Local Commander.

This grand display, in which Yang made full use of every resource he could command to achieve maximum psychological impact, produced at least temporary results and Shen was content for a time to serve the authorities in his new capacity as Local Commander. He is said to have achieved considerable merit defending the frontier against Mongols. However, after a few months, he rebelled again.

There were other less elaborately arranged examples of success for the peaceful surrender policy. One of Yang's subordinate officers pursued a rebel group across the border into northern Szechwan. There he boldly entered their camp, became their sworn brother, and persuaded them to return to their homes in Shensi. Another rebel group surrendered and then confirmed its loyalty by attacking and destroying Chao Sheng, one of the original leaders in the rebel movement.

Unfortunately, balanced against the successes enjoyed by the peaceful settlement policy was a list of undeniable failures. In the first place, some of the rebel leaders refused to consider surrender and continued their operations. Indeed, one of the chief rebels, Wang Chia-yün, in the summer of 1630, managed to capture the important town of Fu-ku located on the Yellow River in the far north of Shensi.[6] He was able to hold the town for three months and undertook to construct fortifications in the area. Thus, he achieved a degree of success and a measure of stability which no other rebel leader had heretofore accomplished. Government forces did manage to oust him from Fu-ku in the fall of 1630 and he reverted to the typical rebel mode of operations: rapid movement from place to place. Fortunately for the government, a year later in the summer of 1631, Wang was killed by his own men in a drunken brawl. However, his band succeeded in surviving the crisis without disintegrating and a successor, Wang Tzu-yung, was selected as the new leader. Furthermore, Wang Tzu-yung was accorded recognition as the leading figure in the rebel movement.

Another category of rebels did not refuse outright to cooperate with the surrender policy and indeed gave lip service to it. But they quite obviously used it to their own advantage, surrendering when hard pressed and on the verge of destruction and subsequently resuming their rebel careers when they had recouped their strength or had put a safe distance between themselves and the official forces. A great deal of popular resentment soon developed against Yang as a result of such actions on the part of the rebels who came to be ironically labeled "official rebels."[7] For a time, Yang was able to suppress news of rebels who had surrendered, been guaranteed protection, and almost immediately revolted again. Also, he managed to override local administrators who advocated more vigorous action. In the long run, however, the situation could not be concealed and strong denunciations of what was termed his coddling of rebels were voiced in Peking itself.

In addition to Yang's trouble with the rebels, he was hard pressed to control his own subordinates, many of whom did not share his Confucian sentiments. For example, the Regional Inspector of Shensi enticed Wang Tso-kua to a banquet at Sui-te and, when he arrived, seized and beheaded him. Another official in northern Shensi also held a banquet for surrendered rebels, but had the opposite intention of impressing the rebels with the advantages of returning to peaceful lives. However, the rank and file of his troops took violent exception to this honor bestowed upon their ex-enemies and a riot ensued.

Other subordinates of Yang hindered his efforts in a different way by alienating the support of the civilian population. Some commanders allowed their troops to plunder and one committed the real atrocity of slaughtering perfectly innocent people in an effort to claim credit for killing rebels.

Another area in which Yang failed was in preventing the uprisings from spreading outside Shensi. By early 1630, several rebel bands, particularly those headed by Lao-hui-hui and I-tzu-wang, had succeeded in crossing the Yellow River into Shansi and plundering several counties. Such operations continued into 1631 during which year it is known that at least twelve Shansi counties suffered looting. The rebels did not confine themselves to the area along the river, but went further afield, pushing to the southeastern corner of the province.

There is little evidence of effective resistance to the rebels in Shansi. Some local *ad hoc* efforts were made, such as that organized by a Mrs. Chang in a village near Ch'in-shui. She emerged as a heroine by refusing to flee and leading the successful defense of the village against a rebel attack. For the most part, however, it is evident that the Shansi authorities had been caught unprepared and they expended a considerable portion of their energies in making acrimonious complaints that Shensi officials were ridding themselves of what was properly their own problem by dumping the rebels on Shansi.

Developments in Peking both aided and hindered Yang in his pursuit of peace for Shensi. On the side of aiding him was the imperial decree

MING DYNASTY PEASANT REBELLIONS

4 LOCATIONS OF PEASANT REBEL ACTIVITY IN **1631**

of late 1630 proclaiming the remission of all unpaid taxes in Yenan Prefecture for 1628 and 1629. In addition, early in 1631, the Emperor granted 100,000 taels to be distributed as relief in the area, finally accepting a proposal which had been made two years previously. This sum was considered by some officials to be grossly inadequate and an unsuccessful effort was made to have it raised to 300,000 taels. The modest size of the relief fund was in part compensated for by the appointment of an able and conscientious Censor, Wu Sheng, to administer it. Wu proceeded immediately to northern Shensi to begin his relief operations and was forced to work under extremely trying conditions which called for the display of a high degree of personal courage.* He was able to exert some temporary calming influence on the situation. Several rebels surrendered to him and two abandoned their sieges of towns after Wu had bestowed relief funds upon them. Unfortunately, he was soon drawn into the political controversy raging around Yang Ho.

Even more forthright economic proposals directed toward Shensi were advanced in Peking. A Ministry of War official advocated a large-scale shipment of relief grain into the area. This would provide jobs for local people as carriers and would make possible the restoration of the region's agriculture, removing one of the prime causes of the rebellion. Furthermore, a Censor proposed that all revenues in northern Shensi be retained locally for the recruitment and training of natives of the area to form an anti-rebel force. He added that merely expending funds was no assurance of success and emphasized the need for good administrators. As an example, he cited Manchuria where millions of taels had been spent, yet the danger was as threatening as ever. Neither of these proposals was accepted.

On the opposite side of the coin, three decisions made in Peking unleashed developments which complicated Yang's problems in Shensi. One of these decisions, reached early in 1631, suspended the flow of grain moving from Shansi into Shensi following the normal trade patterns. This move was made with the assumption that the rebels benefitted from the trade. However, the total effect of the suspension, in worsening the food situation in Shensi, probably did more damage to the government's position than to the rebels'.

Much more disastrous than the grain trade suspension was the famous decision to reduce the number of post stations. The post-station system went back to the beginning of the centralized state in China, and was one

---

* *HLLK* 5/4b pays him the ultimate compliment by offering the opinion that if he had been appointed Supreme Commander, instead of Yang Ho, the problem of the Shensi rebels would have been solved.

of the more essential institutions of imperial rule. It had increased in complexity during Yüan and Ming times, and included a transportation network extending from the capital into every province.* It maintained permanent stations staffed by attendants and stocked with horses, boats, carriages, and other types of equipment. Messages and official personnel were transported along the network at public expense and there is evidence that it was abused by ex-officials and members of the gentry in general who employed the system in a private capacity. Financial support for the system was provided locally and it was considered to be one of the corvée services expected of the people in the areas through which it passed.

Early in 1629, an official of the Ministry of Justice proposed that since grave financial difficulties were now being faced, the number of post stations and the attendants serving at them should be reduced. The Emperor accepted the suggestion and ordered it implemented. The move had the immediate affect of augmenting the rebel ranks in Shensi, as many of the discharged post station attendants, deprived of their livelihood, joined the rebel bands.**

The final extra-Shensi development which hindered Yang's efforts was the 1629 Manchu raid south of the Great Wall and Peking's reacting to it by summoning troops from Shensi and Shansi to come to the defense of the capital. The Manchu raid began in the late autumn and, within a month, a force had pushed to the outskirts of Peking itself. An emergency was proclaimed and help from various quarters was called for. Unfortunately, at least part of the forces from Shensi and Shansi, dispatched in reply to a summons, mutinied a short distance to the southwest of Peking. Most of the mutineers fled back to their native areas in the northwest and many of them joined the rebels. This event was certainly not unprecedented. It has been seen that army deserters from the war in Manchuria had been present in the uprisings from their very beginnings, but probably never before had there been such a massive infusion of army deserters into the rebel cause at any one time.

By the summer of 1631 there were definite signs that Yang's days were numbered as Supreme Commander in charge of pacifying the rebels. The Emperor himself was obviously becoming dissatisfied with his performance. In the beginning, the Emperor had been sympathetic to Yang's views and as late as the beginning of 1631 had issued a proclamation stating that even the rebels were his children and should be given the opportunity to surrender peacefully and not just be butchered. By the

---

* One of the best descriptions of the Ming post system is provided in *MCPL* 5/1b-5b.
** *HLLK* 2/1a and Li Kuang-pi, "Ming-mo nung-min ta ch'i-i," 107. Li estimates that there was a thirty percent reduction in the post stations.

spring of 1631 the imperial attitude had hardened and the Emperor proclaimed the menace was now so serious that the rebels would have to be killed. Yang himself, though, never abandoned his belief in the validity of his policy of political pacification. He did recommend in the summer of 1631 that troops and supplies be brought back from Manchuria to serve in Shansi and Shensi, arguing that the northwest provinces were more important than an area beyond the Great Wall. However, this interest in strengthening the military does not indicate any real abandonment of his primarily civilian approach. Furthermore, Yang's recommendation was not accepted.

Probably the ultimate and crucial event producing Yang's fall from power was a report on the rebel situation submitted in the 8th month of 1631 by the Censor, Wu Sheng, whom we saw had been placed in charge of the distribution of relief funds in Shensi. Wu defended Yang against the more violent critics in Peking who accused him of completely refusing to employ military power in performing his duties. At the same time, Wu argued that the policy of peaceful pacification was a failure and that much more forceful action was needed.[8] He supprted his judgment by a general review of the Shensi situation, stating that the central section of the province from Han-ch'eng west to I-chün and south to P'u-ch'eng had suffered particularly heavily. In this area hundreds of villages had been destroyed, thousands of people killed, and many local officials slain.

Shortly after the receipt of Wu's report in Peking, Yang was deprived of his office and ordered to the capital for investigation. Thus came the downfall of this dedicated man who was a representative of the best in the Confucian humanist tradition and whose program, despite its obvious shortcomings, was a sincere effort to apply his ideals.

Yang managed to evade any significant punishment for his failures, but his usefulness to the government had received a blow from which it never recovered. He died in 1634, some three years after his fall, and misfortune pursued him even beyond the grave. His son, as we shall see, was destined to suffer a still more spectacular failure in attempting to suppress the rebellions and—the ultimate horror—even his bones were scattered when one of the peasant rebel leaders desecrated the family graveyard following his capture of Yang's native area in 1643.

The Pre-rebel Lives of Chang Hsien-chung and Li Tzu-ch'eng and the Launching of Their Rebel Careers

The initial period of the rebellions witnessed the beginnings of the rebel activities of Chang Hsien-chung and Li Tzu-ch'eng. Because of their subsequent importance, their background and the commencement of their careers deserve discussion here.

Information concerning the early life of Chang Hsien-chung is inadequate and conflicting,* a circumstance which is not surprising when one considers the nature of the sources dealing with his rebellion, most of which were written by scholars from the intellectual center of Ming China, southeastern Nan-chihli and northern Chekiang. These men had little, if any, direct contact with Chang's native province, Shensi, and they undoubtedly based their compilations largely on official reports which would contain little information concerning his pre-rebel life.

Even the place and date of Chang's birth are not known with complete certainty, though probably he was born in Fu-shih County in northern Shensi or in Liu-shu-chien, some eighty miles northwest of Fu-shih near the Great Wall. The year of his birth was probably 1606 and one source, describing the celebration of his birthday after he had become famous, states that it occurred on the 9th day of the 10th month. If this is correct, he was born on November 8, 1606.

Growing up, Chang is said to have exhibited unusual strength and to have had such physical characteristics as a tall, thin bodily frame; long, slanting eyebrows; heavy jaws; a pock-marked face; a distinctly yellow complexion; and excessive hairiness. All these traits seem quite plausible and apparently do not represent a historian's stereotype of what a rebel should look like.

Chang's family background is not definitely known, some sources maintaining that he was from a poor family and grew up completely illiterate, while others suggest that his family was in more comfortable circumstances and that he had at least some schooling. One source recounts an elaborate story about how he exhibited a violent temperament even while a schoolboy and went so far as to kill one of his classmates, an action which caused his father to disown him and turn him out of the family. Probably this story is based on nothing more than legends which grew up about Chang after he became famous, and its veracity is doubtful. There may be a measure of truth in the assertion that he had some schooling, as certain indications point to his having been at least semi-literate. For example, there exist crude poems which he is said to have composed in Szechwan near the end of his life. Also, the Jesuit missionaries, with whom he had contact in Szechwan, infer that he acquired some knowledge of Christianity by reading the tracts which they had written.

Probably the most reliable information concerning Chang's family is

---

* The account of Chang's early life and the beginning of his rebellion is based chiefly on *PKC* 1/1a, 7a, 3/5b, 6/3b, 12/6b-7a; *HLLK* 3/6a, 4/11b; *MS* 309/2b, 24b, 32a; *SKCL* 1/1a, 7a, 9/1a, 10/1a-b; *MCPL* 7/9b-10a, 8/6a, 16/13a; and *MSCSPM* 77/43-44, 50.

that it was registered in the Wei-So military system, and it seems certain that he himself became a soldier as a young man. However, his career as a soldier is depicted in two widely differing fashions in the sources. One source maintains that he fought bravely on the frontier and became quite wealthy from the rewards obtained as a result of his military merit. Subsequently, his neighbors, angered at his refusal to lend them money, falsely accused him of having connections with the rebels. As a result of these unjust accusations, he was finally forced into rebellion himself. Other accounts depict Chang's military career as being far less of a glorious success, and indeed he is said to have been sentenced to death by his commander, Wang Wei, after he had been guilty of having committed rape and robbery for the third time. On the execution day, another officer, Ch'en Hung-fan, happened to visit the camp where Chang was stationed, and being struck by the young prisoner's appearance, managed to persuade Wang Wei to substitute a severe beating for the death sentence. Presumably Chang was dismissed from the military forces following the incident. Probably the second more inglorious account of Chang's record as a soldier is essentially correct, given the characteristics he is known to have displayed subsequently as a rebel.

The date for the launching of Chang's rebellion was probably the summer of 1630, apparently only a short time after his narrow escape from execution in the army. He collected around him several hundred men and began raiding villages in the area of Mi-chih in northern Shensi, the general region which had witnessed the beginnings of serious rebel outbreaks two years earlier. He followed the general rebel custom of adopting a nickname, "Eight Great Kings" (Pa-ta-wang), later expanded to "Eight Great Kings of the Western Camp" after the appearance of three other "Eight Great Kings" in the rebel movement.* It has been impossible to determine with certainty what this nickname signifies and why Chang chose it. A possible explanation is that it is an adaptation of the Buddhist Pa-ta-ming-wang, who are bodhisattvas represented in their fierce aspects as guardians of Vairocana.[9] He may have seen paintings of such figures on the walls of temples and been attracted by their fierceness which he wanted to emulate.

Chang's early stature in the rebel movement was a modest one, and he seems to have had a vague subordinate relationship to one of the really pioneer figures in the movement, Wang Chia-yün. His activities and attitudes were in no way really different from any of the numerous other leaders of small bands: he continued roaming about and plundering in

---

* Earlier he had had the nickname "Yellow Tiger," derived from his yellowish complexion.

northern Shensi; upon at least one occasion, when hard-pressed, he reached a temporary surrender agreement with the authorities; and undoubtedly he did not have the vaguest thought of any such grandiose plan as overthrowing the dynasty. However, unlike many of his fellows, he was fortunate enough to survive, and will play a role of increasing importance throughout the following pages.

Li Tzu-ch'eng was born some sixty miles west of the town of Mi-chih, a county seat in far northern Shensi.* The date of his birth varies in the sources. The *Yen-sui-chen chih* is suspiciously overly complete in the information it supplies, placing the birth on September 21, 1597 between 5:00 and 7:00 P.M. Other sources indicate that the year of his birth was 1606.

Li seems definitely to have been of peasant background, though the exact circumstances of his family are a matter of considerable dispute. Some sources depict the family as a poor one and in the process of disintegration, so that Li already at the age of ten had to tend horses for an old Moslem lady. Subsequently, he is said to have held a succession of jobs: a servant in a wine shop, an apprentice to a blacksmith, and a farm laborer. In all these endeavors he is described as being a failure and was dismissed for laziness or misbehavior. Other sources depict his family as possessing some means, and state that he had the opportunity of attending school as a child and youth, though he is described as being far more interested in riding and shooting than in studying.

In another area of Li's personal life as a young man, some of the sources recount a traumatic succession of events revolving around his marriage to a Miss Han, a woman of great beauty but dubious reputation. Upon returning from a journey, he is said to have caught his wife in the act of committing adultery with a local official, and killed either one or both of them, the exact details varying in the sources.

The first definitely certain event in Li's life is his having become an attendant at a post station in his native area around the age of twenty. However, his service at the post station apparently did not last much longer than a year, because, as previously noted, in 1629 the central government ordered the reduction of post stations as a means of relieving localities of some of the burdens of corvée requirements. As a result of this reduction, Li was dismissed, and finding himself without employment, is said to have been appointed a Community Head (Li-chang), because his neighbors considered assigning him this duty was the best way to restrain his proclivities toward violence. His tenure in his new position was

---

* The chief sources for Li's pre-rebel life are: *YSCC* 5/10b-11a, 27a; *PKC* 1/16a; *MCPL* 5/17a-21b; *HS* 4a-b; and *HCL* 5/1a-2b.

again destined to be brief, though the exact circumstances of his removal are uncertain. One source presents his service in a quite favorable light and maintains that he was dismissed because he did not collect the new increased tax levies, but another source states that he misappropriated public funds and had to be removed.

The next stage in Li's pre-rebel life saw a shift from his native area in northern Shensi to the far western section of the province (modern Kansu) where he went to join a government force commanded by an officer named Wang Kuo. Li was accompanied on this move by his nephew, Li Kuo, who was of the same age and had been his constant companion since childhood. It was in western Shensi that Li began his rebellion around 1630 by joining with his fellow soldiers in a mutiny in Chin County apparently as a result of the local magistrate's refusal to grant them supplies. In the mutiny, the commanding officer, Wang Kuo, was killed, and assuming leadership of the group, Li led them east where he attached himself to one of the original rebel leaders, Wang Chia-yün. Following Wang's death, Li joined Kao Ying-hsiang to whom he was to be at least formally subordinate until Kao's death in 1636.

Like all the early rebel groups, Li's band was undoubtedly of modest size and he moved about rapidly over the northern Shensi landscape seeking plunder and safety from the attacks of the government forces. Like Chang Hsien-chung, he was fortunate enough to survive and played an even greater role in the future course of the rebellions than Chang.

Review of the 1627-31 *Period of the Rebellions*

Looking back over the 1627-31 period of the rebellions, several observations are worthy of special attention. In the first place, the military successes of the government forces had not been negligible even though some of them had been achieved against the wishes of Yang Ho. As evidence of the accomplishments of the official troops, all the major rebel leaders who originally launched the uprisings were destroyed within these four years. Wang Chia-yün, Shen-i-yüan, Wang Tso-kua, Miao Mei, and Chao Sheng were all dead. Secondary rebels like Pu-chan-ni ("Unmuddied") also had been killed. Furthermore, the rebels were still confined to the northwest (Shensi and Shansi) which was not a key area. Economically vital regions like the north China plain and the Yangtze Valley had not yet been affected. In addition, none of the rebel leaders had succeeded in acquiring more than a very modest measure of prestige and stability. The rebel bands were essentially collections of plunderers, moving rapidly from place to place. None of them had gained any real support from the gentry.

On the other hand, there were probably more rebels operating in

1631 than there had been in 1627. The destruction of the rebel leaders had not been accompanied by the elimination of their followers who had typically regrouped and either chosen a successor to their dead chieftain or joined another already established rebel band.

Perhaps most important of all on the debit side of the government ledger was the close connection, already quite apparent by 1631, between the uprisings inside China and the threat posed by the Manchus. Besides the obvious disadvantages of the government's being forced to conduct military operations on two fronts, there were the equally important economic repercussions: the continuance and even augmentation of the onerous tax burden, the most significant end result of which was the creation of more peasant rebels. Finally, the 1627-31 period saw the entrance into the rebel movement of the two individuals who eventually were to dominate it, Li Tzu-ch'eng and Chang Hsien-chung.

Chapter II

The Disorganized Raiding Phase of the Rebellions Part I: The Expansion and Initial Climax of the Peasant Uprisings (1631-36)

Appointment of Hung Ch'eng-ch'ou to Head the Rebel-suppression Campaign

Following the dismissal of Yang Ho, the central government elevated one of his subordinates, Hung Ch'eng-ch'ou, to be his successor as Supreme Commander. Hung had even less connection with the northwest than Yang, being a native of faraway Fukien. He did possess an astute political sense and a highly developed organizational ability, qualities which were to stand him in good stead now that he was properly launched on a career which was to keep him playing an important role upon the Chinese historical stage for three decades.*

Hung did not have the basic commitment to Confucian humanism held by Yang Ho and had disagreed with his policies. He had felt that Yang was unrealistic in placing primary emphasis upon getting the rebels to return to their villages, feeling that in too many cases their homes had been destroyed and their lives completely disrupted.[1] He advocated a much more vigorous policy of suppression. He was not, however, so ungentlemanly as to join Yang's bitter enemies who called for severe punishment following his fall from power and even submitted a memorial in Yang's defense which pointed out the particularly desperate situation in Shensi. Hung's motives in submitting this memorial undoubtedly were complicated and probably were not uninfluenced by a desire to erect defenses against a possible future when he might occupy Yang's shoes. Yet it must be counted to his credit that he did not display pettiness toward his fallen ex-superior.

---

* See the excellent short biography of Hung in Arthur W. Hummel, *Eminent Chinese of the Ch'ing Period.*

Hung's policies in Shensi were definitely eclectic.[2] Being a *chin-shih* with a civilian career extending back several years, he could hardly have been expected to adopt a strictly military approach. He announced that efforts would be made to separate real rebels from people who had been forcibly swept up in the rebel bands and that the latter would not be killed. Further, he favored the continuance of relief measures and requested 200,000 taels for this purpose. At the same time, he was not above such Machiavellian plots as the slaughter of 320 rebels after inviting them to what was supposed to have been an amicable wine party. Also, Hung's most trusted lieutenant was the able, but violently swashbuckling, Ts'ao Wen-chao. Ts'ao gained wide fame for his vigorous prosecution of military efforts against the rebels and made no attempt to conceal his intention to exterminate the rebels and anyone connected with them including even those who had been forced to join the movement.

Hung was under no illusions about the difficulties facing him in Shensi. His memorials emphasized the size and formidable terrain of the area for which he was responsible and probably even exaggerated the numerical superiority the rebels enjoyed over him. Other officials were even more pessimistic about the possibilities of restoring order. For example, Wu Sheng, the Censor in charge of relief who remained in Shensi for the first year of Hung's term as Supreme Commander, reported early in 1632 that even though there had been generally good weather and crops during 1631, there had been little benefit as a result. The rebels had simply seized the harvest in the autumn. Some months later, Wu submitted the following even more unfavorable report which, despite its grand displays of rhetoric, still manages to convey a real awareness of the dire situation in Shensi:

On the northern borders of Sian Prefecture are such counties as Yen-ch'ang, Han-ch'eng, Ho-yang, P'u-ch'eng, and Pai-shui which are usually the first victims of a southward invasion of the rebels. During the 5th and 6th months [of 1631], the rebels took all the towns and villages of these counties as their feeding ground. They moved back north toward the beginning of the 7th month. Your Minister went to Lung-fang on the 1st day of the 8th month and learned fully about the actualities of the burnings and lootings that the rebels had committed in that locality. I immediately had the Sian Prefectural Judge, Shih K'o-fa, investigate. In the 9th month, Ku-yüan, Yao, and I-chün were burned by the rebels led by Liu and Shih. The villages were laid waste and I cannot bear to speak of their condition. Your Minister also had K'o-fa investigate the matter. K'o-fa described for Your Minister the conditions of the suffering people. Some were seriously wounded, crawling on the ground and unable to walk. Some were still in swaddling clothes, crying and screaming. Some were starving and suffering from the bitterly cold weather, and as a result, unable to talk. Some were widows, left to themselves, their hearts aching for their dead husbands, and tears of blood running down their cheeks.

Some were sorrowful old people, grieving over the deaths of their beloved children, their livers split and their hearts broken. All members of some families were killed and their corpses left untended. A few survivors, bereft of their families, were wandering around and no one came to their aid. Houses with broken beams and smashed pillars were tottering in the grievous wind and the cold mist. Collapsed houses and scorched walls lay where they had fallen with yellow weeds growing around them. There is no green grass in the open spaces, since it has all been eaten up by horses or destroyed by troops. Upon the trees, suspended against the slanting rays of the sun, stand only crows and hawks, cawing and crying. A picture of several decades of material wealth and civic peace has come down to the grief of the decay of nature. Upon hearing of these things, Your Minister cannot but press his hands to his heart and burst into tears. Alas! Why should the people of Shensi have been visited with such an extreme misfortune as this?[3]

Actual events demonstrated the increased rebel potential.[4] In late 1631 a rebel group captured Kan-ch'üan* in northern Shensi and had the good fortune to seize 100,000 taels which had been sent there to purchase military supplies. Early in 1632 another rebel group, led by K'o-t'ien-fei, defeated a sizable government force near Ku-yüan in west central Shensi and even succeeded in killing a Local Commander. This was one of the most significant rebel victories to date. Subsequently in the summer of 1632 K'o-t'ien-fei and Liu Tao-chiang mounted a quite formidable siege of Ho-shui. Ts'ao Wen-chao himself came to the rescue of the town and finally succeeded in seriously defeating the rebels but only after an exceedingly bitter fight during which at one point he was surrounded and almost killed.

Despite all difficulties, it could be seen by the middle of 1632 that considerable success was coming to Hung in his efforts to clear Shensi of rebels.[5] Discord was encouraged among the rebel groups and in one case a surrendered rebel presented the head of one of his former fellow rebel leaders in order to enhance his own status in the eyes of the authorities. In another instance, a government spy, a Local Commander in disguise, succeeded in getting the rebel rank and file in two groups to surrender after they had killed their leaders, Shih Lin-an and Tu-hsing-lang. Most remarkable of all, Hung himself, in a particularly impressive display of military action, eliminated four important rebel chieftains. By the end of 1632, Hung could boast that virtually all rebel activity in Shensi had ceased. This happy condition was to endure somewhat more than a year during which time the province which gave birth to the rebellions enjoyed a well-earned respite.

Impressive as the Shensi success was, Hung's personal role in achieving

---

* See Map 16 for the location of places mentioned in this chapter.

MING DYNASTY PEASANT REBELLIONS

5   LOCATIONS OF PEASANT REBEL ACTIVITY IN 1632

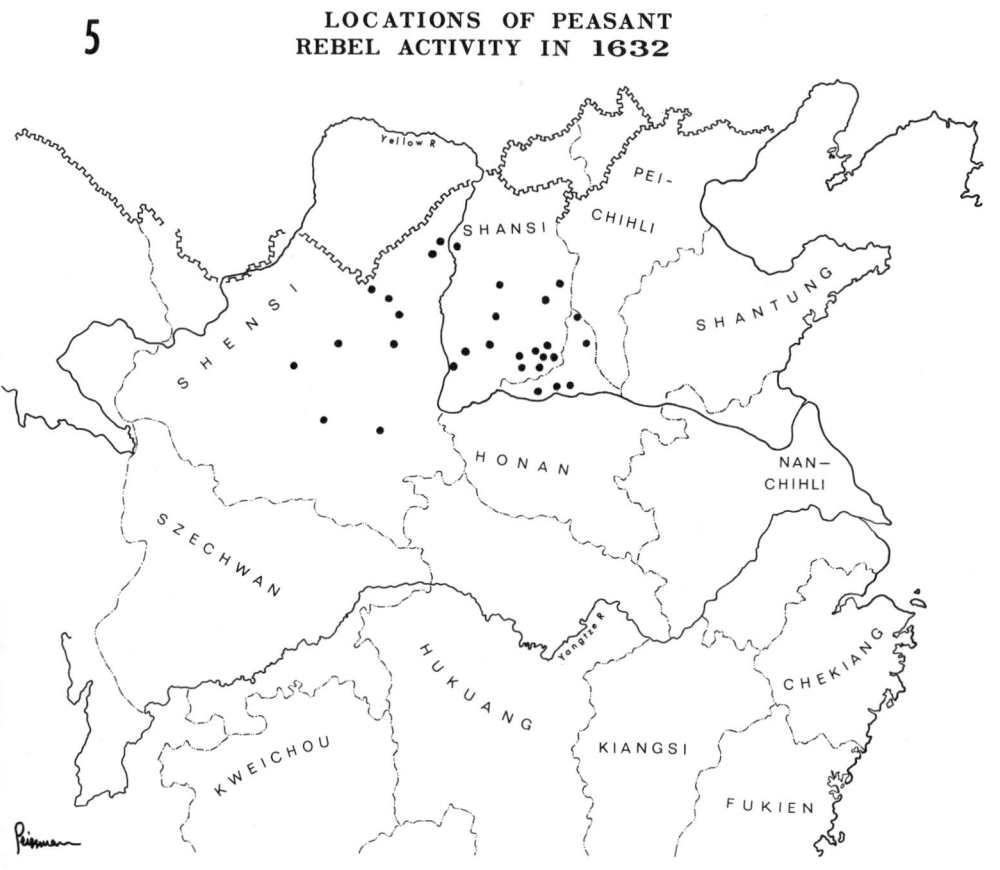

it must not be exaggerated and the unfortunate Yang Ho made to appear even more abject a failure in comparison. Hung was treated generously by the central government, particularly in being allowed to keep 200,000 taels of local Shensi revenue for his military expenses and for the restoration of the area's agriculture. In addition, the two northernmost prefectures in the province, Yenan and Ch'ing-yang, were exempted from paying the onerous new taxes levied especially to finance the struggle against the Manchus and the internal rebels. But most important of all, Shensi was cleared of rebels largely because the focal area of the rebellions shifted to the east.

Eastward Shift of the Rebellions

Several reasons lay behind the eastward shift of the rebellions. In the first place, the move represented a direct continuation of a trend present in the rebellions since 1630 when, as noted, the uprisings in Shensi began spilling over into Shansi. In addition, rebel leaders were attracted to the greater possibilities for plunder in fresh regions hitherto outside their scope of operations. Also, they undoubtedly realized that it would take some time for military operations against them in the new area to reach the state of efficiency they had attained in Shensi.

By the end of 1632 the eastward shift of the rebellions was complete, and for an entire year the center of action remained relatively stable, mainly in southeastern Shansi, and then expanded to include southwestern Pei-chihli (modern Hopei) and northern Honan as well (see Maps 3-6, particularly Map 6). Two of the most significant rebel successes in these new areas were their seizures of the towns of Tse-chou (Shansi) and Hsiu-wu (Honan).[6] The capture of Tse-chou was especially important because of its size and wealth and the fact that one of the defending officers defected to the rebels. To take it, the rebels had maintained a siege for eight days during which time no relief force had come to the town's aid.

The rebel eastward shift posed intensified problems which produced strains at all levels of administration. The central government could hardly have been unaware of the significant fact that the rebels had pushed forth from the relatively unimportant northwest into an area which was much more vital. Indeed, they were within striking distance of the capital. Advice on what should be done poured in.[7] Some of the advice was not particularly imaginative or helpful, consisting of vague ideas about tax reduction or sweeping generalizations about battles against the rebels lost due to the lack of any over-all strategic plan. Other advice showed an awareness of what must be done and, for example, stressed the importance of coordinating the efforts of provincial authorities in the four provinces now affected by the rebellions—Shansi, Pei-chihli, Honan,

MING DYNASTY PEASANT REBELLIONS

6 LOCATIONS OF PEASANT REBEL ACTIVITY IN **1633**

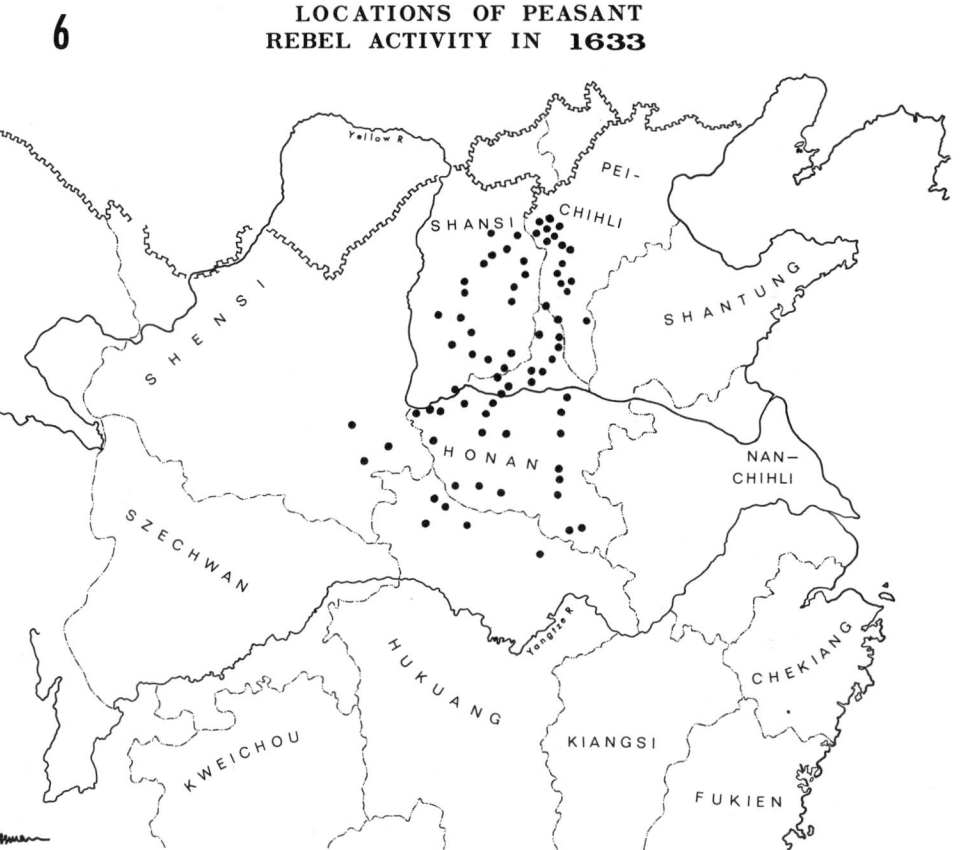

and Shensi. Perhaps the most acute observation of all was made by a Vice-minister in the Ministry of Revenue who noted that the provincial authorities were paying far too much attention to defending towns and cities. In the meantime, the rebels had a relatively free hand in plundering the countryside where they could obtain all the supplies they needed. He suggested that the protection of towns and cities be entrusted to the local magistrates while the provincial officials devoted their efforts to the more important and difficult task of destroying the rebels in the countryside.

There is little evidence that the central government made real use of any of the advice, good or bad, regarding the rebels. The Emperor, still hindered by his youth and inexperience, took some actions which were unfortunate or ridiculous.[8] For example, late in 1632 he ordered officials to contribute horses in an effort to relieve a shortage. Each official of the third rank or above was to contribute one horse and lower officials were to group themselves and jointly present a horse. Apparently the most significant result of this order was to present the palace eunuchs with an excellent opportunity for graft. The eunuchs sold horses to the officials and refused to accept those obtained from other sources. Even more ridiculous was the imperial order, issued in the spring of 1633, castigating the officials for merely playing with the rebels and arbitrarily ordering the rebel threat to be eliminated within three months.

The Emperor's deficiencies were not compensated for by the top echelons of the bureaucracy. The three most influential officials in Peking throughout the first half of the 1630's were the Grand Secretaries, Wen T'i-jen and Chou Yen-ju, and the Minister of War, Chang Feng-i.* While other Grand Secretaries and Ministers were appointed and dismissed with bewildering rapidity, these three remained firmly entrenched, serving longer terms in their respective offices than any other officials during the entire Ch'ung-chen reign period. Unfortunately their staying power was not matched with any marked ability for planning an effective antirebel policy. Grand Secretary Chou's favorite device was concealing unfavorable reports in his office files by labeling them secret and passing them along to his subordinates. Minister Chang based his whole approach to problems on an ostentatious display of servility before the Emperor who, he argued, should decide everything. Upon receipt of bad news from the rebel or Manchurian fronts, instead of planning rational counter-measures, he would resort to dramatic displays before the Emperor, consisting of kowtowing, citing his devotion and unceasing efforts,

---

* *HLLK* 4/10b-11a, 14a. Wen and Chou are listed among the evil officials in the *MS*.

fulminating against disobedient subordinates, and begging that he himself be held responsible and punished in any way the Emperor wished.

The central government eventually did succeed in collecting military forces to oppose the rebels in the newly threatened area.[9] The forces were drawn from several sources: the northern frontier, provincial troops on the spot, the Peking garrison, areas to the south, and Shensi (now seemingly out of danger from the rebels). There were also specially recruited forces consisting of miners and salt workers who were temporarily enlisted for the emergency. This latter group proved to be a mixed blessing. Though the men displayed great bravery and daring, they were also unruly and difficult to manage. At the opposite end of the scale were the Peking garrison troops, who were completely docile, but who won the contempt of the rebels for their lack of fighting spirit.

The main commanders of the newly collected forces were Tso Liang-yü, Teng I, and Ts'ao Wen-chao. Tso had arisen from complete obscurity to his present position of military command as a result of the ability he had displayed on the Manchurian frontier. His last post had been Regional Vice-commander at Ch'ang-p'ing, just north of Peking, and he was now transferred south with 2,400 men and 850 horses and mules to fight the rebels. He was thus launched on a career of rebel pacification which was to last until his death in 1645. Teng was also a completely self-made man, having joined the army in the late Wan-li period when he was only sixteen and rising through the ranks. He was noted for his good sense of strategy, the strict discipline he imposed upon his men, and the excellent field reports which, even though illiterate, he was able to dictate to his clerks. His force was mainly from Szechwan and Chekiang. It was used chiefly for defense, since the troops were not skilled horsemen and thus unsuited to pursue and attack the rebels. Ts'ao was transferred east from Shensi where we saw he was known for his ruthlessness in fighting the rebels.

The problem of coordinating the activities of the various officers fighting the rebels was never satisfactorily solved and no Supreme Commander was appointed.[10] Over-all direction of the campaign was supposed to be in the hands of the Grand Coordinators of Shansi and Honan, but at the height of the trouble, the Shansi Grand Coordinator, already under investigation for neglect of duty in allowing the rebels to move across the Yellow River into his province, was permitted to return home to observe mourning. Considerable difficulty was experienced in replacing him, though the Emperor finally did name Hsü Ting-ch'en to the post. Hsü's latest service had been in the Court of Imperial Entertainments and he possessed no obvious qualifications for the difficult Shansi post. He had trouble getting the troops dispatched from Shensi to obey his orders and also became involved in a dispute with a subordinate officer whom he accused of having treasonable contact with the rebels. Also, he was guilty of concealing the real gravity of the situation in his reports, such as the one submitted early in 1633 in which it is stated that fifty percent of the rebels had been annihilated, thirty percent had been dispersed, and the remaining twenty percent would soon be eliminated according to plans which had been formulated.

The command problem was complicated even further by the Emperor's resorting to a practice long favored by Ming monarchs and dispatching eunuch army inspectors during the summer of 1633.[11] The eunuchs were empowered to investigate the conduct of the campaigns by the various commanders and to distribute 40,000 taels and 1,400 pieces of fine silk cloth as rewards. The inspectors proceeded on their rounds with considerable pomp and circumstance, wearing girdles of jade or rhinoceros skin. Though one source declares that the eunuchs carried out their duties in a reasonably responsible manner, the total impact of the action was unfortunate in intensifying the well-known antagonism between the eunuchs and the regular bureaucracy.

Fortunately for the imperial cause, the rebels were not yet in a position to exploit effectively its weaknesses.[12] The overriding rebel problem was unity and the chaos prevailing within the rebel ranks made the government forces appear like a well-functioning machine in comparison. Wang Tzu-yung was accorded some vague recognition as the possessor of seniority within the rebel ranks, but this recognition meant little in reality. Furthermore, the rebel leader Luan-shih-wang became involved in a bitter dispute with Wang over a woman and entered into a plot with a government agent to assassinate Wang. The plot did not succeed, but did result in a considerable increase of mutual suspicion among the rebel groups. Other government agents had similar success in stimulating rebel discord. In addition, Wang Tzu-yung did die, apparently from natural causes, in the late spring of 1633 and was given an elaborate burial in the mountains of central Honan. There now vanished completely whatever symbolic influence he had exerted for rebel unity.

On the purely technical military level, there was no question that the government still had definite superiority over the rebels. It is true that in many battles the rebels greatly outnumbered the imperial forces, but the superior training and equipment of the latter usually gave them the victory. None of the major government commanders was ever in real danger of a serious defeat and all of them won numerous engagements, succeeding in killing at least six major rebel leaders during late 1632 and 1633. Rebel victories, such as their capture of the towns of Lin-hsien and Tse-chou in Shansi and Hsiu-wu in Honan produced no real advan-

MING DYNASTY PEASANT REBELLIONS

7   LOCATIONS OF PEASANT REBEL ACTIVITY IN **1634**

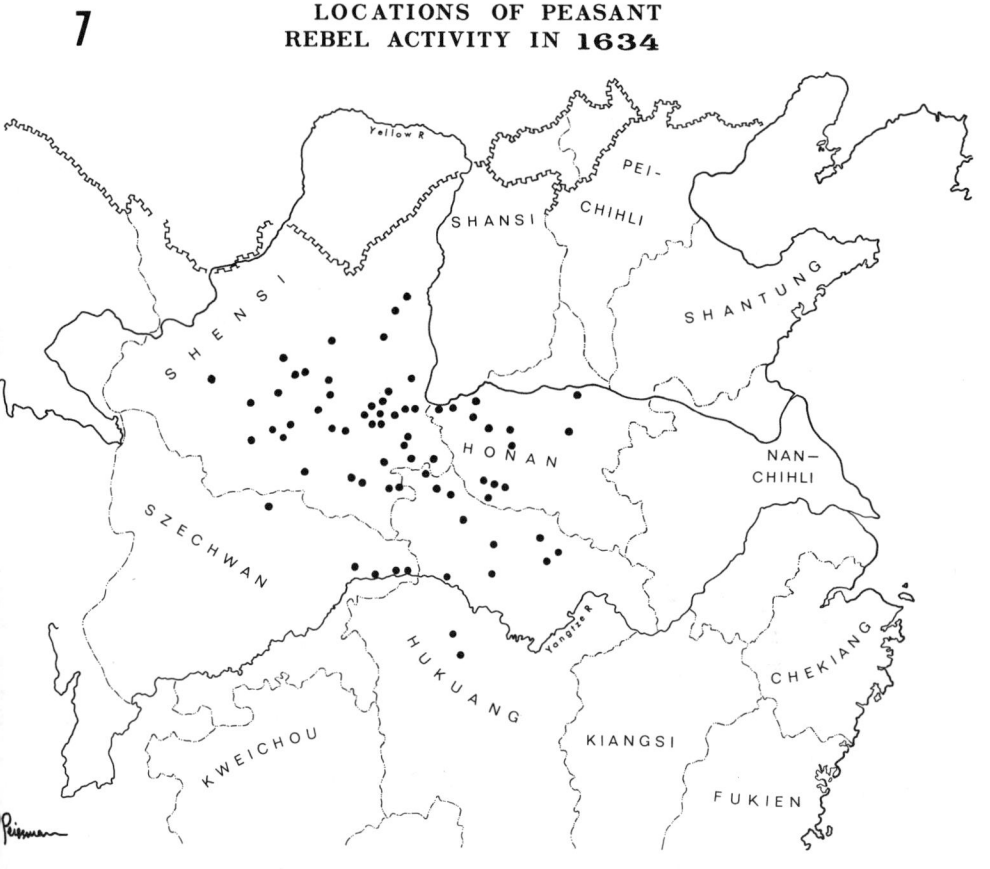

tages for them. None of the towns, with the possible exception of Lin-hsien, was held for more than a few days.

More important than the government's military superiority was the fact that the basic fabric of political and social organization at the local level was not yet seriously disrupted. County officials took vigorous measures for the protection of their areas in many instances, strengthening walls, constructing fortifications, recruiting and arming local defense forces, arranging warning systems, and spying on the rebels' movements. Also, the local areas were called upon to contribute extra supplies to the government forces. There were difficulties in meeting these demands for supplies and one unfortunate county magistrate in Shansi committed suicide because he was unable to provide the materials demanded of him by the army. In general, however, the official forces were adequately provided for without bankrupting local economies.

During the latter half of 1633, the rebels gradually moved out of the area in which their operations had been centered for somewhat more than a year: southwest Shansi, northern Honan, and southwestern Peichihli. They had been unable to withstand the military pressure the government maintained against them and there were no disasters of sufficient magnitude to provoke massive popular discontent which they could exploit to swell their ranks. Thus, the rebel groups pushed south across the Yellow River into central and southwestern Honan. This southward movement was completed during late 1633 and early 1634 when the freezing of the river facilitated crossing it. The abandoned area north of the Yellow River was to remain free of any really serious rebel threat for almost an entire decade, and from 1634 until 1643 the rebels operated mainly within China's vast central region, stretching from the Yellow River in the north* to the Yangtze in the south and from Szechwan in the west to Nan-chihli in the east. Once again, then, the government forces had failed to eliminate the rebel movement, but had succeeded in exerting enough military pressure to force the rebel bands to move, with their strength relatively intact, into another area.

The Focal Area of the Rebellions shifts to the South and West

By the beginning of 1634 the focal area of the rebellions had shifted to central and southwestern Honan, northwestern Hukuang, and particularly central and southeastern Shensi (see Map 7). Thus, wide new areas were engulfed which had previously been outside the rebel-afflicted zone. Even in Shensi, the rebellions pushed into new territory, generally

---

* It should be remembered that in Ming times the Yellow River flowed into the sea south of the Shantung peninsula.

avoiding the impoverished regions in the northern half of the province which had been their birthplace.

In moving into the new area, the rebels had the advantages of rapid movement, the lack of military preparedness on the government's side, and the inexperience of local authorities in dealing with lawlessness of the new magnitude. There was the expected delay in the redeploying of troops to meet the changed situation.[13] At first, 8,000 troops were ordered transferred from the command of Hung Ch'eng-ch'ou in Shensi to Honan, but the pushing of the rebels into Shensi made such a move impossible. Subsequently such temporary expedients as bringing in aboriginal troops from the southwest were resorted to. These troops saw service in both Honan and Hukuang. The major move of the central government, however, was the naming of a Supreme Commander to direct the general assault on the rebels.[14]

As early as the summer of 1633 there had been sufficient realization in Peking for the need to have more unity in the anti-rebel campaign that a proposal had been made to give an overall command position to Hung Ch'eng-ch'ou. The proposal had suggested that Hung move his headquarters to T'ung Pass and assume command of operations against the rebels in Shensi, Honan, and Shansi. The idea had been rejected by the Emperor.

Early in 1634 renewed suggestions were made for Hung to be given a much expanded command, but though the Emperor now had accepted the proposal in principle, Hung was passed over as the one to fill the position, apparently because it was felt that he was indispensable in Shensi. Instead of Hung, Ch'en Ch'i-yü was chosen and named Supreme Commander of Shensi, Shansi, Honan, Hukuang, and Szechwan. For the first time, the anti-rebel campaign had a Supreme Commander whose authority encompassed several provinces.

At first glance it would appear than Ch'en was the most intelligent appointment the government had made thus far in the rebel pacification campaign. A native of Shansi and a *chin-shih* of the late Wan-li period, Ch'en's most recent services prior to his appointment were as Administration Commissioner of Shensi and subsequently as Grand Coordinator of Yenan and Sui-te Prefectures in northern Shensi. Thus, for some time he had occupied high provincial posts in Shensi and certainly must have accumulated considerable knowledge regarding the rebel problem. He had seen military service against the rebels and had to his credit the action which expelled them from their occupation of the Yung-ning Pass.

Ch'en was not strictly committed to pursuing a policy either of political settlement or of extermination through military action.[15] His instructions from Peking empowered him to pursue either policy depending upon his own judgment as to which was most appropriate in any particular case. Furthermore, Ch'en did not have eunuch inspectors in his army, as an imperial order recalled those who had been dispatched the previous year.[16] The Emperor stated that his prior action was taken because of corrupt and incompetent officials, but that conditions had now greatly improved. Eunuch inspectors were left in the border areas, causing the expected continued opposition from the regular bureaucracy. However, the Emperor's action in recalling some of the eunuchs undoubtedly served to improve relations between the court and the officials directing the military campaigns against the rebels in the field.

The initial military efforts directed by Ch'en Ch'i-yü met with considerable success.[17] Incursions into northeastern Szechwan by the rebel leaders Chang Hsien-chung and Lo Ju-ts'ai were quickly beaten back, partly as a result of victories against them by the famous late Ming heroine, Ch'in Liang-yü. In Shensi, Hung Ch'eng-ch'ou, Ts'ao Wen-chao, and Ho Jen-lung were so successful that by the summer of 1634 most of the strongest rebel bands (those led by Kao Ying-hsiang, Li Tzu-ch'eng, Ma Shou-ying, Lo Ju-ts'ai, and probably Chang Hsien-chung) had been bottled up in Ch'e-hsiang Gorge in extreme west central Honan near the Shensi border. The siege of the gorge by the imperial forces continued through the summer during which time the downpours of rain did a great deal of damage to the weapons of the rebels. Even worse, the rebels themselves (said by one source to have numbered 13,000), as well as their horses, were reduced to starvation. Faced with what is described as virtual extinction, the rebels offered their surrender to Supreme Commander Ch'en, and Li Tzu-ch'eng is said to have resorted to the time-honored ritual of binding himself with ropes and appearing in person before Ch'en to present his submission and to beg for mercy.

Why Ch'en accepted the rebel offer to surrender is not satisfactorily explained in any of the sources. One source does state that the rebels bribed members of his staff with large numbers of precious stones and these subordinates brought pressure on Ch'en on behalf of the rebels. There is no suggestion that Ch'en was personally involved in the bribery dealings, and it is probable that he sincerely hoped to end the rebellions in a peaceful manner which did not entail wholesale slaughter. Further, one suspects that the government's military advantage at Ch'e-hsiang Gorge was not as overwhelming as it is made to appear.

Following the rebel surrender, Ch'en assigned some fifty officials to the rebel camps with orders to supervise the return of the rebels to their homes in northern Shensi. Also, Ch'en instructed local authorities along the rebel route of passage not to attack them and to provide them with food.

The surrendered rebels and their official supervisors marched northwest from Ch'e-hsiang Gorge toward the upper Wei River Valley. This was not the most direct route to northern Shensi and it was presumably taken because Ch'en did not want the more important areas of the lower Wei River Valley to become involved in case any mishap occurred in the dealings with the rebels. There was no trouble until the rebel group reached Pao-chi, a town just north of the Wei River in central Shensi, where the incident happened which brought about the collapse of the entire surrender agreement.

Exactly what happened at Pao-chi is unclear, but it is known that the local magistrate killed thirty-six rebels probably as a result of their insistence on entering the town against his wishes. This act enraged the entire rebel group and they dispersed after having slaughtered the official supervisors in their midst. For several months the rebel bands raided widely throughout the whole length of the Wei River Valley while the government sought to assemble its forces once more to attack them.[18] The official task was made more difficult by the actions of one of its own commanders, Tu Wen-huan, who had long been notorious for allowing his men to plunder. His acts now became so flagrant that the Emperor, in response to numerous complaints, ordered an investigation. The report of the investigator charged that Tu had caused a rebellion in central Shensi as a result of looting by his men and that he had tried to conceal his illegal actions by killing innocent people. The final verdict in the case called for the banishment of Tu and the execution of one of his subordinates.

The breakdown of the Ch'e-hsiang Gorge surrender agreement cast a shadow over the future of Ch'en Ch'i-yü as Supreme Commander.[19] He tried desperately to evade the disaster which threatened his career by blaming the magistrate of Pao-chi County for having provoked the surrendered rebels into rebelling again. It took Peking a while to decide Ch'en's fate, but as continued news of wide rebel raiding in the Wei River Valley reached the capital, there could be little doubt that the final decision would go against him. Late in 1634 the blow fell. He was arrested, stripped of his rank, and sentenced to exile. His political oblivion was destined to be permanent, and the end of the dynasty in 1644 saw him still in disfavor. Thus, the third Supreme Commander charged with crushing the rebels lasted only some nine months in his exalted position and ended more a abject failure than one of his predecessors, Yang Ho.

Most of the sources go to considerable lengths in blaming Ch'en Ch'i-yü for having let slip an excellent chance to deal a blow which would have crushed the rebel movement, and he himself is said to have bitterly regretted his decision to permit the rebel surrender. Furthermore, the sources are fond of pointing out the obvious fact that the rebel surrender was based on pure expediency. It is undoubtedly true that the Ch'e-hsiang submission agreement was a mistake and it undeniably had some influence on the future course of the rebel movement. However, it is hardly the crucial turning point of the rebellions, and its importance is exaggerated in the sources. The rebels sustained bitter defeats both before and after Ch'e-hsiang Gorge, always managing to survive. The failure of Supreme Commander Ch'en to insist upon all-out military victory in this one instance hardly meant that the fate of the Ming dynasty was decided in this obscure mountain defile in western Honan.

The Jung-yang Conclave and the Attempt at Rebel Unity

Early in 1635 occurred one of the most interesting events that had taken place thus far in the rebel movement: the great rebel conclave in Jung-yang, a county in central Honan a short distance south of the Yellow River. Unfortunately, the information available about the meeting is scanty and nothing whatsoever is known about the origins of the idea to hold a general assemblage of most rebel groups. Perhaps the government's attempts to unify its pacification campaigns inspired the rebels to pursue a similar course. More probably, it was a quite spontaneous development and resulted in large measure from the fact that most of the rebel leaders were natives of northern Shensi who had known one another for several years and who had cooperated previously in a limited and sporadic fashion. At any rate, in the 1st month of 1635 thirteen rebel groups (*chia*), said to have been composed of seventy-two camps (*ying*) held a general conclave at Jung-yang which lasted approximately two weeks.[20]

The leaders of the thirteen groups were Kao Ying-hsiang, Chang Hsien-chung, Ma Shou-ying, Lo Ju-ts'ai, Ko-kuo-yen, Tso-chin-wang, Kai-shih-wang, She-t'a-t'ien, Heng-t'ien-wang, Kuo-t'ien-hsing, Chiu-t'iao-lung, Shun-t'ien-wang, and Hun-shih-wan. These thirteen, together with Li Tzu-ch'eng who attended the meeting as the chief lieutenant of Kao Ying-hsiang, represent a relatively complete listing of the rebel leadership as of 1635, and those who managed to survive the government campaigns against them were destined to remain important for a decade to come. In fact, no one who did not attend the Jung-yang conclave was able to assume subsequently a top position of leadership in the rebel movement.

Despite the fact that he was technically of lower status than the thirteen rebel "elders," Li Tzu-ch'eng apparently played the dominant role at the Jung-yang meeting. His first accomplishment was the settlement of a dispute which broke out between Chang Hsien-chung and Ma Shou-ying.

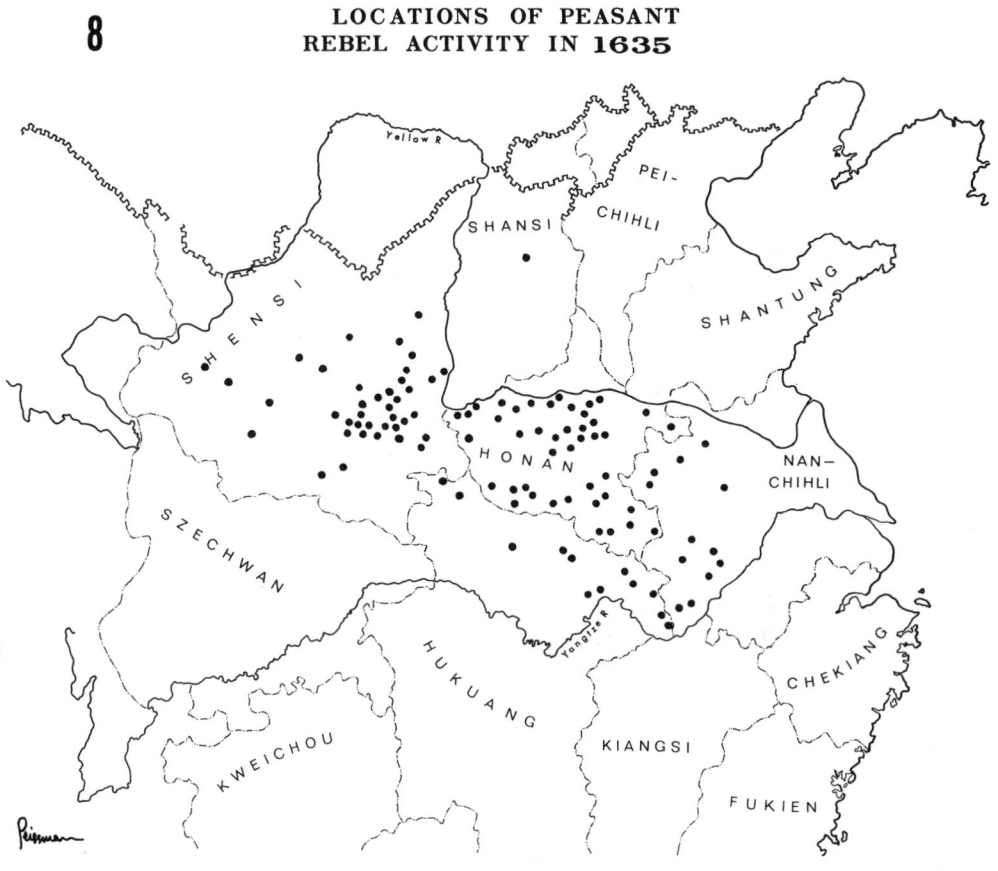

Ma had suggested in preliminary discussions of future operations that concentration should again be on Shansi, an area which had been almost completely avoided by the rebels since 1633. Chang took violent exception to this suggestion, and Li's service as mediator was required. In subsequent talks, Li stressed his belief in the great superiority the rebels had over the imperial forces and he was the moving spirit behind the general plan for opposing the enemy which was eventually drawn up and agreed upon.

The general plan outlined definite assignments and objectives for specific rebel groups: Ko-kuo-yen and Tso-chin-wang were assigned the northern Hukuang area; Lo Ju-ts'ai and Kuo-t'ien-hsing were to remain in central Honan, paying special attention to the defense of the Yellow River; Kao Ying-hsiang and Chang Hsien-chung were to proceed eastward into Nan-chihli; Ma Shou-ying and Chiu-t'iao-lung were to serve as a reserve force and move to the aid of any sector which needed special assistance, and Heng t'ien-wang, Hun-shih-wan, She-t'a-t'ien, and Kai-shih-wang were to move into Shensi. The size of the last force was double that of the others because it was felt that the government troops in Shensi were particularly strong and able.

For some reason, unexplained in any of the sources, one of the thirteen rebel leaders, Shun-t'ien-wang, was given no assignment in the general plan. His career came to an end some three months after the Jung-yang conference when he was captured by a government force in east central Honan.

Apparently the general plan envisaged the group assigned to invade eastward, Kao Ying-hsiang and Chang Hsien-chung, as the most significant attack force. The assignments of the other groups were more defensive in nature. And indeed the Kao-Chang group did manage to achieve a quite spectacular initial success.[21] Moving rapidly across Honan and penetrating into central Nan-chihli, they seized Feng-yang, the native area of the Ming imperial family and the site of important ancestral tombs and temples. The rebels burned and looted some of the tombs, killed several officials, and released a large number of imperial relatives who were being detained on criminal charges.* Among those released was the Prince of T'ang's heir who was later set up as a pretender in Fukien following the collapse of the dynasty. The rebels held the town and the immediate environs for three days, abandoning the area upon learning that a relief force was drawing near.

---

* The imperial family had long used Feng-yang as a closet for hiding family skeletons. For example, following the Yung-lo usurpation, the infant son of the Chien-wen Emperor was sent there and detained for several decades.

The news of the rebel strike against Feng-yang produced consternation in Peking and the Emperor responded with the appropriate ceremonial gestures: wearing mourning, abstaining from sexual intercourse, announcing the disaster in the ancestral temple, and commanding all officials to rectify their conduct. Also, two officials considered especially responsible for the loss of Feng-yang, the Grand Coordinator of the area and the chief eunuch guardian of the tombs, were arrested. The former was executed and the latter committed suicide.

Despite the shock which the loss of Feng-yang caused, the event could hardly be classed as a major accomplishment of the rebels. As noted, they held the town for only three days and withdrew when an enterprising eunuch approached with a relief force. Furthermore, an incident occurred during the looting of the imperial tombs which demonstrated that the rebel efforts at unity were completely premature. The incident involved the possession of some eunuch musicians, performers at tomb ceremonies, who had been captured by Chang Hsien-chung. Li Tzu-ch'eng requested that he be given the eunuchs and Chang was so incensed at the request that he consented only after smashing the musical instruments employed by the eunuchs in their performances. Li responded with an even more brutal display by killing the eunuchs. The incident completely disrupted the Kao-Chang alliance, Kao and Li Tzu-ch'eng returning forthwith to Shensi via Honan and Chang remaining temporarily alone in Nan-chihli. The incident marked the real beginning of strained relations between Chang and Li which were to last for the rest of their lives, though they were not above limited cooperation upon occasion.

Following the collapse of the Kao-Chang alliance, which certainly lasted less than a month, one hears no more of the grand rebel strategy agreed to at Jung-yang. Apparently the other rebel leaders took their assignments just as lightly. Thus, one can hardly consider the Jung-yang conclave as a watershed event in the rebel movement, nor was it unique. There were subsequent meetings, though they were more restricted in participation and more limited in the agreements reached. At the same time, it is impossible to deny the Jung-yang assemblage some real significance. Most important of all, it is one of the earliest manifestations that the late Ming rebels were beginning to have some awareness, however faint, of a purpose more serious than plunder. They began to have some conception of overthrowing the dynasty and marched eastward to Feng-yang with banners proclaiming themselves as adherents of "The True Primal Dragon Emperor" (Ku yüan chen lung huang-ti).[22] Furthermore, the Jung-yang meeting provided the impetus which thrust the rebellions into an important new area—Nan-chihli. With this thrust, the rebels approached two of the most vital points in the entire country: the Grand Canal and the economically, politically, and culturally key region of southeastern Nan-chihli and northeastern Chekiang. Once introduced into Nan-chihli, the rebels subjected the area to periodic plundering for the next decade.

The Rebels Return to Disunity

The downfall of Supreme Commander Ch'en Ch'i-yü in late 1634 was followed by Hung Ch'eng-ch'ou's being appointed to direct the coordinated anti-rebel campaign. This appointment was regarded as a temporary arrangement, and in the 8th month of 1635 Lu Hsiang-sheng was made Supreme Commander of Honan, Shantung, Pei-chihli, Szechwan, and Hukuang.[23] Lu, a native of Nan-chihli and a *chin-shih* of the T'ien-ch'i period, had had considerable prior experience in campaigns against the rebels. He was expected to be responsible for pacifying all the areas east of T'ung Pass, and Hung Ch'eng-ch'ou again would concentrate on Shensi. The two were explicitly directed to coordinate their military moves and aid each other when appropriate.

Both Hung and Lu were well aware of the particular problems which had arisen as a result of the enormous spread of the rebellions and the rapid movement of the rebel bands from one area to another and back again.[24] Already in the 4th month of 1635, Hung had held a conference of his principal lieutenants and discussed policies to be adopted. He pointed out his troops were suffering from exhaustion after chasing the rebels from Shensi to Honan only to find upon arrival that the enemy had rushed back to Shensi. Hung tried unsuccessfully to set up fixed positions for his lieutenants to occupy and serve as bulwarks to prevent the rebels from moving about so rapidly. Shortly following Lu Hsiang-sheng's appointment as Supreme Commander, Hung set up headquarters in southeastern Honan. He directed his attacks southward against the rebel groups in northern Hukuang and tried to keep them separated from the rebels in west central Honan.

Looked at from the rebel side, the rebellions during 1635 and 1636 present a picture of utter confusion. The various rebel groups were operating quite independently with limited and purely localized cooperation and they switched rapidly from one area to another. No degree of planning can be discerned in their movements and they reacted automatically to such considerations of the moment as pressure of government forces and the attractions of more lucrative plundering. A single rebel group would move from central Shensi across Honan to Nan-chihli and back again in a few months' time. In this maze of movement it is absolutely impossible to follow with any degree of certainty the exact route followed by any one rebel leader. Details concerning the movements of the various groups are hopelessly confused in the sources and one can sympathize with the bureaucrats at various levels of government who struggled to make some sense out of the mass of reports which reached them from the field.

During the first three months of 1635, the most active rebel front was in central Nan-chihli.[25] We have noted already the rebel push into this vital province, the breakdown in the attempted rebel cooperation which occurred there, and the return of Kao Ying-hsiang and Li Tzu-ch'eng to Shensi following the breakup of the Kao-Chang alliance. Chang Hsien-chung and allied lesser rebel bands remained in Nan-chihli for at least another month, moving almost due south from Feng-yang, whose capture has been discussed, to the Yangtze River. Then the rebel forces pushed up the river, passing through such important localities as Ho-chou, Ch'ao-hsien, Wu-wei, Lu-chiang, T'ung-ch'eng, Ch'ien-shan, and T'ai-hu in Nan-chihli and Ch'i-chou, Lo-t'ien, Ma-ch'eng, and Hanyang in Hukuang. Apparently only two towns, Ch'ien-shan and Lo-t'ien, actually fell to the rebels and neither was occupied for more than a few days. At Ch'i-chou one of the more important secondary rebel chieftains, P'a-t'ien-wang, was seized and killed by villagers while he was engaged in raiding. He had the reputation of being one of the most brutal rebel leaders and his sons are described as having red hair and eyes as a result of living on a diet of human hearts.

From Han-yang, Chang Hsien-chung and his allies pressed northwestward up the valley of the Han River into southern Honan. He was trailed throughout most of this extended move by government forces under Regional Commander Teng I, but at Fan-ch'eng in the upper Han Valley, Teng's strict disciplining of his troops caused them to mutiny and burn him to death[26] However, the authorities were able to salvage much of his army, and it was eventually amalgamated with the forces of Tso Liang-yü.

In Honan, Chang Hsien-chung met Ma Shou-ying and accompanied him in a move to Shensi, arriving there in the late spring of 1635. Most of the other major rebel groups were already in Shensi and for the next five or six months the main center of rebel activity was again in that province.[27] The rebels concentrated on operations in the Wei River Valley where their major military achievement was the capture of the town of Fu-feng by Kao Ying-hsiang. The town fell after a siege which lasted an entire month. The fact that the rebels were able to mount such a long siege is certainly evidence that their military potential had considerably increased.

Li Tzu-ch'eng and some allied bands pushed north of the Wei River Valley into the familiar northern Shensi area and at Chen-ning achieved what was probably the greatest rebel victory thus far in the rebellions.[28] They surrounded and virtually destroyed a government force of 2,000 men commanded by the swashbuckling Ts'ao Wen-chao. Faced with certain defeat, Ts'ao committed suicide on the battlefield. As noted previously, he had a wide reputation as one of the most vigorous and relentless of the Ming commanders, and his death was a great blow to the morale of the government forces not only in Shensi but also in Honan and Hukuang where he had campaigned.

By the late fall of 1635, Kao Ying-hsiang and several of the principal rebel leaders, with the chief exception of Li Tzu-ch'eng, had moved their bands out of Shensi into western Honan.[29] The town of Lu-shih was occupied for a short time, and subsequently the rebels concentrated briefly in the Ling-pao area before advancing via Ju-chou into the southeastern corner of Honan and attacking the town of Kuang-chou. During the siege of Kuang-chou the rebels are said to have successfully employed two of their twenty cannons in battering down a section of the city wall.

After a short stay in Kuang-chou, Kao and his allies early in 1636 launched a second rebel incursion into Nan-chihli.[30] The rebels reached the Yangtze in the vicinity of Lu-chou, then followed the river northeastward. They made Ch'u-chou their major objective and placed the town under siege. However, they were attacked and defeated by the recently appointed Supreme Commander, Lu Hsiang-sheng. This check forced the rebels to move rapidly northward where they made unsuccessful attempts to capture towns in extreme northern Nan-chihli near the Shantung border. Subsequently, they abandoned Nan-chihli altogether, moving westward into Honan. Thus, the second major rebel invasion of the lower Yangtze area ended as ingloriously as the first and lasted hardly more than a month.

During the half-year period following the rebel withdrawal from Nan-chihli, the main current of the rebellions, amid many minor crosscurrents, flowed slowly southwestward across Honan into northern Hukuang where the movement shifted to the northeast, once more entering southeastern Shensi. Throughout the entire course of this particular rebel move there were numerous encounters between the rebels and the many government units operating in the various areas. In general, it can be said that the government forces in the encounters still demonstrated that they possessed military superiority, though the rebels did manage to deliver a crushing defeat to Regional Commander T'ang Chiu-chou in Sung County in west central Honan. T'ang was killed and his army virtually destroyed. The rebel victory was partly accidental and resulted mainly because T'ang did not receive the support he should have had from Tso Liang-yü and other government commanders. Typically, then, the military encounters resulted in rebel defeats, though never to a decisive degree.

In the economic sphere, closely related to the military situation, the central government, in the spring of 1636, decided to prohibit the trade in grain between Honan and Hukuang. The trade routes led from northern Hukuang into central Honan and because they thus crossed an area which the rebels were constantly passing through, it was possible for the rebels to obtain needed supplies from the traffic. The prohibition evoked a strong protest from the Honan Grand Coordinator who argued that the grain trade was essential for supplying the official forces in central Honan and the prohibition probably never became really effective.

Li Tzu-ch'eng in Shensi

In the autumn of 1635 the rebellions started flowing eastward from Shensi to Nan-chihli and then early in 1636 began moving back to Shensi. Outside of this main trend, Li Tzu-ch'eng remained in Shensi,* mainly in the north, for more than a year following his victory over Ts'ao Wen-chao in the late spring of 1635. He was unable, however, to exploit his victory over Ts'ao and continued to follow the standard rebel practice of continually moving from place to place. In the winter of 1635-36, when food shortages became acute, he attempted to push across the Yellow River into Shansi, but these attempts failed due to the excellent defense of the river organized by the able Grand Coordinator of Shansi, Wu Sheng, whom we met much earlier when he was serving as a Censor in charge of distributing relief funds in Shensi.

Blocked from pushing across the Yellow River, Li turned to wide-ranging movements in northern Shensi. The next six months saw him cover hundreds of miles of territory which extended from his native Mi-chih in the far north to the Wei River and from the Yellow River to Kung-ch'ang in far west-central Shensi. Some of these moves were made by his own band alone, but he was also frequently joined for a time by less important rebel forces and their followers. Throughout this series of moves, sporadic skirmishes were fought with Hung Ch'eng-ch'ou and his various subordinate commanders, but these engagements were no more significant in either enhancing or detracting from Li's power than the scores of similar encounters he had been involved in during the past several years.

---

* *HLLK* 8/37b; *MS* 309/9b; and *YSCC* 5/16a-b. Some of the sources actually have Li accompanying the main rebel current as it moved eastward and returned westward. However, a careful study of the *HLLK*, the most complete of the sources, provides a quite definite indication that Li remained in Shensi. Kao Ying-hsiang, who did move eastward and then returned westward, is easily confused with Li, because of the similarity of their nicknames.

In fact, memorials were submitted in Peking bitterly criticizing Hung for concentrating on campaigns against unimportant minor rebels and leaving Li untouched. There is some justice in these criticisms, for it is apparent that at times the opposition maintained against Li was definitely on a low key. His men are said to have collected outside the city wall of Sui-te to inquire about their relatives inside the town, and the obvious prosperity of the rebels, demonstrated by their fine clothes, evoked such admiration for their good fortune that many more natives of the northern Shensi area were inspired to join the rebel ranks. In addition, Li presented a gift of money to the magistrate of his native county, Mi-chih, to be used for repairing the local Confucian temple. At the same time he assured the magistrate that he would not harm the area.

Li's most serious loss during the somewhat more than one year that he remained in northern Shensi was the surrender to the authorities of one of his ablest lieutenants, Kao Chieh, and his favorite concubine, a lady surnamed Hsing, who is said to have been charged with the management of supplies in his group.[31] These defections did not result from any initiative on the official side, but came about because the concubine and Kao feared that Li would discover the romantic attachment which had developed between them. Kao was given a position of command in the government forces and served the imperial cause rather ably for eight years, reverting back to Li's side early in 1644.

In the late summer of 1636, Li moved into southeastern Shensi to rejoin the main rebel groups which by this time had arrived in that area after a gradual withdrawal from the east. Li had apparently not yet made actual contact with his rebel confederates when the imperial forces under the newly appointed Grand Coordinator for Shensi, Sun Ch'üan-t'ing, achieved one of their more notable victories over the rebels.[32] Sun attacked the rebels in Chih-chih County after they had advanced to the central Wei River Valley from southeastern Shensi. He not only badly defeated the rebels, but also managed to capture Kao Ying-hsiang, the single most powerful rebel leader whose importance is indicated by the fact that the authorities went to the trouble of sending him to Peking for execution.

Li Tzu-ch'eng, who probably was related to Kao and who had served as one of his subordinates for several years, succeeded to the command of Kao's surviving forces and also to his nickname title, "Dashing King" (Ch'uang-wang). Subsequently Li resorted to a hasty retreat from the Wei River Valley and withdrew to far southwestern Shensi.

The late autumn or early winter of 1636 can be said to mark a notable dividing point in the disorganized raiding phase of the rebellions. The rebels had just lost their most important leader and their fortunes were

MING DYNASTY PEASANT REBELLIONS

9 LOCATIONS OF PEASANT REBEL ACTIVITY IN 1636

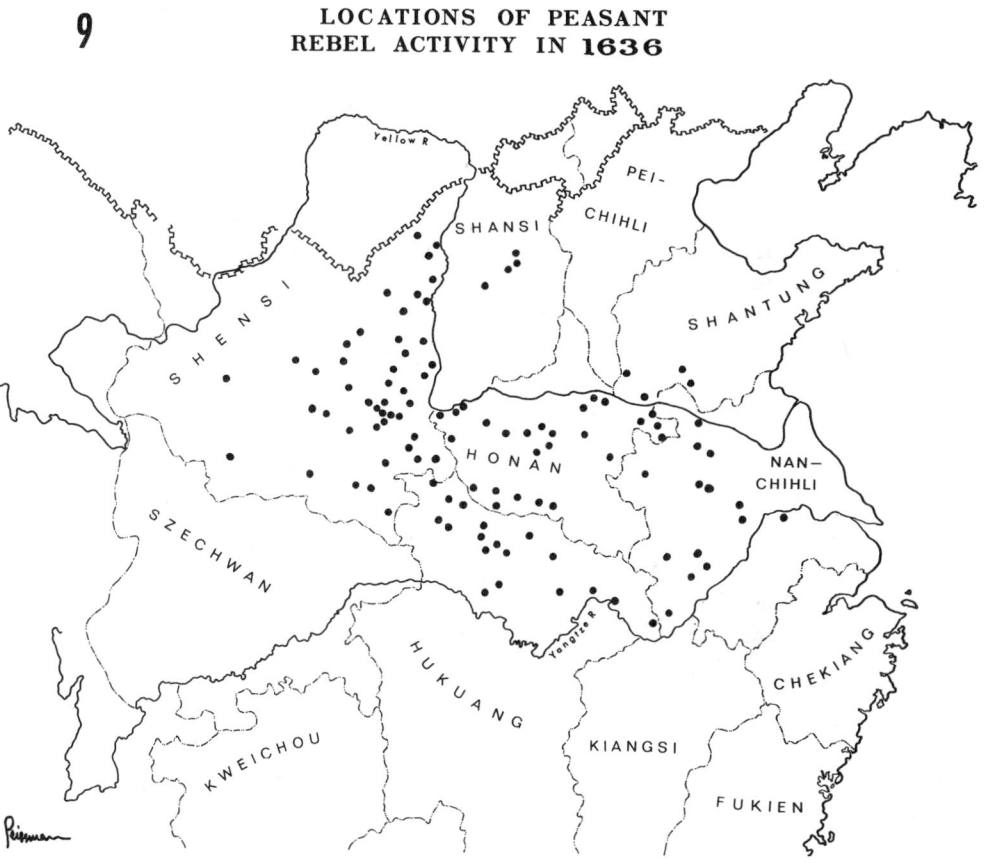

on the verge of beginning a significant, though temporary, decline. On the side of the government, Yang Ssu-ch'ang was in the process of putting the final touches to the consolidation of his influence in Peking, and he was to hold a rather unsteady grip on the fate of the dynasty for the next five years. From the standpoints of both the rebels and the government, events took a decidedly different turn beginning in late 1636. Before considering this next stage of the rebellion, however, the 1631-36 period should be assessed.

General Assessment of the 1631-36 Period of the Rebellions

The situation of the rebellions in 1636 was quite different from that which existed in 1631. Most basic of all, between 1631 and 1636 the rebellions had pushed forth from a relatively confined area in the northwest and become a national problem. Though the rebels had failed to establish themselves north of the Yellow River and to become a more immediate threat to Peking itself, they had succeeded in coursing through most of the central section of China, that vast area between the Yangtze and the Yellow rivers. Accompanying this geographical spread was a considerable increase in the rebels' military potential so that by 1636 even senior officials were admitting openly in memorials that the former overwhelming superiority enjoyed by the government was a thing of the past.

A basic pattern in rebel operations had emerged in a definite fashion by 1636. Particularly important in forming this pattern was the rebel response to the military advantage still held by the government: their resorting to continual movement. The rebel tide swept back and forth from Shensi to Nan-chihli and crosscurrents projected out from this main channel of the movement, forming a crazy-quilt picture of enormous complexity. Such mobility surely indicates that most of the rebels by 1636 were mounted, and rebel seizures of horses and other draft animals must certainly have represented a considerable setback for agricultural production in the huge area affected by the rebellions. The government could not match the rebels in mobility and an official in 1635 estimated that the rebels could move about five times as fast as the official forces.

In this pattern of rebel movement the key area was the border region where the provinces of Hukuang, Honan, and Shensi join. This area was to serve as the epicenter around which the rebellions revolved from 1634 until 1641. It had advantages which the rebels could exploit. In the first place, the population was relatively sparse and there were vast stretches of mountains covered with forests. These forests were so inaccessible that military operations therein by the government forces were extraordinarily difficult to conduct. In a memorial dealing with this subject, Supreme Commander Lu Hsiang-sheng stated that cavalry was of limited usefulness in the area and that infantry could cover only ten or twelve miles per day. Such slow progress greatly exaggerated the problem of supplies which had to be transported into the area. A bearer could carry only a half bushel of grain and be expected to maintain the pace of march. This amount of grain would be consumed by the bearer and one soldier within ten days and it was virtually impossible to conclude a campaign within such a short time. Thus, the rebels could retreat into the area for recuperation and regrouping without any great fears of being attacked. Furthermore, the strategic location of the area made it possible for the rebel groups to use it as a point for launching movements in several different directions. They could move northwestward into the Wei River Valley and northern Shensi, eastward into Honan and Nan-chihli, southeastward down the Han River to the Yangtze, and southwestward into Szechwan.

Another area of importance to the rebels was Huo-shan County (see Map 17) in southwestern Nan-chihli near the Honan and Hukuang borders. It, too, had relatively inaccessible regions to which the rebel groups could retire temporarily during their incursions into the lower Yangtze territory. However, it cannot be compared in significance with the Honan-Hukuang-Shensi area.

One cannot say that either of these two areas, though particularly important to the rebels for recuperation and the staging of incursions, was a real base, properly speaking. A permanent base was an impossibility for the rebels, militarily and ideologically, in 1636 and was to remain so for several years to come. It is certainly true that upon occasion rebels could win victories over government commanders, but such victories were partly chance occurrences without great permanent significance. Only if the rebel groups had been able to achieve real unity would they have had a possibility to maintain a permanent base, and the prospects for such unity were dim indeed in 1636. Furthermore, the rebel leaders did not yet have a conceptual framework which would have impelled them to see clearly the need for such a base and to seek one consciously. Any motivation for the rebels more serious than raiding and staying alive was yet only in its vague initial stages of development.

Looking at the government's efforts to crush the rebellions, the prospect is generally a disheartening one of bad planning, inadequate institutions, and personal failures. In Peking, at the top echelons of leadership, real talent was lacking. The Emperor was dedicated and seriously concerned with the drift of affairs. The self-blaming edicts which he issued quite regularly probably represented a sincere expression of his feelings and were not purely formal gestures. However, his limitations prevented him from being a good judge of character and he placed his confidence in officials of no great ability. His personal deep concern about the situation undoubtedly did more harm than good in that it interjected the imperial will into discussions and decisions concerning details about which he had no real understanding.

The most influential officials serving in Peking during virtually the entire 1631-36 period were the Grand Secretary Wen T'i-jen and the Minister of War Chang Feng-i. The former had a wide reputation for his corruption and the latter's sycophancy toward the Emperor has already been noted. Chang's incompetence is illustrated in a glaring fashion by his reply to a memorial concerning the rebel incursion into Nan-chihli at the beginning of 1635. Chang stated that there was no real need to be concerned about the rebels in Nan-chihli, because being natives of the northwest, they would not relish the kind of food available in the Yangtze Valley or want to feed their horses on local fodder!

The quality of leadership in the middle echelons—the lower officials in the ministries, the Supreme Commanders, and provincial Grand Coordinators—was considerably better than that in the top positions of the central government. Though none of the Supreme Commanders, Hung Ch'eng-ch'ou, Ch'en Ch'i-yü, and Lu Hsiang-sheng, displayed military genius, they did perform in a reasonably competent fashion. Among the Grand Coordinators, Ch'en Pi-ch'ien of Honan and Wu Sheng of Shansi were especially impressive. Wu deserves particular praise and should be awarded a considerable amount of the credit for keeping his province virtually free of rebels while large areas to the south were being overrun. Furthermore, Wu must be absolutely unique among late Ming officials for having once stated in a memorial to Peking that he had all the military supplies he needed! Grand Coordinators in Shantung and Pei-chihli also performed quite competently, joining with Wu Sheng and lower officials in the Ministry of War to plan and execute the successful defense of the Yellow River which was probably the single most notable military achievement of the entire late Ming period. The defense of the river required particularly close attention during the winter when the rebels could take advantage of the ice to cross over. Thus, the defense plans called for a concentration of troops at various points along the northern bank during the critical winter months. With the coming of spring, most of these troops were sent back to their regular assignments or were used to attack the rebels south of the river.

The lower echelons in the military command—the Regional Commanders and Regional Vice-commanders—hardly measured up in quality to their superiors. They were professional military men, some of whom like Tso Liang-yü and Teng I, were of lowly backgrounds and had risen from the ranks solely on their own merits. Generally illiterate, they obviously could not fully share the values of the *chin-shih* Supreme Commanders and Grand Coordinators to whom they were formally subordinate. The chain of command at times virtually ceased to function and the distraught Honan Grand Coordinator, Ch'en Pi-ch'ien, wrote a friend that to send a subordinate officer on a campaign against the rebels was like inviting a guest to one's home: the officer had to be entreated to undertake the mission; he could not be ordered to. For earlier periods of Ming history there are abundant illustrations of the complete dominance of high civil officials over professional military men who were often subjected to all kinds of indignities, but in the present circumstances the tables were beginning to turn.

The troops serving under the Regional Commanders and lower officers increasingly tended to be recruited on an *ad hoc* basis with the initiative for enlistment being taken by the individual commander. Some of the armies, particularly that of Tso Liang-yü, began to assume more and more of the characteristics of a personal army over which the Supreme Commanders and Grand Coordinators had a declining amount of control. The discipline in these semi-personal armies was lax and at times even the commanders could not control their own troops. It has been noted that no less important a Regional Commander than Teng I met a horrible fate at the hands of his own men who burned him to death as a result of their resentment over his attempts to control them strictly. Teng's troops, following his murder, refused to accept the new commander assigned them by Hung Ch'eng-ch'ou and on their own initiative attached themselves to the army of Tso Liang-yü.

The sources abound in citations of events illustrating the failure of the troops of the professional commanders to perform their military assignments and, even worse, their committing atrocities. One of the most frequently mentioned atrocities is the familiar one, extending back virtually to the very beginning of the rebellions: the slaughter of completely innocent peasants, sometimes even in collusion with the rebels, so that the official forces would be able to present heads as fake evidence of having gained a victory. There are also numerous accusations charging troops with looting and raping. It is said to have been common knowledge that Tso Liang-yü made little effort to restrain his troops and in fact enjoyed great popularity among them for demanding only a modest share of the loot.

It cannot be maintained that the professional military commanders were dominated completely by low motives or that they did not perform some real service to the imperial cause. Their loyalty was relatively firm and was demonstrated by the fact that very few of them at this time defected to the rebel side. Commanders like Tso Liang-yü had some real military ability and though it could hardly be said that he would have been willing to risk everything for the dynasty and he often was dilatory about pressing attacks, he nevertheless undertook numerous reasonably successful campaigns and probably was responsible for destroying more rebels than any other late Ming officer. Though he demanded of his troops little except slaughtering rebels and paid virtually no heed to their discipline, he did not completely outrage gentry sensibilities. Many stories, undoubtedly partly apocryphal, credit him with grandiose gestures which would have appealed to the gentry. For example, one story concerns a *chu-sheng** who appeared at his camp to complain that his wife had been kidnapped by Tso's troops. Tso promised that the woman would be given back if the man could find her. However, the wife refused to return with her husband, explaining that she preferred her present life and had no desire to go back to her past relative poverty. Tso comforted the man by presenting him with another woman and then when he was a short distance from the camp, sent him a bag containing his wife's head. Such gestures certainly made Tso one of the most colorful late Ming commanders, but they could hardly cancel out the unfortunate impact on popular morale produced by the violent acts which his troops committed. Tso must bear a considerable share of the responsibility for the late Ming popular saying, "The rebels comb with a coarse comb, but the official forces comb with a fine-toothed comb."

To sum up the military condition at the middle and lower levels of command during the mid-1630's, it can be said that a dangerous bifurcation was developing between the high civil officials charged with military responsibilities and the professional military men some of whom were self-made upstarts. The breakdown in discipline among the official troops, particularly in the semi-personal armies of the professional commanders, was almost as important as the depredations by the rebels in sundering the fabric of local political and social order.

Concerning a more technical military problem, the government in the mid-1630's was faced with the need for obtaining more and better troops. There seems no question that the rebels outnumbered the imperial forces, though officials in their own interests undoubtedly exaggerated the disparity between the two. As early as the summer of 1634, Hung Ch'eng-ch'ou had memorialized that the official forces in Shensi numbered less than 20,000 while the rebels totaled some 140,000.[33] Furthermore, all the rebels had horses while only thirty percent did on the government side. Two years later, Hung submitted more detailed figures. The official cause in Shensi, he stated, was supported by only 18,000 troops of whom

---

* The lowest Ming official degree.

13,000 were local troops (both infantry and cavalry) and 5,000 (all cavalry) had been dispatched from Szechwan.[34] For the rebel side, Hung cited four major groups, numbering from 20,000 to 40,000 and coming to a total as high as 120,000. Because of this disparity, he urged a crash program for enlisting recruits and obtaining supplies.

Some of the advice submitted to Peking on the subject of meeting the need for more troops stressed the familiar theme of local initiative and the sources are fond of mentioning acts of bravery performed by local people. For example, a beggar emerged as one of the heroes in the successful defense of T'ung-ch'eng, Nan-chihli, in 1636. Also, it is claimed that construction of defense works at the village level in Szechwan was one of the reasons why there had been few rebel incursions into that province up to 1636. The arguments for local self-defense, though appealing as a basis for dispensing with lawless professional armies, hardly provided a sufficiently immediate answer for a general threat of great urgency.

Both Peking and the provincial authorities turned to several directions for raising additional forces, undertaking a broadening process which had potential merit. During the first four or five years of the rebellions, the main military effort to crush them was made by forces from the northwest and the reputation of these forces was high. Subsequently, however, a partially justified suspicion emerged to the effect that since the northwest forces and the rebel leaders were natives of the same area, there were instances of collusion or near-collusion between them. Thus, there was added impetus to recruit other elements into the army fighting the rebels. Various sources were tapped: aborigines from the southwest, troops from the Manchurian frontier, surrendered rebel groups, and levies from all the various provinces, particularly those most directly affected by the rebellions.[35] Aboriginal troops were employed in some numbers and one garrison in Hukuang alone is said to have had 5,000 of them, but there is no evidence that their contribution to the campaigns against the rebels was really significant except possibly in Szechwan where they were operating in more familiar territory and mostly under native leaders. The troops from Manchuria, some of whom were probably non-Chinese, received quite favorable comments for their fighting abilities, being especially effective as cavalrymen. However, they had little experience campaigning in forest-covered mountains and had almost no success serving in the key Shensi-Honan-Hukuang border area. Furthermore, they were difficult to control and typically were said to have been on bad terms with the local people of the areas in which they served. In addition, their service against the rebels could never be considered as permanent, since any dangerous increase of Manchu pressure on the northeastern frontier would make their recall necessary. The provincial recruits varied considerably in quality. For example, there was a great deal of criticism of the Szechwanese troops. Also, the Emperor himself sent a message to Wu Sheng, the Shansi Grand Coordinator, protesting about the performance of a Shansi force dispatched to fight the rebels in Honan. The Emperor stated that although the troops had been granted special pay, they had given very poor service. Wu replied that in future more care would have to be taken in recruitment and that recruits should be required to have a sponsor who would be held accountable if they ran away. In assessing the government's efforts to strengthen the armed forces, it might be said that some temporary alleviation of the problem was attained, but this was hardly sufficient security for the future.

In a very real sense the climax of the disorganized raiding phase of the rebellions was attained during 1635 and 1636 (see Maps 8 and 9). Never before or afterwards were so many large independent rebel groups operating at one time and never again was so much territory subjected to widespread rebel incursions during such a short time span. By 1636, the rebels at one time or another had coursed through a huge section of central China and it was not until 1643 that there were really substantial additions to the rebel-affected area.

Beginning in late 1636 and early 1637, following the 1635-36 climax, the rebellions started to decline and were not to regain their momentum until 1641. During this four-year interval, the dynasty made its final effort to save itself by re-establishing internal stability.

Chapter III

The Disorganized Raiding Phase of the Rebellions Part II: The Temporary Decline of the Rebellions, their Resurgence, and the Failure of the Government's Last Chance for Suppression (1636-41)

Rise of Yang Ssu-ch'ang to Power

In the 9th month of 1636, the Minister of War, Chang Feng-i, committed suicide, finally overcome by the accumulation of failures and disasters which had occurred, internally and on the Manchurian frontier, during the four long years he had occupied that vital office. A month later, the Emperor turned once again to the Yang family of Wu-ling, Hukuang, and appointed Yang Ssu-ch'ang, son of the now-deceased Yang Ho, as the new Minister of War. For the next four and a half years Yang was to be the single most influential official in the government.

Yang Ssu-ch'ang's past record in the bureaucracy was impressive. He had obtained his *chin-shih* degree in 1610 and his first service was in educational posts in Hangchow and Nanking. Following that, he was a Director in the Ministry of Revenue. His career was interrupted during the period of eunuch dominance in the T'ien-ch'i era, but was resumed under the new Emperor in 1628 when he was appointed to a subordinate provincial post in Honan. In 1631 his responsibility for military affairs began with an appointment to a post at Shanhaikuan. Just after assuming this position, his father's political career came to its disastrous end, and Yang performed the filial gesture of submitting a memorial in which he requested that he be allowed to bear his father's guilt. Despite his father's difficulties, Yang was retained in office and in 1632 was advanced to become Grand Coordinator of Yung-p'ing Prefecture and Shanhaikuan, a very vital post in view of the increasingly serious Manchu threat. In

1634 he was made Vice-minister of War and concurrently Supreme Commander of northern Shansi and a special district in northwestern Peichihli. Shortly after his appointment, he was forced to retire for the observation of the period of mourning made necessary by his father's death, and it was only in the autumn of 1636 that his career was resumed after a two-year hiatus.

Yang seems to have caught the special attention of the Emperor first during his brief tenure as Vice-minister of War when he advised opening up gold, silver, copper, and tin mines to obtain funds for fighting the rebels, and following his recall to Peking in 1636, he rapidly consolidated his influence at court. His chief assets were his bureaucratic experience, reputation for honesty (apparently deserved at least in a financial sense), excellent calligraphy, brilliance in expressing himself orally, and knowledge of history.

Unfortunately, there was a more negative side to Yang's qualifications for deciding the dynasty's fate. Perhaps most serious of all were his lack of practical military experience and his passion for detail, causing him to keep voluminous records and draw up proposals which seemed brilliant on paper, but which were never translated into effective action. He was also a stickler for form and caused considerable amusement in official circles by his refusal to use the character "ho," his father's given name. When the character occurred in the names of others who had to be referred to in his official correspondence, he would omit the left half, producing the character *niao* (bird). Furthermore, he displayed no real ability at choosing competent subordinates and the alterations he made in the command positions were generally unfortunate. For example, Lu Hsiang-sheng was transferred to the northern Shansi frontier and replaced as Supreme Commander of the anti-rebel campaigns by Hsiung Wen-ts'an whose abilities were much overrated by Yang. His appointments of Grand Coordinators were hardly any better and the frequency with which these key officials were changed during his period of dominance created added instability.

During his service on the northeastern frontier, Yang had advocated a policy of appeasement toward the Manchus, citing precedents from past history to support his suggestion for permitting expanded Sino-Manchu trade. However, now that he was responsible for the policy to be pursued toward the rebels, Yang seemed as uncertain as the Emperor himself who, as late as 1636, was still issuing occasional proclamations that even the rebels were his children, and that since they had been forced into illegal actions due to the terrible conditions prevailing, they should be allowed to surrender and return home. At the same time, the Emperor was involved daily in details concerning the military efforts to crush the rebels.

Probably it would be fair to say that Yang's rebel policy was, from the beginning, a patchwork based mainly on appeasement to which was added some element of a tough-minded military posture. Certainly his policy does not impress one as having the integrity of that of his father which was grounded on a genuine commitment to Confucian humanism.

One of Yang's early actions after assuming the headship of the Ministry of War was the supremely futile gesture of quite artificially setting a three-month time limit for the suppression of the rebellions, and when this period expired without any significant accomplishment against the rebels, bureaucratic protocol required him to submit an offer to resign. The Emperor, as expected, refused to accept the offer and instead ordered Yang to prepare an elaborate appraisal of the various officers leading the anti-rebel campaigns. Thus, there is ample evidence in Yang's actions from the very beginning of a lack of realism which was to characterize most of his future moves and lead finally to his total failure.

Yang's first formulation of a major anti-rebel plan was completed in the summer of 1637 after he had succeeded in restoring some order to Ministry of War affairs which had been left in chaos by his predecessor. The plan, truly comprehensive in scope, envisaged two types of armies, defensive and offensive, operating in coordination to end the rebel menace.[1] The defensive forces would occupy strategic positions in the rebel-infested regions, by their presence retarding rebel movements and keeping the rebels confined to a more restricted area. The defensive forces were to be composed of ten armies, each commanded by a Grand Coordinator. They would be placed in the following locations:* (1) Shang-nan and Lo-nan, Shensi (Shensi Grand Coordinator); (2) Shan-chou and Ling-pao, Honan (Shansi Grand Coordinator); (3) Yen-chin, Honan (Pei-chihli Grand Coordinator); (4) Hsiang-yang and Yün-yang, Hukuang (Yün-yang Grand Coordinator); (5) Te-an and Huang-chou, Hukuang (Hukuang Grand Coordinator); (6) Huang-mei and Kuang-chi, Hukuang (Kiangsi Grand Coordinator); (7) Ying-shan and Liu-an, Nan-chihli (An-ch'ing Grand Coordinator); (8) Ch'ien-shan and T'ai-hu, Nan-chihli (Nanking Grand Coordinator); (9) Ying-chou and Po-chou, Nan-chihli (Feng-yang Grand Coordinator); (10) Hsü-chou and Su-chou, Nan-chihli (Chiang-tung Grand Coordinator).

The offensive force, headed by a Supreme Commander, would operate within the defensive ring, particularly in its center, southern and central Honan. It would be highly mobile and would carry the attack against the rebels wherever they went. The Supreme Commander would have

---

* The places are underlined on Map 17. Also, see Map 17 for the location of all places mentioned in this chapter.

under his direct command a body of crack troops moved south from the northern frontier. He would be assisted by a eunuch commander leading troops taken from the Peking garrison and by the Honan Grand Coordinator under whom would be such professional commanders as Tso Liang-yü.

Yang's ambitious program called for the recruitment of 120,000 additional troops and the price tag attached to this increment in strength came to 2,800,000 taels. Taking advantage of his favored position with the Emperor and invading the sphere of the Ministry of Revenue, Yang himself proposed that the 2,800,000 tael sum be raised in the following manner: (1) the land tax would be increased to bring in an additional twelve ounces of grain per *mou*, producing a total tax increment of 929,000 taels; (2) special taxes on certain types of land would result in 406,000 taels; (3) 200,000 taels of the sum saved from the reduction in the post stations would be turned over to the recruitment program; and (4) hopefully most of the remaining 1,265,000 taels could be raised by the sale of studentships in the Imperial Academy which would have to be renewed each year.*

Yang's financial proposals came at a time when considerable discussion was being evoked in the face of the obvious economic crisis confronting the dynasty. The most radical suggestion concerning the financial situation was made by a little-known holder of a military degree who submitted a memorial proposing that heavy taxes be levied on wealthy office-holding families.[2] This proposal produced a bitter response from the Grand Secretary, Ch'ien Shih-cheng, who pictured the wealthy families as bulwarks standing between the common people and disaster. He bolstered his outrage by resorting to history and cited two examples of wealthy people who were not bothered even by such tyrants of the past as Ch'in Shih Huang-ti and Han Wu-ti. Ch'ien's views were supported by other officials.

More modest financial proposals were contained in other memorials.[3] One such memorial was submitted by a private scholar without office, Huang Ch'ang-chi, who saw a solution to the economic problems in military reorganization and the elimination of official corruption. He felt that a smaller well-trained army should replace the present larger forces that were designed to look impressive only for inspections and in reality had little military potential. A more routine memorial was submitted by Supervising Secretary Yen Chi-tsu who opposed any tax in-

---

* *HLLK* 10/15b-18a; *PKC* 3/3a-b; and *MS* 272/2a-b. Imperial Academy studentships (*chien-sheng*) had been sold at various times earlier in the Ming dynasty when the central government experienced financial difficulty. See Ping-ti Ho, *The Ladder of Success in Imperial China*, 32-33.

creases but advocated a rigid policy of collecting current and back taxes with penalties for failure to pay. At the same time, he advocated adequate salaries for officials to prevent corruption, sufficient supplies for the army to avoid mutinies, and government aid to peasants in rebel-afflicted areas to restore agricultural production.

In the end, Yang's proposals for a tax increase were accepted, though with some genuine reluctance, by the Emperor who at the same time insisted that there should be a rigid prohibition against the customary practice of the officials draining off some amount of the taxes into their own private coffers. Thus, Yang's economic program was adopted formally, though it is highly doubtful that it was any more effective in reality than his ambitious military plan which the economic program was designed to support.

Rebel Operation During 1637

During the first year and a half that Yang occupied the dominant position in Peking, the movements of the rebel groups were slower than in recent years and less territory was covered in their raiding expeditions. Furthermore, the rebel groups continued to operate in areas which were familiar to them and no new regions became involved. Leading the campaigns against the rebels were such long-time commanders as Hung Ch'eng-ch'ou (in Shensi) and Tso Liang-yü (moving about as an attack force in Honan, Nan-chihli, and Hukuang). In addition to these old forces, there was now a new Supreme Commander, Hsiung Wen-ts'an, who was appointed in the early summer of 1637 and established his headquarters initially in northwestern Hukuang at Yün-yang, a strategic point within the key Honan-Hukuang-Shensi border area.

Hsiung Wen-ts'an was one of the relatively few natives of the remote southwestern province of Kweichow who succeeded in obtaining a *chin-shih* degree and having an important political career during Ming times. Prior to his appointment as Supreme Commander, his chief claim to fame was his service against the pirates along the Fukien and Kwangtung coasts. He conducted the negotiations which resulted in the formal submission to the government of the famous Cheng Chih-lung, father of Cheng Ch'eng-kung (Koxinga). Subsequently, with the assistance of Cheng Chih-lung, he won several victories over Kwangtung pirates. These accomplishments won him the admiration of Yang Ssu-ch'ang who became his mentor and was chiefly responsible for his appointment as Supreme Commander in charge of military affairs in Hukuang, Nan-chihli, Honan, Shensi, Shansi, and Szechwan, which was the entire rebel-afflicted area.

There is no evidence that Hsiung ever seriously attempted to put into effect Yang Ssu-ch'ang's elaborate plan of encircling the rebels within a defensive ring and attacking them. There were attack forces technically under his command, including those of Hung Ch'eng-ch'ou and Tso Liang-yü who continued their campaigns against the rebels. However, both of these commanders went on operating almost entirely independently and Tso was on very bad terms with Hsiung from the very beginning, refusing to obey Hsiung's orders and even encouraging his men to attack a Cantonese contingent in Hsiung's army. In addition, a force of 12,000 troops under a eunuch commander was dispatched to Honan from the Peking garrison, but his force achieved no significant military victories and was virtually destroyed in the winter of 1637 when the rebels attacked during a snowstorm in southeastern Honan. Hsiung himself showed no real taste for military efforts and apparently from the very beginning envisaged his role as one which would seek to repeat in central China the negotiating successes he had achieved among the pirates of the south China coast.

The most important rebel activity and movement beginning early in 1637 was a push down the Han River Valley and on into Nan-chihli.[4] Three major rebel leaders, Ma Shou-ying, Lo Ju-ts'ai, and Chang Hsien-chung, participated in this push which marked the third time that a major eastward incursion had been staged. In their drive down the Han Valley the rebels succeeded in occupying briefly Sui-chou and Ying-ch'eng and reached the Yangtze near Huang-chou. Subsequently they pushed northeastward to the Shu-ch'eng area where they were attacked and defeated by Tso Liang-yü. This check caused them to retire for most of the summer of 1637 into the mountains between T'ai-hu and Ch'ien-shan where, according to one source, the rebels suffered the loss of one of their most important senior leaders, Ma Shou-ying, nicknamed "Old Moslem," who died a natural death. This report of Ma's death may be an error, for there are later references to an "Old Moslem" in other sources for several years. However, the report is probably correct and the subsequent references to an "Old Moslem" merely indicate that a successor to the original one had been chosen and had adopted the nickname of his predecessor.

In the late summer of 1637, the rebel groups in Nan-chihli moved out of the mountains of T'ai-hu and Ch'ien-shan and pushed rapidly down the Yangtze, reaching as far east as Liu-ho which they succeeded in capturing. The fall of Liu-ho caused considerable uneasiness in Nanking which was only a short distance away, but the city remained safely beyond the rebels' grasp, being on the southern side of the Yangtze, a river so formidable that it would be several years yet before any really important rebel group possessed the ability to cross it. The rebels did threaten for a time to push from Liu-ho to Yangchow, a move which would have made it possible for them to disrupt traffic on the Grand Canal for the

MING DYNASTY PEASANT REBELLIONS

10   LOCATIONS OF PEASANT REBEL ACTIVITY IN **1637**

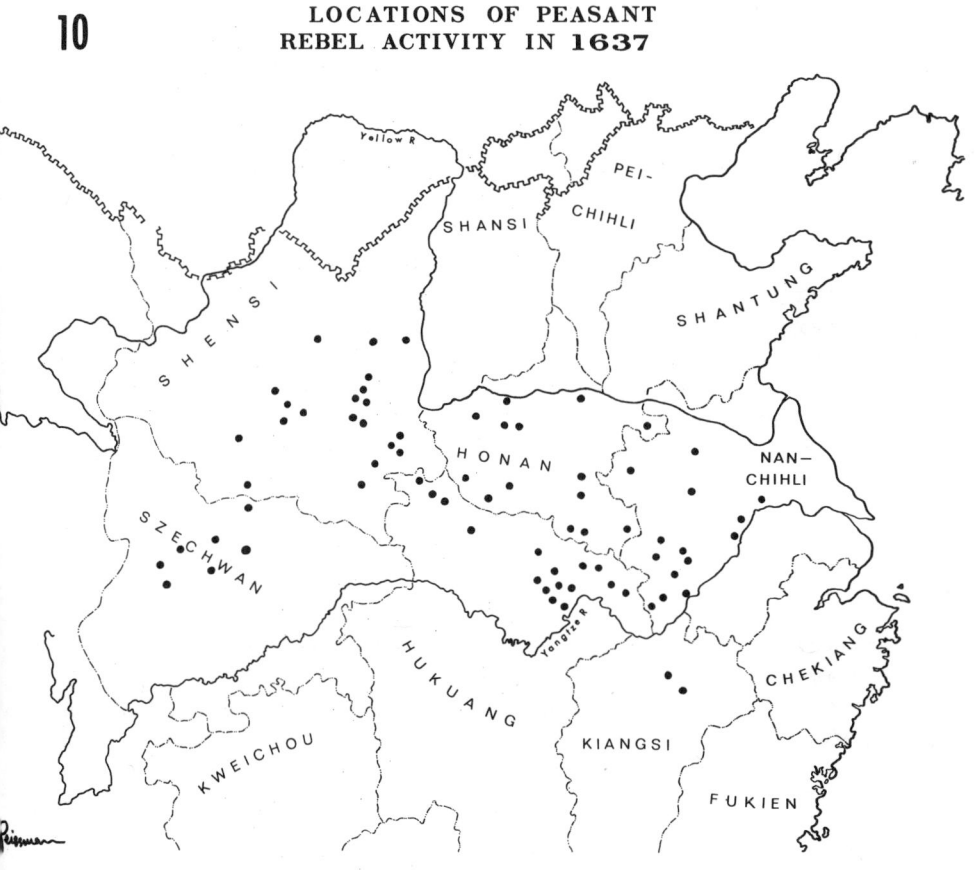

first time. However, a concerted effort, generously supported by contributions from the great merchants of Yangchow, succeeded in stopping the rebel advance. Subsequently, most of the rebels withdrew from Nan-chihli after having remained there for considerably longer than they had during the two earlier eastward incursions. Generally retracing their steps up the Yangtze and Han Rivers, they returned to northern Hukuang and southern Honan.

Adhering to his two-year-old practice of remaining outside of the main rebel movement, Li Tzu-ch'eng continued to stay in southwestern Shensi throughout most of 1637.[5] He remained relatively quiet until the 9th month when he joined several lesser rebel leaders in an attack upon Han-chung, the most important town in extreme south-central Shensi near the Szechwan border. The town's garrison was secretly reinforced with troops dispatched by Hung Ch'eng-ch'ou and the rebel attack was easily defeated.

After the Han-chung failure, Li decided to seek his fortune southward and launched the most extensive incursion into Szechwan as yet attempted by any rebel group. Moving through an unguarded pass southwest of Han-chung, Li rapidly advanced past such towns as Kuang-yüan, Tzu-t'ung and T'ung-ch'uan to the provincial capital, Chengtu, which he besieged for twenty days without success. Having failed to take Chengtu and undoubtedly hearing that Hung Ch'eng-ch'ou was moving south into Szechwan to attack him, Li decided to abandon the siege and return to Shensi. While retreating northward early in 1638, he was caught by Hung Ch'eng-ch'ou at Tzu-t'ung and defeated. Hung's tactics were to place his Szechwanese troops, whom he considered of inferior quality, in the center of his line. They withdrew under the rebel attack, leading the rebels into an ambush where they were pounced upon by Hung's crack Shensi unit.

Escaping from the battlefield with part of his army, Li succeeded in reaching southern Shensi where he received another severe blow in an attack by one of Hung's subordinates. With his strength now greatly reduced, Li fled to far southwestern Shensi and was to remain relatively inactive throughout most of 1638.

Defeat and Surrender of Chang Hsien-chung

In the autumn of 1637, Chang Hsien-chung withdrew from Nan-chihli and settled in the Nan-yang area of southwestern Honan. He was attacked there by Tso Liang-yü, and a personal encounter between Chang and Tso occurred. In the clash, Chang was struck between the eyes by an arrow and was slashed on the face with a sword. He might well have been killed had he not been rescued at the last moment by one of his most trusted lieutenants, Sun K'o-wang. Withdrawing from the battlefield,

MING DYNASTY PEASANT REBELLIONS

11 LOCATIONS OF PEASANT REBEL ACTIVITY IN **1638**

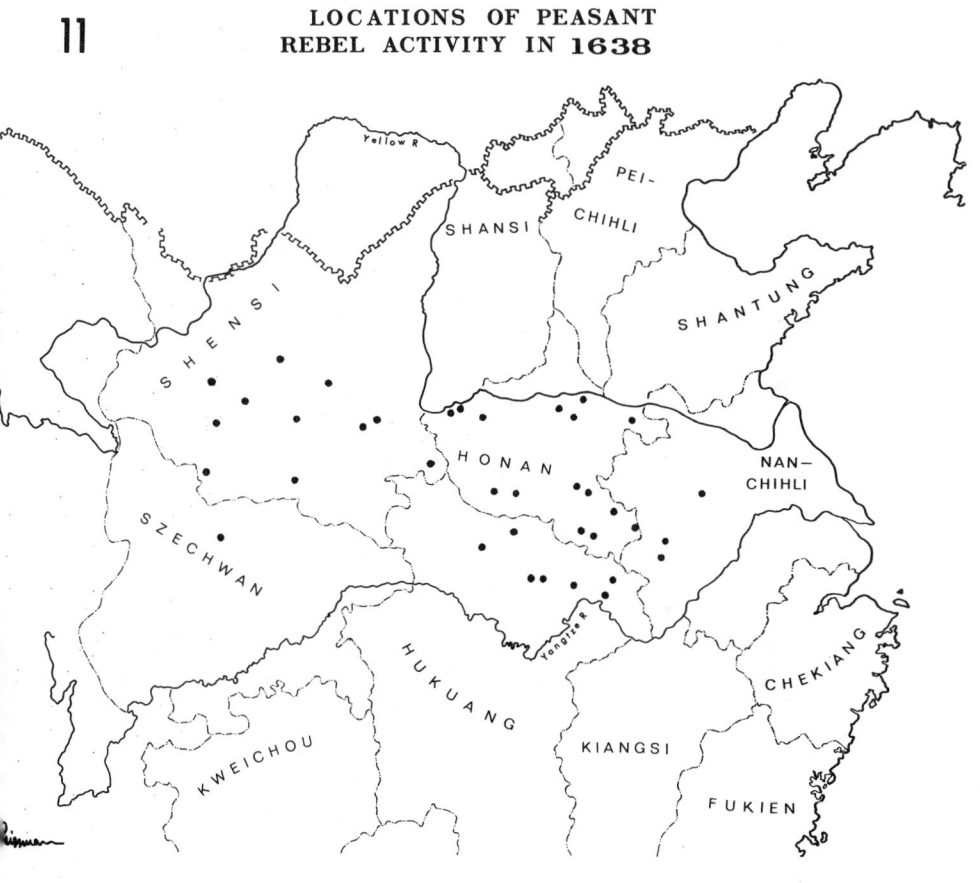

Chang staged a hasty retreat down the Han Valley and remained for some three months in the Ma-ch'eng area of Hukuang near the Nan-chihli border. Tso Liang-yü attacked him again there early in 1638, defeating him severely and causing him to flee once more up the Han Valley. He is said to have covered 250 miles in two days and nights of continuous flight. He finally established a new headquarters at Ku-ch'eng in northwestern Hukuang.

Having occupied the town of Ku-ch'eng, Chang decided upon a shift in policy and set in motion the first of a series of negotiations which would lead to his formal surrender.[6] Apparently the chief architect of this new policy was one of his chief lieutenants, a man named Hsüeh. Virtually nothing is known of Hsüeh, except that he was a native of northern Shensi and (the most significant fact) he had a relative, Hsüeh Kuo-kuan, who was currently occupying the exalted position of Grand Secretary in Peking. Hsüeh had long argued that with his own influence inside the court through his relative, Chang Hsien-chung would find it highly to his advantage to come to terms with the government. Now that Chang had suffered two severe defeats within three months, he was finally in a mood to accept his lieutenant's advice.

In addition to any influence which could be exerted in Chang's behalf by Grand Secretary Hsüeh in Peking, the immediate situation facing Chang in Hukuang was favorable toward his being allowed to surrender. As noted earlier, Supreme Commander Hsiung's policy was primarily based on appeasement. Furthermore, Hsiung now had as one of his chief subordinates an officer named Ch'en Hung-fan who had known Chang for a decade and, as noted previously, had once saved him from being executed (see p. 17). Thus, Chang had a valuable personal tie with a highly placed government commander.

In the late spring of 1638, Chang dispatched one of his most able and literate lieutenants, Sun K'o-wang, to institute the negotiations for his surrender. Sun took with him from Chang a flattering message addressed to Ch'en Hung-fan and valuable presents, including silk cloth, beautiful women, and jewels, for both Ch'en and Supreme Commander Hsiung. After talking with Sun, Ch'en Hung-fan recommended the acceptance of Chang's offer to surrender and experienced no difficulty in persuading Hsiung to accept his recommendation.

The informal terms of the surrender permitted Chang to continue his occupation of Ku-ch'eng and recognized him as a government commander who would be granted supplies to support an army of 20,000 men. Actually Chang's army at this time probably numbered less than 5,000, but he claimed to have 100,000 and his request to be granted supplies for this large number raised an issue which was never settled. Also implied in the surrender was Chang's obligation to place himself under the military command of Supreme Commander Hsiung and to serve, as other surrendered rebels had, in the campaigns against the remaining rebels. This obligation was never implemented even in a token fashion. Finally, Chang had to accept at Ku-ch'eng a small garrison force, dispatched by Hsiung and assigned the impossible task of supervising the surrendered rebels.

Chang bolstered his position following his so-called surrender by dispatching his lieutenant, Hsüeh, to Peking where he is said to have succeeded in bribing all highly placed officials except Yang Ssu-ch'ang. Chang also distributed large numbers of bribes to provincial and local officials in Hukuang. When he was on the verge of resuming his rebellion, he took great glee in publishing a detailed account of his bribery activities, complete with names of recipients, exact dates, and amounts. In all of these dealings, Chang is depicted as a wily and polished operator who was a master of deceit and political maneuver. It is obvious that he had changed considerably from the illiterate or semi-literate peasant and common soldier who had headed a petty local uprising in northern Shensi a decade previously.

Chang's behind-the-scenes maneuvering stood him in good stead, for several of the more astute officials and military commanders considered his surrender to be a patently false posture. His enemy *par excellence*, Tso Liang-yü, regarded the present situation, with Chang settled in a fixed position and deprived of his mobility, as an excellent opportunity to destroy him. Tso actually requested permission to attack Chang, but Hsiung who regarded Chang's surrender as his crowning achievement, refused Tso's request.

It is impossible to say with certainty exactly what Chang's personal attitude was toward his so-called surrender. He may have been genuinely willing at the outset to agree to a relatively permanent understanding with the government as long as his interests were not flagrantly contravened. More probably, he quite cynically regarded his surrender from the very beginning as a purely temporary expedient resorted to in order to gain time to recover from his recent defeats and to build up his power. Certainly Chang's actions at Ku-ch'eng showed little desire to reach a genuine and enduring accommodation with the government.[7] He boasted of his ability to bring order to all of northern Hukuang and requested that he be given as his personal preserve a band of territory extending northward from Ku-ch'eng across Honan to the Yellow River. He would guarantee that this area would be kept free of rebels. In addition, Chang took over virtual control of the county administration, thrusting the regular governmental units into the background. At the same time, he improved his economic position by erecting a kind of customs house on the Han River and collecting several thousands of taels per month as duties on the products being shipped on the river. More obviously threatening were such acts as continuing to recruit and train troops, manufacture weapons, and maintain underhanded contacts with other rebel groups, some of whom had also surrendered. Furthermore, at Ku-ch'eng, Chang began to have his first really extensive contact with members of the gentry and three now joined him as advisers. The three, P'an Tu-ao, Hsü I-hsien, and Wang Ping-chen, were holders of only lower degrees (P'an and Hsü were *chu-sheng* and Wang was a *chü-jen*) and there is no evidence to suggest that any of them were members of really powerful and prominent families. Even so, their joining Chang is an indication that his prospects must have appeared sufficiently bright to have exerted some real appeal. Chang derived from them potentially valuable advice. Hsü seems to have been particularly helpful, instructing Chang in military science which he had made his specialty.

Chang remained at Ku-ch'eng in the midst of his varied activities for an entire year. In the meantime, other currents in the rebel movement continued to flow on all sides of his Ku-ch'eng enclave and occasionally impinged upon it.

Activities of Other Rebel Groups during 1638

The surrender of Chang Hsien-chung, who was considered to be the single most powerful rebel leader in 1638, exerted a considerable effect upon the rebel movement in general. Most immediately noticeable were the even further decline in the momentum of rebel raiding and the confining of rebel activities to more restricted areas (see Maps 11 and 12). Nevertheless, throughout the greater part of 1638, most of the familiar rebel leaders remained active, with northeastern Hukuang and southwestern Honan the favorite areas of concentration. Nan-chihli was largely untouched during both 1638 and 1639, except for a few districts near the Honan and Hukuang borders. Some military pressure against the rebel groups was maintained by Hsiung Wen-ts'an, Tso Liang-yü, and their subordinate commanders, and Hsiung briefly transferred his headquarters from northwestern Hukuang to southeastern Honan in order to be nearer the center of rebel concentration. A series of minor victories was gained by the official forces, but they were not of sufficient importance to signify that Hsiung was abandoning his basic orientation toward appeasement.

In far western Shensi, throughout the first half of 1638, Li Tzu-ch'eng was struggling to escape from being destroyed by Hung Ch'eng-ch'ou and his able subordinate, Ts'ao Pien-chiao. In the summer of 1638, the military pressure against him became so strong that he abandoned western Shensi and moved southwestward to the Szechwan border, but did not succeed in achieving a breakthrough. He then moved to the Han-chung area where he decided to retrace his route to the far west. Finding his path westward firmly blocked, Li was forced to reverse directions and decide upon an incursion into Honan where he had not been in three years. After attempting unsuccessfully to enter Honan via one of the southeastern Shensi passes, he had to turn north toward the T'ung Pass, the main avenue of communication between the two provinces. Hung Ch'eng-ch'ou and Ts'ao Pien-chiao had anticipated that he would try to escape via the T'ung Pass and had carefully laid several ambushes into which he fell in the 10th month of 1638. Li suffered a disastrous defeat and was precipitously plunged to the nadir of his rebel career.[8] His wife and daughter were captured by the official forces and his army was cut to pieces. He managed to flee the battlefield accompanied by only nineteen men among whom was included his most faithful follower and intimate associate, Liu Tsung-min.

Li was fortunate in that his defeat occurred relatively near the Honan-Hukuang-Shensi area, the favorite region for the rebels to seek refuge in times of dire need, and it was to extreme southeastern Shensi that he fled. Li's mood upon first reaching the refuge area is described as one of profound despair, and in a deserted ancestral temple he is said to have proposed a macabre bargain to Liu Tsung-min. Li asked him to divine the future and if the divination proved to be unfavorable, Liu should decapitate him and surrender. However, three successive divinations produced favorable results and Li's life was saved. His spirits improved markedly and he is said to have attempted to revive the flagging enthusiasm of his followers by comparing himself with the founder of the Han dynasty who at times had faced similar extremities.

After spending some time in the southeastern Shensi refuge, Li went to Ku-ch'eng for a conference with Chang Hsien-chung. Since Chang was now enjoying the greatest prosperity of his career, Li undoubtedly hoped that he would assist him in making a comeback. According to one source, Chang at first received Li in a cordial manner and treated him to a magnificent banquet. However, even if this initial cordiality actually was displayed, the long-standing tension between them rapidly reasserted itself and Li soon fled from Chang's camp in fear of being murdered.

From Ku-ch'eng, Li eventually went to eastern Hukuang and sought from Lao-hui-hui the assistance which Chang had refused him. Upon reaching the headquarters of Lao-hui-hui, Li became ill and was forced to remain inactive for several months. At the end of this time, Lao-hui-hui gave him a few hundred men to serve as a nucleus around which to build a new army, and with this small force he returned to Shensi.

The Nadir of the Rebellions and the Increase of Manchu Pressure

The last few months of 1638 and the first half of 1639 marked the nadir of the disorganized raiding phase of the late Ming rebel movement. Chang Hsien-chung ostensibly honored his surrender agreement and remained settled at Ku-ch'eng; Lo Ju-ts'ai reached an accommodation with Supreme Commander Hsiung and remained stationary in northwestern Hukuang after ostentatiously declining Hsiung's offer of a military title and declaring that he wanted to be a mere peasant; and Li Tzu-ch'eng, after having been brought to the very brink of destruction, seemed to have few prospects of reviving his career. Thus, none of the three principal rebel leaders was actively pressing the fight against the government in late 1638 and the first half of 1639. Several of the secondary rebel leaders also surrendered and though a few of them remained active, there was a drastic deceleration in their momentum and they were affecting only quite restricted areas (see Maps 11 and 12).

Looking over the rebel scene early in 1639, Yang Ssu-ch'ang (by now promoted to Grand Secretary, but still in substantial charge of Ministry-of-War affairs) and his protege, Hsiung Wen-ts'an, may well have been convinced that the rebellions had been virtually crushed. Unfortunately, any such view was far too hopeful and was based on a very superficial analysis of the rebel situation. In actual fact, none of the rebel leaders, except Li Tzu-ch'eng, had suffered a really shattering military defeat. Chang Hsien-chung and Lo Ju-ts'ai were inactive not because they did not have the power to conduct military campaigns, but because they had chosen temporarily to accept Hsiung's appeasement offers. They were soon to rescind their acceptance and demonstrate the shallow foundation on which Hsiung's ostensibly successful rebel policy was based.

Events on the Manchurian frontier also served to help pull the rebellions back from their 1638-39 slump and assist them in regaining their momentum and power. Manchu raids, as has been noted, had occurred from time to time from the beginning of the Ch'ung-chen period, and in the latter part of 1638, probably as a reflection of their greater confidence following their 1636 victories in Korea and in the islands off the southern coast of Manchuria, the Manchus staged their deepest raid yet into Chinese territory.[9] They pushed to Kao-yang, some 140 miles south of Peking, and in the fighting the dynasty lost one of its most capable commanders, Lu Hsiang-sheng, who had served briefly as Supreme Commander of the anti-rebel campaign. Lu died a hero's death on the battlefield, but his arch-rival, Yang Ssu-ch'ang, who disagreed with Lu's advocacy of a vigorous military stance in Manchuria, temporarily prevented appropriate honors being bestowed upon him.

MING DYNASTY PEASANT REBELLIONS

12   LOCATIONS OF PEASANT REBEL ACTIVITY IN **1639**

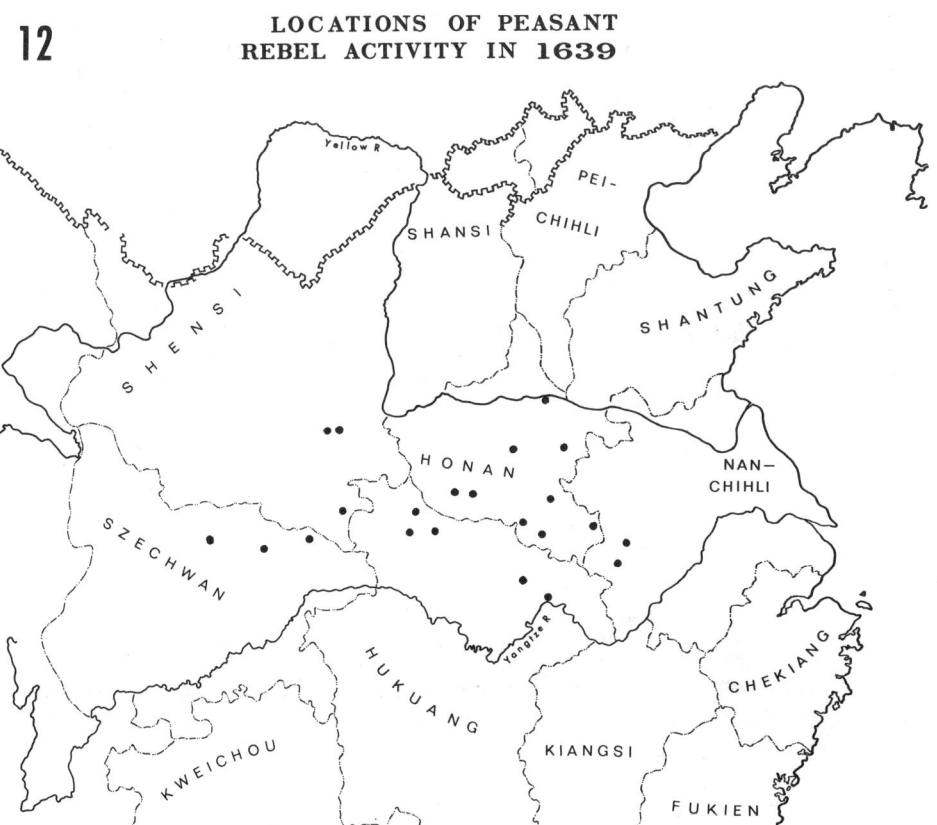

Early in 1639, the Manchus repeated their former successful raid on an even larger scale. They pushed all the way into central Shantung and briefly occupied the provincial capital, Tsinan, where they took captive the Prince of Te.

Thoroughly alarmed over the Manchu raids, the central government decided that the military talents of Hung Ch'eng-ch'ou were more needed on the northern frontier than fighting rebels in Shensi and in the 12th month of 1638, he was ordered to assume the position of Supreme Commander of a section of the Manchurian border area. He may well have been pleased with this transfer, for he had been on bad terms with Hsiung Wen-ts'an and his achievements had been slighted by Yang Ssu-ch'ang. However, the removal of the most experienced and successful major figure in the anti-rebel campaigns, after a decade of continuous service, decreased the chances of the government's achieving victory in the future.

Revival of the Rebellions and Yang Ssu-ch'ang's Assumption of the Field Command against the Rebels

On June 6, 1639, Chang Hsien-chung openly resumed his rebellion at Ku-ch'eng and ended the year-long surrender agreement he had negotiated with Supreme Commander Hsiung Wen-ts'an.[10] It is unclear exactly what prompted Chang's action to come at precisely this time, but for some months before the final event, it had become increasingly clear that he had every intention of making such a move. He had continued to build up and equip his army; had maintained close contacts with Lo Ju-ts'ai who had settled a short distance to the northwest of Ku-ch'eng following his own formal surrender; and had had the audacity to try and force a Censor at Ku-ch'eng to submit a memorial to the Emperor requesting that the important city of Hsiang-yang be granted to him as his personal preserve. Also, he had shown increasing resentment at Hsiung's attempts to squeeze fatter bribes out of him while at the same time ignoring his own requests for an increase in the sums granted him for the support of his troops.

In resuming his rebellion, Chang released all the prisoners at Ku-ch'eng; rifled the government warehouses; forced the local garrison to join him; burned the county government buildings; and murdered the county magistrate before that unfortunate official had been able to complete his attempted suicide, but not before he is said to have delivered himself of some appropriate Confucian maxims. Following these acts of violence, Chang abandoned Ku-ch'eng and moved a short distance to the west where, by pre-arrangement, he joined forces with Lo Ju-ts'ai.

The combined forces of Chang and Lo moved slightly to the southwest and attacked the town of Fang-hsien which was ably defended by the magistrate, Shih Ching-ch'un, in command of a greatly outnumbered garrison hastily reinforced by civilians.[11] The siege continued for a week during which time the rebels made several futile attempts to scale the walls with ladders. Chang took a leading personal role in the attack and at one point had a very narrow escape when his horse was killed beneath him and he was struck in the face by a fire arrow. The town might well not have fallen at all if one of the defending officers, who had had previous connections with Lo Ju-ts'ai, had not defected to the rebels and opened one of the gates.

After a brief occupation of Fang-hsien, Chang and Lo moved westward into the heavily forested mountain region near the Shensi border and it was into this area that Hsiung Wen-ts'an ordered Tso Liang-yü to go in pursuit of them. Tso responded to the order with a great deal of bitterness, angrily reminding Hsiung that he had long ago proposed an attack on Chang. Tso also branded Hsiung's whole approach to Chang as as foolish as deliberately releasing a tiger and then ordering a subordinate to recapture it.

Despite his bitterness, Tso complied with Hsiung's order and moved into the mountains in search of Chang.[12] Reaching Mt. Lo-ying near the Shensi border, he fell into a carefully planned rebel ambush and found himself besieged. Already weakened by a shortage of supplies, the official forces were completely overwhelmed by the rebels on August 24, 1639 and the resulting victory for Chang was the greatest as yet achieved by any rebel leader. 10,000 government troops were killed or dispersed, military supplies valued at 100,000 taels were abandoned, and Tso's chief subordinate officer was overwhelmed and hacked to death. Tso himself managed to escape after throwing away most of his personal possessions and his official seal.

Tso returned to his headquarters where he soon had to face a stern reprimand from Peking which demoted him and ordered him to redeem himself with future victories over the rebels. Probably he would have been punished more severely had he not submitted a detailed report concerning the long dispute he had had with Hsiung in regard to the policy to be adopted toward Chang Hsien-chung. Even Yang Ssu-ch'ang agreed that he should not be blamed too seriously for what had happened.

The disaster at Mt. Lo-ying provided the final blow needed to topple Hsiung Wen-ts'an from power.[13] Hsiung's position had long been insecure and he had been subjected to severe attacks from the very beginning of his service as Supreme Commander. For example, in the autumn of 1638, Hung Ch'eng-ch'ou had accused Hsiung of failing to cooperate in joint attacks on the rebels operating in the Honan-Shensi border area. Officials in Peking had taken up Hung's accusation and impeached Hsiung with the result that the Emperor began to have doubts about the competence of his Supreme Commander. More serious losses of face for Hsiung occurred when Chang Hsien-chung and Lo Ju-ts'ai resumed their rebel activities and were followed by most of the secondary rebel leaders who had also surrendered. However, prior to the Mt. Lo-ying battle, Hsiung could rely on the protection of his mentor, Yang Ssu-ch'ang. After Lo-ying, even Yang was powerless to save him and an imperial order was issued for his removal from office and arrest.

Because of the close connection between the two men, Hsiung's downfall could not help affecting the prestige of Yang Ssu-ch'ang who had few supporters among the officials at Peking and whose power was based almost solely upon his personal influence with the Emperor. As early as the 1st month of 1639, Yang began to be subjected to bitter criticism, one memorial even calling for his execution on the grounds that he had failed to prevent the Manchu raid into Shantung. Yang responded to this memorial with a request to retire, but this was refused by the Emperor who continued to give him full support. After the disaster at Mt. Lo-ying, however, Yang apparently concluded that drastic action was necessary if his own downfall was not to follow shortly upon that of Hsiung Wen-ts'an. He requested, possibly after some imperial pressure, to be allowed to take the field himself as Supreme Commander against the rebels.[14] The Emperor indicated his pleasure in accepting the request by the magnificence of the gifts bestowed upon Yang: a large amount of silver, various kinds of silk cloth, and many banners. Shortly thereafter, when Yang was ready to depart for Hukuang, there was a gala banquet during which the Emperor personally poured Yang three cups of wine and presented him with an original poem in his own highly admired calligraphy.

In the late autumn of 1639, Yang reached Hsiang-yang and formally assumed the duties of Supreme Commander. One of his first acts was the unpleasant one of holding a long conference with Hsiung Wen-ts'an and subsequently arranging for him to be conveyed as a prisoner to Peking. He undoubtedly realized that nothing could now save Hsiung from severe punishment and he made no direct intercession in his behalf. But he did seek to provide some indirect justification by pointing out in an early report on Hsiung that during the two years he had served as Supreme Commander, he had received 100,000 taels less than the amount actually due him for the support of his forces. This faint appeal for leniency, if such it was, apparently had no effect and though a decision on Hsiung's case was a long time in coming, he was finally executed in the 10th month of 1640.

Yang arrived in Hukuang in possession of what he hoped would be sufficient resources, both military and economic, to cancel out all the failures of the past and crush the rebellions.[15] Accompanying him south were forces from the Peking garrison and from Manchuria, later augmented by troops from Yunnan and Hukuang who were to serve under his personal command. This army was to be the nucleus of the anti-rebel drive and was to be joined by the forces of such professional officers as Tso Liang-yü and Ho Jen-lung.

On the level of overall military planning, Yang left in Peking another of his grandiose outlines for the maintenance of a 730,000-man army, the bulk of which (573,000) would be scattered along the northern frontier and the remainder would be given various assignments within the country for service against the rebels. To support this army, Yang persuaded the reluctant Emperor to agree to the retention of the tax increases which had been imposed the previous year and initially had been regarded as merely temporary in nature. This ambitious plan shared the fate of most of Yang's grand schemes in never being really implemented.

In the more restricted realm of the problems faced by Yang upon his arrival at Hsiang-yang, the initial headquarters for his rebel-pacification campaign, his first major effort was directed toward restoring discipline and a sense of direction among the professional officers who had grown accustomed to the laxness characterizing Hsiung Wen-ts'an's period in command. Yang had one officer publicly whipped, disciplined several more, and summoned most of the principal commanders to attend a conference at which he delivered an exhortation designed to restore morale and to instill a fighting spirit. Subsequently, there was a ceremony at which the commanders took a solemn oath pledging devotion. Yang was now ready to launch one of the last major anti-rebel efforts prior to the downfall of the dynasty.

The Anti-rebel Campaign of Yang Ssu-ch'ang

The major fact in the rebel situation which Supreme Commander Yang had to face from his Hsiang-yang headquarters was a general westward shift of the rebellions.[16] Szechwan, for the first time, became the main area of rebel concentration, and was destined to remain so throughout most of 1640 (see Map 13). Chang Hsien-chung, following his victory at Mt. Lo-ying, had moved some distance to the southwest and crossed over the border into northeastern Szechwan; and early in 1640 at least eight other rebel leaders, including such familiar figures as Lo Ju-ts'ai, Kuo-t'ien-hsing, and Sao-ti-wang, had pushed toward the Hukuang-Szechwan border area. Like most of the earlier major rebel shifts, the current movement westward did not result from a careful and coordinated assessment of the military situation by the rebel leaders. Rather, it was largely a spontaneous, unconscious development and produced no greater unity and stability in the rebel ranks.

Reacting to the rebel push toward the west, Supreme Commander Yang formulated a plan for confining them within the relatively wild area of eastern Szechwan and western Hukuang north of the Yangtze.[17]

After confinement had been made complete, the powerful groups would be attacked and destroyed while the weaker ones would be broken up and allowed to surrender. Three major command groups would be assigned the task of keeping the rebels hemmed in. Tso Liang-yü would be stationed in the Hsing-an, P'ing-li, and Chu-ch'i districts of the Shensi-Hukuang border area and would block the rebels from pushing across Hukuang into Honan. The Szechwan Grand Coordinator, Shao Chieh-ch'un, would be stationed near K'uei-chou, Szechwan, preventing any in-depth invasion of Szechwan. Yang himself would guard against any rebel attempt to advance eastward down the Yangtze. In order to carry out this assignment effectively, early in 1640, Yang began shifting his large personal force, said to number between 30,000 and 40,000, southward from Hsiang-yang. By the 3rd month of 1640, Yang had established his headquarters at I-ling on the Yangtze.

Yang's confinement plans did not receive the support of his most powerful subordinate commander, Tso Liang-yü. Tso was unimpressed with Yang's strategy suspecting that it was designed to keep him frozen in an inactive guard position while other commanders achieved the glory of destroying rebels. Furthermore, his pride still rankled from his defeat by Chang Hsien-chung and he wanted revenge. He requested permission from Yang to be allowed to move into northeastern Szechwan and attack Chang, still acknowledged by all to be the single most powerful rebel leader and the prime target of Yang's campaign.

Yang rejected Tso's request for mixed reasons. In the first place, he did indeed have personal animosity toward Tso. He had assigned another general, Ho Jen-lung, to head the chief attack force against the rebels in eastern Szechwan and western Hukuang and had even planned to deprive Tso of his title, "Rebel-pacifying General" (P'ing-tse chiang-chün) and confer this title on Ho. On the other hand, there were legitimate reasons for Yang's ordering Tso to assume a guard position in the Shensi-Hukuang border region. Most importantly, Shensi's military position had been considerably weakened when Hung Ch'eng-ch'ou had been transferred to the Manchurian frontier and had taken some of his troops with him. There was a very real threat that the rebels would push north from Szechwan into Shensi.

Deliberately disobeying Yang's orders, Tso decided to follow his own plans and moved southeastward to seek a confrontation with Chang Hsien-chung. Such a confrontation soon occurred on remote Mt. Ma-nao in the wilds of northeastern Szechwan where a battle of considerable significance took place.[18] Chang had been occupying Mt. Ma-nao for some weeks and had constructed on it a fortified camp from which he sent out raiding parties to obtain needed supplies. Tso, acting in coordination

MING DYNASTY PEASANT REBELLIONS

13 LOCATIONS OF PEASANT REBEL ACTIVITY IN **1640**

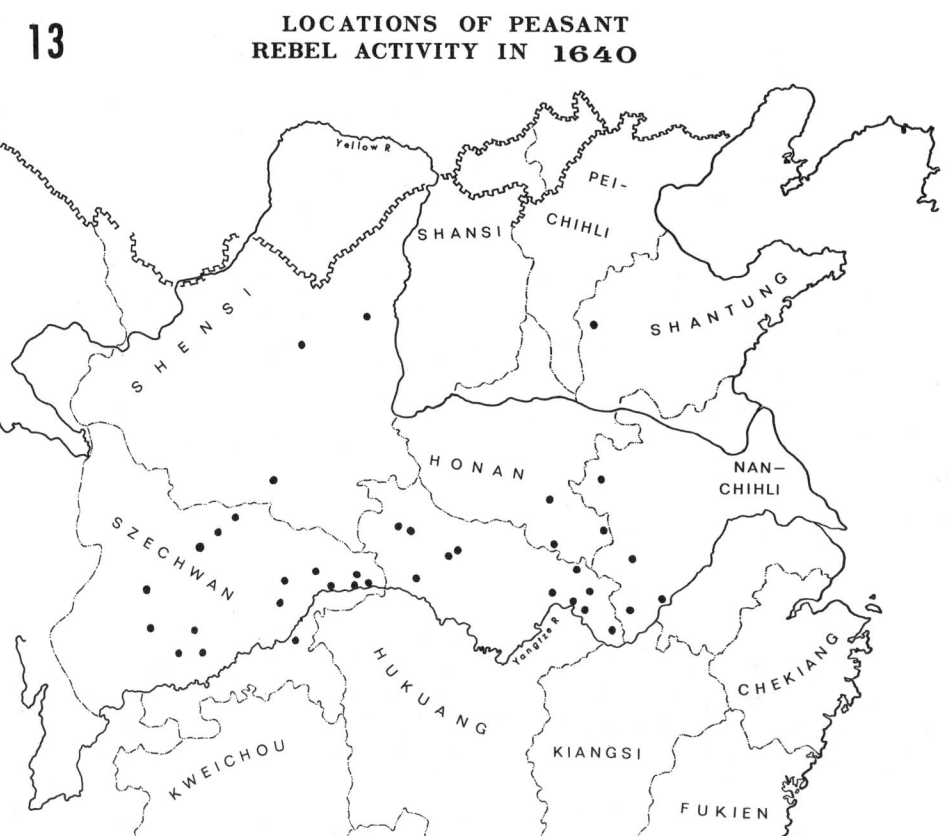

with troops under the command of Ho Jen-lung, converged upon the area from two directions. Arriving nearby, Tso planned a ruse initially to attack the rebels inside their encampment and subsequently to slaughter them on all sides as they fled in confusion. Tso's plan was put into operation on March 28, 1640 when the ex-rebel, Liu Kuo-neng, now serving in the official forces, disguised his troops as rebels and was admitted into Chang's camp where they were taken as a returning raiding party. Completely suprised when Liu's forces attacked following their admission within the fortification, Chang's men were seized by panic and a rout ensued. Chang himself did manage to make good his escape, followed by a force of several hundred. The rest of his army, including a few of his principal lieutenants, was killed, captured, or dispersed, and a large amount of supplies was seized. His wives and the gentry advisers who had attached themselves to him at Ku-ch'eng were taken prisoner and Tso had the personal satisfaction of again obtaining possession of his own official credentials and other documents which had been captured by Chang at the Mt. Lo-ying disaster.

Escaping from Mt. Ma-nao, Chang's remnant force suffered other defeats in a series of brief skirmishes. However, he succeeded finally in breaking into the clear and fled over the border into Hukuang. For some three months he remained quietly in a remote forested area of western Hukuang. He expended some of his gold and silver hoard to purchase supplies and information from the mountain people and proceeded gradually to rebuild his shattered military strength.

There was great rejoicing in Peking upon the arrival of Yang Ssu-ch'ang's report on the Mt. Ma-nao victory. Silver amounting to 50,000 taels and a large quantity of cloth were dispatched to Yang for distribution to the troops. In addition, Yang was granted the exalted honorary title of Grand Guardian of the Heir Apparent and Tso Liang-yü was made Junior Guardian of the Heir Apparent. Lesser titles and rewards were conferred on the subordinate commanders.

The Mt. Ma-nao victory was destined to remain the most significant military achievement of the government forces during Yang Ssu-ch'ang's tenure as Supreme Commander, and no credit for the victory can be awarded Yang personally. Ironically enough, it was won in the wake of a direct violation of Yang's orders. Furthermore, the victory was not followed up to destroy Chang Hsien-chung completely, and within half a year Chang's strength had recovered to the point where it was almost on a par with what it had been prior to Mt. Ma-nao. The responsibility for the failure to destroy Chang must be shared by several. Yang, from his headquarters at I-ling did dispatch a force to seek out Chang in western Hukuang. However, this force, confronted with the difficulties of the terrain, made only a cursory search and returned without accomplishing its mission. At the same time, Tso Liang-yü and Ho Jen-lung stood on the sidelines and took no effective action partly because of their personal animosity toward Yang. Tso was miffed because Yang had planned to deprive him of his title of "Rebel-pacifying General" and give it to Ho, and Ho felt cheated when Tso's victory made it impossible for Yang to carry out his plan to transfer the title. In addition, some of the sources maintain that Tso felt it was not in his own best interests to destroy Chang Hsien-chung completely.[19] Absolute success against the most important of the rebels, Tso is alleged to have reasoned, might remove the foundations upon which his own position of influence rested.

Following the Mt. Ma-nao battle, Yang Ssu-ch'ang found his attention increasingly concentrated on Szechwan as rebel activity came to be centered there. Several minor rebel groups had been operating in Szechwan already early in 1640 and in the summer of that year a major breakthrough occurred which saw such powerful rebel leaders as Lo Ju-ts'ai, Kuo-t'ien-hsing, and Chang Hsien-chung, allied for the moment, push up the Yangtze into Szechwan. By this time, Chang had made a substantial recovery from the near-disaster at Mt. Ma-nao and had pieced together an army from several sources. He had been rejoined by some of his men who had fled from Mt. Ma-nao and dispersed into the forests; he had been assisted with grants of troops, horses, and supplies by Lo Ju-ts'ai; and he had been joined by some of the forces of the rebel leader, Cheng-shih-wan, who refused to follow him when he surrendered to Yang Ssu-ch'ang.

The breakthrough into Szechwan by Chang, Lo Ju-ts'ai, and Kuo-t'ien-hsing was blamed primarily upon Szechwan authorities, particularly the Grand Coordinator, Shao Chieh-ch'un, and two officers defending the Hukuang-Szechwan passes whose personal animosities resulted in one pass being left undefended and the rebels being permitted to slip through. Also, the Szechwanese troops are said to have performed badly in general, failing to carry out military duties assigned them and increasing the difficulties of the Hukuang and Shensi troops.

In response to the rebel westward shift and the failure to defend the Hukuang-Szechwan passes, Yang Ssu-ch'ang decided to transfer his headquarters up the Yangtze in order to be nearer the center of action. Advancing slowly under difficult conditions, by the autumn of 1640, Yang had reached K'uei-chou, Szechwan, and by winter had proceeded on to Chungking where he remained only a short time before returning east.

Once beyond the fortified Hukuang-Szechwan passes, the rebels followed their customary practise of rapid movement punctuated with sporadic skirmishes with the official forces. However, for some two months the rebels were kept confined to a relatively restricted area in extreme eastern Szechwan north of the Yangtze. Within this area the fight against them was carried on by Grand Coordinator Shao Chieh-ch'un, assisted by the heroine Ch'in Liang-yü who was now quite pessimistic about the possibility of victory over the rebels, and a professional officer, Chang Ling. Despite his seventy years, Chang was one of the ablest commanders in Szechwan and his death from wounds, received while winning one of the more significant skirmishes with Lo Ju-ts'ai and Kuo-t'ien-hsing, was a blow to the government cause.

By the late summer of 1640, sufficient military pressure had been brought against the rebels in Szechwan to initiate a series of significant rebel surrenders and produced in Yang the illusion of possible success.[20] Kuo-t'ien-hsing, Hun-shih-wang, Hsiao-ch'in-wang, Wang Kuang-en and Hua-kuan-so all surrendered. Wang Kuang-en and Hua-kuan-so submitted directly to Yang himself, performing the customary ritual of kneeling at his feet, weeping, and begging to be permitted to die in his service. Kuo-t'ien-hsing, whose surrender was the most significant and was destined to be permanent, submitted to Tso Liang-yü who was ordered by Yang to incorporate the rebel troops into his own army. Hsiao-ch'in-wang and Hun-shih-wang were assigned garrison tasks in northwestern Hukuang. Thus, by the autumn of 1640, only two major rebel leaders, Chang Hsien-chung and Lo Ju-ts'ai, remained active in Szechwan and even Lo at one point entered into negotiations with the authorities and toyed with the idea of surrendering. However, Lo did not surrender and joined with Chang to bring about a resurgence of rebel power in Szechwan.

In the 9th month of 1640, Chang and Lo broke out of the eastern Szechwan area and moved rapidly northwest via Ta-chou to Kuang-yüan. Their plans were to abandon Szechwan and cross over into Shensi, only a short distance north of Kuang-yüan. However, finding the border passes well garrisoned, they were forced to alter their plans and turned southwestward, plundering up to the outskirts of Chengtu which was besieged briefly.

Supreme Commander Yang arrived in K'uei-chou, Szechwan, at about the same time that Chang and Lo launched their westward push. He was infuriated at what he regarded as the military incompetence exhibited by the provincial authorities and meted out stern punishment. He executed one of the professional military officers and did not spare even Grand Coordinator Shao Chieh-ch'un who was arrested and executed in spite of the broad chorus of pleas requesting that he be spared. After this display of severity, Yang ordered all-out pursuit of the rebels, rejecting a plan suggested by one of his chief subordinate officers, Wan Yüan-chi, that the army be divided up and assigned three roles: pursuit, reserve, and guard (the last group particularly instructed to prevent a future incursion of the rebels back toward the east).

By this time, Yang Ssu-ch'ang had occupied the position of Supreme Commander for a full year and though certain accomplishments had been achieved, even his most enthusiastic admirers, of which there were few indeed, could hardly claim that his mission had been successful. Violent attacks against him, at least partly justified, began circulating in Peking along with truly malicious rumors.[21] The most valid criticism involved his military competence, which certainly could be questioned. Conducting the anti-rebel campaign like the genuine bureaucrat he was, he kept voluminous records and attempted to center all command decisions, even minor ones, in his own hands. As one of the more sensible memorials attacking him pointed out, the rebel situation was likely to alter drastically in a very short time, since the rebels deliberately sought to exploit fully their mobility. Local officers should be given more freedom of action and initiative. The memorial concluded on an ungracious note by pointing out that the Mt. Ma-nao victory would not have been won if Yang's orders had been heeded.

The rumors attacking Yang depicted him as stupid, lazy, irresponsible, and provincial. He was said to have spent his time at the I-ling headquarters drinking, writing poetry, looking at scenery, and calculating *Fengshui*. Also, he was accused of having been guilty of the ultimate insult to Confucian rationalism by recommending the reading of the fourth chapter of a Buddhist work, the *Hua-yen-ching* (*Avatamsaka Sutra*), as a means of warding off locusts. The dominant theme in his entire campaign was attacked as being based on narrow provincial considerations. That is, he was said to have been mainly concerned about keeping the rebels out of his native Hukuang, not particularly caring about what happened to Szechwan. Finally, he was depicted as not having real control over even his own headquarters, a fact supposed to have been shown by the alleged response to his offer of 10,000 taels of silver and a marquis title to anyone who would kill or capture Chang Hsien-chung. The day following this offer a sign was said to have been found on the walls of Yang's office offering three-tenths of a tael to anyone who would kill Yang himself. All of these rumors were based on the most flimsy foundations, if indeed they had any foundations at all. For example, concerning the last-mentioned rumor, Chang Hsien-chung, noted for his heavy-handed humor, probably did make the satirical gesture of offering three-tenths of a tael for Yang's head after hearing of the handsome reward Yang had offered for his own. However, it is highly doubtful that Chang had supporters within Yang's staff who were so brazen as to post a notice of this mock reward on the office wall. As for Yang's special concern for Hukuang and neglect of Szechwan, there may have been a measure of truth in such a charge. But Yang's motives in this instance need not have been based entirely on narrow provincial interest. There were valid military reasons for attempting to confine as many of the rebels as possible to relatively isolated sections of Szechwan where they posed no threat to really strategic areas.

Yang was certainly aware of the intensifying attacks against him and undoubtedly the memory of the failure which had overtaken his father served to deepen his anxiety. At one point in the fall of 1640, he even considered a completely cynical suggestion, offered by one of his subordinates, which was designed to improve his official image. The subordinate recommended that Yang transfer his attention from Szechwan to the Honan-Hukuang-Nan-chihli border area where military success would be easy, because the rebel groups were weak and the terrain posed no real problems. To his credit, Yang finally rejected this suggestion and remained in Szechwan trying to cope with the strongest rebel groups while events moved toward the ultimate disaster.

Pursuing their raids in western Szechwan, Chang Hsien-chung and Lo Ju-ts'ai continued their rapid movements, usually succeeding in keeping a safe distance between themselves and the pursuing official forces. By the beginning of 1641, they had reached the Yangtze and briefly occupied Lu-chou after having followed an irregular route southeast from the vicinity of Chengtu. At Lu-chou the government forces attempted to trap the rebels, the city being surrounded on three sides by the Yangtze and thus easily bottled up. However, Chang and Lo succeeded in abandoning the city before the official force arrived to set up its blockade.

After departing from Lu-chou, Chang and Lo retraced their steps northwestward, returning again to the vicinity of Chengtu. Then, they changed directions and pushed rapidly eastward to Pa-chou which they captured. Once more altering directions, the rebels moved southeastward from Pa-chou to K'ai-hsien, a move which indicated that they had decided to abandon Szechwan and advance down the Yangtze to Hukuang.

Since Yang Ssu-ch'ang had ordered all the official forces in Szechwan to pursue Chang and Lo after their movement to the west, no strong garrison existed in eastern Szechwan to oppose the rebels now that they had returned to that area. A government army did manage to overtake the rebels near K'ai-hsien after a forced march from the west. In the ensuing battle the rebels won a complete victory, thus removing the last remaining block to their push through the Yangtze gorges into Hukuang. Upon hearing the news of the K'ai-hsien defeat, Yang Ssu-ch'ang also moved toward Hukuang as rapidly as possible, but was hopelessly outdistanced by the rebels.

After entering Hukuang, Chang Hsien-chung assigned his ally, Lo

MING DYNASTY PEASANT REBELLIONS

14 LOCATIONS OF PEASANT REBEL ACTIVITY IN **1641**

Ju-ts'ai, the task of opposing a government army which was soon encountered, while he himself planned a dramatic seizure of Hsiang-yang before that important city had had time to receive word of the disasters the imperial cause had suffered in Szechwan. Covering a hundred miles in a rapid move lasting a day and a night, Chang hurried toward Hsiang-yang and along the route had the good fortune to capture a messenger from one of the subordinates of Yang Ssu-ch'ang. The crucial element in Chang's plan to take the city was to plant agents within the walls who would create a disturbance during the night and amid the resulting confusion would open one of the gates to permit the entrance of the main body of rebel troops. The plan worked perfectly and agents were smuggled into the city under at least two guises. One group used the credentials of the captured messenger to pose as an official force and another group pretended to be refugees who had fled from the rebels. Once inside the city, the agents carried out their assignment and Hsiang-yang was occupied during the early hours of March 15, 1641.[22] Only eight days previously Chang had been some 365 miles away near K'ai-hsien, Szechwan.

Chang Hsien-chung remained at Hsiang-yang for two days during which time he killed several officials and chose as his most important victim the local district prince, the Prince of Hsiang. That unfortunate descendant of Ming emperors was made the butt of a macabre joke. Chang occupied the place of honor in the main hall of the palace and forced the Prince to sit below him. After the Prince had been served a cup of wine, Chang made the following mock pronouncement: "I want to cut off the head of Yang Ssu-ch'ang, but Ssu-ch'ang is far away in Szechwan. Thus, I must borrow the Prince's head. This will cause Ssu-ch'ang to suffer the punishment of the law for having been responsible for the loss of a district prince. The Prince must exert his strength and finish this cup of wine."[23] Subsequently, the Prince was killed and his body burned.

Chang's other activities at Hsiang-yang included looting the property of Tso Liang-yü which had been stored there for safekeeping, releasing his own wives and gentry advisers from prison where they had been placed following their capture at Mt. Ma-nao, seizing all the military equipment that his forces had need of and could carry away, and rifling the prefectural treasury. From the silver obtained from the treasury, he contributed 150,000 taels to aid famine victims, an act of generosity re-reported without explanation in the sources. It was possibly urged upon him by his gentry advisers who undoubtedly wanted to create for him a more benevolent image.

The shortness of Chang's stay at Hsiang-yang was dictated by his fear of Tso Liang-yü whose army was quartered at Yün-yang, some 150 miles to the northwest. Chang knew that Tso would immediately march against him and he abandoned Hsiang-yang to move eastward over the border into Honan.

Li Tzu-ch'eng Moves into Honan

Simultaneously with Chang Hsien-chung's wide-ranging activities in Szechwan, his eruption into Hukuang, and the dramatic seizure of Hsiang-yang, rebels in other areas were enjoying increasing success. The tempo of lawless acts committed by minor local rebels was on the rise even in provinces like Shantung and Pei-chihli which had been relatively free of such activity previously. Also, Tso-chin-wang and Ko-kuo-yen were still active in their favorite haunts in the Honan-Hukuang-Nan-chihli border region and no really serious efforts had been made to crush them while Yang Ssu-ch'ang was directing his major efforts toward destroying Chang Hsien-chung. Most serious and most laden with future danger, however, was Li Tzu-ch'eng's push into Honan in late 1640 and his subsequent success there.

Following the disaster which befell Li in the winter of 1638, he remained relatively inactive in southern Shensi and the Shensi-Honan border area for two years, barely managing to escape being crushed by the official forces. His prospects dramatically altered late in 1640 when he moved from Shensi into west central Honan. Taking advantage of serious unrest evoked by famine conditions in the area, he rapidly acquired a large following, the size of which partially compensated for its lack of training and discipline. Furthermore, he attracted to his cause a member of the gentry, Li Yen, who was destined to become one of the chief architects of his subsequent successes.

Early in 1641, Li captured the two towns of Yung-ning and I-yang and proceeded to besiege Loyang (Honan-fu) on March 7, 1641.[24] The defense of the city soon collapsed after two subordinate officers surrendered to Li and the garrison troops, resentful over inadequate rations, mutinied. Following the city's fall, Li launched a systematic effort to extract as many items of value from both official and private sources as possible. He paid especial attention to the possessions of the local district prince, the Prince of Fu, who was well-known for his vast wealth, greed, ostentatious living and obesity. The Prince himself at first managed to escape, but was soon captured after having been abandoned by everyone except a thirteen-year-old eunuch servant. He suffered a horrible fate at Li's hands. His blood was mixed with that of a deer to form what the rebels, making a pun on the word for "deer" and combining it with the Prince's title, mockingly termed "Happiness and Prosperity Liquor" (Fu-lu-chiu). The Prince's flesh was also said to have been mixed with deer meat and eaten by the rebels after it had been offered as a sacrifice in a religious ceremony. Thus ingloriously ended the life of the second son of the Wan-li Emperor who in happier days had been one of the key figures in the struggle for determining the successor to his father.*

Li's savage treatment of the Prince represented more than the mere personal resentment of a peasant against the rich and favored. It was designed to enhance his own leadership charisma by appealing to popular sentiment against the Prince in Honan. The proclamation issued following the killing of the Prince demonstrated the broader implications of the event quite clearly. Li stated in the proclamation, "The Prince was a wealthy man. He oppressed the people and looked upon their cold and hunger unfeelingly. Consequently I killed him because he was like that."

After contributing one-tenth of the loot he had obtained at Loyang to aid local famine victims, Li withdrew from the city, bearing with him a large amount of booty. He pushed eastward, bent on even more ambitious conquests. However, he did not abandon Loyang, leaving behind Shao Shih-ch'ang, a minor official who had joined Li's cause, to maintain control over the city in his behalf. Shao recruited a garrison force from among the famine victims, but all his efforts proved to be abortive. The Grand Coordinator of Honan soon dispatched a force which easily recaptured the city. Shao surrendered and was executed. The Emperor ordered public decapitation for the Regional Commander held responsible for the fall of Loyang to Li.

Death of Yang Ssu-ch'ang

The twin disasters of Hsiang-yang and Loyang propelled Supreme Commander Yang Ssu-ch'ang toward the final tragedy of his career.[25] Continuing his move down the Yangtze, begun following Chang Hsien-chung's breakthrough toward the east, Yang eventually halted at Ching-chou in central Hukuang. Enroute to Ching-chou, he had heard of Chang's seizure of Hsiang-yang and, following his arrival, the even more depressing news of Loyang's fall reached him. He became terribly despondent, refused to eat, and told his most trusted lieutenant, Wan Yüan-chi, that he could never face the Emperor again. On April 10, 1641 he committed suicide, apparently by taking poison, leaving Wan Yüan-chi in command of his army. Wan moved one part of the army under his own personal command to extreme eastern Hukuang and sent other detachments to northern Hukuang and southern Honan.

---

* One of the bitter political issues of the Wan-li era was the designation of an Heir Apparent. The Emperor was suspected of supporting his second son who was the child of his favorite concubine. Eventually, however, the officials succeeded in forcing the Emperor to name the first son as Heir Apparent and the second son as the Prince of Fu.

When the news of Yang's suicide reached Peking, the Emperor refrained from any display of resentment. He rejected the memorial of the Vice-minister of the Ministry of Rites who suggested that Yang's coffin be broken open and his corpse whipped. Also, the Emperor entertained a message from Yang's son who sought to exonerate his father and was so moved by the appeal that he had several dreams in which Yang knelt before him and wept. As a result, the Emperor ordered that Yang's crimes be forgiven and that he be buried with the rites appropriate for a high official. Subsequently, however, Yang's corpse did suffer a horrible indignity. In 1643, Chang Hsien-chung, carrying his bitter hatred of Yang even beyond death, exposed and slashed his corpse as part of the general desecration he visited upon the Yang ancestral graveyard.

General Assessment of the 1636-41 Period of the Rebellions

Surveying the rebellions during the 1636-41 period, one conclusion which can be drawn is that the apparent prospects for the government to crush them were entirely illusory. It is true that during most of 1638 and the first part of 1639 there was a definite decline in rebel strength and activity. The strongest rebel groups were either induced to accept a formal accommodation with the government or suffered serious defeats, and many minor rebel groups were either destroyed or forced into a quiescent state. However, at no point, even during this 1638-39 low point of the rebellions, were the upholders of the official cause operating from a sure foundation of strength and much of the superficial success they achieved was based on flimsy political maneuvering rather than military power. The rebellions remained merely semi-dormant, waiting a resurgence in the future.

As for the area affected by the rebellions, no major changes had occurred by 1641 over what had been true in 1636. Szechwan was brought more definitely within the rebel-afflicted sphere, especially during 1640. On the other hand, Nan-chihli and northern Shensi were less subjected to rebel incursions than they had been during the 1631-36 period. In general, however, the rebels still coursed through the huge central section of China between the Yangtze and Yellow Rivers, though their movements within this vast area were less rapid and probably less devastating than formerly.

Considering the quality of official leadership at the upper echelons during the 1636-41 period, one cannot say that there was any demonstrable improvement over the earlier period. The Emperor maintained his customary dedication and seriousness of purpose. It was undoubtedly true that he worked as long and as hard as any ordinary member of the bureaucracy. Unfortunately, aside from attempting to deal with matters for which he had no real competence, he also wasted his energies by giving

MING DYNASTY PEASANT REBELLIONS

15   LOCATIONS OF PEASANT REBEL ACTIVITY IN **1642**

attention to petty details which should have been left in the hands of subordinates. Two classic examples might be cited.[26] One case involved three minor military positions in Hukuang dealt with in a report by the provincial Grand Coordinator. The report noted that the positions were vacant and not only made recommendations as to who should fill them but also requested that the ranks of the new appointees should be raised. The Emperor eventually gave his personal attention to this petty matter, accepting the recommendation of who the new appointees should be, but rejecting the request that their ranks be raised. The second case involved a minor military officer in Szechwan who had been sentenced to be executed for failing to attack the rebels and plundering the common people. In carrying out the sentence, a dispute arose between the Ministry of Justice and the Ministry of War as to the proper time for the execution. The former argued that the officer should be executed immediately and the latter maintained that there should be a delay until the autumn. Intervening in the dispute, the Emperor scolded the two ministries for not consulting one another and agreeing; then he ended the case by accepting the Ministry of Justice's position and ordering the immediate execution of the officer.

Ranking just below the Emperor in the leadership scale was Yang Ssu-ch'ang whose influence extended throughout the 1636-41 period. No one can deny Yang's good intentions, honesty, and competence as a bureaucrat. Undoubtedly he would have functioned quite adequately as a Vice-minister or Minister, but he was certainly beyond his depth as principal Grand Secretary enjoying the full support of the Emperor. His most glaring mistake was the assumption of field command where, despite his best efforts, he displayed abject incompetence in technical military matters. In sum, Yang's entire term in power might be said to be a classic example of the weaknesses inherent in one of the most fundamental assumptions underlying Ming institutions: strict civilian superiority. Yang's failure really meant that the last real chance for the dynasty to save itself had been lost.

In the middle echelons of power, the caliber of men employed during the 1636-41 period does not measure up to that of the previous period. Hsiung Wen-ts'an, in particular, was incompetent and his selection demonstrated Yang Ssu-ch'ang's poor judgement. Hsiung's only contribution was the achieving of a temporary lull in the rebellions by means of political maneuvering and appeasement. Hung Ch'eng-ch'ou would have given far better service as Supreme Commander than Hsiung. Even though Hung was hardly a military genius, he was gifted with a stubborn persistence and had a decade of experience fighting the rebels. It was certainly the height of folly for Yang Ssu-ch'ang to ignore Hung's long

16

THE LATE MING PEASANT REBELLIONS 1628-36

17

THE LATE MING PEASANT
REBELLIONS
1636 - 41

experience and, because of his personal dislike of Hung, have him transferred to the Manchurian frontier where his talents were improperly used and indeed were eventually placed at the service of the Manchus.

In addition to the continuing leadership deficiencies, the government during the 1636-41 interval failed to solve any of the other pressing problems which had appeared all too obvious earlier. Troop inadequacies, both in number and quality, remained. In particular, desertions by Hukuang and Yunnan troops during the Szechwan campaigns are said to have seriously hampered the effectiveness of the government forces. There was also the old problem of the increasing attachment of some of the government military units to their own leaders who became semi-independent wielders of power and were not always responsive to government direction. The discipline problem in these semi-personal armies continued to be especially acute, though certainly this problem manifested itself throughout the government forces generally. For example, a special imperial order to a military officer in Shensi instructed him to launch an attack on the rebels and to obtain supplies in the areas through which he passed. He was expressly forbidden, however, to take his force inside a town. He and his men were to remain in the countryside and have the supplies delivered to them there.

The long-range interaction between the internal rebels and the Manchu threat continued. The dynasty was bleeding to death on two fronts, and increased peril on one could not help but lessen the prospects of success on the other. The last major effort against the Manchus was launched early in 1641 and it ended in failure at about the same time that Yang Ssu-ch'ang's efforts to suppress the rebels were collapsing.

Most serious of all the problems which the dynasty failed to solve was the economic one. Not only was there no disposition to stop the policy of ruinous taxation, but on the contrary, the policy of increasing taxation was actually intensified with Yang Ssu-ch'ang's raising the tax rate to even higher levels. Yang's tax hike was a gross misfortune in two respects: on the one hand, it produced very little additional revenue and, on the other hand, it demoralized the bureaucracy even further and pushed the peasants toward more desperate extremes. Government efforts to alleviate the increasingly desperate economic situation were totally inadequate and were confined to such ineffectual measures as formally ordering military commanders to have their men settle down on land and produce their own food. Such orders were never effectively implemented.

The early part of 1641 was a crucial period for the late Ming rebellions and marked the beginning of an important shift in emphasis and direction. This change was first made manifest in the activities and posture of Li Tzu-ch'eng and subsequently was discernible to a lesser degree for

Chang Hsien-chung as well. Basically, the change involved an increased rebel military potential and an enhanced seriousness of purpose. Throughout the ensuing three years, Li was never again really threatened by a Ming army. The days were gone when he had to flee desperately from place to place, always in fear of being defeated and destroyed by a government army. Instead, beginning in early 1641, the most that the Ming generals could attempt was to hold Li in check, hoping vainly that if they could only maintain their defensive posture long enough, Li's force would disintegrate and his power position would collapse. In sum, early 1641 saw the rebel movement progress from the disorganized raiding phase to the dynastic ambitions phase. The dominant theme of the next chapter will be Li Tzu-ch'eng's attempt to achieve supreme power.

Chapter IV

The Dynastic-Ambitions Phase of the Rebellions: Li Tzu-ch'eng's Drive to Peking and Chang Hsien-chung's Power Centers in Hukuang and Szechwan (1641-44)

Li Tzu-ch'eng in Honan (1641)

Honan was the focal point of the rebellions for 1641 and 1642, and Li Tzu-ch'eng was unquestionably the dominant figure in the movement there, rapidly enhancing his power and leaving behind the misfortune of the past. This new status for Li was in some measure quite fortuitous, a result of his being in the right place at the right time. We have already seen his move into Honan at the end of 1639 and his taking advantage of famine conditions to build up a large following almost overnight. We have also noted his capture of Loyang* in March, 1641, which was the most significant victory of any rebel leader up to this time. And even more important than the capture of Loyang was the fact that Li made at least some effort to hold it permanently. Although this effort did not succeed, the fact that it was made at all indicated that Li now definitely had a new seriousness of purpose. He was abandoning his old orientation toward random plundering and now had the ambition to acquire a more stable base.

Another indication of Li's changed status was the new type of followers he was attracting. Particularly significant was the joining of his cause by Li Yen, a native of Chi-hsien, Honan (a short distance southeast of Kaifeng). He was the holder of a *chü-jen* degree and a member of a wealthy and prominent family, his father having been a minister during the T'ien-ch'i period. Li Yen did not attach himself to the rebel cause as the result of a momentary fancy but only after a long series of events had

---

* See Map 18 for the location of places involved in Li's career from 1641 to 1645.

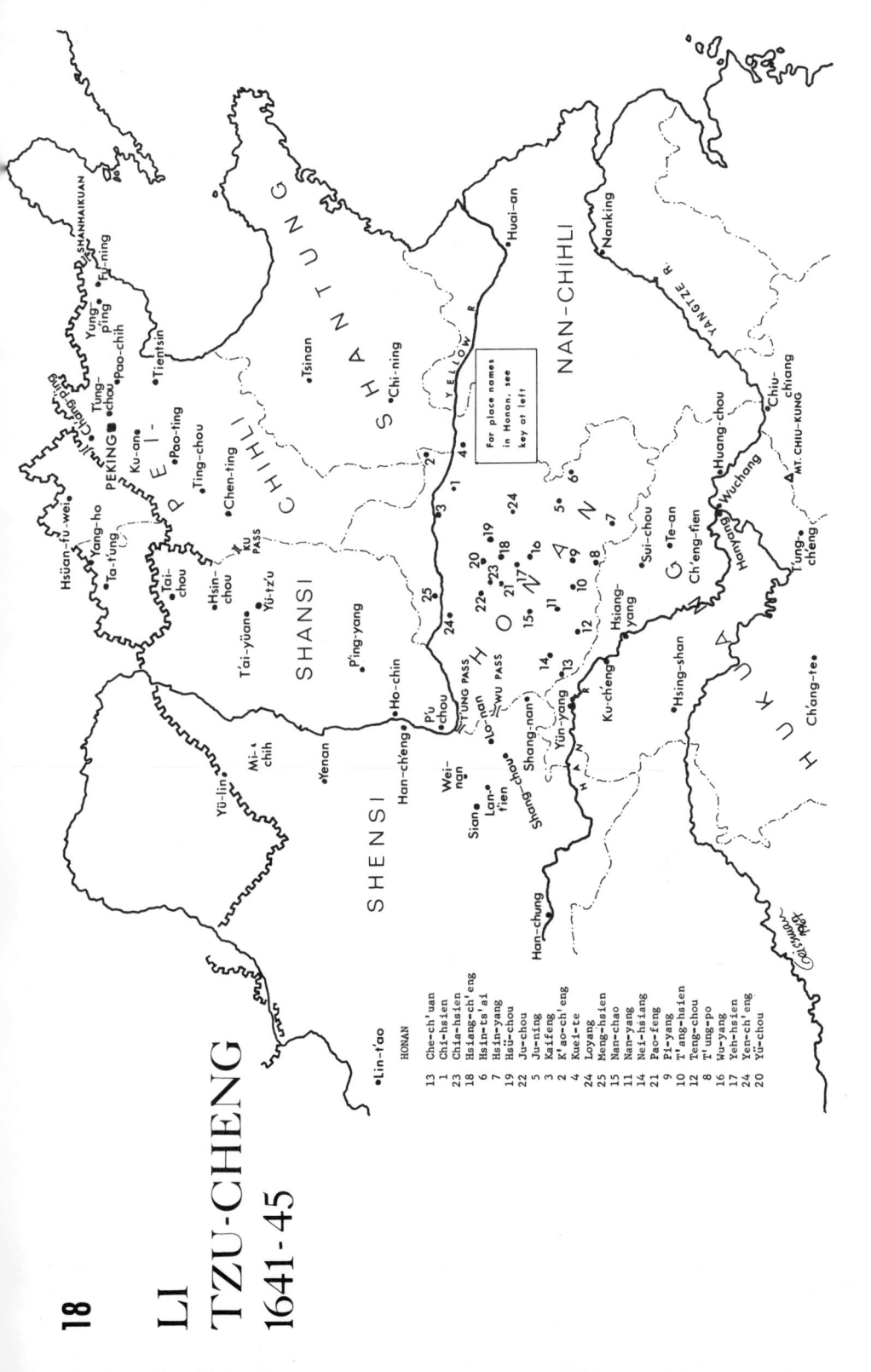

provided background motivation.¹ The initial event of the series involved the philanthropic activities of the Li family. These activities began in the late 1630's when famine conditions became critical in Honan and Li Yen contributed more than five hundred bushels of grain for public relief. This act consolidated the general reputation for benevolence the family already had and Li Yen found himself the center of increasing popularity among the peasantry of east-central Honan. This popularity was not appreciated by his gentry neighbors who found themselves under pressure from mobs to make similar contributions of grain; if they refused, their storehouses were looted. At this point, a touch of romance entered the story when Li Yen was kidnapped by a petty rebel group headed by a woman acrobat and tight-rope walker nicknamed Hung-niang-tzu, who is said to have wanted to marry Li Yen. Eventually, he managed to elude his captors and returned home where the evil reputation he had acquired among his gentry peers soon placed him in a difficult position. He was accused of having rebel sympathies and was imprisoned by the local magistrate. The imprisonment caused a violent reaction in the area, and a mob temporarily seized control of the town. The magistrate was murdered and the prison was broken into, giving Li Yen and his fellow inmates their freedom. After being liberated, Li Yen addressed the mob and informed them that the proper course to follow now was to join Li Tzu-ch'eng. After burning his home, presumably as a public demonstration of a complete rupture with his past life,* he went to west central Honan where he offered his services to the man whom he was to assist so significantly in becoming the dominant figure in the rebel movement, Li Tzu-ch'eng.

Li Yen had a crucial contribution to make to the career of Li Tzu-ch'eng and his counterpart is to be found in every past Chinese peasant rebellion which achieved any real importance. He was the educated Confucian bearer of the dominant elements of his country's traditional values, and his idealism and sense of dedication demonstrated the continued vitality of the tradition. Furthermore, he was of very real assistance to Li Tzu-ch'eng in the realm of practical politics. The wide reputation he had achieved in Honan for his benevolence certainly enhanced the appeal of Li Tzu-ch'eng and the two men became inextricably linked together in the minds of Honan peasants, a confusion made all the easier by their having the same surname.

Li Yen's influence on Li Tzu-ch'eng took the expected direction of urging moderation, restraint, and the alleviation of pressing burdens on the people. In one of their first interviews, Li Yen centered his arguments

---

* Li Yen also made another gesture symbolizing a break with the past: changing his given name. Originally, it was Hsin, but after joining Li Tzu-ch'eng, he changed this to Yen.

around the Confucian formula for obtaining the empire: to gain the hearts of the people by acting benevolently. Shortly thereafter, Li Yen started a deliberate campaign to circulate popular slogans which would create for Li Tzu-ch'eng a new image and win him widespread support. There appeared such slogans as "Equalize land," "Three years remission of taxes," "Not a single person killed," "Equal buying, equal selling," "Welcome 'Dashing King' and do not pay taxes." Some of the slogans were put to music by Li Yen and they became so popular that even children sang them.

In the spring of 1641, at about the same time that he captured Loyang, Li Tzu-ch'eng was joined by another member of the gentry, Niu Chin-hsing, a native of Lu-shih in extreme west-central Honan. Niu was a holder of the lower degree of *kung-sheng*, but his family was not really prominent. He had little of the Confucian idealism of Li Yen and there was considerable rivalry subsequently between the two men. Niu was recommended to Li Tzu-ch'eng by a physician named Shang Chiung who had been a member of Li's group for some time and was greatly respected by Li. Apparently one of the chief reasons for Niu's joining the rebel cause was his difficulty with the local authorities who had sentenced him to be exiled to the frontier.

An additional important figure to join Li Tzu-ch'eng early in 1641 was Sung Hsien-ts'e who was not, however, a member of the gentry. He was a fortuneteller and a native of Yung-ning, Honan, where he had a wide reputation for his ability in divination. In physical appearance he conformed to what apparently was one of the ideals for a shaman in China, being terribly crippled and so stunted in stature that he was only three and a half feet tall. He pleased Li Tzu-ch'eng by predicting that an "eighteenth grandchild" (shih-pa-sun-erh) would obtain the imperial throne, and this prediction was considered to refer to someone possessing the surname Li.* Sung came to exert considerable influence over Li Tzu-ch'eng, and although he represented a tradition at least partly antithetical to the Confucianism of Li Yen, relations between Sung and Li were cordial.

Reviewing Li Tzu-ch'eng's position in the spring of 1641, one can say that he was on the threshold of a new direction. He had achieved a major military triumph in capturing Loyang, a city with venerable connections with past Chinese history and one of the most important cities of the north China plain. In addition, he had acquired an augmented

---

* *YSCC* 5/20b-21a. Similar predictions had occurred earlier in Chinese history. Usually, however, these earlier predictions involved an "eighteenth son" (shih-pa tzu), since these three characters, when joined together, form the character for the surname Li.

staff which now contained men who possessed talents largely unavailable to him previously.

From Loyang, Li Tzu-ch'eng marched his forces due east to Kaifeng.[2] He placed the city under siege, bent upon an even greater victory than the previous one and determined to bring about the fall of the first Ming provincial capital to a rebel force. The defense of Kaifeng at first was in a state of confusion. The Honan Grand Coordinator was absent on a mission north of the Yellow River to suppress local bandits in Pei-chihli and had difficulty persuading his men to march to the defense of threatened Kaifeng. Even when he did win their consent and arrive on the scene, the local Kaifeng authorities refused to allow them within the city walls. The local Regional Commander, Ch'en Yung-fu, whose troops were mostly Kaifeng natives, had gone to Loyang in a vain attempt to prevent its fall. He did finally manage to return to Kaifeng in time to participate in its defense. In the meantime, the local authorities had taken some action. The magistrate had ordered all the nearby residents and provisions moved inside the city so that the area outside the walls presented a scorched-earth aspect to the rebels. The local district prince, the Prince of Chou, much wiser than his unfortunate distant cousin at Loyang, had contributed the generous sum of 500,000 taels to a reward fund, and it was announced that anyone killing a rebel would be rewarded fifty taels. In addition, the defense was aided by an invention produced by a local *sheng-yüan*. This was a cage-like wooden device projecting horizontally from the top of the wall. Each device was capable of containing ten soldiers and fifty of them were constructed. The soldiers in the structures were able to shoot down on the rebels attacking the wall while themselves being protected by the wooden floors and sides.

After some rather desultory attempts to dig holes in the city wall, the rebel enthusiasm for continuing the siege cooled markedly. Furthermore, the defenders, led by Regional Commander Ch'en Yung-fu, attacked Li's camp at night with considerable success. In the fighting, Li Tzu-ch'eng narrowly escaped death when he was struck in the eye by an arrow from the bow of Local Commander Ch'en Te, the son of the Regional Commander. Li never regained sight in the injured eye and after the incident one of the popular nicknames bestowed upon him was "Blind Ch'uang."

At the end of seven days, the rebel siege of Kaifeng was abandoned. Li retreated to the southwest and spent several months relatively inactively in east-central Honan, recovering from his eye injury. The official forces made virtually no effort to attack him, despite reinforcements arriving from Pei-chihli. To make matters worse, the Honan Grand Coordinator became involved in a dispute with a subordinate and was ordered arrested and sent to Peking by the Emperor. Faced with what must have seemed a dire fate, the Grand Coordinator hanged himself.

The threat posed by Li Tzu-ch'eng in Honan exerted pressure on the Peking authorities to try and patch together another defensive arrangement and at least to appoint a successor to the late Yang Ssu-ch'ang as Supreme Commander. In the 4th month of 1641, the imperial decision was announced and Ting Ch'i-jui was made Supreme Commander of Shensi, Hukuang, Honan, Szechwan, and portions of Nan-chihli.[3] Ting had the advantage of being a native of east central Honan, the very area where Li was now operating, and also he had had valuable experience serving as Grand Coordinator of Shensi. An army of 30,000 men was ordered pieced together to be placed under his personal command, though it is highly doubtful that it ever reached anything like full strength.

Ting was destined to have a relatively brief tenure in office and the campaign he waged was decidedly lackluster. Indeed, the whole idea of Supreme Commanders was now being questioned in Peking. One memorial pointed out that provincial Grand Coordinators were vitally necessary and the Emperor himself instructed the Ministry of War to place more power of decision in the hands of local commanders who were intimately acquainted with rebel conditions.

Throughout the summer and autumn of 1641, there continued a process, underway since at least early in 1641, for the consolidation of rebel leadership around Li Tzu-ch'eng in Honan.[4] The most important rebel chieftain to attach himself to Li was Lo Ju-ts'ai whose loose series of alliances with Chang Hsien-chung had always been tenuous and had frequently been dissolved. The final rupture with Chang came in the 8th month of 1641 and Lo moved his forces from Hukuang to join Li in Honan. Several other leaders also submitted to Li, among them Lao-hui-hui, Hu Ch'uang-tzu, Cheng-shih-wang, and Ko-liao-yen. Some of the leaders did not actually join forces with Li, but remained in Hukuang and arranged informal alliances with him from a distance. Thus, part of Li's increasing stature and success was the result of a development within the rebel movement where the trend was away from the original chaotic diversity and in the direction of unity and consolidation.

In the autumn of 1641, with his military position strengthened by the submission of the previously independent rebel leaders, Li Tzu-ch'eng resumed action against the government forces.[5] He attacked an army in the area of Hsin-ts'ai near the Nan-chihli border in east-central Honan. The army was jointly commanded by a former Minister of War recently released from prison, Fu Tsung-lung, who as Supreme Commander of Shensi had been ordered to come to the assistance of Honan, and by Regional Commander Yang Wen-yüeh who had been dispatched to Honan from Pei-chihli. Shortly after the beginning of hostilities, Yang departed from the area with a portion of the troops and refused to heed subsequent appeals for aid made by Fu. Knowing that Fu was in an untenable position, Li besieged his force, erecting a siege barrier to prevent its escape. After all his supplies were exhausted, Fu made a desperate sortie to break out of the encirclement, but the attempt failed completely and Fu himself was captured. Li used his prisoner in a ruse by which he hoped to bring about the downfall of nearby Hsiang-ch'eng. Fu was taken outside the town wall by rebel troops posing as an official force from Shensi and requesting permission to enter. Fu, however, failed to perform as expected, bravely defying his captors by shouting a warning which revealed the entire scheme to the town defenders. Exacting revenge, Li had Fu slain in a particularly brutal fashion and went on to overwhelm the town as well.

From Hsiang-ch'eng, Li Tzu-ch'eng turned westward and in the 11th month of 1641 attacked Nan-yang, the major city of southwestern Honan, which was stoutly defended by a professional military man known only by his nickname Meng-ju-hu ("Fierce As a Tiger"). Meng had given many years of dedicated service to the official cause, his most recent field of action having been in Szechwan against Chang Hsien-chung. Meng exacted a heavy toll on the attacking rebels, but was finally overwhelmed and killed after having faced north and paid his last respects to the Emperor. Following the fall of Nan-yang, Li went on to capture most of the principal towns in the surrounding area of southwestern Honan. No significant opposition from government forces was encountered anywhere. A eunuch general was dispatched from Peking to aid Nan-yang, but he accomplished nothing. Indeed, his troops seem to have set something of a record in looting, kidnapping women, and slaughtering innocent peasants whom they claimed to be rebels. Their actions became so flagrant that an investigation was ordered, and the eunuch general eventually was executed.

Li Tzu-ch'eng Moves toward Enhanced Power in Honan (1642)

Following his seizure of Nan-yang, Li Tzu-ch'eng's attention once again was attracted to the northwest, Kaifeng's capture continuing to be his great ambition. Enroute from Nan-yang to the Kaifeng area, he paused long enough in central Honan to occupy Yeh-hsien after the ex-rebel leader, Liu Kuo-neng, had put up a stiff fight in its defense. Li attempted to persuade Liu to surrender following his capture and reminded him of their long friendship and association in the past. Liu spurned Li's efforts and met his death with dignity, soon to be joined, according to one perhaps overly romanticized account, by his eight-year-old son who preferred suicide to submission to Li.[6]

From Yeh-hsien, Li proceeded on to besiege Yen-ch'eng where Tso Liang-yü was currently garrisoned. Tso adopted a completely defensive policy and Li, soon losing interest in the siege, abandoned it and attacked

Hsiang-ch'eng which had formerly been in rebel hands, but had recently been recaptured by the Shensi Grand Coordinator, Wang Ch'iao-nien. Li had a bitter personal hatred of Wang who had played a leading role a short time earlier in the desecration of the graves of Li's ancestors in Shensi. Thus, Li pressed the attack on Hsiang-ch'eng with particular vigor, and not only captured the town, but also killed Wang and destroyed most of his army. Li is said to have taken especially dire vengeance against local gentry members who had played a leading role in bringing about the city's recapture by Wang. Li apparently killed 190 prominent local citizens and one of them, considered particularly active in aiding the official cause, suffered the slaughter of his entire clan.

Pressing on northwestward from Hsiang-ch'eng, Li took five towns to the south and east of Kaifeng and in the middle of January, 1642, launched his second attack upon the city.[7] Li was able to concentrate directly on surmounting the city wall itself, as there was no real threat that he would be attacked from the rear by forces coming to the aid of the beleaguered provincial capital. Tso Liang-yü was some fifty miles away at Chi-hsien and refused all pleas that he attack Li. Tso did have some justification for his refusal, arguing that his presence at Chi-hsien would serve as a check on Li and prevent him from mustering all his efforts on attacking the city. Li, in fact, did send troops from his army at Kaifeng to attack Tso at Chi-hsien, but this did not seriously hamper the rebel siege efforts. As for Supreme Commander Ting Ch'i-jui, he did come to Kaifeng's aid, despite the opposition of local authorities. He was finally permitted inside the walls and a disaster almost resulted when a gate was opened to admit his troops. The rebels chose this moment to attack and nearly succeeded in their attempt to seize the gate.

One of Li Tzu-ch'eng's first major offensive efforts was the erecting of a huge platform a short distance from the city wall and higher than the wall. On this platform he mounted cannons which could shoot down on the defenders, thus posing a serious threat. Responding with a countermeasure, the government commanders marshalled a large labor force inside the city and overnight erected a platform of their own on top of the wall. This platform towered above the rebel platform and with cannons mounted on it, the defenders succeeded in destroying the rebel structure.

Li's next move was a more conventional attack on lunar New Year's Day, the date having been purposely chosen with the hope that the celebration of the holiday would distract the attention of the defenders. Only a few rebel troops succeeded in gaining the top of the wall and they were all quickly captured, summarily decapitated, and their heads exposed on the wall for the rest of Li's army to see. The success gave a considerable boost to the defenders' will to resist. Their morale was enhanced even further by the unearthing of a cannon on which was an inscription stating that the weapon had been manufactured during the Hung-wu period and giving instructions to employ it for the purpose of fighting rebels. In actual fact, the cannon had been buried only recently by one of the local officers who had subsequently engineered its "discovery" in the hope that it would be accepted by the populace as a demonstration of supernatural support for the official cause.

Having failed in all his initial offensive moves, Li Tzu-ch'eng abandoned efforts to capture the city by more conventional methods of scaling the walls and turned his attention toward achieving a breach in the wall. He ordered his men, protected by armor, to burrow into the wall and no man was to be allowed to return from the wall to the rebel camp without bringing at least one brick with him. This task was a formidable one indeed, as the Kaifeng wall, following its reconstruction during the Chin dynasty (12th century), was a truly monumental structure, measuring some 120 feet in width. However, after a massive rebel effort, involving the labor of thousands of men for at least a week, some thirty-six holes were dug in the wall large enough to contain a hundred men each. Then ropes were attached to the sections of the wall which remained intact between the holes and these were pulled by hundreds of rebel soldiers from a distance, resulting in a further collapse of the wall. The Grand Coordinator offered a reward of 2,000 taels to anyone who could force the rebels out of the holes and a private local citizen succeeded in accomplishing the task, permitting the official commanders to fill the holes with their own troops and successfully resist rebel efforts to recapture the positions. Furthermore, the defenders tried to frustrate any more rebel digging efforts by boring small holes down from the top of the wall to connect with the rebel-made cavities and then pouring poisonous substances through the openings.

Probably Li would have succeeded in breaching the wall had he persisted and proceeded with greater caution. Instead, he made a drastic miscalculation which resulted in a disaster for the rebels. He decided to place gunpowder in other holes dug by the rebels, calculating that when it exploded a considerable section of the wall would be completely destroyed. All preparations for this plan were completed and a large body of rebel troops was assembled outside the wall ready to rush into the city immediately after the explosion. As it happened, the main force of the explosion blasted outward rather than inward, leaving the wall relatively intact and destroying large numbers of rebel troops. This was a great blow to rebel morale, and on the following day, February 12, 1642, Li abandoned the siege and moved south, leaving behind 30,000 sick animals which were slaughtered and given to the famine victims.

Li's second attack on Kaifeng had lasted slightly less than a month but was considerably longer than the first, a year earlier, which had en-

DYNASTIC AMBITIONS PHASE (1641-44)

dured only a week. The rebel siege force is said to have consisted of 30,000 picked troops and 400,000 auxiliaries. It was said that 2,873 rebels were killed.

The second failure at Kaifeng probably was due mainly to Li's own errors, indicating that his technical military competence still needed considerable improvement. However, the successful defense of the city also reflected to the credit of those chifly responsible for directing the government forces, particularly the Magistrate, Wang Hsieh, and the Grand Coordinator, Kao Ming-heng. In addition, the Prince of Chou continued to display a high sense of public responsibility and provided a considerable portion of the economic support needed for the defense. Unfortunately, the defenders' victory was destined to be quite temporary and Kaifeng had gained merely a respite. Its eventual fate was undoubtedly far more devastating than that which would have befallen it had Li Tzu-ch'eng succeeded in capturing it on February 11, 1642.

For three months after abandoning his second attack on Kaifeng, Li Tzu-ch'eng conducted campaigns to the south and east.[8] His main camp was maintained at Sui-chou and he captured five towns in the general area, the most important of which was Kuei-te, said to have been defended only by an *ad hoc* force of local civilians. In attacking the town, he successfully used gunpowder to blast the wall, an indication that he must have profited by the experience gained from the disaster at Kaifeng. Also, his forces crossed the Yellow River and occupied K'ao-ch'eng, located a short distance north of the river. The rebel occupation of K'ao-ch'eng was very brief, but has a certain significance in that it represented the first thrust north of the Yellow River by a major rebel group in a decade.

This series of campaigns by Li placed a considerable strain on the Shantung forces attempting to defend the border area. The Shantung Grand Coordinator memorialized that large numbers of people were fleeing from Honan into Shantung and it was impossible to distinguish real refugees from disguised rebels. In general, however, the Shantung forces managed to maintain the Yellow River line and no major rebel incursion into the province occurred at this time.

During the campaigns of the late winter and spring of 1642, Li Tzu-ch'eng gave particular attention to storing food to support a more sustained siege of Kaifeng whose fall he was determined to bring about. In May 1642, Li decided that adequate preparations had been made and the third siege was begun after the main rebel force had been concentrated some twenty miles west of the city.[9] Remembering past mistakes and failures, Li decided that this time there would be no attempts at storming the wall. The attack plan would be based entirely on an attempt to sever the city's lines of communication with the outside and to starve it into submission. The rebel troops would simply wait behind their entrenchments surrounding the city and would fight only to destroy any opposition force coming to the aid of the city or to repel any sorties launched by the defenders from inside the walls. The rebels sought to worsen the food situation for the city by reaping the surrounding wheat fields and burning those which they were unable to reap, but the defenders did manage to salvage some 56,000 bushels of wheat and beans.

Though considerably outnumbered by the rebels, the government forces in and around Kaifeng were still impressive: two armies, commanded by Tso Liang-yü (whose forces had been augmented by the surrender of a local rebel who had joined him) and by Wu Ta-wei, were to the east of the city; and two additional forces, commanded by Supreme Commander Ting Ch'i-jui and Yang Wen-yüeh, were to the west. Tso's army was probably the strongest and was followed by that of Yang Wen-yüeh which was from Pei-chihli and had been more liberally supplied with firearms. However, its effectiveness was impaired by a shortage of gunpowder and provisions.

The government generals were unable to agree on the strategy to be adopted to defend Kaifeng, Ting Ch'i-jui proposing an active policy of attack and Tso Liang-yü advocating the wearing down of rebel morale by remaining on the defensive. As it turned out, neither policy was pursued to any really effective degree, since all the commanders were soon defeated and forced into retreat by Li Tzu-ch'eng. The first to be defeated was Tso Liang-yü who abandoned an attempt to construct protective entrenchments and began what he hoped would be an orderly withdrawal. Unfortunately, in negotiating the retreat, he found himself trapped behind rebel fortifications where his army suffered such a severe mauling that he fled with his remaining forces all the way to Hsiang-yang in Hukuang.

Tso's defeat was a harsh blow to the morale of the remaining official forces who, after some resistance, particularly by the army of Yang Wen-yüeh, retreated to the Ju-yang area. Thus, the government forces around Kaifeng not only were defeated by the rebels, but also betrayed their responsibilities by retreating to regions so distant from the city that they could not possibly serve even remotely as a counterweight to the rebel pressure. It is obviously unrealistic to have expected the government commanders to destroy Li Tzu-ch'eng, but they could have adopted more effective delaying and harassing tactics.

As for Peking's reaction to the defeat of its generals outside Kaifeng, little could be done beyond the issuance of an imperial decree ordering that Supreme Commander Ting Ch'i-jui be imprisoned and Regional Commander Yang Wen-yüeh be recalled. A different approach was taken toward Tso Liang-yü whose power and semi-independent status meant that he had to be handled carefully. Tso's long-time benefactor and mentor in the upper bureaucratic echelons, Hou Hsün, was released from prison and reinstated as Vice-minister of War. His special task was to employ the personal ties he had with Tso in order to make him more responsive to government orders.

Following the defeat of the government commanders in the Kaifeng area, no real success was achieved in relieving the city. A Hukuang relief force disintegrated after hearing the news of the disaster which had befallen Tso and the other generals, and a Shantung force, though it did approach relatively close, decided it would be wise to remain north of the Yellow River. No force existed within the entire empire which could save the doomed city, and in the space of a little more than a month after the beginning of the third rebel siege, Kaifeng was compelled to rely mainly upon its own resources.

Early in the summer, shortly after the defeat of the government forces outside the city, the rebels attempted to weaken the defenders' will to resist by offering favorable terms for an immediate surrender. At the same time, the rebels threatened to cut the Yellow River dike and flood the city if resistance was maintained. However, neither the rebel offer nor the threat had any significant effect on the defenders.

As the summer of 1642 wore on, very little military action occurred around Kaifeng. Some help did manage to cross the river, particularly the army of Regional Commander Liu Tse-ch'ing who succeeded in winning several minor victories. However, internal frictions within Liu's forces soon made it necessary for him to retreat back across the river. Also, the government commanders constructed 3,000 special armored carts for transporting provisions from north of the river through the rebel lines. In addition, a few sorties were staged from the city by the defenders. All these efforts produced small successes, especially in providing limited amounts of badly needed supplies, but they never posed any real threat to the rebel stranglehold. Thus, both sides waited, the rebels counting on starvation to bring about the eventual collapse of their opponents and the defenders desperately hoping that the rebels would have supply problems of their own and that their patience eventually would be exhausted.

By the middle of the summer, the pinch of the rebel blockade was being acutely felt inside Kaifeng, and riots began to occur at food distribution centers when the public granaries, whose supplies were low from the very beginning as a result of previous illegal sales of public grain by corrupt officials, began to find their stores of grain depleted entirely. Toward the end of summer, after all the public grain had been distributed, soldiers and spontaneously formed gangs began making raids on the private grain hoards of wealthy citizens. However, such supplies were limited when compared to the need, and the sources enumerate a long list of items which the starving citizens devoured in the desperation of their hunger: bark, leaves, roots, grub-worms, rats, birds, horses, human beings, cows, donkeys, dung, dried tea, maggots, leather, drugs, and fur coats. Some relief was found by opening the gates and allowing the people to forage outside the walls or to escape from the area entirely, but this was at best a stopgap measure and was terminated when the authorities decided that the rebels were gaining valuable information about conditions inside the city by capturing people who had been allowed to flee. Despite the desperate situation, with people actually dying of starvation in some numbers, there does not seem to have been any marked lessening of the determination to resist, and a traitorous goldsmith, caught trying to smuggle some arrows and a message to the rebels outside of the city, was stabbed repeatedly by the enraged populace after he had been captured and nailed to a board by his feet and hands.

By the end of summer both sides, for different reasons, had been driven to such extremes that they were willing to carry out the measure of ultimate desperation: cutting the Yellow River dike a short distance north of Kaifeng. The position of the defenders could hardly be maintained for much longer and even though the rebel besiegers were obviously in a better situation, cracks in their patience were beginning to appear. Li Tzu-ch'eng's chief subordinate ally, Lo Ju-ts'ai, in particular, was becoming restive and was advocating the abandonment of the siege. Attempting to exploit the possibilities of a rift between Li and Lo, the Honan Grand Coordinator, Kao Ming-heng, sent the latter a message which contained the deliberately falsified information that he was going to be granted a high post by the court. This message fell into the hands of Li Tzu-ch'eng and did nothing to allay the suspicions he already had about Lo. However, Li was astute enough not to allow a rupture with Lo to occur at this point and he bought Lo's consent to continue the siege by giving his ally some of the supplies which he needed from his own stores and by promising him the eastern section of Kaifeng to loot once the city had fallen.

The opposing sides, both official and rebel, must share the responsibility for cutting the Yellow River dike. Certainly the idea had occurred to both sides virtually from the very beginning of the siege and we have noted that the rebels threatened the defenders with such an eventuality early in the summer when they were pressing for a surrender. However, initially the rebels probably had no serious intention of carrying out their threat. They wanted to capture the city as intact as possible in order to preserve its wealth for plundering. Thus, apparently it was the official side which first actually adopted cutting the dike as a policy, calculating that the strong walls of Kaifeng would protect the city from being inundated while at the same time the rebels in their encampments surrounding the city would be overwhelmed. The government efforts to cut the dike occurred toward the end of August and were carried out under the orders of the Honan Grand Coordinator. According to one source, the rebels discovered the plan before it was completed, chased away the government cutting crew, and finished the task themselves after the rebel forces had been ordered to higher ground. At this time, no disaster resulted. The water rose only moderately in Kaifeng and even conferred the unexpected benefits of washing some fish into the starving city and forcing the rebels to retreat some distance further from the walls. Li was enraged at this outcome and ordered the execution of the adviser who had suggested that the dike be cut.

The real disaster began on October 8 when the dike was cut a second time at another point. Apparently this second cutting was undertaken solely by the rebels who had finally come to the end of their patience and had been disturbed by unfounded rumors that a formidable relief force had been dispatched from Shensi. The river had been rising noticeably as a result of autumn rains and it broke through the deliberately weakened section with a tremendous roar, said to have been audible for miles. Kaifeng was almost completely inundated and large numbers of people were drowned. Even a few of the rebels outside the city were caught by the torrent and swept away, though most of them had retreated to ground sufficiently high to be out of danger.

Chaos reigned in the stricken city for some weeks following the inundation. Several daring officials from bases north of the river came in boats to bring relief supplies and carry out survivors, including the Prince of Chou who had taken refuge on a roof together with several hundred members of his household entourage. The survivors were collected at centers north of the river and granted 100,000 taels as a relief fund.

In the midst of the rescue operations, private bands of looters were active and at one point the rebels moved in and held vague control over the city for a brief period. Li Tzu-ch'eng was anxious to obtain some recompense for maintaining the long siege and took away anything of value that could be discovered. However, the devastation was so complete that little worth having remained and quite soon he was only too glad to abandon the area with its enormous problems of restoration.

The Kaifeng siege is the most famous military event of the late Ming rebellions and the inundation of the city is clearly one of the greatest disasters of the era. Probably several hundred thousand people died in the flood and in the preceding period of starvation. According to one source, only 100,000 citizens of the city presented themselves for relief following the flood and this number represented only ten percent of the city's population prior to the siege. Therefore, 900,000 people had been drowned or starved to death. Undoubtedly, this figure is considerably exaggerated and does not take into account the large numbers who escaped from the city just prior to the siege or during its course. Jesuit accounts, for example, infer that most of the small community of Christian converts had abandoned the city in good time and it was only his devotion to his calling, rather than lack of opportunity, which made the Portuguese father, Rodregue De Figueredo, refuse to abandon his post in Kaifeng.* Yet even if one acknowledges that the 900,000 figure is exaggerated, the Kaifeng siege and inundation still must be ranked as a disaster of massive proportions.

As for the effect of the Kaifeng disaster on the fortunes of Li Tzu-ch'eng, one might say that it enhanced his prospects in a negative way by pushing a crucial province, Honan, closer toward chaos and thus further undermining the dynasty. Any more positive contribution that the city's fall might have bestowed upon Li was washed away in the swirling waters of the Yellow River. Certainly if Li had managed to accomplish the early rebel ambition of capturing the city relatively intact and had followed the advice of Li Yen in treating the people with leniency, he undoubtedly would have attracted a considerable following among the local gentry and greatly increased his stature. Under these circumstances, Kaifeng might well have become the center of his power and served as a springboard for a direct march on Peking, producing a Ming collapse in 1643. Instead, Li's disappointment over finding little except devastation at Kaifeng turned him south and southwest, rather than north, and delayed the campaign to Peking.

Following his decision to abandon the Kaifeng area, Li Tzu-ch'eng considered crossing the Yellow River some distance west of Kaifeng and attacking Huai-ch'ing. Apparently, this move was not pursued for very long or very seriously and was soon abandoned when light opposition was met. Li then turned in the opposite direction and went to Nan-yang, a city which he had occupied a year earlier but where whatever power he had remaining was currently being threatened by the Supreme Commander of Shensi, Sun Ch'üan-t'ing, who was destined to be his last major Ming opponent.[10]

Sun Ch'üan-t'ing was one of the abler officials who saw service in the campaigns against the rebels, and it will be remembered that, while serving as Grand Coordinator of Shensi in 1636, he succeeded in capturing the rebel leader, Kao Ying-hsiang. Later, he had been appointed Supreme Commander of Shantung and parts of Pei-chihli in 1639, but had been

---

* Since Father Figueredo was never heard from following the flood disaster, he is presumed to have drowned. See Louis Pfister, *Notices biographiques et bibliographiques sur les Jésuites de l'ancienne Mission de Chine*, 158-159.

summarily dismissed and imprisoned by Yang Ssu-ch'ang after serving only four months. Recalled in the spring of 1642, he was made Supreme Commander of the northern section of Shensi. In Shensi he first tried to consolidate his position by executing, on secret orders from Peking, Ho Jen-lung. Ho, after Tso Liang-yü, was probably the most powerful of the semi-independent professional military commanders and shared several characteristics with Tso. He possessed real military talent, but also maintained only very loose discipline in his forces, was recalcitrant, and obeyed orders only when it suited him. We have already noted the difficulties Yang Ssu-ch'ang had with him during the campaigns of 1639 and 1640. More recently, Ho had deserted his post in Honan in 1641 and thus contributed to the destruction of the official force commanded by Fu Tsung-lung. Furthermore, Ho was a native of the same county as Li Tzu-ch'eng, Mi-chih, Shensi, and was long suspected of having secret connections with the rebels. Ho's execution at first threatened to produce a mutiny among his troops, but Sun pacified them with assurances that the old command structure would be left intact. For the successor to Ho, the choice went to a professional commander with an even more dubious background, Kao Chieh, an ex-rebel who had formerly served under Li Tzu-ch'eng.

Following the execution of Ho Jen-lung, since there was virtually no rebel activity in Shensi, Sun was ordered to devote himself to the difficult task of crushing the rebellion at its main center in Honan. He moved into southwestern Honan and established himself near Nan-yang where he was attacked by Li Tzu-ch'eng in the late autumn of 1642. The first encounter between Sun and Li ended indecisively, though with some advantage for Sun. However, the government supply wagons had not been able to keep up with Sun's forces and his men are said to have been reduced to subsisting on persimmons, a circumstance which resulted in the popular appellation "Persimmon Garden Campaign" being applied to Sun's moves against the rebels. Unable to solve the supply problem, Sun was so seriously defeated in the second engagement with the rebels, also fought in the Nan-yang area, that he was forced to retreat back into Shensi.

Having successfully repulsed the government's challenge to his position in Nan-yang, Li next moved eastward and turned his attention to the destruction of the last official force which possessed any real military potential in Honan.[11] This force was located in Ju-ning Prefecture and was composed of remnants of the three government armies which had retreated there following their defeat by Li at Kaifeng in the early summer (1642). The main commanders of the force were Yang Wen-yüeh and Wu Ta-wei. Li rapidly disposed of the government army in Ju-ning. Wu Ta-wei was killed in the fighting and Yang Wen-yüeh was captured.

Refusing to heed Li's attempts to persuade him to accept the new after having done his best in a vain effort to sustain the old, Yang was executed and accorded an honorable burial.

By the end of 1642, Li Tzu-ch'eng effectively had destroyed Ming military potential in Honan. At the same time, he had continued to consolidate power within the rebel movement in his own hands and most of the remaining semi-independent rebel leaders, some of whom had already indicated submission to Li, now made their acceptance of his authority more explicit[12] Most of these subordinate rebel chieftains were instructed by Li to take up positions in southwestern Honan and northeastern Hukuang where they were assigned the task of helping to combat the official forces in Hukuang and Nan-chihli. Also, they were supposed to maintain some surveillance over Chang Hsien-chung, the one rebel leader who refused to relinquish his independence and submit.

After demonstrating his military potential by sweeping aside all really serious opposition in Honan south of the Yellow River, and after assuming more definite dominance over the rebel movement internally, Li Tzu-ch'eng was faced with two major choices: remain in Honan and construct a system of political control to match his military power (for despite his victories, Li cannot conceivably be considered as exercising real control over Honan) or extend his sphere of influence outside of Honan and, instead of control in depth over a restricted area, seek a more superficial control over a larger area. Li chose the latter alternative and, in doing so, may well have made the most costly mistake of his career.

Li Tzu-ch'eng in Hukuang (1643)

In late 1642, Li Tzu-ch'eng decided to expand his sphere of influence southward from Honan and pushed into Hukuang, striking at the obviously crucial target, Hsiang-yang, the key to the northern section of the province.[13] Hsiang-yang was defended by that redoubtable veteran of the anti-rebel campaign, Tso Liang-yü, who had retreated there following his abandonment of all attempts to defend Kaifeng six months earlier. And in Hsiang-yang, Tso's army, never noted for its discipline and effectiveness, reached a new low. In numbers it was still formidable (said by some sources to have been as high as 200,000 men), but probably no more than 20,000 at most had any real military potential. The rest of the army was a rabble of diverse origins, particularly surrendered rebels and refugees.

The plundering by and general lack of discipline in Tso's army had rather thoroughly dissipated the popular support Tso had enjoyed earlier in the Hsiang-yang area. Local groups now actively aided Li Tzu-ch'eng when his forces arrived and guided him around the   rtified positions

Tso had established on the Han River. In addition, the local populace burned a large number of the boats in the fleet which Tso had prepared for his retreat down the Han River, forcing him to make himself even more unpopular by seizing merchant vessels. Thus faced with no more effective opposition than Tso's demoralized and thoroughly unpopular army, Li's seizure of Hsiang-yang was accomplished with relatively little expenditure of military effort.

Abandoning Hsiang-yang, Tso retreated down the Han Valley in the direction of Ch'eng-t'ien Prefecture where the Hukuang Grand Coordinator, Sung I-ho, at first refused to have any dealings with him at all, apparently regarding Tso's force as almost as great a threat as the rebels themselves. A short time later, Sung changed his mind and attempted to incorporate Tso's army into a united government force which would block Li's expansion southward from Hsiang-yang. This attempted unification of forces failed, since Tso had decided that it was futile to resist Li and did not halt his retreat until he reached Wuchang where he felt sufficiently safe to stop for a short time.

Li Tzu-ch'eng did not bother to pursue Tso in his southward retreat. Instead, he first consolidated his position at Hsiang-yang and the immediate area. Following that, he divided up his army and dispatched several of his principal lieutenants on separate expeditions which, in the course of a few weeks, had succeeded in expanding Li's sphere of influence, at least in a preliminary fashion, throughout most of northern Hukuang.[14] This sphere of influence extended from Hsiang-yang northwest to Ku-ch'eng, southwest to Hsing-shan, and southeast to Hanyang and Huang-chou. One of Li's units even succeeded in pushing south of the Yangtze and occupying Ch'ang-te, a city particularly noted for its wealth.

Very little serious opposition was offered by the official forces to Li's drive for expansion in Hukuang. The only important exception was at Ch'eng-t'ien where Grand Coordinator Sung I-ho put up a stout defense. Sung had occupied his office since the mid-1630's and previously had been noted chiefly for his voluminous and rather unrealistic reports to the Emperor regarding his anti-rebel activities. One of the reports had so exasperated the Emperor that Sung had been accused of gross procrastination and ordered to assume a more aggressive stance. Now, Sung demonstrated that he was capable of at least attempting to be more than a mere bureaucrat and he gave his life in a vain effort to prevent the fall of Ch'eng-t'ien.

Many of the successes which Li's forces achieved so easily in their expansion drive from Hsiang-yang proved to be quite ephemeral. Hanyang, for example, was occupied by the rebel troops for only a few days and Huang-chou and Ch'ang-te for only slightly longer. Thus, the area over which Li exercised any really marked control extended only approximately halfway down the Han Valley from Hsiang-yang.

Following his initial expansion drive, directed mainly southwestward and souteastward from the Hsiang-yang center, Li turned to the northwest where he wanted to open up an invasion route to Shensi. Here, his earlier triumphs were not repeated and he never succeeded in capturing the key city of Yün-yang whose garrison troops had long been noted for their superior fighting abilities. Furthermore, the Regional Commander in charge of the defense of Yün-yang, Wang Kuang-en, was one of the ablest generals of the late Ming period.

Li's first attempt to capture Yün-yang occurred in the 3rd month of 1643 when his favorite lieutenant, Liu Tsung-min, was dispatched from Hsiang-yang to attack it. Liu besieged the city for two months at the end of which time he suffered the humiliation of having the defenders issue forth and defeat him so severely that he was forced to retreat. Two subsequent rebel attacks, apparently directed by Li personally, also ended as complete failures, forcing Li to revamp his military plans and return to considering Honan as a launching place for an invasion of Shensi.

The rebel failure to take Yün-yang is indicative of continuing basic weaknesses in Li's military potential and demonstrates that his successes, past and to come, were less due to his own real strengths than to the incompetence, disorganization, and demoralization of his official opponents. More specifically, the successes of Regional Commander Wang Kuang-en in defending Yün-yang made Tso Liang-yü's dereliction of duty even more glaringly apparent. Tso certainly could have assumed a defensive posture in blocking Li's advance down the Han River instead of completely abandoning his responsibilities and fleeing to another area.

At roughly the same time that Li launched the first unsuccessful attempt to capture Yün-yang, there occurred a significant series of events at Hsiang-yang: the assassinations of Lo Ju-ts'ai, Ko-kuo-yen, and Tso-chin-wang, the erstwhile independent rebel leaders who most recently had been serving as somewhat restive subordinates of Li.[15] The first victim of this blood purge was Ko-kuo-yen. Li long had harbored suspicions about him and these had become critical when Ko returned from a campaign in eastern Hukuang during which he had had the good fortune of being able to incorporate into his army many stragglers from the demoralized forces of Tso Liang-yü. Furthermore, upon his return Ko made the mistake of first going for a conference with Lo Ju-ts'ai, an action which made Li think that the two were plotting against him. Having determined to take drastic action, Li invited Ko to a banquet, and after the guest had become thoroughly drunk, he was seized and killed. His force was incorporated into that of Li.

The assassination of Lo Ju-ts'ai was more complicated. In the first place, Lo was by all odds Li's most important and valuable ally-subordinate. The alliance between them had endured for almost two years and they had known one another since virtually the very beginning of the rebellions. Following their alliance, their talents had been quite effectively pooled and their cooperation had contributed greatly to the success of the rebel cause. Li's greatest strength was said to have been in the area of overall planning while Lo's was in executing specific military requirements of a particular campaign. However, despite the complementary nature of their abilities and the successes derived from their cooperation, tensions between them existed, particularly on Li's side. Perhaps most basic of all were the personality differences. Li gave the utmost in dedication to the success of his rebellion, was rather puritanical in his personal life, and was beginning to conceive more and more clearly the grand goal of the founding of a dynasty. For Lo, the rebellions were a profitable venture and the gains should be enjoyed. He made no effort to conceal his gourmet proclivities or his inordinate delight in fine clothes and beautiful women. His harem of several hundred ladies was made up of the choice beauties of several provinces. Such sensuality evoked supreme contempt from Li. Furthermore, Lo was incapable of conceiving serious goals. Once when Li proposed to him that they seize Shensi and divide it up between them as a permanent base, Lo replied that moving about in an almost unlimited area was a great delight and he saw no reason why they should confine themselves to any particular territory. It is obvious, then, that Lo, despite certain technical military talents, was a person of restricted horizons. He would never on his own have moved beyond the disorganized raiding rebel phase, and now that he was attached to the soaring ambitions of Li Tzu-ch'eng, he was becoming expendable.

Apparently the final events which pushed Li into deciding to destroy Lo were the deliberate efforts by underlings in both camps to create trouble between them. Lo's chief gentry adviser, a *chü-jen* from Shensi, was continually warning about the threat posed by Li. Lo may have paid some vague heed to these warnings, as he is said to have given very tentative consideration to arranging a quite profitable surrender deal by presenting Li's head to the authorities. There was also the troublemaker, Ch'en Sheng, a man with a foot in the camps of both Li and Lo, but who considered his first loyalty to the former. Ostensibly to increase organizational efficiency, he suggested to Lo that he divide his horses into four groups (left, right, front, and rear) and mark them accordingly. Lo followed this suggestion and subsequently Ch'en spread the rumor that Lo had secret plans to surrender, because one group of his horse bore the mark "left" which was the same character as the surname of Tso Liang-yü. Probably, Li Tzu-ch'eng did not believe this far-fetched accusation and may even have masterminded it as a means of creating support for his eventual move against Lo, for even without the horse-marking incident, there were sufficient reasons to make Li destroy his ally.

Lo Ju-ts'ai was invited to the same banquet which Ko-kuo-yen attended and met his doom, but Lo, suspecting Li's actual plans, declined the invitation on the excuse of illness. The following morning, Li resorted to direct action and secretly dispatched a twenty-man assassination squad to surprise Lo at his headquarters. The plot worked completely according to plan and Lo, caught unarmed and combing his hair, was overpowered and decapitated. His head was exhibited to his men who were told that he had plotted to betray the rebel cause. This explanation did not prevent a riot among his troops and they began to be quieted only when Li promised Lo's lieutenants that the command structure in the army would remain intact. This promise, however, was not completely honored and Li's own appointees were given positions of supervisors in the army. This breach of the agreement, plus a residue of other bitterness, resulted in some of Lo's forces deserting the rebel cause and surrendering to various officials. For example, the garrison at Yünyang was strengthened by being joined by troops from Lo's army.

The details concerning the assassination of Tso-chin-wang are unclear, but since he had been closely associated with Ko-kuo-yen, it is possible that the two were killed at the same banquet.

In addition to destroying Lo, Ko, and Tso, Li eliminated a former subordinate-ally, Yüan Shih-chung, who for the past year had been attempting to create an independent power base. Unlike Lo, Ko, and Tso, who were all probably natives of northern Shensi and had been active in the rebel movement from the very early years, Yüan was a native of Pei-chihli and had risen in rebellion only in 1640. He had allied himself with Li in 1641 and the two rebel leaders had become so warmly attached to one another that Yüan had been given Li's ward as a wife. Subsequently, relations between them cooled and Yüan, after deserting Li during the attack on Kaifeng early in 1642, had pursued an independent career of the disorganized raiding type in northwestern Nan-chihli and some of the adjacent areas across the border in Honan. By early 1643, Yüan found himself in the uncomfortable spot of being impinged upon by Li on the one hand and the government forces on the other. Faced with these two pressures, Yüan decided that it was safer to attempt to come to an understanding with the official side than to reconstruct his alliance with Li. Accordingly, he handed over to the government one of Li's emissaries who had been sent to treat with him, hoping that this gesture would enhance his chances for favorable surrender terms. Unfortunately for Yüan's plans, Li became so enraged that he sent a strong force which attacked and killed him.

Li's destruction of the four rebel chieftains represented further progress toward a consolidation of power within the rebel movement, a trend which, as has been noted, had been underway since early 1641. The marked diversity which characterized the early years of the rebellions was now past and if one considers the thirteen rebel leaders who participated in the great conclave at Jung-yang, Honan, early in 1635, only Chang Hsien-chung continued to play a significant role independent of the now-dominant Li Tzu-ch'eng. The other twelve leaders had suffered various fates: two had been killed by the government forces, two had deserted the rebel cause and surrendered, one had died, three had just now been destroyed by Li Tzu-ch'eng, and four had simply disappeared from the historical stage, probably dying obscure deaths in the remote areas to which the rebels retreated during times of ill fortune. The unity which the rebel leaders sought so fleetingly and ineffectually at Jung-yang had now become a reality derived from their own deaths, surrenders, and oblivion.

In the midst of consolidating rebel leadership more firmly within his own hands, carving out a substantial sphere of influence for himself in northern Hukuang, and continuing to exercise some degree of control over scattered areas in Honan south of the Yellow River, Li Tzu-ch'eng at Hsiang-yang also made the first definite moves toward the establishment of a formal administrative structure.[16] The initial step was taken in the 1st month of 1643 when Hsiang-yang was renamed Hsiang-ching and elaborate military titles were proclaimed for both Li and his soon-to-be-eliminated ally, Lo Ju-ts'ai. Li's title was "Long-accumulated Worshipping-Heaven Leading-in-righteousness Generalissimo" (Lao-fu feng-t'ien ch'ang-i ta-chiang-chün). Shortly thereafter the Generalissimo element in the title was elevated to Commander-in-chief (Ta-yüan-shuai). At the same time, lower-level military appointments were made to achieve a more definite organization.

In the realm of civil government, Chang Kuo-shen and Niu Chin-hsing were given some recognition as chief ministers, the former being assigned the title of Upper Minister of State (Shang-hsiang-kuo) and the latter Minister of the Left (Tso-fu). In addition, skeleton staffs were assigned to each of the traditional six ministries: Personnel, Revenue, Rites, War, Justice, and Works. Something of a capstone to the new administration was added on April 27, 1643 when Li proclaimed himself Prince of Hsin-shun (Hsin-shun Wang). There was even some sentiment for Li to take the further step of declaring himself Emperor, but the move was opposed by Niu Chin-hsing whose advice Li decided to heed.

It is highly doubtful if this formal governmental structure was much more than window-dressing. Some of the appointees, for example Niu Chin-hsing, exercised considerable influence, but it was an influence derived from their longstanding personal relationship with Li Tzu-ch'eng rather than their actual occupancy of one of the newly created offices.

By the early summer of 1643, Li Tzu-ch'eng's momentum in Hukuang had come to a halt and indeed his influence in the southeastern section of the province was receding. To the northwest, Yün-yang continued to resist all of Li's efforts to capture it and blocked his invasion route to Shensi. The governmental structure established at Hsiang-yang was hardly functional and the local administrations, set up at various places in the upper Han Valley, had little basic support other than military power. Conditions, then, demanded that fundamental decisions be made to determine the future couse to be followed.

Throughout the early summer of 1643, lengthy discussions were held in Li's Hsiang-yang palace and eventually three views of what should be done emerged.[17] The most radical proposal was championed by Niu Chin-hsing who advocated that Li mobilize his forces and march straight across Honan and Pei-chihli for a direct attack on Peking. The other two proposals were more conservative. One was advanced by Yang Yung-yü, a former Erudite in the Directorate of Astronomy. He advised a push down the Han and Yangtze to seize Nanking and the lower section of the Grand Canal. Such a move, he argued, would bring about the economic collapse of Peking. The third view was advocated by Ku Chün-en who attacked Niu's proposal as too rash and Yang's as too indirect. Instead, he suggested that Peking be attacked by approaching it from the west after the rebels had first made themselves masters of Shensi and Shansi. He supported his plan by arguing that in attacking Shensi the rebels would be aided by the fact that they would be operating in familiar territory and also the area could serve as a place for retreat and regrouping in the event of a defeat at Peking. It is hardly suprising that Li accepted this last plan, appealing as it did to his provincial pride as a Shensi man.

In the late summer of 1643, Li withdrew from Hsiang-yang and moved northward into southwestern Honan. This move was dictated most immediately by Li's acceptance of the Ku Chün-en plan, the first phase of which called for a Honan-based seizure of Shensi. There were also other reasons which caused Li to make the decision to withdraw from Hukuang. Most importantly, his position in Honan was deteriorating. Recently, his forces had been compelled to abandon both Ju-ning and Hsin-yang, retreats which had virtually eliminated his influence in the southeastern section of the province. Obviously, Honan was badly in need of attention if his power there was not to collapse entirely. In addition, events occurred at Hsiang-yang which, even though they are undoubtedly exaggerated in the sources as portents showing divine disapproval of rebels, probably did exert a considerable psychological impact on Li and convinced him that Hsiang-yang was indeed a place of ill-omen. The first event was the collapse of a partially completed new palace which Li had ordered constructed in honor of his recently assumed princely title. The second event was the metallurgical failure which resulted when artisans unsuccessfully attempted to cast coins for the new regime.

Following the withdrawal to Honan, Li's position in most of Hukuang collapsed almost overnight, a signal illustration of the flimsy foundations on which his power rested. Surviving Ming forces, particularly those at Yün-yang, and local *ad hoc* groups compelled Li's garrisons to withdraw from most of the areas they still occupied and within a few weeks virtually the only Hukuang territory still controlled by Li was around Hsiang-yang itself. Even Hsiang-yang was besieged for a short time by Regional Commander Wang Kuang-en from Yün-yang. Thus, in Hukuang, as earlier in Honan, Li demonstrated once again the same fatal weakness: the inability to translate initial military dominance into solid support extending down to the local level. It would have been far wiser for him to have rejected, or at least postponed, all three of the grand schemes suggested to him for seizing national power. First, he should have constructed a firm foundation for control in northern Hukuang and southern Honan.

Peking's Last Attempts to Organize Resistance to Li Tzu-ch'eng

By the beginning of 1643, the mood in Peking moved closer toward numb indecision and hopeless desperation. The Manchus had just pressed to the vicinity of the capital and subsequently succeeded in launching another raid into central Shantung where the local district prince, the Prince of Lu, was frightened into committing suicide. News from the rebel front reaching Peking was equally depressing and one report states that people from all social strata spoke openly of surrendering when the rebels arrived.

The wheels of the Peking bureaucracy ground on, although one suspects increasingly on the basis of merely mechanical momentum, and the Emperor was as overworked as ever. A great deal of bureaucratic and imperial energy continued to be wasted on petty details: a request from a group of Wuchang citizens for armed protection; an accusation made by one officer against another who was charged with improper conduct and gross neglect of duties; and a recommendation by a Shensi Regional Commander that meritorious officers be rewarded with gifts of money and fine silk cloth embroidered with three-toed dragons. In addition, the bureaucracy at times descended to ludicrous actions.[18] For example, in the late spring of 1643, the Minister of War suggested that the Emperor assume personal command of the anti-rebel campaign. Again, at approximately the same time, the Ministry of War replied to an imperial command that the rebellions be suppressed within a period of ten days by stating in a routine fashion that the order had been passed on to the proper authorities to be carried out.

On the other hand, the Peking bureaucracy was still capable of some attempt at rational deliberation, and part of the information it received from its provincial and other officials was realistic and astute.[19] For example, the Censor in charge of the tea and horse trade along the northern borders reported quite frankly that trading had virtually collapsed at the very time when the need for horses was particularly acute. This trade collapse had reached really critical proportions by 1643 when the large-scale rebel operations in Honan and Hukuang had disrupted traffic on the trade routes along which tea had been transported from central China to the northern border regions.

Another incisive memorial was submitted by the Grand Coordinator of Honan who, despite certain literary devices obviously meant to appeal for sympathy (aged ladies so improverished that they had to accept employment as village watchmen), gave a reasonably straightforward assessment of the Honan situation. He reported that there were only 9,000 troops in the province with any military potential and that only 200,000 of the 500,000 taels, supposed to be available for military expenditures, had actually been made available. Furthermore, administration at the prefectural and county levels had broken down to such an extent that appointees refused to take up their official duties. The memorial ended with an appeal for special funds in order to obtain adequate supplies for the existing troops, to recruit additional forces, and to restore agricultural production.

A third astute assessment of the 1643 situation was made by the Supreme Commander of Feng-yang, Nan-chihli, who submitted a list of the strengths and weaknesses of Li Tzu-ch'eng. The strengths included Li's absolute devotion to his rebel career and his relative lack of interest in luxuries; the hard core of the rebel group being composed of desperate outlaws who faced death if they failed and thus were compelled to support the rebel cause vigorously; some groups in Honan and Hukuang being forced into the rebel camp because they felt compromised as a result of their association with the rebels and their failure to defend effectively the government position; the rebels being well furnished with horses and their weapons being the equal of those of the official forces; and the rebels having succeeded in perfecting the technique of attacking walled cities. The weaknesses included a failure to attract capable men to fill the political and military needs of the rebel cause; the rebels having abandoned one of their principal military assets when they ceased to be mobile and began to settle down in relatively fixed positions; the rebel centers in Honan and Hukuang having experienced a virtually complete breakdown of agricultural production which would soon result in the rebels facing a critical shortage of supplies; Li's high-handed measures to consolidate his power within the rebel movement having created internal frictions which could be exploited; and the eye wound which Li received the previous year during the Kaifeng siege having been so serious that he would probably not live more than another year.

With the exception of the last one (almost certainly derived from wishful thinking and supposition rather than any real medical diagnosis), these assessments of Li's strengths and weaknesses have merit. Furthermore, the recommendation which the Supreme Commander made, based on the assessments, was probably the best policy that Peking could have pursued. He recommended that the government adopt a strictly defensive stance with the official forces blocking Li by holding positions in Nan-chihli, along the Yellow River, and in Shensi and Szechwan. Virtually no action should be taken against him within the Hukuang-Honan area except for sporadic raids launched from Yün-yang and one should simply await the time when Li's weaknesses (particularly his supply problems) outweighed his strengths and his military power disintegrated. In the final analysis, though, Peking decided against a policy of cautious defense and attempted to piece together a final military offensive.

Only two available armies might have the military potential required for the offensive against the rebels that the central government was discussing during the spring and summer of 1643: the army of Supreme Commander Sun Ch'üan-t'ing in Shensi and possibly that of Tso Liang-yü in the central Yangtze area, though the condition of the latter was the cause of much concern. As noted earlier, the demoralization of Tso's forces reached a critical stage following his precipitous retreat from the upper Han Valley in the face of Li Tzu-ch'eng's invasion, and matters were not improved by Tso's having been the target of an imperial edict which blamed him for the loss of Hsiang-yang and demanded that he redeem himself by achieving success against the rebels in the future.

Throughout the first part of 1643, both regional and central government officials struggled with the problem of Tso Liang-yü: how to decrease the economic and political disruption which the presence of his large army in the central Yangtze area had caused and how to revive the military potential of his army to the extent that it could serve a useful role in fighting the rebels.[20] Retreating from Hsiang-yang, Tso had not halted until he reached the Wuchang area where he promised the local district prince, the Prince of Ch'u, that he would assume responsibility for the defense of the area against both Li Tzu-ch'eng and Chang Hsien-chung if he were given support for 100,000 troops. The Prince refused to have any dealings with Tso, who, as a consequence, allowed his men to loot the city and the surrounding countryside. Despite these ravages, Tso apparently never even considered abandoning his formal loyalty to the Ming, and indeed actually rejected a specific appeal made by Li Tzu-ch'eng for him to join the rebel cause. This appeal reached Tso at Wuchang and was delivered by one of Li's officers, Wang Ssu. Wang had been given Tso's daughter as a concubine following her capture, along with other members of the family, by the rebel forces at Hsü-chou, Honan. Wang brought with him to Wuchang a personal letter to Tso from his family in the hope that the chances of his accepting Li Tzu-ch'eng's offer would be enhanced. However, Tso adamantly rejected Li's appeal.

After the Wuchang area had been rather thoroughly ravaged, Tso and his army continued their depredations down the Yangtze to Chiu-chiang, Kiangsi, even looting government salt boats, and it was not until the late spring of 1643 that any kind of control was reasserted over the marauding troops. This stabilization resulted only after Tso had been subjected to strong political and military pressures. The military pressures even reached the point of outright attacks upon his troops by garrisons in the area which had been strengthened with private forces recruited by powerful local families. The political pressures were exerted mainly by the Censor, Li Pang-hua, who had been specially dispatched from Peking to negotiate with Tso. Li promised Tso to defend him before the Emperor and ordered the Chiu-chiang authorities to give him 150,000 taels. In exchange, Tso swore to remain loyal; released 4,000 captives, probably mainly women, who had been kidnapped by his troops; returned 500 stolen boats; and executed four of his men for looting.

By the summer of 1643, then, a partial solution to the problem posed by Tso Liang-yü had been achieved in the reassertion of some degree of official control over his troops. On the other hand, Peking was destined to be frustrated in its hope that the military potential of his army could be restored to a degree that would enable it to play a significant role in the anti-rebel campaigns. Tso's forces remained in the central Yangtze area and exerted some influence, mainly indirect, upon the movements of Chang Hsien-chung, but never again did Tso enter the struggle against Li Tzu-ch'eng. The final military effort of any real importance which the dynasty was able to make against Li had to be based entirely upon the Shensi forces of Sun Ch'üan-t'ing.

The Struggle between Li Tzu-ch'eng and Sun Ch'üan-t'ing for Mastery of Honan

In the autumn of 1643, Sun Ch'üan-t'ing was probably the official with the most experience in the anti-rebel campaigns who still occupied a position of real power. As noted earlier, Sun had served briefly against the rebels in 1636 and again in 1639, but his really significant role did not begin until early 1642 when he was named Supreme Commander in Shensi and subsequently tried to destroy Li Tzu-ch'eng in Honan.

Following his defeat by Li in late 1642, Sun withdrew from Honan to Shensi and showed talent in building up an effective military force, basing his efforts almost entirely on local and provincial initiative and receiving little assistance from Peking.[21] Sun launched land-reclamation projects, levied a special tax of fifty taels on three-family units to hire troops, and required localities to construct their own defense works and man them. Remembering that supply problems had been one of the chief reasons for his defeat by Li the previous year, Sun took particular interest in a project for constructing 20,000 carts. These carts, called "fire carts," were designed to serve military purposes in addition to the primary one of transport. That is, Sun planned to use them as a means of blocking attacks by rebel cavalry and as protective screens behind which his infantry could obtain shelter.

By the autumn of 1643, then, Sun had built up the most effective force in China with the exception of some of those facing the Manchus on the northeastern frontier. There was some concern expressed in Peking about Sun's two chief lieutenants, Kao Chieh and Pai Kuang-en, both of whom were professional military men outside the regular bureaucracy. As already pointed out, Kao was an ex-rebel and Pai had acquired such an unsavory reputation for disobedience while serving on the northern frontier that he had been deliberately transferred to Shensi. However, despite obvious character defects, Kao and Pai had military competence and Peking could hardly take the risk of creating the serious unrest which might result if they were removed. In the final analysis, the central government accepted Sun's army as constituted and confined its discussion to the question of deciding how it should be used.

Two views emerged concerning the deployment of Sun's army. One view, held by Sun himself and shared by a minority group of officials in Peking, was that the army should be kept in Shensi and employed almost entirely in a defensive fashion. Sun argued that rebel supply problems were becoming so acute that Li Tzu-ch'eng's forces would soon begin to disintegrate. Furthermore, if Li attempted to invade Shensi from Honan, the defenders would have a distinct advantage. The opposing view, held by a majority of Peking officials, advocated ordering Sun to move his army into Honan and attack Li there. These officials felt that the time was now opportune for destroying Li. Their position was supported by an influential group of Shensi gentry among whom Sun was very unpopular because of the heavy exactions he had placed upon them to support his army and whose main aim was to get Sun out of the province by any means.

Finally bowing to the pressures generated both in Peking and locally in Shensi, Sun reluctantly accepted the plans for an offensive against Li in Honan. He held a public departure ceremony in Sian on September 13, 1643 and at its conclusion led his army eastward. Four days later he passed through T'ung Pass and proceeded on into Honan where he would strike the last major blow that a Ming force ever delivered against Li Tzu-ch'eng.[22]

Pressing forward down the Yellow River Valley, Sun paused briefly in the vicinity of Loyang, where he was joined by some of the remnant official forces that had managed to survive in Honan, and made his final plans of operations against Li. One view urged him to make Loyang his main base, stall for time, and gain the renown of restoring the city which had such venerable connections with past Chinese history. Sun rejected this proposal and decided to proceed directly into an engagement with the rebels. At the same time, Tso Liang-yü was ordered to move his army from Chiu-chiang, Kiangsi, to Ju-ning, Honan, joining with Sun in a pincer movement. Such an operation had merit, but as has been noted, Tso's army had not been restored to real operational capacity and Tso never obeyed the order to move to Honan. Sun alone, then, pushed southward from Loyang and the first battle of the campaign occurred.

Li Tzu-ch'eng, following his move from Hukuang to southwestern Honan, had first planned to press into southeastern Shensi (in the area of Shang-nan and Lo-nan), thus outflanking the T'ung Pass where strong resistance could be expected. However, Sun's rapid thrust into Honan and his strengthening of the garrisons south of the T'ung Pass forced Li to abandon his original plans and move his army northeastward into central Honan. Li set up his main base at Hsiang-ch'eng where he erected permanent fortifications and recalled even more of the forces from Hukuang that he had originally intended to leave there as garrisons.

The rebel and government armies met in Ju Sub-prefecture and in a sharp engagement on October 20, 1643, Sun won a clear-cut victory, almost succeeding in capturing Li Tzu-ch'eng's personal flag, a ploy in which the heroes were former rebels who had served under Lo Ju-ts'ai and thus felt a particularly bitter hatred toward Li. The victory, the first in more than a year for the official cause, produced elation both in Sun's army and in Peking. However, the astute Vice-minister of War warned that Li's defeat was not decisive and again urged that the dynasty's last reliable army south of the northern frontier should be held for long-range goals and not lightly exposed to disaster.

Sun followed up his Ju Sub-prefecture success with victories over Li in Pao-feng County and Chia County. Furthermore, he sent a detachment to T'ang-hsien in southern Honan where the rebels had one of their more permanent camps in which lived the families of many of the rebel leaders. Sun's force captured T'ang-hsien and destroyed the rebel camp. Thus, the first month and a half of the Honan campaign had seen events go decidedly in favor of the government. But in early November, difficulties began to catch up with Sun, particularly again the old problem of supply. Because of the virtual collapse of agricultural production in Honan for more than a year, as well as the deliberate scorched-earth policy pursued by the rebels, it was impossible for Sun's force to obtain adequate provisions in Honan itself, and although Shansi, Shensi, and Pei-chihli were supposed to render assistance, little was forthcoming. Another of Sun's problems was an internal split within his own army. His subordinate, Pai Kuang-en, felt it was now time to shift to a defensive policy, while Kao Chieh supported Sun himself in advocating a continuance of the present offensive policy. Also, Sun's plot to employ subversion against Li failed. This plot hinged upon one Ch'iu Chih-t'ao, a member of a prominent Hukuang gentry family who had surrendered to Li and, despite his youth, had been appointed to a high post in the skeleton administration set up by the rebels. Ch'iu maintained secret communications with Sun and promised to serve as an agent for the government cause. Ch'iu's plan was soon discovered and he was cut to pieces on Li's orders. At the same time, some of the ex-rebels, who had surrendered to Sun, maintained contacts with their former associates and if the advantage ever seemed to be slipping toward the rebel side, they were certainly willing to abandon their allegiance to the official cause.

In early November of 1643, the tide turned suddenly against Sun and the favorable position he had achieved disappeared more rapidly than it had been erected. The rebels reoccupied Ju-chou and Sun began a retreat toward the southwest. To protect his forces during the retreat, Sun ordered Kao Chieh to perform a rear-guard role and Pai Kuang-en to set up an ambush to trap the pursuing rebel troops. Pai failed to carry out his orders and instead began a withdrawal of his 8,000 men toward T'ung Pass. He was miffed because his earlier advice to adopt a defensive policy had not been followed and in addition had decided that Honan should be abandoned entirely. Deprived of Pai's support, Sun's retreat turned into a rout when Li attacked him, virtually destroying his army and seizing a large quantity of his equipment. Sun managed to collect a remnant band of troops and hastily withdrew northward to the Yellow River. Subsequently, he turned west and went to T'ung Pass where he sought desperately to erect some kind of defense against the rebel attack which he knew would soon come. Thus, Sun's Honan offensive lasted only two months (September-November, 1643) and ended in a complete disaster, a result which probably indicates that he was correct in opposing the campaign and calling for a policy of defense.

Li Tzu-ch'eng Seizes Control of Shensi

Having defeated Sun Ch'üan-t'ing in Honan, Li Tzu-ch'eng could turn his full attention to the Ku Chün-en plan for attacking Peking via Shensi and Shansi. He moved quickly to exploit his victory and advancing up the south bank of the Yellow River, he captured the gateway to Shensi, T'ung Pass, on November 16, 1643.[23] The triumph was partly due to Li's resorting to the stratagem of having a portion of his troops pose as a government force by disguising them in official uniforms captured from Sun. However, he undoubtedly would have captured the pass in any event, since Sun's army was demoralized and outnumbered. Sun fled from the defeat at T'ung Pass and made a final effort to block Li's advance up the Wei River Valley by making a stand at Wei-nan. He was again defeated and bravely laid down his life in the brief battle at Wei-nan. Most of his subordinate officers, except Kao Chieh, soon surrendered to Li, the last holdout being Ch'en Yung-fu who was afraid to surrender because it was his son who had shot out Li's eye during the Kaifeng siege early in 1642. However, Li broke an arrow and took an oath that past actions would not be held against Ch'en and that his surrender would be accepted. Having received this assurance, Ch'en capitulated. Kao Chieh managed to escape across the newly frozen ice on the Yellow River into Shansi.

With the collapse of the feeble and hastily organized resistance of Sun Ch'üan-t'ing, Li pushed on to his first major objective, Sian, encountering very little further opposition enroute. He arrived outside Sian on November 21, and the defending general shot an arrow into the rebel camp bearing his offer to surrender.

At Sian, Li occupied the palace of the local district prince, the Prince of Ch'in, who was treated leniently and was even granted an exalted honorific title. Subsequently, Li proceeded to take additional steps, supplementary to those previously taken at Hsiang-yang, to demonstrate his increasingly serious ambitions for imperial status.[24] He changed the name of Sian to Ch'ang-an, an obvious attempt to appeal to provincial pride by evoking memories of past glories during the T'ang dynasty. The city was to have the alternate name of Hsi-ching, "Western Capital," in addition to Ch'ang-an. Also, Li ordered the holding of an official examination for the selection of office-holders and made some effort to place his administrative structure on a firmer foundation.

Li's initial moves in Sian seem to have obtained for him some real popular sympathy and support. Aside from his appeals to the public on the basis of his being their fellow provincial, he also strictly forbade violence and performed such charisma-producing ceremonial functions as visiting the aged. Undoubtedly the moderating hand of Li Yen can be seen in the formulation of these policies. Unfortunately, crosscurrents were soon evident and, according to one source, the period of good will between Li and the Sian populace lasted less than a month. Subsequently, his men began seizing women and resorting to other acts of violence. Li himself, following the advice of his Minister of Justice, the former Circuit Intendant, Chang Kuo-shen, began a systematic policy of squeezing funds from wealthy ex-officials in the area. Those who had held high office in the central government were required to present 50,000 taels and lesser sums were expected from holders of lower offices, down to a minimum of 5,000 taels to be paid by those who had served as county magistrates.

Li's major energies at Sian, however, were expended in bringing the entire province under his control. At least three main expeditions were sent out from Sian: one under T'ien Chien-hsiu to the southwest with Han-chung as the principal objective, another under Li Yu to the far west with Lin-t'ao as the main objective, and a third under Li Kuo to the north with the original spawning grounds of the rebellions as the major objective. At some point Li himself joined the northern expedition, apparently mainly for sentimental and ceremonial, rather than military, considerations.

Very little active opposition was encountered by any of the expeditionary forces, except at Yü-lin in the far north on the Great Wall. Li had expected trouble at Yü-lin and had sent a large bribe to the local Regional Commander who had accepted it and agreed to surrender the city. However, the populace rose in rebellion at this betrayal, forced the Regional Commander to flee, and selected a retired military officer living in the city as his replacement. Bitter fighting, in which even women are said to have participated as defenders, raged around the city during a thirteen-day siege at the end of which the rebels succeeded in boring through the wall on January 6, 1644. Even then street fighting continued and mopping up activities lasted for several days longer.

With the fall of Yü-lin, Li had succeeded in extending some degree of control over most of Shensi. The control was obviously hastily asserted and was far from being solidly based, but it was somewhat more substantial than the control he had exerted over areas in Honan and Hukuang earlier in his career.

Peking was completely incapable of making any effective response to halt the expansion of Li's power in Shensi and there is no evidence that a single soldier entered the province from the outside to help defend it. The central government officials did not even have reliable information about what was happening, which encouraged the more unrealistic ministers to look upon the rebel activities as events that were happening far away and that would dissipate before reaching the capital. The central government's total response to Li's attacks on Shensi seems to have been two futile appointments. The Vice-minister Yü Ying-kuei was appointed to succeed the dead Sun Ch'üan-t'ing as Supreme Commander and was given 50,000 taels from the Emperor's personal funds. However, he never assumed office, stopping across the Yellow River in Shansi. Another Peking official was appointed to a military supervision post in Shensi, the appointment being made on the basis that he was a native of the province and thus intimately acquainted with conditions. On being informed of his appointment in an imperial audience, the poor man burst into tears in the presence of the Emperor and protested that nothing could be done to save his native province now that Sian had been lost to Li Tzu-ch'eng.

While in northern Shensi, Li Tzu-ch'eng's main interest was a visit to his native county, Mi-chih, which he had not seen in almost a decade.[25] He entered Mi-chih in grand style, accompanied by 10,000 cavalry, and embarked upon a series of actions designed to enhance his imperial pretensions. He changed the county's name to T'ien-pao ("Heaven-protected"), and the name of Yenan, the prefecture to which Mi-chih was subordinate, was also changed to T'ien-pao. In addition, Li rewarded his fellow clansmen with titles and gifts of silver and also restored the Li family tombs which had been desecrated by the authorities. Taking revenge for this desecration, Li had two prominent Mi-chih citizens, whom he considered to be especially responsible for initiating the action, quartered in the streets of the town.

Most importantly, Li bestowed imperial titles on his ancestors and his wives. His great-grandfather, grandfather, and father were given the title of Emperor and his mother (née Lü) was made Empress Dowager.

His principal wife (née Liu) was made Empress and his secondary wife (née Ch'en) was accorded the rank of Precious Concubine. The given names of his great-grandfather, grandfather, and father, as well as his own, were altered to quite obscure characters, which were all tabooed.

After the conclusion of the Mi-chih ceremonies, Li returned to Sian, arriving there on December 31, 1643. In Sian, he continued his efforts to consolidate his control over the province, stabilize his administration, and enhance his image as the founder of a legitimate dynasty. On the first day of the lunar New Year (February 8, 1644) he was formally installed as Prince of Shun.[26] At the same time, he proclaimed a new dynasty to be called Ta Shun and announced that his reign title was to be Yung-ch'ang. Other actions included an order for the preparation of a new calendar and an offering of sacrifices to the three generations of his ancestors.

It is curious that Li should have refrained from mounting the throne and proclaiming himself emperor during the New Year's festivities. Indeed, it seems hardly possible in traditional Chinese terms for a new dynasty and a beginning reign period to come into existence without a new emperor. Furthermore, one wonders why Li found it necessary to assume another princely title when he had already proclaimed himself the holder of a similar one, Prince of Hsin-shun, at Hsiang-yang some eight months previously. The sources provide no answers to these questions, though possibly a lack of proper advice lay behind this display of dubious protocol. On the other hand, Li's refraining from taking the ultimate step of ascending the throne may indicate that he had some as yet unresolved doubts concerning the future role which he should play.

Whatever the reason for Li's restraint in proclaiming himself emperor, the future still must have appeared to him full of promise on that New Year's Day in 1644. He had eliminated all effective opposition in Shensi and at that very moment his men had already crossed the Yellow River and were pushing forward in Shansi. The capture of Peking, after years of restless wanderings and near-disasters, seemed a virtual certainty.

Li Tzu-ch'eng's Drive to Peking

Following his proclamation of a new dynasty, Li Tzu-ch'eng turned his attention to affairs in several spheres.[27] Most immediately taken up was the awarding of new titles of nobility to his most prominent lieutenants. These titles were quite generously distributed and eight marquises, seventy-two earls, thirty viscounts, and fifty barons were created. In addition, new coins were minted and an official examination was held. Thus, three gestures were quickly made to promote the aura of legitimacy surrounding the new regime.

In another sphere, the campaigns to spread Li's authority in Shensi were continued, and though subsequent events were to prove that his power in the province was based on shallow foundations, certainly he exercised more effective control over Shensi by early 1644 than he had ever wielded over an area of comparable size previously. Furthermore, Li was determined to maintain his position at least to some extent in Honan, though it is difficult to know precisely how successful he was in doing so. It seems certain that the districts in western Honan along the Yellow River were quite firmly in his control. The officials whom he had appointed governed the counties in the area and the notice proclaiming his new dynasty was circulated and accepted. In fact, an official in Peking reported with consternation that Li's officials were all cultured members of the gentry whose teachers had failed to inculcate in them the proper feelings of loyalty. The dismayed official went on to suggest that this state of affairs was of sufficient gravity to merit a full discussion by the appropriate ministries. Other sources also frankly admit that Li's propaganda about alleviating the tax burden had had real appeal in Honan and in some areas there had been a completely peaceful transfer of power from Ming local officials to those appointed by Li. Such peaceful transfers had been accompanied by roughly the same formalities which were exchanged between incoming and outgoing Ming local magistrates. On the other hand, there is quite definite evidence that Honan counties in the Hukuang and Nan-chihli border areas were mostly restored to Ming control, and apparently Yen-ch'eng in the central section of the province, where Li is said to have maintained a 2,000-man garrison, marked the eastern limit of his really effective authority.

As for Hukuang, there is no evidence to suggest that Li's control was maintained anywhere except at Hsiang-yang. He did launch a campaign from Sian to seize Yün-yang, the stronghold in extreme northwestern Hukuang which had defied all his efforts to capture it in 1643. The proximity of Yün-yang to Shensi definitely made it a threat to Li's position there. However, the attempt to take it early in 1644 ended, as had the previous ones, in complete failure.

Amid all the other activities, Li's main attention at Sian was riveted on the eastward thrust to Peking, and in mid-January of 1644 the first contingents of his army pushed across the Yellow River from Han-ch'eng, Shensi, bringing about the collapse of the long-held government defense line based on the river and beginning the rebel conquest of Shansi where relative stability had been maintained for a decade.[28]

Moving northwestward following the successful crossing of the river, Li's forces captured in rapid succession Ho-chin, P'u-chou, and P'ing-yang. Only light opposition was encountered: the Grand Coordinator withdrew to T'ai-yüan; the Regional Inspector fled; and Kao Chieh, the last of the professional officers serving under Sun Ch'üan-t'ing who had not surrendered to Li, abandoned his defense position along the river and retreated to southeastern Shansi. Within the space of a mere two weeks, the government's control in the entire southwestern corner of Shansi had collapsed.

Li's forces continued northeastward from P'ing-yang toward their first major objective, T'ai-yüan, and were joined early in March by Li himself who, after leaving behind a garrison in Sian, assumed personal direction of the drive to Peking. The attack on T'ai-yüan was launched on March 16 and the city was soon entered after one of the defending commanders surrendered and the rebels shattered a section of the wall with cannon fire. Furthermore, the sources maintain that the wind was so strong and so laden with dust that the defenders on the walls were unable to open their eyes. Thus, even the elements are made to appear to have been on the side of the rebels. Sporadic street fighting did continue for a short time, but really effective counterattack against the rebels was not possible.

Li paused only briefly in T'ai-yüan, determined as he was to preserve the momentum of his drive on the capital. However, he did take time to issue one of his most comprehensive propaganda pronouncements, which had been prepared for him by a recently acquired gentry follower, Chang Sui-jan.[29]

From T'ai-yüan, Li moved farther north, his progress at times resembling a triumphal procession with communities offering presents of meat and wine. Hsin-chou was occupied and no serious opposition was encountered until he reached Tai-chou where Regional Commander Chou Yü-chi held out as long as possible and inflicted numerous casualties upon the invaders before he was forced to retreat to nearby Ning-wu Pass for a last-ditch stand. At Ning-wu Pass, Chou fought until he saw the imperial cause was hopeless and then deliberately sought his own death by jumping down from the wall in the midst of the rebels and fighting in hand-to-hand combat until he was slain. Chou was virtually the only hero on the government side during the entire Shansi campaign, and even Li Tzu-ch'eng admitted that the rebel cause would not have reached its present position had the dynasty been generally served by officers as capable as Chou.

With the fall of Ning-wu Pass, there were only two remaining fortified points in Shansi which might serve as potential obstacles to Li's advance: Ta-t'ung and Yang-ho. In actual fact, at neither place was anything more than token resistance offered. The Regional Commander and magistrate at Ta-t'ung surrendered immediately at Li's approach and the

Grand Coordinator, after a hopeless attempt to organize opposition to the rebels, was taken prisoner. Li occupied the city on April 7. The situation at Yang-ho was certainly no more favorable to the imperial cause than what had prevailed at Ta-t'ung. The last report submitted a day or so prior to Yang-ho's fall by Supreme Commander Wang very aptly described the impossible position in which he found himself. The report states that the common people openly advocated surrender to Li, the troops were on the verge of mutiny, and the officers had made secret contacts with the rebels. Desperate efforts had been taken by Wang to rally the troops and populace: anyone advocating surrender had been threatened with execution and the officers and officials had been assembled at the Kuan Ti Temple for a speech on loyalty. After neither threats nor exhortation had evoked any response, the town fell virtually without resistance and its capture marked the end of Li's Shansi campaign. Within the space of three months the government's defense position in Shansi had been shattered and a rebel path of conquest had been cut across the entire province from Ho-chin to Yang-ho. Li was now poised to move into Pei-chihli and attack Peking itself.

Faced with its approaching doom as the rebel army pushed across Shansi, the central government frantically considered, and in some instances tried to put into effect, a wide variety of proposals. One involved the transferral of the imperial court to Nanking, a move whose principal champion was Li Ming-jui.[30] The suggestion was initially given serious consideration by the Emperor who summoned Li to the palace for a lengthy conference at night during which such specific details as the route to be taken and the forces to be employed as guards were discussed. Subsequently the Emperor seriously considered dispatching two ministers to Tientsin and to Shantung to make preliminary preparations for the move south, but was dissuaded from doing so after being convinced that the ministers would throw their responsibilities to the winds and flee back to their homes once they got outside of Peking. In the discussions about the move south, the Emperor displayed an increasing shortness of temper and at one point expressed his famous opinion that his own qualities made it unjust for him to be forced to preside over the collapse of a dynasty, but that the baseness of his ministers made it appropriate for them to be in office at such a time.

In the end, the entire proposal to move to Nanking was dropped, apparently after the Emperor decided that the abandonment of Peking would deliver a fatal blow to the prestige of the dynasty. Also, the move gained little support from officials in the capital. Even a side suggestion derived from the main proposal was rejected. This plan would have had the Heir Apparent alone sent to Nanking where he would have been in a position to ascend the throne in case a disaster happened at Peking.

In another area, the Emperor resorted to a favorite device of his ancestors and turned to the eunuchs as the element upon which he felt he must lean for support in a dire emergency.[31] He announced that since the provinces were not submitting grain tax payments on schedule and since there was a desperate need for supplies, it would be necessary to appoint eunuch supervisors to alleviate the critical situation. In addition, eunuch army inspectors were dispatched to most of the key army units in Pei-chihli and in some of the neighboring provinces as well. These appointments evoked the expected outcries from the regular bureaucracy with claims being made that the eunuchs would only worsen an already critical supply condition and cause a division of responsibility. In actual fact, the appointments came so late that they probably had little effect on the situation either one way or the other.

Undoubtedly the question which attracted the most attention in Peking was the financial one.[32] Desperate appeals for funds poured in and one exasperated Grand Coordinator strongly protested to the Ministry of War that his many memorials asking for funds had been greeted either with silence or merely perfunctory replies. Some attempt at least was made to satisfy these demands for support in most instances, however. At first, the officials clung to the hope that vast treasures were stored within the Imperial City and that the Emperor would release them when conditions became really desperate. After one audience, when the Emperor invited the officials for tea and a discussion of problems in a more informal setting, one of the officials stated that it was now necessary to depend on the Emperor's personal funds. The Emperor's reply was a tearful assertion that no such funds existed in any quantity. Subsequently, pressure was again exerted on the Emperor upon occasion to release personal funds and the rumor spread that the eunuchs, refusing to forgive the Emperor for bringing about the downfall of the eunuch strongman, Wei Chung-hsien, had managed to conceal the fact that large stores of precious metals existed within the Imperial City. This rumor was probably without any foundation and certainly no dramatic alleviation of the dynasty's financial plight ever came from the discovery of an imperial hoard of gold and silver.

Another direction turned to in the search for funds was an attempt to improve the collection of taxes by a resort to rewards and punishments. An imperial decree provided for promotions to be granted to all officials who collected their full quotas, and, conversely, any official who failed to collect at least 90% of the taxes in his area was to be dismissed.

Apparently the only measure which achieved even a modest degree of success in raising funds was pressure for contributions exerted upon wealthy imperial relatives, officials, and eunuchs. Approximately 200,000 taels are said to have been obtained from these sources. The campaign for contributions was launched when the Emperor dispatched a eunuch, Hsü Kao, to solicit a contribution from Chou K'uei, the father of the Empress. Initially, Chou refused to give anything and a rather acid exchange resulted between Hsü Kao and him with the eunuch demanding to know what use Chou's vast wealth would be after the dynasty had collapsed. Following a personal appeal by the Emperor, Chou agreed to contribute 10,000 taels, though actually he persuaded the Empress, his daughter, to supply half the sum. Chou's large fortune remained virtually intact, but within two months he was in his grave after Li's henchmen had seized from him a reputed fortune of 520,000 taels in gold and silver and several hundred thousand taels worth of art objects.

Several of the wealthy eunuchs were more generous in making contributions and two are said to have given as much as 50,000 taels each. However, the single richest eunuch gave only 1,000 taels and, like Chou K'uei, soon saw the rest of his fortune fall into the hands of Li Tzu-ch'eng.

A final source of badly needed funds was the Peking populace and modest sums were offered by ordinary citizens who, the sources indicate, were dominated solely by patriotic motives. For example, one aged man contributed 400 taels which represented his life's savings. He was rewarded with a title in the Embroidered-uniform Guard.

In the more general area of political action, several moves were taken by Peking in a desperate attempt to bolster the deteriorating situation.[33] A generous monetary reward and a marquis title were offered to anyone who would present the head of Li Tzu-ch'eng; Peking merchants and wealthy gentry members were promised preferential treatment in official assignments if they stored as much as 8,400 bushels of grain in their warehouses; private citizens who raised armed forces on their own initiative and freed a sub-prefecture or county from rebel control were to be made magistrates of the liberated areas regardless of whether or not they had an official degree; district princes and members of the gentry were threatened with punishment if they fled from their native areas without living up to their responsibilities of resisting the rebels; an amnesty was proclaimed for certain ex-officials who had been deposed and imprisoned as well as for those who had surrendered to the rebels provided they would revert to supporting the dynasty; and as one of his final acts, the Emperor issued the last in a long series of self-blaming edicts in which he took upon himself the onus for the official corruption, military debacles, and the crushing tax burdens. Furthermore, the edict ordered the abolition of all the special taxes.

In the military sphere, Peking was able to do virtually nothing to protect itself against the rebel advance.[34] Several old suggestions were renewed in memorials: to benefit from the lessons derived from the destruction of the army of Sun Ch'üan-t'ing in Honan and adopt a strictly defensive posture against the rebels; to re-orient the entire military policy in the direction of reliance solely upon local militia forces responsible only for the defense of their own immediate area; to win the support of minor rebel groups in Honan and Pei-chihli that had managed to remain independent and employ them in the struggle against Li; and to recruit aborigines from the southwest who had the reputation of being particularly skilled in the use of firearms. Furthermore, an actual order was issued to the Jesuit missionary, Adam Schall von Bell, directing him to accompany the newly appointed Grand Coordinator to Shansi in the capacity of military adviser with the particular responsiblity for constructing cannons.* Nothing, was accomplished by this order, since the military collapse of the government forces in Shansi was too far advanced.

As for the disposition of military forces, the various commanders paid little heed to orders issued from Peking. A general order to come to the aid of the capital, directed especially to Wu San-kuei on the Manchurian frontier and to Liu Tse-ch'ing in central Pei-chihli, was not obeyed. Wu did move some of his forces south of the Great Wall as a gesture of compliance, but made no attempt to block Li's advance on the capital. Liu quite openly abandoned all efforts to defend Peking and moved south to avoid the rebels. A minor general, T'ang T'ung, did advance to the capital and was honored by being given an imperial audience after which he was dispatched north of Peking to bolster the defense of Chü-yung Pass. Furthermore, the Grand Secretary Li Chien-t'ai made a grandiose and completely unrealistic gesture to save Shansi, his native province. He told the Emperor that he was willing to sacrifice his entire family fortune to support the military effort and was put in command of several thousand troops. His departure from Peking was preceded by an elaborate ceremony during which he was given three cups of wine by the Emperor himself. However, he never came close to achieving his military objective and in fact did not even manage to reach Shansi. His army began deserting when he was no more than thirty miles from the capital and towns along his route refused to receive him. Overcome with despair and illness, within two months he was captured by the rebels.

---

* Father Schall had had considerable experience in casting cannon for the Ming military forces. See his *Historica Relatio*, 80-92.

In every area, then, the dynasty's last exertions to save itself failed and the rebel advance continued without meeting a single instance of resistance strong enough to threaten its forward thrust.

Li moved into Pei-chihli by two routes: a smaller force, consisting mainly of cavalry, entered via Ku Pass and captured Chen-ting on March 31; and the main rebel army, under the personal command of Li, proceeded eastward from Ta-t'ung to occupy Hsüan-fu-wei on April 17. With the fall of Hsüan-fu-wei, only one possible obstacle remained before Peking itself was reached, and this was Chü-yung Pass where Regional Commander T'ang T'ung was stationed and to which Wu San-kuei had been ordered, though he did not comply with the command. The pass fell on April 21, following the surrender of Regional Commander T'ang to Li, and within one day the rebel tide had pushed forward to Ch'ang-p'ing, only some forty miles north of Peking. The news of the fall of Ch'ang-p'ing reached the court during an imperial audience, causing the Emperor to conclude the session abruptly and rush from the hall. In the meantime, the smaller rebel force was moving toward Peking from the south and by April 19 had seized Pao-ting where Grand Secretary Li Chien-t'ai was captured.[35]

The court found itself poorly or even mistakenly informed about all these rebel advances, since its information-gathering agents had virtually ceased functioning and in some instances had defected to the rebels. On the other hand, Peking teemed with rebel agents so that the plans of the government were soon known in Li's camp.

From Ch'ang-p'ing, Li dispatched the ex-Supreme Commander Wang Yung-chi to initiate negotiations with the Ming court. Li's actual terms and intentions are vague, though he is said to have instructed Wang to demand either a partition of the country or the appointment of himself as the regent for the Emperor with the title of "Great General" (Ta chiang-chün). There is no evidence to suggest that Wang met with any success in conducting the negotiations or indeed that, given the chaotic conditions in Peking, they were actually conducted.

With Peking facing imminent siege, the Emperor determined to place even heavier dependence upon the eunuchs, one of whom, Ts'ao Hua-shun, was given primary command of the city's defenses, despite the fact that he had been closely associated with the eunuch strongman, Wei Chung-hsien, for whose downfall the Emperor had been partly responsible. In addition, most of the regular officials were denied the right to mount the city wall. Even in the death throes of the dynasty, the long-standing tension between the eunuchs and the regular bureaucracy was heightened.[36]

On April 23, Li arrived on the outskirts of Peking and the Three Great Camps, the military organization which was responsible for the defense of the capital but whose present military potential was virtually nonexistent, promptly surrendered. Subsequently, Li began an immediate siege of the city after setting up his headquarters outside the Chang-i Gate.[37]

One of Li's first moves after establishing himself outside the Peking wall was to shoot a message into the city by arrow offering to negotiate. Again, Li's motives for desiring negotiations are hazy. He could hardly have doubted his ability to capture Peking and must have known that the defense was on the verge of collapsing. At any rate, the court accepted his offer and Li appointed Tu Hsün, a eunuch who had been one of the Emperor's closest confidants but who had surrendered to Li at Chü-yung Pass, to represent him in the negotiations.

After having been hoisted over the wall, Tu proceeded to the palace and into the presence of his former imperial master. Tu frankly advised the Emperor that the rebels were invincible and that he must accept their terms. The terms included the conferring of a princely title on Li, granting him control over the northwest (presumably Shansi and Shensi), and a reward of 1,000,000 taels of silver. In return, Li would promise to rid the empire of all enemies, both internal and external.

After the presentation of the rebel terms, the Emperor turned to ask the opinion of Grand Secretary Wei Tsao-te, but Wei refused to break his silence. Thereupon, the Emperor replied directly to Tu, telling him that he would be informed within a short time of the imperial decision. Tu was then allowed to leave after a plan to seize him had been abandoned when more astute officials pointed out that any harm done Tu would bring destruction to the Prince of Chin and the Prince of Tai who had been captured in Shansi and were being detained in Li's headquarters outside the city. Following Tu's departure from the audience hall, the Emperor flew into a rage, overturned the throne, and bitterly rebuked Grand Secretary Wei for his failure to formulate some plan which would rescue the dynasty from its present peril.

There is no further mention of the negotiations in the sources, and probably the Emperor did not even bother to convey a formal rejection of the rebel terms to Tu Hsün. The whole incident produced no results and its chief importance lies in the indication which it gives that probably some indecision still remained in Li's mind concerning his concept of his future status and course of action.

After the fruitless negotiations, the Emperor turned once again to his officials and two final court sessions were held to discuss actions to be taken.[38] The first session is described as a pathetic one with the Emperor and officials facing one another in tears and showing little disposition for discussion. Someone did manage to propose the granting of the title of baron to Regional Commander Liu Tse-ch'ing in the hope that the gesture would induce him to move his army north and attack the rebels. Also, it was suggested that Peking citizens be mobilized to fight, but this suggestion was dropped when a more realistic official said that they would flee immediately once fighting started.

The second and last court session was mainly concerned with the possibility of a last-minute flight to Nanking and the conclusion was reached that such a flight was now completely out of the question due to the fact that reliable troops in sufficient numbers to break through the rebel siege lines simply were not available. Thus, it was apparent that no possible avenue of escape remained and one official reported having seen a formal notice signed by many prominent officials and eunuchs who agreed to welcome Li the following day.

On the evening of April 24, the eunuch chiefly responsible for the defense of Peking, Ts'ao Hua-shun, opened the Chang-i Gate, allowing the rebel troops to enter the city and move toward the walls of the Imperial City itself after defeating a Moslem guard unit. Faced with this disaster, the Emperor decided upon desperate action. Summoning the Empress and other members of his family to a farewell meeting, he had wine poured and after drinking it, smashed his jade cup by throwing it on the floor. The Empress then bitterly upbraided the Emperor for failing to listen to her advice, embraced her sons, and retired to her own quarters to hang herself. The Emperor ordered his sons to take refuge outside the palace and attempted to kill his daughter with a sword, but succeeded only in cutting her severely on the arm. Subsequently, he wandered rather aimlessly about the palace grounds, and after his ministers failed to heed a summons to an audience, he ascended Coal Hill and hanged himself in a pavilion. One faithful retainer, the eunuch Wang Ch'eng-en, joined him in committing suicide.[39]

At noon on April 25, a few hours after the suicide of the Emperor, Li Tzu-ch'eng entered Peking via the Te-sheng Gate and took possession of the Imperial City. A long-delayed rebel goal thus had been achieved and the fortunes of Li's Shun dynasty had attained their apex.

Li Tzu-ch'eng in Peking

Li Tzu-ch'eng took possession of a chaotic Imperial City which could not even supply him with reliable information concerning the fate of the late Emperor. At first, it was assumed that the Emperor had fled in disguise and taken refuge among the common people. To insure his prompt discovery, Li ordered a generous reward of 10,000 taels of silver and the title of baron for news about his whereabouts, and dire punishment for anyone who would dare conceal him. Soon, it was established that the Emperor had indeed committed suicide and his body was conclusively identified.

Subsequently, Li turned his attention to interviews with surviving members of the imperial family to whom he showed considerable sympathy and restraint. He ordered his chief lieutenant, Liu Tsung-min, to take charge of the Emperor's daughter and see that the serious wounds she had received at the hands of her father were given medical attention. Also, he did not become enraged at the imperious manner adopted toward him by the three sons of the Emperor, the Heir Apparent, the Prince of Yung, and the Prince of Ting, though their impoliteness was probably not nearly so gross as is depicted in the sources.*

Outside the Imperial City, Peking itself had to grow accustomed to its new masters, although as would be expected, the sources cite numerous examples of persons who refused to accept the changed order and sacrificed themselves to the old.[40] However, for the most part, Peking citizens adapted to the new situation with what seems to have been no great enthusiasm, but at the same time, no notable opposition. Upon entering the city, the rebel regime had issued a proclamation calling for the common people to continue business as usual and promised that rebel troops would be prevented from committing any depredations. An early incident gave this promise greater credence: two rebel soldiers, caught looting a cloth shop, were hacked to death on the spot. Thus, the first fortnight of the rebel occupation of Peking saw the city maintaining relative quiet. Local people were forced to put up with the inconvenience of having to quarter and feed rebel soldiers in their houses, but there do not appear to have been any massacres, large-scale looting or raping, or active underground opposition to the rebels.

Within a short time, however, relations between the rebel regime and the Peking populace began to worsen partly as a result of the failure of the new authorities to institute any very positive measures to elicit support and partly because of an increasing number of depredations committed by rebel soldiers. From the very beginning, there had been some definite sentiment among the rebels that the spoils of Peking were to be seized and enjoyed. Indeed, the informal agreement, arrived at prior to the city's fall, provided for Li Tzu-ch'eng himself to have the Emperor's property, Liu Tsung-min and Li Yen that of the imperial relatives, Niu Chin-hsing and Sung Hsien-ts'e that of the civil officials, and the lesser rebel leaders that of the private wealthy families. Furthermore, after the city fell, the low-ranking rebel officers were given a hundred taels of

---

* *PKC* 9/7b-8a. The three princes are said to have refused to dismount at the palace gate and insisted on riding their horses into the hall itself where they conducted the interview while remaining on horseback. Also, they are depicted as rejecting Li's offer of food and drink. Given the ages of two of the princes, eight and twelve, it is hardly likely that they acted so flagrantly impolite toward Li. The entire episode is at least partly a reflection of the pro-Ming sympathies of the *PKC* and traditional sources in general.

silver and eleven yards of cloth. Neither the minor officers nor the common soldiers were happy with the rewards accorded them and this dissatisfaction increased the difficulty of maintaining discipline, particularly since large numbers of troops continued to be quartered inside the city and Li Yen's suggestion that all soldiers be transferred outside the city walls was not accepted. In addition, the maintenance of discipline did not have the unqualified support of all the major rebel leaders. Li Tzu-ch'eng himself, Li Yen, and, to a lesser extent, Niu Chin-hsing could be counted on the side of restraint and responsibility, but Li Tzu-ch'eng was increasingly isolated in the Imperial City, and his most trusted lieutenant, Liu Tsung-min, openly stated to Li Yen and Niu Chin-hsing that he was chiefly concerned with preventing mutinies among the troops and would not pay any great heed to the people. Even when Li Tzu-ch'eng appealed to Liu Tsung-min and the other rebel commanders, still suffering from a freebooters' psychology, to restrain their troops, no real results were gained. The commanders frankly told Li that, having gained the empire for him, they now should be allowed to enjoy and enrich themselves.

Other evidence of the estrangement between the rebels and the Peking populace is provided by the anti-rebel tales and rumors which became prevalent and by the lowering of rebel morale. One of the popular tales concerned the late Emperor's daughter who is said to have dreamed of her father's having conversed with Shang-ti and having been assured by that deity that the rebels would soon be defeated. At the same time, a rumor which gained wide circulation concerned the imminent arrival of Wu San-kuei who would destroy the rebel regime with his crack frontier army. It was said that Wu would order the populace to distinguish themselves from the rebels by wearing a white garment of a particular cut, and as a result there was such a run on white cloth at the shops that it became virtually impossible to obtain such material. The lowering of rebel morale is indicated by the story of a man who was picked up on the Peking streets by a group of illiterate soldiers and forced to accompany them to their quarters where they made him write a letter to their relatives in Shensi. After the letter had been written, the soldiers conversed frankly with the man, expressing regrets that they had ever joined the rebel cause and voicing the opinion that Li's forces would soon be crushed by Wu San-kuei and Tso Liang-yu.*

Even though his regime was failing to engender any great enthusiasm

---

* *PKC* 10/8a and *HLLK* 18/4a. The element in this story which makes it appear true is the mention of Li's being attacked by Tso Liang-yü. The compilers of the *PKC* and *HLLK* certainly would have known that Tso's military potential had declined markedly and would hardly have mentioned him had they invented the story.

in Peking and indeed was suffering from a worsening of relations with the populace, Li Tzu-ch'eng still showed no disposition to be conscious of failure and continued his efforts in several directions to place his administration on a stable and permanent basis.[41] One series of actions might be described as ceremonial, and the most important item in this category was the question of Li's ascending the throne. Some uncertainty surrounds this and it is unclear whether or not he ever actually had the enthronement ceremony properly performed. It appears definite that he sat upon the throne during audience and made provisions for such other requirements of a new dynasty as regulating official dress, cutting an imperial seal, proclaiming the name of the dynasty and the reign period, and tabooing characters connected with himself and his ancestors. However, it seems probable that he left the final requirement for formalizing a new dynasty, the enthronement ceremony, unfulfilled at least until the last chaotic moments of his occupation of Peking.

Another important ceremonial obligation faced by Li was the burial of the late Emperor and Empress as well as the treatment accorded his imperial predecessors generally. Such ceremonials had important political connotations, because they were able to influence the support obtained from adherents of the fallen dynasty. In arranging the burial of the Emperor and Empress, a reasonably proper level of performance was maintained. The corpses were encoffined wearing imperial robes, though the coffins were made of quite ordinary willow wood, and Li himself as well as his Minister of Rites, Kung Yü, paid homage to the deceased imperial couple. Some two or three weeks later, the coffins were placed in a tomb, which had already been constructed for a dead concubine of the late Emperor, in the Western Hills. This final ceremony apparently was quite forlorn, and there were only four participants: the three sons of the deceased imperial couple and a minor rebel official. No officials of the fallen dynasty are said to have attended, though they were not forbidden to. As for the attitude toward the earlier Ming emperors, Li had the tablets of most of them removed from the ancestral temple and burned. Only the tablet of Emperor T'ai-tsu, the founder, was spared and placed in the temple which contained tablets for the most famous emperors throughout all Chinese history. In general, it would seem that Li Tzu-ch'eng did not really outrage traditional mores in his treatment of his imperial predecessors, but at the same time, his failure to display any marked generosity hardly enhanced his stature.

Another ceremonial undertaken by Li was an audience for the aged who were received in one of the palaces and formally questioned about the hardships of the common people.

In the arena of more practical politics, Li gave at least some attention to a variety of problems: holding official examinations, coining money, and adopting policies to be pursued toward the officials of the fallen dynasty.[42] Two official examinations were held: one for the *chu-sheng* degree and one for the *chü-jen*. Of the seventy candidates taking the *chü-jen* examination, fifty passed and all were assigned posts. Furthermore, it was announced that county examinations would be held in every province by the coming autumn.

The coinage efforts do not seem to have been altogether successful, though misfortunes in casting the coins undoubtedly are exaggerated in the sources to prove that divine authority was opposing the rebels. At any rate, it is claimed that the rebel coins were not only heavy and unwieldy, but also, due to an error in casting, bore the characters for the T'ai-ch'ang reign period, instead of the Yung-ch'ang.* This error is said to have so enraged Li that he ordered the artisans responsible executed.

Probably the most important political decisions made by Li were those determining the policy to be adopted toward the officials who had served the Ming.[43] Possessing no adequate administrative structure of his own, Li's future could have been substantially aided by effectively integrating into his regime the organization surviving from the fallen dynasty. Li's first order to the Ming ex-officials was for them to come to an audience on April 27, two days after Peking's fall. The officials arrived as ordered for the audience, dressed in the clothes of criminals, but Li allowed them to remain waiting in the palace all day without receiving them. And during their fruitless vigil, the ex-officials were harassed by the taunting remarks of rebel troops. Subsequently, Li did begin seeing the ex-officials, mainly on an individual basis, and one of his first interviews was with former Grand Secretary Wei Tsao-te. He asked Wei why he had neglected to commit suicide when he had been so close to the Chung-chen Emperor, and Wei made the sycophantic reply that he wanted to remain alive in order to serve Li. Later, Li held other interviews, and during all of them he is said to have maintained an attitude of studied and even insulting informality, wearing quite ordinary clothes and sitting crosslegged on the throne.

As for the formulation of a policy toward the ex-officials, one of the earliest general suggestions was advanced by Li Yen who advocated a three-fold division: the corrupt ones should be tortured until they offered up their fortunes and then handed over to judicial processes; those who refused to surrender should have their property confiscated and handed over to justice; and the incorrupt ones should not be blamed for their past connections and should contribute what they could to the rebel

---

* T'ai-ch'ang was the reign period title for Emperor Kuang-tsung who ruled only approximately one month during August-September, 1620.

regime. The only portion of this suggestion which was implemented to any effective extent was that which pertained to milking the ex-officials of their fortunes, and a quite systematic effort was instituted to obtain as many precious metals and other valuables as possible. Liu Tsung-min was placed in charge of this extortion process and set up an elaborate headquarters, complete with torture chambers, where the ex-officials were detained while their cases were under investigation. A rough schedule of expected "donations" from the ex-officials was established: 100,000 taels from those who had served in the Grand Secretariat, 70,000 taels from heads of ministries, and 30,000 to 50,000 from lower ranking ministry officials. These sums, of course, were supplemented by others extorted from imperial in-laws and private wealthy persons who had held only titular official positions or none at all. The single most important of such victims was Chou K'uei, father of the late Empress. His palatial mansion was occupied by Li Yen who tortured him and forced him to work as a servant in which capacity he was so mistreated that he soon died.

Considerable success, at least monetarily, was achieved in the campaign to squeeze the ex-officials and wealthy families generally, though many deaths came about as a result of it, including that of such a prominent person as former Grand Secretary Ch'en Yen whose flattering memorial urging Li Tzu-ch'eng to ascend the throne failed to save him. Liu Tsung-min achieved notoriety as being especially bloodthirsty, and at the height of the extortion campaign he is reported to have had 2,000 persons detained at his headquarters. Of this number half eventually lost their lives. Li Tzu-ch'eng is reported to have been so horrified when he visited Liu's torture chambers that he urged him to moderate his actions.

As for the amount of precious metals squeezed from the victims of the rebels, one source mentions the impossible figure of 18,500,000,000 taels, and after melting down this huge bulk and casting it into 37,000,000 ingots, the rebels are supposed to have attempted to transport the entire amount to Sian either before or during their flight from Peking. As the compiler of the *P'ing K'ou Chih* points out, it would have required virtually every transport animal obtainable to have moved such a mass of metal. A more conservative estimate of the rebel loot, though still probably greatly exaggerated, is 700,000,000 taels of which thirty percent was said to have come from the aristocracy (including the imperial in-laws), thirty percent from the eunuchs, twenty percent from former officials, and twenty percent from wealthy merchants.

In another area of political activity, Li's attitude toward the eunuchs earned him moderately favorable comments in the sources, for although the eunuchs had contributed toward his success in seizing Peking and were employed by him to some extent subsequently, he drove thousands out of the city and left them to fend for themselves.

A general assessment of Li's political actions following the fall of Peking must lead one to conclude that he was unimaginative and lacking in leadership potential. The main rebel effort was concentrated on the rather sterile endeavour of taking possession of the money and property of wealthy ex-officials and others. And although this milking process undoubtedly resulted in some monetary gains, it did not solve any of the basic financial problems of the rebel regime. No effective effort was made to strengthen the new administration by attracting really firm support from abler ex-officials of the Ming. Thus, there were no political breakwaters to be depended upon later when military disaster struck.

Of necessity, Li Tzu-ch'eng's main attention at Peking was centered on military affairs. One direction this took was the expansion of his power into Shantung, a province which had remained more outside the main stream of rebel activity than any other area in north China, though it had been affected by local rebel action. Li dispatched troops from Peking to Shantung and managed to capture and hold briefly such places as Tsinan and Chi-ning.[44] Also, there was an attempt to extend rebel authority into northern Nan-chihli, and Li appointed a magistrate to Huai-an Prefecture. However, the rebel magistrate was soon captured and executed by Ming loyalist groups.

Li's main military concern was the situation in the northeast[45] where Wu San-kuei and the Manchus were engaged in a complicated series of maneuvers to gain the utmost advantages for themselves. It is uncertain precisely when Wu made the definite decision to ally himself with the Manchus against the peasant rebels, but the alliance was probably in the final stages of being agreed upon at the time Li Tzu-ch'eng captured Peking. Certainly Manchu ambitions vis à vis China were well known by the spring of 1644, and on April 21 of that year, the Manchu Emperor had issued an open letter to Ming generals in north China, inviting their adherence to the Ch'ing cause. This was undoubtedly a deliberate effort to compete with the peasant rebels for the support of prominent Ming military figures following the dynasty's collapse.

Although Wu's decision to cast his lot with the Manchus was probably reasonably definite by late April of 1644, two other contestants for power were still courting him in the hope of winning his valuable support: Ming loyalists and Li Tzu-ch'eng. Li's appeal to Wu came at about the same time he was sending messages inviting surrender to such other Ming generals as Liu Tse-ch'ing and Tso Liang-yü, but Li's efforts to win over Wu were much more seriously pressed than those directed toward Liu and Tso. Li combined appeals to filial piety with offers of honors and wealth in attempting to persuade Wu to join his cause. That is, he had

Wu's father, Wu Hsiang, write a letter in behalf of the rebel regime and combined this with a marquis title bestowed upon Wu and a monetary reward. Also, Li contributed a large sum, said by one source to have been 1,000,000 taels of silver, to be given to Wu's army at Shanhaikuan. Furthermore, Li's approach to Wu probably contained a veiled threat against the Wu family most of whose members were in Peking and therefore at the mercy of the rebels.

Wu San-kuei's response to the overtures made to him by Li Tzu-ch'eng offer little indication that he was interested in reaching an agreement with the rebels. Though he accepted the presents bestowed upon him by Li, he adamantly rejected his father's appeal for him to surrender, replying in rather acid tones that his father had always taught him to be loyal and thus he could not now accept advice which would have him be disloyal to the Ming. Undoubtedly Wu's decision to reject the rebel overtures was based mainly on what he considered his own best interests and those of the traditional values he upheld. However, the decision may have been influenced to some degree by more narrow personal considerations. There is, for example, the famous story that Wu became enraged when the rebel leader, Liu Tsung-min, seized his favorite concubine, Ch'en Yüan, a former Nanking sing-song girl and a noted beauty. Also, Wu is said to have been misled into believing that the rebels had mistreated his father. It is doubtful, though, if these personal factors exerted a major influence upon Wu.[46]

When the negotiation with Wu failed to promise success, the rebel authorities in Peking decided to begin military pressure against him. At first, this pressure was slight, and a small rebel army under T'ang T'ung was ordered to Shanhaikuan. T'ang was defeated and driven away on May 5 by Wu who was perhaps given some aid by the Manchus. T'ang thereupon was reinforced by another rebel army commanded by Pai Kuang-en and a second battle occurred on May 10. Again the rebels were defeated and Wu pursued them as far as Yung-p'ing before returning to Shanhaikuan. In addition, Wu issued a strong proclamation expressing in no uncertain terms his intention to exterminate the rebels.

Faced with what was obviously complete failure in attracting or forcing Wu to join their cause, the rebel authorities in Peking were obliged to decide upon an alternative policy, and on May 14 a conference of all the major rebel leaders, except Li himself, was called. The conference was presided over by Niu Chin-hsing and two questions were discussed: a military expedition against Wu and the date for Li's ascending the imperial throne. No decision was reached on either subject and no help was obtained when divination was resorted to, since the predictions were unfavorable.

Two days later, on May 16, Li himself called a conference in the palace, but apparently the chief subject discussed was the arrangement to transport bullion and other items of value from Peking to Sian. Li announced that the precious metals looted from various sources in Peking had been melted down and cast into tens of thousands of ingots each weighing a thousand taels. All of these ingots would be shipped to Sian for which Li expressed a decided preference, saying it was worth ten Pekings. However, he recognized that the threat posed by Wu San-kuei made it impossible for him to abandon Peking under the present circumstances.

It is probable that the May 16 palace conference also discussed military operations against Wu, but the subject is not mentioned in the sources which subsequently quite suddenly state that on May 18, Li left Peking for Shanhaikuan after having ordered that grain stores be shipped by sea from Tientsin to supply his army when it had reached its destination. Li was accompanied on the campaign by two of his favorite lieutenants, Liu Tsung-min and Li Kuo. Also carried along, for safekeeping and as a means of exerting pressure on Wu, were Wu's father, several district princes, and the three sons of the late Emperor. The actual number of rebel troops is said to have been 50,000, though the claim was made that there were 100,000. Advancing via T'ung-chou, the rebel forces reached Yung-p'ing on May 22, and proceeded on northeastward a short distance to a point near Shanhaikuan where the battle which was to decide Li's fate was destined to take place.[47]

With Li's army arriving in the vicinity of Shanhaikuan, Wu San-kuei on May 25 sent an urgent message requesting aid from Prince Dorgun, the Manchu Regent. Marching rapidly southward, Prince Dorgun on May 26 took up a position some three miles north of Shanhaikuan where the first skirmish between the rebels and the Manchus took place. The rebel force was commanded by T'ang T'ung who was apparently the only one of Li's lieutenants to succeed in entrenching himself north of the Great Wall. However, T'ang was unable to maintain himself in this advance position for very long, because he was soon defeated by the Manchus.

On May 27, Prince Dorgun entered Shanhaikuan itself, was welcomed in person by Wu San-kuei, and the two leaders launched into a discussion of the tactics to be employed against the rebels. At first, it was proposed that the Sino-Manchu force be deployed directly in front of the rebels who were occupying a line running from southwest of Shanhaikuan to the sea. This plan was abandoned in favor of one which concentrated the offensive blow upon the flank of the rebel force after Wu's troops had been incorporated into the right wing of the Manchu army and had been instructed to wear pieces of white cloth on their shoulders so that they could be distinguished from the rebels by the Manchus in the confusion of battle.

DYNASTIC AMBITIONS PHASE (1641-44)

Following the determination of the battle plans, the Sino-Manchu force launched a sudden attack, probably somewhat aided by having their first moves concealed by a violent dust storm which, however, soon subsided. Li Tzu-ch'eng was directing operations from his headquarters atop a small hill and was apparently not fully aware that the Manchus had joined his Chinese opponents. It was only after a large band of cavalry flying strange white banners arrived on the battlefield and were identified by a Buddhist monk in his entourage that he realized he was fighting the Manchus.

The Shanhaikuan battle lasted only a few hours and ended in an overwhelming defeat for the rebels, despite the fact that Li was in personal command of the rebel forces. Abandoning the battlefield in great disorder, Li's troops embarked upon a rapid retreat toward Yung-p'ing, and this movement might well have turned into a rout had the Sino-Manchu force not halted its pursuit after some twelve miles. The chief reason for this sudden and complete rebel defeat was the disparity in quality between the rebel soldiers and those of the Sino-Manchu army. The Manchus had the benefit of a hardy frontier environment, a vigorous military tradition, and the background of practical experience during more than a generation of successful campaigns. At the same time, the army of Wu San-kuei provided a valuable supplement to Manchu strength, for it was undoubtedly the best of the surviving Ming forces, and one source claims that a single soldier in Wu's command was the equal of ten rebels. In addition, there may well have been a numerical balance disadvantageous to the rebels, though the evidence here is equivocal. The *Ch'ing Shih-lu* claims that Li's force totalled 200,000, but this figure is probably deliberately exaggerated to enhance the glory of the Manchu victory. The Chinese sources indicate that Li had somewhere between 50,000 and 100,000 men, the former figure probably being more nearly accurate than the latter. Opposing Li, the Manchus had around 50,000 in their army and Wu is said to have had 40,000 regular troops and 70,000 to 80,000 recruited on an *ad hoc* basis locally. Faced with opponents clearly superior in quality and probably superior in numbers, Li suffered a defeat so decisive that he was never able to recover from it.

Retreating from Shanhaikuan to the vicinity of Yung-p'ing, Li paused briefly to collect his scattered forces before continuing the withdrawal to Peking, his temporary goal. Before he was able to bring any real order to his battered army, Wu San-kuei resumed his pursuit and attacked at Fu-ning and Pao-chih. In desperation, Li sent one of his chief officials to enter into negotiation with Wu and won a very short respite after he pretended to acquiesce to Wu's demands that he hand over the Ming Heir Apparent, promise not to destroy the Ming ancestral temple, and agree to abandon Peking.* However, by the time Li reached Peking on May 31, Wu was again exerting pressure on him and he found himself under semi-siege. He sought to force Wu to retreat by displaying his father, Wu Hsiang, on top of the city wall and threatening to kill him. Wu responded by having his troops riddle the two rebel soldiers guarding his father with arrows, an act which so enraged Li that he had the entire Wu family, totalling thirty-eight persons, executed. Following this bloodbath, Wu Hsiang's head was cut off and hung on the city wall, a spectacle which is said to have so affected Wu San-kuei that he fell from his horse.

The next three days were spent by Li Tzu-ch'eng in frantic preparations to abandon Peking and probably in hasty arrangements for his formal assumption of the imperial position. The enthronement ceremony apparently took place on June 3 and seems to have attempted to conform with proper etiquette, though it must have been conducted with undue speed, for the very next day witnessed a general rebel departure from Peking.

Li marched his forces out of Peking in the early morning hours of June 4, leaving behind him a city which had been stripped of vehicles and draft animals and many of whose palaces and other public buildings were in flames. Numerous Peking citizens were forced to accompany the rebels to compensate for losses suffered at Shanhaikuan and elsewhere. The rebel army moved rapidly, knowing that Wu San-kuei was hovering in the background and was likely to attack. Thus, the scene was quite different from the one almost six weeks earlier when the rebels were moving in the opposite direction to occupy the capital. In the interim, Li's fortunes had taken a drastic turn downward and he must have suspected the disaster which was eventually to come.

The Activities of Chang Hsien-chung and Minor Rebel Groups in 1641

Chang Hsien-chung's capture of Hsiang-yang in March, 1641 was a brilliant coup, but it signified nothing really basic and marked no turning point in his career. He merely abandoned the plundered city two days after capturing it and moved on to raid other areas, his actions in no way different from past practices. During the subsequent half year, he covered hundreds of miles, moving about in territory by now thoroughly familiar to him: southern and southeastern Honan and virtually the entire length of the northern border region of Hukuang.

---

* The negotiations with Wu never got beyond a very preliminary stage and Li did not hand over the Heir Apparent whose final fate is unknown, although he probably was killed during the confusion of Li's retreat from Peking to Sian.

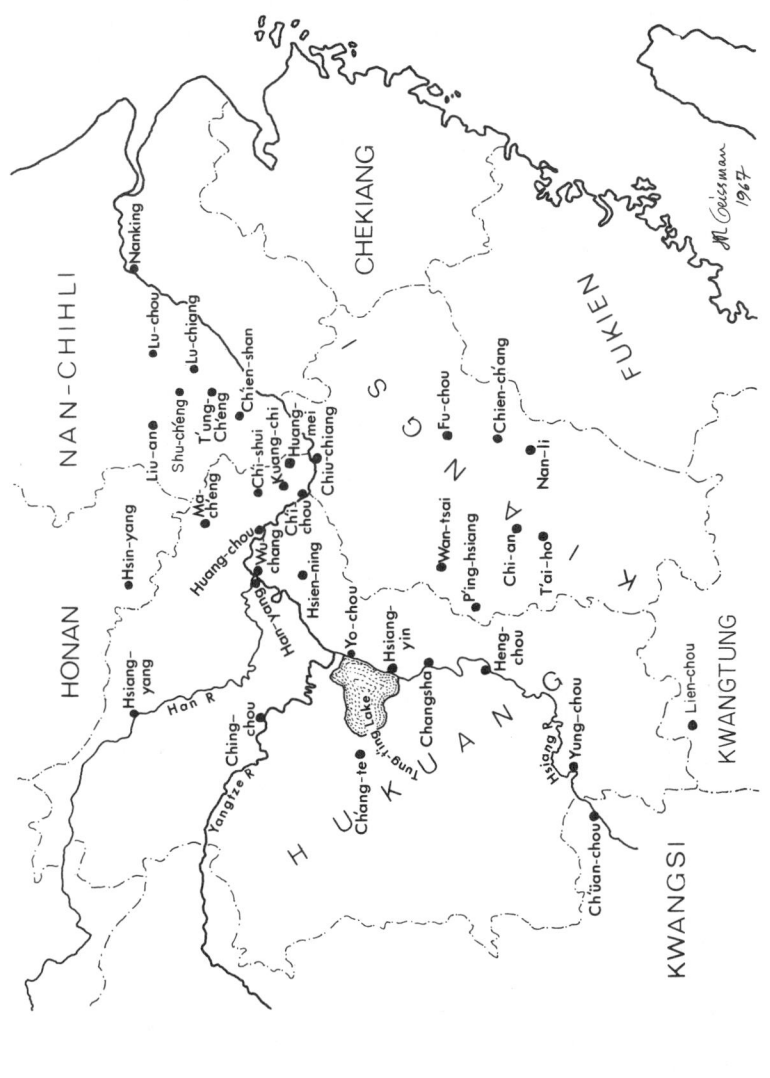

19 CHANG HSIEN-CHUNG 1642-44

Chang's plundering successes came to an abrupt halt in the 8th month of 1641 when he was caught at Hsin-yang* in southeastern Honan near the Hukuang border by his old enemy, Tso Liang-yü, who was still quite willing to attack Chang in order to even past scores, even though he was studiously avoiding an encounter with the now powerful Li Tzu-ch'eng. Tso succeeded in seriously defeating Chang who had just been deprived of the support of his former ally, Lo Ju-ts'ai, now in Li's camp. Chang fled from the battlefield with only a few hundred men and eventually felt forced to seek protection from Li Tzu-ch'eng in central Honan.[48]

Chang's flight to Li must have been considered a bitter humiliation by the recently defeated rebel leader. Chang's long rivalry with Li and the tension existing in the relations between the two have been noted several times already. Furthermore, Chang had considered himself, from the very early days of the rebel movement, to be Li's superior and this assessment previously had been generally accepted by the rebels and the official side alike. Certainly throughout the late 1630's and all of 1640, Chang had been judged the major rebel figure, and following his capture of Hsiang-yang, he had openly proclaimed his superiority to Li. Now, Chang found Li escalating toward power which no Ming rebel had ever possessed, while he himself had suffered the latest of his many near-fatal defeats.

Following Chang's arrival at Li's camp, there were inconclusive negotiations for him to be accepted as a subordinate in Li's forces. The pill proved too bitter for Chang to swallow and Li seems to have toyed with the idea to have his proud rival assassinated. Finally, though, Lo Ju-ts'ai persuaded Li that Chang could perform valuable diversionary service if he were sent to strengthen the rebel activities north of the Yangtze in Nan-chihli, an area which he knew quite well. Accordingly, Lo gave Chang a few hundred troops and he went to join Tso-chin-wang and Ko-kuo-yen, the two rebel leaders who had long been operating in eastern Hukuang and western and central Nan-chihli. In this area Chang once more resumed successful raiding and eventually, as we shall see, achieved considerable stature, though he was never again destined to surpass Li Tzu-ch'eng.

One area which had been relatively unaffected by the rebellions (except for minor local incidents) prior to 1641 was the scene of considerably intensified rebel activity during that year.[49] This was Shantung. One source, resorting to a quite obvious flourish of literary exaggeration, states that desolation reigned supreme over a space of six hundred miles in the province. The region was said to have been covered with white

---

* See Map 19 for places involved in Chang's career which are mentioned in this chapter.

bones and deserted villages, and cannibalism had become so rampant that even fathers committed the cardinal sin of devouring their own children.

In addition to such patently untrustworthy claims of total disaster, there are more solid reports which demonstrate increased rebel activity. For example, one group of Shantung rebels succeeded in pushing across the Yellow River into Nan-chihli. There they burned one of the city gates at Hsü-chou, destroyed sixteen boats on the Grand Canal, and plundered as far south as the Yangchow area before returning to Shantung. Furthermore, the Shantung Grand Coordinator submitted a report dealing with the deteriorating defense of the Yellow River. He cited the case of one garrison which on paper was credited with having 3,600 troops, but actually had only 700. Also, long stretches of the river were said to have no protection at all. Despite the increased rebel activity in Shantung, the province was a long way from becoming another Honan, and early in 1642, the situation in Shantung moved toward greater stability when the major local rebel leader, an ex-butcher named Li Ch'ing-shan, was killed. The more able-bodied men in his group were enrolled in the official forces and the others were ordered to return home. To help eradicate any lingering effects of the troubles, the Emperor granted 200,000 taels as a relief fund. Thus, the Ming authorities were still rather firmly in control of Shantung and there was no serious disruption of traffic on the Grand Canal. None of the principal national rebel leaders had ever set foot in the province and it was to be at least two years before Li Tzu-ch'eng's power in Shantung became at all significant.

Chang Hsien-chung in Nan-chihli (1642)

Following the grant of several hundred troops, bestowed upon him by his former ally, Lo Ju-ts'ai, Chang Hsien-chung pushed into Nan-chihli, an area where he had operated on three prior occasions for relatively short periods of time. Now, the province was destined to remain the center of his operations for more than a year.

Entering Nan-chihli in late 1641 via the northwestern corner of the province, Chang pushed rapidly southward and throughout 1642 his activities were confined to a relatively restricted area in southwestern Nan-chihli north of the Yangtze.[50] His first major military effort was directed against Shu-ch'eng in the 3rd month of 1642. He was joined in the attack by Tso-chin-wang and Ko-kuo-yen with whom he had been briefly allied upon occasion in the past, but who were destined in the latter part of 1642 to form more definite ties with Li Tzu-ch'eng. Shu-ch'eng had the misfortune not only of having inadequate defense forces, but also of not even having a magistrate. The defense was organized on a somewhat *ad hoc* basis by a Hanlin Recorder, Hu Shou-heng, who had assumed leadership of the city for the past several months. Hu infuriated the rebels by burning their surrender demand, shot into the city by arrow, on the wall, and gave every indication of an intention to maintain a stout defense. However, the city's fall to the rebels was virtually assured when the Local Commander, K'ung T'ing-hsün, joined them with his force of some 1,000 men. K'ung had been on bad terms with the local authorities who had refused to allow his army to come inside the city after his troops had resorted to displays of violence. Augmented by the former garrison, the rebel attackers overcame the defenders after a three-day siege. In celebration of the victory and illustrating the new status he was trying to give himself, Chang ordered that the city's name be changed to Te-sheng ("Attained Victory") and that its status be raised from county to subprefecture. These changes were quite meaningless, since Chang had no real intention of occupying the city on a long-term basis, and indeed had abandoned it by the time government troops belatedly arrived about a month after its fall.

Two months after his capture of Shu-ch'eng, Chang, bent on greater military glories, turned his efforts toward Lu-chou, one of the most important cities in Nan-chihli. Possessing a strong wall and deep moat, Lu-chou had succeeded in frustrating all previous rebel efforts to capture it, including two attempts made by Chang himself. Now dissension, centering around a corrupt magistrate, had resulted in a weakening of the city's defenses although it undoubtedly could have fought off an attack which was openly pressed. Thus, Chang, duplicating the tactics he had employed two years earlier in capturing Hsiang-yang, set in motion another of his famous ruses for smuggling a rebel fifth column into the city. It so happened that just at this time a prefectural-level official examination was scheduled and there was a great deal of activity in and about the city. In the confusion, considerable numbers of Chang's troops are said to have infiltrated the city disguised as students and travelling merchants. It seems highly unlikely that rebel soldiers could have posed successfully as students, so this element in the story is undoubtedly popular fiction. But a rebel fifth colum was indeed planted within the city and, according to a prearranged schedule, launched an attack on the night of June 2, 1642 just as the main rebel force surprised the garrison by attacking from the outside. The city's defenses collapsed almost immediately and it was soon occupied. During the next few days the rebels killed the magistrate and several other officials and looted the city. They made no attempt to hold it, and by the time a relief force had arrived from a nearby city a few days later, Chang and his troops had withdrawn.

Following the fall of Lu-chou, Chang briefly occupied Lu-chiang where, in one of the exaggerated flights of fancy so typical of the sources when they want to emphasize rebel brutality, he is said to have virtually exterminated the entire population of this thriving city, leaving only a few hundred inhabitants alive. What makes this description even more incongruous is the prior dispassionate statement of fact that Chang captured the local magistrate, but released him unharmed! After the fall of Lu-chiang, Chang settled into relative inactivity during the height of summer and undoubtedly was made jealous by reports of Li Tzu-ch'eng's success in defeating all his opponents around Kaifeng and continuing with the siege of that important city.

In the 8th month of 1642, Chang concentrated his attention for a time on what was, for him, a quite new activity. He settled in the area of Lake Ch'ao, a short distance southwest of Lu-chou, where he captured boats, had additional ones constructed, and began recruiting and training a naval force to stage an invasion south of the Yangtze against Nanking where he would proclaim himself Emperor. The rumors of these plans spread rapidly throughout the lower Yangtze area, producing considerable uneasiness and evoking memorials calling for more adequate river defense. As it turned out, Chang's push across the Yangtze and assault on Nanking never came near to being translated into reality. He seems to have lost interest in the idea after doing little more than ordering the preliminary naval training, having an imperial seal cut, and accepting into his service some men who had made themselves eunuchs in order to obtain positions within his palace after the fall of Nanking. However, the interlude of naval interest on the part of Chang does have some long-range significance. It indicated that Chang had made a start toward breaking with the strictly land-oriented attitude which his north China background had imposed upon him and was beginning to adjust to the milieu of the middle and lower Yangtze where water transportation and naval power were crucial. Also, his Lake Ch'ao nautical efforts undoubtedly were the foundation for the real naval power which he did succeed in developing later and which enabled him to become the first and only late Ming rebel leader to succeed in building up a significant sphere of influence south of the Yangtze.

After abandoning his naval interests on Lake Ch'ao, Chang turned west and captured Liu-an near which he defeated a government force commanded by Regional Commanders Liu Liang-tso and Huang Te-kung and by a eunuch officer Lu Chiu-te. Then, he moved southward and on September 30, 1642 launched an unsuccessful attack on T'ung-ch'eng, the official forces arriving much sooner than expected and forcing his withdrawal. Ironically, this alacrity on the part of the government forces is attributed to a local sing-song girl who was a great favorite of Regional Commander Huang Te-kung. When the rebels appeared, the local authorities persuaded the girl to send a message to Huang urging him to come to the aid of the city, and Huang, responding to the personal appeal, reached the city in less than five days, instead of the ten expected by the rebels.

Chang's bad luck at T'ung-ch'eng dogged him subsequently when he moved southwestward to the area of Ch'ien-shan and established a fortified camp on a mountain slope, evidently intending to remain in the spot for some time to rest and recuperate. Liu Liang-tso and Huang Te-kung made a surprise attack on the camp after approaching it from the rear. In describing the succeeding melée, the sources present a picture of complete disaster for Chang: 10,000 rebels killed, including some of his closest advisers; several 10,000 horses and mules seized; and several thousand women and children captured. Given Chang's rapid recovery and subsequent activities, it is hardly possible for the victory of the official forces in the surprise attack to have been as overwhelming as the sources indicate. Probably Chang succeeded in escaping with the bulk of his troops. Still, the attack was a blow to his increasingly ambitious plans and is a signal demonstration of how far removed he was from attaining a stature equal to that of Li Tzu-ch'eng.

During the final months of 1642, Chang remained in the same southwestern Nan-chihli area, accomplishing few significant feats beyond finally capturing T'ung-ch'eng which had been left without protection when the government forces had been obliged to go north to repel an incursion by one of the minor rebel leaders allied with Li Tzu-ch'eng. Early in 1643, Chang decided to move out of Nan-chihli and the province was never to see him again, his destiny leading him further and further westward.

Leaving Nan-chihli, Chang went to Hukuang, the area which seemed now to offer the greatest prospects of success. Just at this time (early 1643), Li Tzu-ch'eng was firmly entrenching himself in northwestern Hukuang and Ming power was in the process of disintegrating there. Furthermore, the collapse engendered by Li in the northwest was spreading to other sections of the province, and Chang felt he now had an excellent opportunity to carve out an area of influence in eastern Hukuang similar to the one Li had erected in the northwest. He was to achieve at least partial success in his plans and Wuchang was to be the setting for his earliest more serious dynastic ambitions.

Chang's activities during 1642 were still essentially "old style" and he had not really moved beyond disorganized raiding to mature political intentions and greater power. It is true that he remained in a relatively circumscribed area for a longer time than was usual in former years. However, his objective in capturing cities in Nan-chihli was still primarily to provide an opportunity for plunder, rather than to secure permanent bases, and his quite fanciful dynastic pretensions, which came to nothing, were probably mainly a deliberate attempt to compete with Li Tzu-ch'eng. Chang's rebellion, in development, was approximately a year behind that of Li, and indeed Chang may never have progressed to the stage of dynastic ambitions at all had Li not been available both as an example and as a power for destroying Ming military potential.

Chang Hsien-chung's Power Center in Hukuang

By the beginning of 1643, Chang Hsien-chung was the only important rebel leader who had succeeded in maintaining himself completely independent of Li Tzu-ch'eng and was able to continue pursuing his own aims. As previously noted, Chang had spent most of 1642 in southwestern Nan-chihli where he generally adhered to his old pattern of random plundering. There were, however, two significant deviations from the familiar plundering pattern: he gave at least some thought to the idea of attacking Nanking and declaring himself emperor and he started developing a naval force, a necessity for military success in the Yangtze area.

Early in 1643, Chang turned his direction westward and moved across the border into eastern Hukuang.[51] This move was decided upon largely as a result of events which had produced general turmoil in the province. As already seen, Li Tzu-ch'eng occupied a substantial section of northwestern Hukuang from his center at Hsiang-yang beginning in late 1642. Furthermore, the semi-independent government commander, Tso Liang-yü, fleeing from Li Tzu-ch'eng with his large demoralized army, had created chaos and confusion as they retreated down the Han and Yangtze rivers. Amid such unsettled conditions, it was with relative ease that Chang pushed up the Yangtze and took, within the space of some two months, Huang-mei, Kuang-chi, Ch'i-chou, and Huang-chou. Chang halted briefly at Huang-chou, which fell on May 10, 1643, and occupying the prefectural government headquarters, proclaimed himself "Prince of the West" (Hsi wang). This step was taken thirteen days after Li Tzu-ch'eng had announced a princely title for himself at Hsiang-yang and Chang's move may have been a deliberate attempt to place himself on the same level with Li.

From Huang-chou, Chang turned northwestward to Ma-ch'eng, an area noted for its wealthy families. One source states that four of the most prominent local families each had between 3,000 and 4,000 underlings, slaves, servants, and hangers-on. Considerable unrest had been prevalent in the area for some time, and three local leaders, T'ang Chih, Chou Wen-chiang, and Li Jen-hui, had headed an uprising. T'ang and Chou were both members of the gentry, the latter being the holder of a *chu-sheng* degree; and Li seems to have been a servant of one of the wealthy families. The three leaders had accumulated a numerous following, 27,000 according to one source, and promptly joined forces with Chang when he appeared at Ma-ch'eng. With this considerable increment to his troop strength, it was possible for Chang to launch a campaign to capture the major prize in all Hukuang, the provincial capital of Wuchang.[52]

The authorities in Wuchang were quite aware of the threat posed to the city by Chang as soon as he had moved into Hukuang from Nan-chihli and had made some efforts to build up a defense force. Their efforts had to face formidable difficulties: many of the local offices were unfilled, funds were lacking, and the area had never really recovered from the turmoil produced when Tso Liang-yü passed through it. The financial problem was partially solved by resorting to the local district prince, the Prince of Ch'u, who was reputed to possess a fortune of 2,000,000 taels and who, after considerable pressure, made a modest contribution to support the recruiting of a defense force. Unfortunately, the sources turned to for raising the defense force were the various groups of refugee troops in the city. These men were veterans of several government armies, particularly that of Tso Liang-yü, which had broken apart in the fight against the rebels. Their presence in Wuchang certainly produced a great deal of unrest and the attempt to give them a useful function to perform was highly desirable. However, their demoralization and rootlessness made it impossible to turn them into an effective defense unit in the short time available, and indeed some of them may have had sympathies and pre-arranged ties with the rebels.

Moving southwestward from his highly profitable occupation of Ma-ch'eng, Chang pushed west along the northern bank of the Yangtze and seized Hanyang with virtually no resistance. At Hanyang, he paused in order to assemble his naval units and transport his army across the Yangtze for the first time in his long rebel career. The Wuchang authorities indirectly aided his plans by deciding to ignore the recommendation of one of the more astute officers who advocated defending the river bank and the islands in the Yangtze. Instead, a much more restricted defense posture was adopted which was based solely upon the walls of Wuchang itself. This policy was accepted partly because it was feared that the newly raised defense units would immediately desert if they were not carefully watched. Chang was permitted to cross the Yangtze with only slight opposition and promptly placed Wuchang under siege. The city's defenses rapidly fell apart and, except for a brief sortie led by one of the few responsible officers, very little fighting took place. The city fell on July 15, 1643 after some members of the newly recruited defense force opened two gates. Chang occupied his first provincial capital and opened the way for his first expansion south of the Yangtze.

The sources take particular pains to depict the horrors which ensued following the downfall of Wuchang. Thousands of people are said to have been massacred and other thousands drowned after being forced to jump into the Yangtze. One source even goes so far as to state that there was not a single inhabitant of the city who escaped death or some form of mutilation and that the fish in the river devoured so many corpses as to become unfit for food. On the other hand, it is stated that Chang contributed a considerable sum from the wealth he seized from the Prince of Ch'u to aid the starving refugees in the city. Undoubtedly a balanced view of Chang's actions in Wuchang would lie somewhere between the above extremes. Certainly there were atrocities, the treatment of the Prince of Ch'u being the prime example. Chang had the Prince brought before him and in a mocking interview, reminiscent of the similar one held with the Prince's distant cousin two years earlier in Hsiang-yang, Chang pronounced his imperial prisoner indeed stupid in being unable to utilize his great fortune to provide for a successful defense of Wuchang. Subsequently, the Prince was placed in a bamboo cage and drowned.

Chang's main interest at Wuchang was to advance his imperial ambitions by beginning the assembly of a bureaucracy and by using the city as a nucleus for a power center. In his capacity as "Prince of the West," he occupied the palace of the Prince of Ch'u and proclaimed Wuchang to be his capital under the new name of T'ien-shou. Furthermore, he announced that such offices as the Six Ministries and the Five Chief Military Commissions would be established for a central government and various appointments would be made to fill prefectural, subprefectural, and county offices in the area of eastern Hukuang over which he exercised some control. Actually only one appointment of a minister seems to have been made and that was to the Ministry of War which Chou Wen-chiang, the Ma-ch'eng *chu-sheng* who had joined Chang during the attack on the city, was appointed to head.

Other expected actions taken by Chang in the direction of forming a bureaucracy included the holding of an official examination and an order to various localities demanding that their records be submitted to Wuchang. After the official examinations, twenty examinees were awarded the *chin-shih* degree and forty-eight the two lower degrees. All of these new degree-holders were assigned offices at the prefectural, subprefectural, or county levels.

Chang's administration was obviously a very flimsy structure and had even less of a solid foundation than that of Li Tzu-ch'eng. Furthermore, it had hardly had a chance to begin operations before Chang decided to expand southward and his position at Wuchang was destroyed.

Chang's decision to push south from Wuchang resulted both from his ambition to increase the size of his power area and from the insecure military position he found himself occupying in the city. In the military sphere, dangers threatened him from two directions: Li Tzu-ch'eng in northwestern Hukuang and government forces, particularly the army of his old enemy, Tso Liang-yü, whose military capabilities had been partially restored, in northern Kiangsi. As seen earlier, Li had ambitions to expand into eastern Hukuang and a rebel leader allied to him had actually occupied Huang-chou and Hanyang briefly a short time prior to Chang's move into the area. Furthermore, Li had planned a campaign to take Wuchang and became quite upset when Chang seized the city before his own plans were put into operation. Thus, Li sent Chang a mock congratulatory message which pointed out that he had eliminated Lo Ju-ts'ai, Ko-kuo-yen, and Tso-chin-wang and that Chang's turn would soon come. Also, Li announced a reward of 1,000 taels of silver to anyone who would capture Chang. For his part, Chang attempted to placate his rival and dispatched some three hundred cavalrymen with valuable gifts for Li who, however, remained angry and detained Chang's troops. Finally, though, no clash between Chang and Li occurred. Instead of moving down the Han River, Li as we know, turned north and was no longer interested in competing with Chang for power in Hukuang.

Trouble from the government forces to the east did develop for Chang and an army under Regional Commander Fang Kuo-an advanced up the Yangtze.[53] By early September (1643), Fang's army was approaching Huang-chou after having destroyed all the local administrations and garrisons which Chang had set up in eastern Hukuang. Chang made no effort to defend his area against Fang, a failure which certainly does not speak very highly of his political and military sagacity. In fact, while Fang was advancing from the east, Chang was devoting all his attention to plans for launching a campaign to the south. This campaign was begun on September 7, 1643 when Chang departed from Wuchang at the head of a force consisting of both land and naval units. At Wuchang he left a garrison commanded by Chang Ch'i-tsai, one of his recently acquired subordinates and probably a native of the area. Apparently

Chang felt that Chang Ch'i-tsai would be able to defend Wuchang, but in fact the latter abandoned it eleven days later (September 18) as Fang Kuo-an was approaching the city. Thus, Chang's center at Wuchang came to an inglorious end after only a brief existence.

Displaying no real concern about the loss of Wuchang, Chang concentrated his efforts upon capturing Yo-chou, the first major objective of his southward push.[54] He met no really formidable resistance on the move south and occupied Yo-chou on the same day that his garrison was abandoning Wuchang (September 18).

From Yo-chou, Chang, after setting up a garrison and a local administration, continued south along the eastern shore of Tung-t'ing Lake to capture Hsiang-yin. Then, he ordered campaigns in two directions: one to push south to seize Changsha, the major city of central Hukuang; and the other, a naval expedition led by himself, to cross Tung-t'ing Lake and proceed up the Yangtze to occupy Ching-chou, the possession of which would protect his western flank and help secure his control of the entire Tung-t'ing Lake region. The latter expedition ended in complete failure. A violent storm was encountered on the lake and Chang ordered a return to Hsiang-yin after several boats had capsized. After reaching Hsiang-yin, he vented his anger upon the boats by ordering them burned, apparently because he considered them ill-omened. Following this holocaust, said to have been visible for miles, he marched south to join his other expeditionary force in the attack upon Changsha which fell, after minor resistance and the surrender of two of its defending officers, on October 7. Almost immediately, Chang continued his advance up the Hsiang River with Heng-chou, occupied on October 11, as the major objective. Following the Heng-chou victory, Chang returned with part of his army to Changsha.

Chang set about building Changsha into a new center to replace the lost Wuchang, and though he did not repeat all the actions expected of a dynastic founder, at least he ordered the holding of an official examination and the construction of a palace. Changsha became the focal point of his activities for three months and served as the base from which he attempted to expand his control in all directions.[55]

The first direction of expansion from Changsha was a continuation of the southward advance from Heng-chou, a campaign conducted entirely by lieutenants and not participated in by Chang himself. This southern thrust pushed along the Hsiang River to engulf Yung-chou and Ch'üan-chou across the border in Kwangsi. In addition, there were campaigns which went outside the Hsiang River Valley to Pao-ch'ing (west of Heng-chou) and to Lien-chou in northern Kwangtung. The occupation of

Lien-chou, though unimportant in itself and lasting only a few days, has a certain special interest in that it marks the southernmost point reached by the late Ming rebellions.

Another area into which Chang's forces expanded from Changsha was central Kiangsi, one of the key regions of Ming China, important culturally, economically, and politically. Chang himself apparently participated in only one of the Kiangsi campaigns and that extended just to P'ing-hsiang which is immediately over the border from Hukuang. However, his lieutenants succeeded in capturing for him at least seven of the important towns in central Kiangsi: Wan-ts'ai, Yüan-chou, Fu-chou, Chi-an, Chien-ch'ang, T'ai-ho, and Nan-li.

The third area of expansion from Changsha was to the northwest with Ch'ang-te as the major objective. This campaign was personally commanded by Chang who had a special reason for wanting to capture the area, it being the native prefecture of his former arch-enemy, Yang Ssu-ch'ang. During the campaign, Chang took particular pains to perform the desecration of the Yang family graves which has been referred to previously.

Looked at on a map, Chang's expansion from his Changsha center appears quite impressive, but it was destined to be ephemeral and collapsed as rapidly as it had been accomplished. Pressure against Chang's conquests was exerted from two principal directions: southward in Hukuang down the Yangtze and Hsiang Rivers from Wuchang and southward into central Kiangsi from Chiu-chiang. The latter pressure was directed mainly by Supreme Commander Lü Ta-ch'i and Tso Liang-yü, though Tso's troops, undisciplined as always, caused so much resentment among the local populace in central Kiangsi that they were soon recalled. Despite this difficulty, the pressure of the government forces did succeed in preventing the garrisons and local administrations loyal to Chang in central Kiangsi from functioning effectively. Probably there was not a single Kiangsi town which his troops were able to control for longer than a month without interruption and several of them changed hands at least four times within two months. In Hukuang, a government force, moving south from Wuchang, even managed to capture Yo-chou, killing the officials appointed by Chang and posing a direct threat to Changsha. A short time later, one of Chang's lieutenants did succeed in recapturing it.

Late in 1643, Chang began withdrawing his forces from the areas of expansion which were still in his control.[56] He first concentrated his recalled troops at Changsha and then abandoned that city on January 15, 1644 to move north, mainly by boat, to Yo-chou. This northward push produced great alarm in Wuchang, since it was assumed that his goal was to reconquer that area. As it turned out, he had quite a different

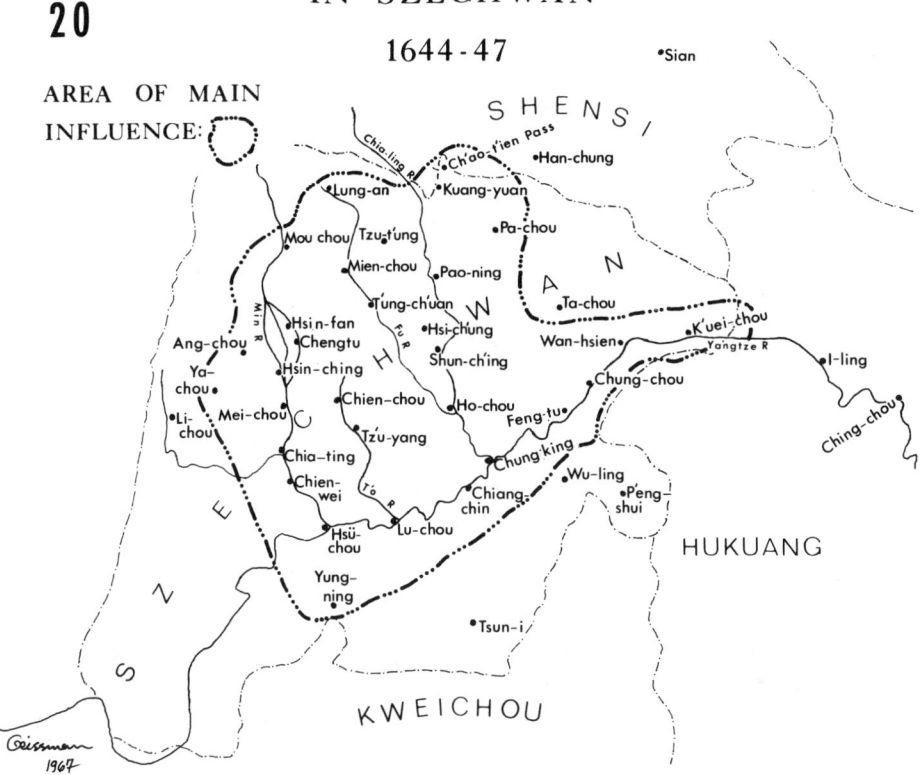

objective, and on February 2, 1644, he abandoned Yo-chou and moved northwestward up the Yangtze to Ching-chou.

Various government commanders subsequently re-occupied all the districts from which Chang had withdrawn[57] and the reports which they submitted made pleasant reading in Peking, even though the more astute officials in the capital must have realized that no decisive military victory had been achieved. Peking was now grasping at straws and one can hardly blame the hard-pressed court too severely for its misplaced generosity in bestowing upon Tso Liang-yü the grandiose honorific title of Junior Preceptor to the Heir Apparent as a reward for his anemic Hukuang victory.

Transfer of Chang Hsien-chung's Power Center to Szechwan

Chang Hsien-chung had several motives for abandoning Hukuang, though the dominant one seems to have been the virtual stalemate which had developed there between his own forces and those of the various government commanders. Neither side had ever pressed for a decisive military outcome and gingerly confined the conflict to peripheral clashes. And after a year of inconclusive maneuvering, Chang apparently decided that it was impossible for him to eliminate Tso Liang-yü and Supreme Commander Lü Ta-ch'i and that a move to an entirely different area must be made. Furthermore, his attempts to found a viable bureaucracy were even more pathetically ineffective than those of Li Tzu-ch'eng. He simply did not have the patience or political vision to build solid strength outward from a base area. Thus, there were no political successes to compensate for the military stalemate. Also, Chang was possibly personally unhappy about operating for the first time south of the Yangtze where he was a complete stranger and where even language differences must have intensified his feeling of isolation. In sum, finding himself faced with indifferent military and political prospects and possibly being personally dissatisfied with a quite novel locale, it is not surprising that Chang, given his past history of almost constant movement, should decide to abandon his Changsha base.

It is more difficult to account for Chang's specific choice of Szechwan as the area into which he would move once the decision had been made to leave Hukuang. There is some evidence to suggest that he was not unaware of the strategic deficiencies of Szechwan whose isolation made it unlikely that the province could ever be used as a springboard for attaining national power. In addition, Chang had subordinates who advised him to push east down the Yangtze into the wealthy area of southern Nan-chihli or to move south into Kwangtung whose northern border had been penetrated by his troops. There was also the possibility, though it does not seem to have ever been seriously considered, to push north along the Han River, a route taken by Chang several times in the past.

In the final analysis, the three possible alternatives to Szechwan must have appeared to Chang to possess notable disadvantages. Viewed ideally, southern Nan-chihli, of course, offered definite attractions. Being the economic and cultural key area of the Ming state as well as exerting great political power, the area obviously could serve as a base from which national power could be attained.* However, Chang did not possess the political talents needed to exploit effectively the possibilities of southern Nan-chihli. Furthermore, moving to Nan-chihli would have brought no relief from the military stalemate which he faced in Hukuang. Had Chang attempted to push east, Tso Liang-yü and Supreme Commander Lü Ta-ch'i would undoubtedly have been forced at last to present him with really determined opposition. The second alternative, Kwangtung, probably was never seriously considered by Chang. It was on the periphery of the Ming state, possessing a sub-culture and language of it own. It represented for Chang an unknown and almost foreign quantity. Finally, the possibility of a thrust up the Han River into the familiar areas of northern Hukuang and perhaps southern Honan had few attractions. The economic resources of the area had been rather thoroughly utilized by Li Tzu-ch'eng and few remained. Also, a move into the area would have brought Chang into conflict with remnant forces left behind as garrisons by Li. Thus, none of the three alternatives was selected by Chang and Szechwan was chosen instead.

Chang abandoned Yo-chou early in February of 1644 and pushed westward.[58] He did not even make the pretense of appointing officials to remain behind in the Hukuang area, and any of his officials who attempted to maintain themselves on their own were soon destroyed or captured by the official forces. However, the government commanders made no serious effort to pursue and attack Chang. They were probably heartily glad to see him move to another area where the responsibility of defeating him could be shifted to others. Thus, with no real threat of being attacked in the rear, Chang moved up the Yangtze and halted briefly at Ching-chou where an attempt against his life was made by a sing-song girl who formerly had been in the household of a district prince. The girl offered Chang a cup of poisoned wine, but was forced to take an initial drink of it herself and immediately fell dead.

Continuing up the Yangtze with large land forces on both the nor-

---

* For a brief treatment of the special importance of the lower Yangtze area during Ming times, see my article, "The Ming Dynasty Bureaucracy: Aspects of Background Forces," 354.

thern and southern banks and naval units on the river, Chang entered the pass leading into Szechwan* with virtually no opposition, a fact noted with loud laments in the sources which maintain that a relatively small force could have defended the pass successfully. Light opposition was met once he was in Szechwan, but the provincial Grand Coordinator, Ch'en Shih-ch'i, who had actually been relieved of his office but was still exercising its powers while awaiting the arrival of a successor, chose to remain at Chungking with the main portion of the official forces. Furthermore, the defense of the province was made more difficult by the demoralization which ensued following the arrival of news of the suicide of the Emperor and the fall of Peking to Li Tzu-ch'eng on April 25, 1644. These disasters made it apparent to the provincial authorities that no assistance could be expected from the outside.

The only major impediment Chang met during the initial stage of his invasion of Szechwan came in Wan County where heavy rains forced him to halt his advance for some two months. Following this delay, he resumed his march and after overcoming opposition at Chung-chou and Feng-tu without difficulty, pressed on toward his first principal target, Chungking.[59]

Chungking's main defensive outpost was at T'ung-lo Gorge, some fifteen miles down the Yangtze to the east, and upon reaching this point, Chang divided his army into two groups. One group, mainly naval in composition, was assigned to attack the gorge itself and the other group, composed entirely of land forces, was led by Chang in a bypass westward around Chungking to seize Chiang-chin, some fifty miles up the Yangtze. After capturing Chiang-chin, Chang's group reversed directions and approached Chungking from the west while the other force was pressing upon the city from the opposite direction after having overwhelmed T'ung-lo Gorge. Faced with attack from both sides, the defenses outside of Chungking collapsed and the city itself was besieged. The siege lasted only four days during which time the rebels succeeded in digging a hole in a relatively weak section of the wall. They filled the hole with gunpowder which was exploded by fire arrows. Following the explosion, the attackers stormed through the breach in the wall and the city was occupied on July 24, 1644.

Following the city's fall, Chang is said to have instituted a widespread massacre, and among his more prominent victims were Grand Coordinator Ch'en Shih-ch'i, the prefectural magistrate, the county magistrate, and the Prince of Jui who had taken refuge in Chungking after fleeing from Han-chung, Shensi, to escape the forces of Li Tzu-ch'eng. Chang, who seemed to take a special delight in tormenting district princes, chided

---

* See Map 20 for places involved in Chang's activities in Szechwan, 1644-47.

the Prince for being foolish enough to flee to Szechwan and boasted that his own strength exceeded that of Li Tzu-ch'eng.

Chang halted only briefly in Chungking and sought to aid his forthcoming push westward by announcing that no locality would be harmed if the people would seize the officials and surrender without resistance. Subsequently, Chang ordered that Chungking be held by a small garrison force commanded by a lieutenant, Liu T'ing-chi, and led the rest of his army toward the second major objective, Chengtu, the provincial capital in the heart of the fertile Red Basin.[60]

From Chungking, Chang pushed up the Yangtze to Lu-chou and then northwestward through such towns as Tz'u-yang and Chien-chou. A second force probably was sent north from Chungking along the Chia-ling River to Shun-ch'ing and then due west to Chengtu. No serious opposition was met until Chengtu itself was reached and even there the defense was ineffective. The Chengtu authorities had had some six months to organize resistance to Chang after learning of his incursion into Szechwan, but had failed miserably. The local district prince, the Prince of Shu, had hesitated for a considerable time to contribute funds for defense, citing the prohibitions against princes interfering in political matters and pointing out his family's long reputation for docility and respect for dynastic precedents. Eventually he was persuaded to contribute some funds, but few recruits proved to be available and the garrison was hopelessly outnumbered when Chang's army arrived. Even the city moat was allowed to remain dry and a project to bring in water was never successfully completed. Furthermore, something of a final blow to the morale of the defenders came in the attempted flight from the city of the Prince of Shu who wanted to take refuge in Yunnan and was prevented from doing so only at the last minute by the Regional Inspector.

Chang's army reached Chengtu early in September, 1644 and he attempted to negotiate the city's surrender. The attempt was adamantly rejected by the authorities who even executed the rebel envoys. Following the failure of negotiations, Chang attacked in full force, repeating the siege techniques he had utilized at Chungking by blowing up a section of the wall with gunpowder after holes had been dug in it. The city was occupied on September 9, 1644, and though the county magistrate was persuaded to surrender, most of the prominent officials either committed suicide or were killed. A special effort was made by Chang to induce the Regional Inspector, a fellow native of Shensi, to submit, but the effort ended in failure. As for the Prince of Shu, he joined several members of his household in drowning himself in a well.

Apparently from the very beginning of his Szechwan invasion, Chang had planned on occupying Chengtu for an extended period of time and using it as a base for establishing a government.⁶¹ Following his capture of the city, he began a series of campaigns which were destined to extend his control at least to some degree as far north as the Shensi border and as far east as Pa-chou.

Simultaneously with the campaigns to extend his area of control, Chang in Chengtu was attempting to establish an administration and provide himself with more of the formal trappings of power. Such offices as the Six Ministries and Grand Secretariat were set up, and Chang subsequently proclaimed himself Emperor of the "Great Western State" (Ta Hsi Kuo).⁶² The name of Chengtu was changed to "Western Capital" (Hsi-ching), the characters for Chang's personal name were ordered tabooed, and the various buildings making up the compound formerly occupied by the Prince of Shu were accorded imperial appelations. Thus, within less than a year after beginning his invasion of Szechwan, Chang had expanded his control over a considerable portion of the central section of the province and had launched his most ambitious effort to found a new dynasty. The abject failure of his imperial pretensions and his eventual fate will be dealt with in the next chapter.

Chapter V

The Collapse of the Rebellions (1644-47)

Retreat of Li Tzu-ch'eng from Peking to Sian

After making the patently false claim that he was departing from Peking* to crush Wu San-kuei, Li Tzu-ch'eng abandoned the city in the early morning hours of June 4, 1644. He did not retrace the northern route which had led him to the capital, and instead turned south-southwest, his objective being to enter Shansi via Ku Pass.¹ When he reached the outskirts of Peking, Li was attacked almost immediately by Wu and a series of running skirmishes ensued in which Li found himself at a decided disadvantage due in part to the fact that his troops were demoralized and were burdened with a large amount of booty from Peking which they were desperately trying to retain until they could reach safety. Exploiting the rebel weaknesses, Wu maintained heavy military pressure against his opponents, and Li's retreat turned into a virtual rout. As the situation deteriorated, rebel order disappeared and the troops began throwing away their booty in such a wholesale manner that the roads leading from Marco Polo Bridge near Peking to Ku-an are said to have been littered with abandoned weapons, women, silk cloth, and other valuables. Presented with such a golden opportunity to enrich themselves, Wu's soldiers temporarily interrupted their pursuit of the rebels and began collecting the abandoned loot. However, Wu was able to resume his attacks against Li after a short delay and was aided by local *ad hoc* groups who were anxious to rid the area of the rebels and to obtain a share of the rebel loot for themselves. Particularly telling blows were delivered against Li's disintegrating army at Ting-chou and Chen-ting. In the Ting-chou battle, several thousand rebels are said to have been killed, including such prominent leaders as Ku Ta-ch'eng and Tso Kuang-hsien, and more than 10,000 surrendered. During the Chen-ting engagement, Li himself was

---

* See Map 18 for places involved in Li's career which are mentioned in this chapter.

struck by an arrow and knocked from his horse. After this narrow escape, Li sought refuge in a nearby house only to have the neighborhood people set fire to it and force him to flee as rapidly as possible through the Ku Pass into Shansi. At this point, he gained a badly needed respite, for Wu continued the pursuit only up to the pass and then retraced his steps to Peking where he undoubtedly had many affairs to discuss with his Manchu allies.

Li's flight from Peking, and indeed all his moves subsequent to the crucial defeat at Shanhaikuan, were essentially automatic responses to a desperate situation and show little evidence of attempts to formulate positive policies beyond a vague conception of obtaining safety and regrouping his shattered forces at Sian. The abandonment of Peking was complete and no attempt was made to leave a garrison behind to hold it. As a result, the city remained without any regular authority for two days, that is, between Li's departure on June 4 and the arrival of the Manchus on June 6. Furthermore, Li was unable to take any effective action to preserve his authority in the newly submitted areas in Shantung or even in Honan and Hukuang, where his control had been erratic and vacillating, but in some regions had existed for two years.[2] In Shantung, his power was destroyed almost immediately after his flight from Peking, though local rebels, who had submitted to him and had been integrated to some extent into his administration, managed to hold out in remoter regions for a few months, continuing to use his reign period title and to give him formal recognition. Such remnant holdouts occupied no really important areas, were a passing phenomenon, and were not able to offer real resistance to the Manchus into whose orbit the province gradually slipped after the Southern Ming cause failed to rally firm support.

The disappearance of Li's authority in northern Hukuang and in Honan proceeded more slowly, but nevertheless the drift away from him was inexorable. Tso Liang-yü, in one of his last spurts of action, temporarily restored Ming control over Te-an Prefecture and Sui Subprefecture in northern Hukuang, and the Ming loyalist magistrate of Nan-yang Prefecture in southwestern Honan forced Li's officials to flee from the counties of Pi-yang, Wu-yang, and T'ung-po. However, Li's officials still managed to maintain themselves in the southwestern Honan localities of Teng Sub-prefecture, Nei-hsiang County, Che-ch'uan County, T'ang County, and Nan-chao County, and in such central Honan areas as Yü Subprefecture and Hsiang-ch'eng County. But the upholding of Li's authority in these areas was doomed and probably in no locality did it manage to survive longer than the winter of 1644.

The slipping away of Honan from Li's control produced as a side effect the destruction of Li Yen who was probably the ablest member of the gentry attracted to the rebel cause. As a native of Honan, Li Yen was particularly appalled at the collapse of rebel strength there and requested of Li Tzu-ch'eng that he be permitted to take 20,000 troops and restore control in Honan. This request aroused Li Tzu-ch'eng's suspicions and his fears were exploited by Niu Chin-hsing who had always been jealous of Li Yen and was afraid that his influence would come to dominate Li Tzu-ch'eng. Niu managed to convince Li Tzu-ch'eng that Li Yen was plotting to head a rebel movement of his own. No other prominent rebel leader was able to counteract Niu's influence, and it is particularly unfortunate that the influential Liu Tsung-min, who had always been friendly toward Li Yen, had not yet sufficiently recovered from serious wounds, received during the retreat from Shanhaikuan to Peking, to play his customary role as an adviser. Thus, Niu persuaded Li Tzu-ch'eng to have both Li Yen and his younger brother, Li Mou, executed. The loss of Li Yen was a particularly heavy blow to the rebel cause, removing as it did one of the most potent influences for moderation. His death intensified internal friction within the rebel leadership, Liu Tsung-min and Sung Hsien-ts'e in particular feeling strongly that Niu Chin-hsing had done serious harm to the rebel cause. However, it is highly doubtful that Li Yen could have halted or even delayed the rebel collapse even if he had managed to escape the fate which overtook him the summer of 1644.

While his position was collapsing in Shantung, Honan, and Hukuang, Li Tzu-ch'eng himself was continuing to lead his army in a retreat across Shansi which he had entered via Ku Pass. He pushed on to Yü-tz'u County and to T'ai-yüan where he paused briefly and left behind a garrison headed by the former officer of the Ming, Ch'en Yung-fu. By the time he had reached T'ai-yüan, Li had recovered somewhat and was attempting to stabilize the situation and bring about an end to the semi-panic which had seized his forces.

From T'ai-yüan, some of Li's units proceeded westward and crossed the Yellow River into northern Shensi. He himself probably turned southwestward to P'ing-yang and crossed the Yellow River to Han-ch'eng, Shensi. It was from this vicinity that he sought to restore his military momentum and direct operations in a quite widespread area.[3] To the north, his nephew, Li Kuo, attempted to insure rebel control in the old homeland of the rebellions (northern Shensi); in south-central Shensi a campaign against Han-chung was successful, bringing the last major urban area in the province under Li's control; and at T'ung Pass there was not only an effort to establish an effective defense posture, but also rebel forces were sent outside the pass to reinvigorate their cause in Honan.

Li's efforts in all these areas had some initial success, and in south-central Shensi, his commanders even attempted to push his area of control into northern Szechwan, though in making this move they came into conflict with the interests of Chang Hsien-chung and were soon forced to retreat. The final area in which Li launched an attack was Yün-yang in extreme northwestern Hukuang. Here, his old enemy, Wang Kuang-en, who had frustrated his conquest attempts so often before, held firmly and the rebel offensive was defeated.

Throughout the summer of 1644, the Manchus consolidated their control in Pei-chihli and began to extend into Shansi, winning the adherence of such provincial and local officers and commanders as T'ang T'ung who had served both the Ming and Li Tzu-ch'eng.[4] Also, in August, 1644, Prince Dorgun announced the abolition of all the special land taxes, an action which could not fail to have considerable popular appeal.

By the fall of 1644, Manchu strength and prestige were sufficiently strong to launch a major offensive in Shansi, and T'ai-yüan was captured virtually without resistance after Li Tzu-ch'eng's garrison commander fled. Following this victory, a two-pronged assault against Li's main stronghold in Shensi was planned: one force would be dispatched from Honan against T'ung Pass and another would be sent across the Yellow River into northern Shensi and subsequently sweep south.[5] This pincer movement was started early in 1645 when Prince Dodo and Wu San-kuei crossed the Yellow River in Meng County, Honan, and pushed to T'ung Pass. And at approximately the same time, Prince Ajige crossed from Shansi into Shensi and attacked Yenan which was unsuccessfully defended by Li Kuo. The crucial battle occurred at T'ung Pass where Li Tzu-ch'eng's commander, Ma Shih-yao, put up a spirited defense. The battle raged for three days and apparently resulted in considerable casualties occurring on both sides, though one cannot take seriously the general figure of 200,000 fatalities cited in one of the sources. In the end, the rebel efforts were in vain and they retreated up the Wei River following the battlefield death of their commander. At the same time, Prince Ajige triumphed over Li Kuo in Yenan and launched his sweep south.

The defeats of the rebels at T'ung Pass and in the north of Shensi delivered the final blows which made recovery by Li Tzu-ch'eng impossible, though his chances for a comeback even before these most recent reverses were already slim. Following the defeats, he could only revert to the unplanned and desperate wanderings which had been characteristic of his earlier years.

Final Months of Li Tzu-ch'eng

Following the rebel defeats at T'ung Pass and Yenan, Li and his surviving lieutenants collected their decimated forces for a brief sojourn in Sian where the troops were invited to take whatever they liked from the stores of valuables which had been accumulated there. Then the city was abandoned after Li had ordered a subordinate, T'ien Chien-hsiu, to burn it. T'ien did not carry out the orders for destruction for both humanitarian and practical reasons, arguing that the people of the city had already suffered enough horrors and also that an undestroyed city would tempt the Sino-Manchu opponents of the rebels to linger in it and thus delay their pursuit.

Li Tzu-ch'eng's retreat route from Sian led him southeast through Lan-t'ien County and Shang Subprefecture to Wu Pass and on into Honan.[6] Had the time been four or five years earlier, he would undoubtedly have taken refuge in the familiar Shensi-Honan-Hukuang border area where so many rebels, including Li himself, previously had sought safety. Now, his following was still too large to be supplied in such a remote area, and there was not any continuing collapsing situation to be taken advantage of after recuperation, for it must have been apparent that Manchu power was on the verge of increased consolidation and strength. Thus, Li did not even pause in the Shensi-Honan-Hukuang border area, but instead crossed southwestern Honan and proceeded on into Hukuang.

Passing by Hsiang-yang, where in happier days almost three years earlier he had taken the first tentative steps toward establishing an administration of his own, Li continued on down the Han Valley and probably paused for several weeks in the Wuchang area before crossing the Yangtze and proceeding on to T'ung-ch'eng in extreme eastern Hukuang near the Kiangsi border. According to an alternative account, he went first to Ch'en Prefecture, south of the Yangtze in west central Hukuang, where rebel headquarters were established. When supply problems arose there, Li left Li Kuo in command of the main camp and himself led a small band eastward to T'ung-ch'eng. Probably this confusion as to what Li's movements actually were arose from the fact that his army disintegrated following the flight from Sian and scattered out to various places. It is certain that at one point a portion of his forces did go to Ch'en Prefecture, but it is doubtful if Li himself was with this group. Also, it is probably untrue that Li ever seriously considered going to Szechwan and joining Chang Hsien-chung, as is stated in some of the sources.

The final fate of Li Tzu-ch'eng is shrouded in considerable uncertainty.[7] Perhaps the *Ch'ing Shih-lu* contains the most authoritative account, as it is based on a memorial by Prince Ajige who participated in the campaign against him following his retreat from Sian. The memorial states that the Sino-Manchu army pursued the fleeing rebels down the Han Valley, defeating them several times enroute. Finally, Li, with only some twenty followers remaining with him, took refuge on Mt. Chiu-kung in extreme eastern Hukuang on the Kiangsi border. There he was surrounded by a group of enraged peasants and finding himself on the point of being overwhelmed, he hanged himself. However, by the time the Manchu forces obtained possession of the corpse, it was so decayed that recognition was impossible even though Li's wife, concubines, and two relatives had been captured and could have been used as witnesses.

Other accounts do not mention Li's having committed suicide, but maintain that he was trapped in muddy terrain by angry peasants and beaten to death with hoes.* While this action was taking place, the peasants had no idea that they were attacking Li Tzu-ch'eng, and it was only after he had been killed that they suspected who he was by his gold seal, fine clothes, and missing left eye. The peasants took Li's body to the Southern Ming Supreme Commander, Ho T'eng-chiao, who decapitated it. Subsequently, Li Kuo obtained the major portion of Li's corpse (presumably during the negotiations for his surrender to the Southern Ming) and gave it an elaborate burial after providing it with a straw head and jade cap.

A third account of Li's death, contained in the *Yen-sui-chen chih*, states simply that after Li and his small band succeeded in escaping from the peasants on Mt. Chiu-kung, his group scattered into remote areas and his eventual fate is unknown.

Considering all the above evidence, it is probable that Li, after fleeing down the Han Valley and crossing the Yangtze, finally sought refuge on Mt. Chiu-kung and was killed there by a peasant band some time during the early summer of 1645.

Apparently the only one of Li Tzu-ch'eng's principal subordinates to survive him and retain a certain importance was his nephew, Li Kuo, who was chosen to lead the small remnant rebel group which still remained together as a unit following the death of Li himself. Li Kuo proceeded to arrange a formal submission to the Southern Ming and was granted a title of nobility by the Ming Pretender, the Prince of T'ang.

The fates of most of Li Tzu-ch'eng's other lieutenants are unknown, their names simply disappearing from history. It does seem probable, though, that his longstanding favorite, Liu Tsung-min, was captured and killed by the Sino-Manchu force during the retreat down the Han Valley. Also, it seems definite that T'ien Chien-hsiu, one of the most moderate of the rebel leaders, succeeded in surrendering to the Manchus.

---

* The place of his death is given as either Mt. Chiu-kung or Mt. Lo-kung. Lo-kung is said by one source to be an alternate name for Chiu-kung, but no evidence can be produced to prove this. The name "Lo-kung" does not appear in *Chung-kuo ku-chin ti-ming ta tzu-tien*.

Chang Hsien-chung and the Establishment of a Rebel Regime at Chengtu

Following his capture of Chengtu* on September 9, 1644, Chang proclaimed the formation of a "Great Western State" with the reign title of Ta-shun.** It seems that he did not formally ascend the imperial throne until some three months later on December 4, though he did set about establishing and immediately filling such offices as the Prime Ministry of the Left, Prime Ministry of the Right, the Grand Secretariat, and the Six Ministries, not waiting for his assumption of the imperial position.[8] The persons selected to fill these various offices were mostly native Szechwanese who had had only a brief relationship with Chang, and in at least two instances outright force was applied to secure their services for the rebel regime. The cases of enforced service involved Chiang Ting-chen, a *chin-shih* and a Szechwanese, who was coerced into allowing himself to be named Minister of Rites, and Kung Wan-ching, also a *chin-shih* and a Szechwanese, who was forced to accept the post of Minister of War. Chiang Ting-chen's tenure in office as Minister of Rites was destined to be brief, for he took the earliest opportunity to return home where he proceeded to burn himself and his entire family to death, an act which so enraged Chang that he ordered the ashes from the conflagration thrown into a nearby river.

Actually, Chang's civil bureaucracy never succeeded in wielding real power and remained only semi-functional at best. Wang Chao-ling was its only member who was truly important and his status was based upon his well-established personal relationship with Chang. A member of a Nan-chihli gentry family, Wang had been captured by Chang's group some years previously and came to exert great influence over his master. As will be seen subsequently, Wang's influence was decidedly unfortunate, pushing Chang toward greater extremes of violence, instead of restraining him.

There is no detailed information concerning appointments to lesser offices either for the central government or at lower levels. It is clear, though, that some effort was made to establish county administrations

---

* See Map 20 for places involved in Chang's career in Szechwan, 1644-47.
** Two of the sources, *MCNL* 12/37a and *PKC* 12/8a, give the reign period's name as I-wu, rather than Ta-shun.

loyal to the Chengtu regime. These local governments were hastily constructed, with officials being appointed to serve in them by uneducated rebel commanders whose selections probably were made more or less at random from among the local people who attached themselves to the rebel cause. Furthermore, no real attempt was made subsequently to achieve a systematic integration of the local administrations with the central government, a failure which was particularly unfortunate and was one of the most important reasons for the collapse of Chang's Szechwan regime.

Given the relative impotence of his civil administration on both local and central government levels, it is obvious that Chang's authority was still based mainly on his military forces, and it was to them that he continued to give most of his attention.[9] In the first place, he incorporated into his army many Szechwanese troops, totalling, according to one source, 140,000 men. Also, he sought to organize his forces in a more rational fashion, and is said to have provided for divisions into 120 camps. It should be noted that quite unlike the civil administration, where new adherents predominated, the upper echelons of command in the army remained in the firm control of those who had had long experience in the rebel movement. Four commanders, Sun K'o-wang, Liu Wen-hsiu, Li Ting-kuo, and Ai Neng-ch'i, all of whom had been associated with Chang since the early years of his rebellion, were singled out for posts of special importance. Sun was named "General who Pacifies the East" (P'ing-tung chiang-chün), with command over nineteen camps; Liu "General who Soothes the South" (Fu-nan chiang-chün), with fifteen camps; Li "General who Bestows Peace upon the West" (An-hsi chiang-chün), with sixteen camps; and Ai "General who Stabilizes the North" (Ting-pei chiang-chün), with twenty camps. The bestowal of these grandiose military titles not only obviously carried with it the implication of nation-wide conquest, but according to a Jesuit account, the spheres of projected conquest included foreign areas as well.[10] Sun was responsible for conquering Shantung, Pei-chihli, the eastern section of Mongolia, Korea, and Japan; Liu for Nan-chihli, Chekiang, Fukien, Kiangsi, Hukuang, Kwangsi, Kweichow, Yunnan, Indo-China, and the Philippines; Li for Shansi, Shensi, and the western section of Mongolia: and Ai for Honan and the northern section of Mongolia. The titles were conferred on the four rebel commanders after each had drawn lots to determine which particular title should be his, and Chang Hsien-chung declared the results to be precisely as he had thought they should be, a fortunate conjunction which he believed foretold success for his plans. Subsequently, Chang is said to have delivered an impassioned speech which was so eloquent that even the recalcitrant civil officials, against their own wills, found themselves believing that he would indeed succeed.

Other actions taken by Chang, more or less appropriate for a dynasty founder, included the coining of money, the installation of an Empress, the holding of an official examination, the attempt to win the support of non-Chinese elements, and the establishment of a municipal administration for Chengtu.[11] Bronze for coinage was obtained from melting down religious figures in Chengtu and nearby temples as well as vessels seized in the residence of the Prince of Shu. The money is described as well minted and was in completely traditional style, having a hole in the middle and bearing the inscription "Ta-shun t'ung-pao."* For his Empress, Chang chose a lady from one of the top Szechwan families whose father, Ch'en Yen, had served as Grand Secretary from 1640 to 1644 and had been killed by Li Tzu-ch'eng. Her reception in Chengtu was the occasion for an elaborate ceremony and included, according to one source, a specially constructed and gaily decorated temporary bridge which was built over the wall and designed to enable her to enter the city without passing through one of the ordinary gates. The official examination was held for the selection of *chih-shih*, and 120 candidates are said to have succeeded in obtaining the degree. There is considerable dispute concerning the name of the candidate who was awarded first place in the examination, but according to one source it was Kung Chi-min who was selected because Chang liked his given name, "Aiding-the-people." The support of non-Chinese elements was especially important for Chang, since large sections of the more remote areas of Szechwan were still dominated by them in Ming times, and the system of native officials (T'u-ssu) was a well-recognized part of local control. Chang is said to have followed the long-established practice of awarding golden seals, inscribed with titles and ranks, to native officials who consented to surrender. His surrender appeal is said to have had some success, though it failed to attract the most famous native official of all, the heroine Ch'in Liang-yü, who was able to maintain control over her area in extreme eastern Szechwan south of the Yangtze. Finally, in establishing a municipal administration for Chengtu, Chang showed particular interest in turning the city into a suitable military base, in achieving firm local control, and in discovering potential opposition. There were put into force such measures as broadening the city streets to allow for the easy movement of troops, the establishment of a strict *pao-chia* system to make neighbors responsible for one anothers' actions, and the development of a spy system. Movement out of and into the city was carefully regulated, with guards at the gates

---

* A reproduction of one of the coins is contained in *MMNM* 6; and Donnithorne, in "The Golden Age and the Dark Age in Szechwan," 162, states that the coins are still to be found in Szechwan.

obtaining names and occupations of all persons leaving the city, as well as dates of their return. Strict punishment was meted out if any of this information proved to be false.

Amid all the many responsibilities in connection with founding an administration at Chengtu, Chang also found time for a private activity—the establishment of a relationship with two Jesuit fathers, Gabriel de Magalhaens and Louis Buglio, who had been engaged in missionary work in Szechwan for some years.* The relationship between Chang and the fathers is somewhat more than an historical curiosity. Most importantly, it provides a non-Chinese view of Chang, and even though such a view is unfortunately not extensively recounted and does not differ fundamentally from the traditional Chinese assessment of him, it is nevertheless of considerable value.

It is difficult to make any general estimate of Chang's initial efforts at establishing an administration, particularly in view of the general prejudice against him in the sources. Certainly his government had very basic weaknesses and, as will be seen, was ill-prepared to meet subsequent challenges. However, it was hardly as dismal a failure as depicted in the traditional accounts, and the only known surviving original official pronouncement of his government indicates a considerable measure of balance and restraint, as can be seen in the following translation:

This administration is just and law-abiding. Its commands and ordinances are rigid. Civilians and military personnel emphatically are expected to hold to their respective positions and be peaceful toward one another. There shall definitely be no falsehood of any kind. . . . Several ordinances are made as listed below, and if there is anyone who violates them, the law shall be carried out in accordance with the stipulations. It is specifically announced:
(1) It is not allowed to raise an army on one's own initiative without receiving clear authorization from this administration. People of any locality are allowed to detain and deliver to the military courts those who disturb or do damage to that locality so that the law may be carried out. If lawlessness is

---

* The two principal sources for the relationship between Chang and Fathers de Magalhaens and Buglio are sections from the following works: Martin Martini, S.J., *Bellum Tartaricum*, and Thomas Dunin Spot, S.J., "Collectanea Historiae Sinensis." The sections which deal with Chang and the Jesuit fathers in both works are based on an original account by Father de Magalhaens entitled "Relacao das tyranias obradas por Cang-hien chungo." This work was never published and the manuscript was brought from China to Europe by Father Martin Martini in the 1650's. The manuscript was supposed to have been deposited in the archives of the Society of Jesus in Rome. However, a search of the archives, made in 1951, failed to discover it and it is presumed to be lost. The work by Dunin Spot also exists only in manuscript in the archives of the Society of Jesus. The authorities of the archives were kind enough to supply the author with a microfilm of that portion of the work which is based on the original account by Father de Magalhaens.

hidden with connivance and not reported to the authorities, the people of that locality themselves shall be held guilty.
(2) It is not alowed to loiter in or around the government buildings. Nor are any of the government employees, while at leisure, allowed to use, without official sanction, the horses and the soldiers at the post stations. Once discovered, the violators shall be tied up and flogged.
(3) It is not allowed for the military officers in charge of local defense to accept lawsuits brought in by the people. Violators shall be impeached and prosecuted.
(4) It is not allowed to disturb or do damage to any locality by falsely pretending to act in the name of the Heavenly Troops. Officials in charge of local affairs shall investigate and make reports about this kind of thing, upon receipt of which the authorities will prosecute and issue a warning to the public.
(5) It is not allowed to let hoodlums come in the camp and submit groundless suits against innocent people. Violators shall be tied up and flogged.
(6) It is not allowed for either civil or military officers in charge of [characters missing] to take women of this area for wives and concubines. If this ordinance is violated, prosecution and investigation shall be pursued.[12]

Ta-shun 2nd Year 3rd Month
March/April, 1645

Furthermore, a Jesuit source indicates a generally favorable initial reception for Chang's government, stating:

... he began his rule with such liberality, justice, and magnificence by which he captivated all hearts, that many mandarins, famous both in civic or in military affairs whom fear was keeping concealed, left their hideouts and flew to his side. And surely he was so equipped by nature with such virtues that had not clemency been wanting and more than beastly savagery and inhuman cruelty taken its place in his soul, he had seemed made king by nature.[13]

Expansion of Chang's Area of Control in Szechwan

In September, 1644 when Chengtu fell to Chang Hsien-chung, he exercised effective control over only a small portion of the province, mainly the invasion route between Chungking and Chengtu. There is not even any definite evidence that he left substantial garrisons along the Yangtze between Chungking and the Hukuang border, the route which he took when he first moved into Szechwan. Thus, his control over the wilder eastern section of the province was vaguely exercised and was more negative than positive.

Following his capture of Chengtu, Chang began making more systematic efforts to extend his area of control, using Chengtu as the focal point.[14] The sequence of events in connection with this expansion is far from clear, due undoubtedly to the fact that the Ming administration in Szechwan had broken down and only scanty records were kept on which subsequent historical accounts could be based. It seems certain that the initial campaigns were mainly north and northeast from Chengtu, toward the Shensi border, with Chang's four chief lieutenants, Li Ting-kuo, Ai Neng-ch'i, Liu Wen-hsiu, and Sun K'o-wang, playing the leading role in their conduct. This north-northeastward thrust was dictated by both economic and strategic reasons, part of the area being quite well developed as a center of agricultural production and the remainder, that portion lying nearest the Shensi border, being the region through which an outside thrust against Szechwan most probably would come.

Chang's opponents in this expansion from Chengtu were local bandits, remnant Ming forces, and troops attached to the cause of Li Tzu-ch'eng under the command of Ma K'o. Ma had been active in northern Szechwan for some time and represented a southward thrust from Li's main power center in Shensi. However, the deterioration in Li's fortunes following the decisive battle of Shanhaikuan made it impossible for Ma to maintain himself in Szechwan, although he did have some initial success against Chang's armies. By late 1644, he had been compelled to retreat across the border into Shensi. The local bandit gangs, known as the Yao-Huang group which operated mainly in the northeastern section of the province, were not formidable foes and Chang soon reached an accommodation with them. The remnant Ming forces, also, could offer little effective opposition initially to Chang, and were thrust beyond the edges of his sphere of control. Generally speaking, then, Chang experienced little difficulty in the northern campaigns of expansion, and seems to have used with considerable success the technique he had employed during earlier campaigns in Szechwan: promising not to harm communities in exchange for their voluntary submission.

Chang's personal role in the northern campaigns seems to have been relatively restricted, and he is known to have participated in only two: the attack on Ma K'o at Mien-chou during the fall of 1644 and the unsuccessful attempt to take Han-chung in southern Shensi during the summer of 1645. The attack on Han-chung was one of the most ambitious campaigns ever launched by Chang and probably more than 100,000 men were involved in it. Its failure was an important milestone in the beginning of Chang's decline.

Following the campaigns to the north and northeast, there were less ambitious thrusts toward the west and south from Chengtu,[15] and by early 1645, Chang's area of control had reached its ultimate extent, making it possible to say that some degree of authority was exercised over most of the economically significant and militarily strategic areas of the province (see Map 20). The wilder areas of the northeast, southeast, south, and west were completely outside of Chang's control, and it was here that opposition to his regime could take root.

Development of Opposition to Chang in Szechwan

Opposition to Chang Hsien-chung in Szechwan had to develop almost entirely from sources within the province, since conditions prevailing in other sections of the country generally precluded the dispatch of forces from the outside. The Southern Ming regime at Nanking did name the ex-Grand Secretary Wang Ying-hsiung to the position of Supreme Commander and placed him in charge of military affairs in Hukuang, Szechwan, Kweichow, and Yunnan, ordering him to put special emphasis on restoring Szechwan to Ming control. In carrying out these instructions, Wang proceeded to Tsun-i in extreme southern Szechwan, an area which never came under Chang's control, and established headquarters from which he directed an ineffectual campaign against the Chengtu-based rebel regime. Wang depended almost entirely on forces raised locally in Szechwan, since the Southern Ming Nanking government had more than it could do in attempting to resist the southward thrust of the Manchus, and no troops could be spared for faraway west China. Indeed, the Nanking regime was destroyed in June, 1645 when the city fell to the Manchus and the Hung-kuang Pretender was subsequently captured and executed. The successor to the Hung-kuang Pretender, the Prince of T'ang, set up in Fukien, could do even less about the situation in Szechwan, though he did go through the formality of making a few appointments for the province.

As for Manchu opposition to Chang, because of troop limitations and the enormous geographical area involved, Szechwan could not be reached until the latter part of 1646. Thus, for more than two years, Chang had to face only local Szechwan opponents.[16]

The leading foes of Chang in Szechwan were mostly surviving Ming military officers or civil officials who had succeeded in escaping death or capture during the rebel invasion. Some of them had managed to preserve a few of their original forces and had withdrawn to more remote areas until they were able to gain wider support and strengthen their forces with new recruits. In theory, all these anti-Chang leaders were Ming loyalists and thus subject to the authority of Supreme Commander Wang Ying-hsiung in Tsun-i. However, the position of Supreme Commander Wang was largely nominal, and the supposedly pro-Ming leaders in Szechwan in reality functioned essentially as warlords who built up followings on their own initiative and operated more or less independently. The general principle under which all the anti-Chang leaders functioned was to begin on the periphery of Chang's area of power and gradually move toward the center as his regime progressively collapsed under the weight of problems which it could not solve.

The single most successful anti-Chang leader was Local Commander Tseng Ying who at the time of the rebel invasion was in command of a small force near K'uei-chou in extreme eastern Szechwan. Fleeing from K'uei-chou, Tseng established himself in the P'eng-shui and Wu-ling districts of the southeastern section of the province, and in this area, entirely free of Chang's influence, Tseng proceeded to build up a considerable force.

By the spring of 1645, Tseng was strong enough to attack and capture Chungking itself, the main rebel base in central Szechwan. The loss of such an important position was a serious matter, and when the news arrived in Chengtu that his garrison had been forced to abandon Chungking, Chang took quick action to recover the city by sending Liu Wen-hsiu, one of his four favorite lieutenants, to attack Tseng Ying. The rebel army, said to have numbered 30,000, advanced southeastward from Chengtu to Ho-chou where it was divided to attack Chungking with both land and naval forces. Tseng, after arranging for subordinates to meet this two-pronged attack, personally led a small force in a secret march around the rebels and attacked them from the rear. The rebel force suffered a severe defeat and forthwith retreated back to Chengtu. Chang, displaying the familiar rebel weaknesses of lack of persistence and failure to realize the necessity for obtaining an unchallenged position in a stable base, made no further efforts to recapture Chungking and thus his authority over most of eastern and central Szechwan was eliminated less than a year after it had been originally established. On his part, Tseng Ying made no real effort to extend his power westward from Chungking, being content with possibilities opened up for him in his small area of power. Cooperating with local members of the gentry, he became quite wealthy and played politics at the Southern Ming court so successfully that he was awarded the title of "Marquis who Pacifies Rebels" (P'ing-k'ou hou) by the Prince of T'ang. Ironically enough, his final fate was death at the hands of forces led by his old opponent, Liu Wen-hsiu, who attacked Chungking shortly after Chang Hsien-chung had been killed.

After Tseng Ying, the second most important leader of forces opposing Chang was Yang Chan, a native Szechwanese officer who held a military degree and who had long been active in the campaigns to suppress the rebels, having served under Yang Ssu-ch'ang and also having participated in the unsuccessful defense of Chengtu against Chang. Following the fall of Chengtu, some 2,000 troops fled and established themselves temporarily at Hsin-ching where they were joined by Yang Chan who succeeded in escaping from Chengtu after having been held briefly as a prisoner by the rebels. Assuming command of the remnant Ming force, Yang realized that it would be impossible to maintain a position so close to Chengtu, and in several stages moved south to Hsü-chou on the Yangtze. Early in 1645, Chang's lieutenant, Sun K'o-wang, pushed southward from Chengtu, forcing Yang to retreat south of the Yangtze to Yung-ning. Even this relatively remote area could not be held against the rebels, and after enduring great hardships, Yang eventually succeeded in reaching safety at Supreme Commander Wang Ying-hsiung's headquarters in Tsun-i.

Later in 1645, with the recession of Chang's power, Yang Chan was able to reoccupy Yung-ning, and beginning in early 1646, with the accelerating collapse of Chang's power at Chengtu, Yang moved back up the Min Valley, assuming control over such places as Chia-ting, Mei-chou, Ya-chou, and Ang-chou. Later, it was Yang who succeeded in restoring formal Ming authority over Chengtu itself after the city had been abandoned by Chang.

There were many minor leaders opposing Chang Hsien-chung, and the entire scope of the operations conducted by these men presents a very confused picture in the sources. Among these secondary figures, three seem to stand out to a degree which makes them worthy of mention: Wang Hsiang, Ts'ao Hsün, and Chu Hua-lung. Wang operated almost entirely in the south and was the main military support of Supreme Commander Wang Ying-hsiung. Ts'ao Hsün, like Yang Chan, was captured following the rebel victory at Chengtu, and joined with Yang in a successful escape. Following the escape, Ts'ao and Yang cooperated briefly, but after Yang's move south, Ts'ao pushed westward and established himself in the area of Li-chou from which base he launched several partly successful attacks upon the rebel-held districts to the east. Finally, Chu Hua-lung operated along the northwestern fringes of Chang's area of influence, destroying rebel control over Mou-chou and Lung-an only a few months after it had been asserted. Late in 1645, Chu made the astute move of coming to an agreement with the Manchus who had established themselves in Shensi upon the abandonment of the province by Li Tzu-ch'eng.

Summing up the opposition to Chang, it can be said that none of his rivals ever succeeded in posing a really serious direct military threat to him. Indeed, none ever attempted to launch a frontal attack against his main base at Chengtu. However, Chang's opponents did manage to keep the Szechwan situation in continual imbalance, hacking away, month after month, at the periphery of his domain. The fluid military conditions combined with and reinforced Chang's political ineptitude in bringing about the failure of his attempt to establish a viable regime at Chengtu.

Adoption of Terroristic Policies by Chang's Chengtu Regime

Earlier, when considering the establishment of Chang's regime in Chengtu, we noted the Jesuit contention that during an initial period there was considerable support for the new administration. Subsequently, however, circumstances developed which swept away all the indications of success and demonstrated in a glaring fashion Chang's political ineptitude, causing him to throw any attempt at moderation to the winds and adopt policies based mainly upon sheer terror and force.[17] Such brutal policies had the predictable effect of producing increased opposition so that a vicious cycle resulted with an intensification of terror being made necessary. Inexorably, the end product of this progression of events was the complete failure of the Chengtu regime.

The most apparent reason for the Chengtu failure was Chang's personal deficiency in leadership: he could never successfully make the transition from the roving plunderer of the earlier years to the founder of a stable government. He simply did not possess the steadfastness of purpose or the moderation required for such a transition. Nor did he have anything more than a vague understanding of the values which a dynasty founder had to subscribe to in the traditional Chinese context.

Specific events occurred which exacerbated Chang's leadership deficiencies, making the collapse of the Chengtu regime more certain and speeding up the process. Undoubtedly the most serious development which produced violent reactions on Chang's part was the emergence and increase of the armed opposition to his rule. In addition, Chang was greatly angered by the failure of the army to capture Han-chung, Shensi during the summer of 1645. The attack was against remnant forces of Li Tzu-ch'eng, plus other local groups, and success would have meant the extension of Chang's power to include the most important urban center of sorthern Shensi. Not only did the attack fail after a short siege, but also a large body of Chang's Szechwanese troops, said by one source to have numbered 40,000, defected to the enemy.

Other incidents which increased Chang's disposition toward violence included an assassination attempt and secret efforts by a group of prominent Chengtu citizens to persuade Li Tzu-ch'eng to invade Szechwan and crush Chang. The latter incident occurred in late 1644 when Li still held tenuous power in Shensi. The plot failed when the message to Li was intercepted by Chang's border guards in northern Szechwan.

It is most difficult to arrive at any balanced picture of the specific manifestations of the terroristic policies inaugurated by Chang, because of the prejudice of the sources against him. Indeed, most of the sources fairly seem to vie with one another in piling gore on gore, and as a result, Chang emerges as an example *par excellence* of ruthlessness and savagery. Many of the atrocity stories are undoubtedly based on nothing more than legends which grew up about Chang after his death, as is shown in the following rather extreme example from the *Shu pi*.[18] According to the *Shu pi* account, once when he was ill, Chang promised that if he recovered, he would offer two "heavenly candles" as a sacrifice. At the time that he first spoke of such an offering, no one understood what he meant by "heavenly candles." When he did recover, he ordered the small bound feet of many women cut off and placed in two piles, and since the feet of one of his own concubines were unusually small, he had them severed and placed on top of each pile. Then, oil was poured on and both piles set afire in fulfillment of his promise to offer two "heavenly candles."

There are many other examples of similar horror stories, so that a superficial view of Chang's Chengtu regime makes it emerge as a series of senseless slaughters. Actually, as has been pointed out, there are reasons for the terroristic brutalities which make some sense especially when one considers the limitations of Chang's background. Furthermore, there seem to have been two more or less logical stages in the formulation and application of the terror policy. The first stage occupied the period when Chang was employing terror as a means of consolidating his control and thus was somewhat moderate. The second stage began after Chang decided to abandon Szechwan and determined to make the province valueless to anyone else by means of systematic destruction.

During the initial stage of restricted terror, Chang made some effort at rational control by establishing a spy system to ferret out possible threats and sought to make the *pao-chia* institution of mutual responsibility a real deterrent to the arising of opposition. Terror was directed mainly against groups that might be expected to furnish leaders opposing the Chengtu regime. Naturally the gentry was particularly suspect, and Chang devised an especially ingenious plan to strike such a telling blow against them that they would be incapable of plotting to destroy him. The incident is described by Martini as follows:

[Chang] called all the students of the country to be examined for their degrees, promising to give those honours to whomsoever should deserve them best, and the Chinese are so bewitched with the desire for these dignities that they did not conceive the perfidious strategem of the tyrant. There appeared therefore in the public hall deputed for that ceremony about eighteen thousand persons all of which he commanded his soldiers to massacre most barbarously, saying that these were the people who by their cavilling sophisms solicited the people to rebellion.[19]

There are other indications of the violent dislike Chang harbored against the gentry. For example, once he proclaimed that he killed only the officials, including their wives, children, relatives, friends, and connections, and not the common people. He went on to claim that the oppression of the officials was so all-pervasive that even dogs and chickens had not escaped it. Since the officials had been guilty of slaughtering and oppressing people, they could not object now that they were meeting their own fate at his hands. Also, he is said to have ordered the execution of one of his chief officials because he was infuriated at the sight of the grand mansion owned by his family.

Subsequently, Chang directed violence against other groups considered dangerous, such as diviners, physicians, and Buddhist monks. A thousand of the latter were killed in a single temple when it was discovered that they had concealed a member of the Ming imperial family. Also, a leading monk was killed at Chang's court in the very presence of the two Jesuit fathers. In addition, Chang took some rather drastic actions against the Szechwanese troops who had been incorporated into his army, being particularly angered at the defection of Szechwanese units during the attack on Han-chung. It is impossible to make any realistic estimate of how many troops fell victim to the terror policy. The *Ming shih* mentions the fantastic figure of 980,000, and even though this number is completely unbelievable, the loss of life among the provincial military units must have been considerable.

By early 1646, Chang's Chengtu regime was on the verge of a complete collapse as a result of the extension of the terror policy. His authority over areas outside the immediate vicinity of Chengtu had broken down, and one source maintains that within four months ten officials appointed by Chang in a single county were slain by groups opposing him. In this increasingly deteriorating situation, Chang resorted to more and more violence, even turning against the officials whom he had appointed to serve in his central administration. It is known that at least three of the high officials of his government, Minister of Rites Wu Chi-shan, Minister of War Kung Wan-ching, and Grand Secretary Yen Hsi-ming, were killed as a result of trivial disagreements. Even such an erstwhile favorite as Chang Ta-shou who had been selected for top honors at one of the official examinations and subsequently showered with presents and recognition, suddenly fell from favor and was executed without explanation. Lesser officials' also often suffered the same fate, and Chang is said to have adopted the bizarre policy of calling vicious dogs into court sessions and killing the officials whom they sniffed at. The Jesuits report that of a thousand officials at the outset of the rebel regime, all but twenty-five were eventually killed. At the same time, terror began to be employed quite indiscriminately against the general population following the decision to abandon Chengtu entirely.

Abandonment of Chengtu by Chang Hsien-chung and His Eventual Fate

With his government toppling around him and with daily evidence accumulating that the situation was progressing beyond remedy, Chang began considering future moves. He is said to have looked back with nostalgia at the simple early years of his rebellion and compared his present situation unfavorably with the past, boasting that formerly, with a mere 500 men, he had struck fear in the hearts of as many as 20,000 government soldiers. Now, even though he possessed the imperial title and commanded many thousands of troops, victory escaped him.

Chang's decision to abandon Chengtu came in the summer of 1646, though the move had undoubtedly been under consideration for some time. The decision was arrived at for a variety of reasons: Chang's disillusionment with serious attempts at stable government; his personal nostalgia for returning to his native province, Shensi; his recognition that Szechwan was a backwater which could not serve as a base from which to launch a drive for national power; and what must have been a serious supply problem, the resources of the Chengtu area undoubtedly having been thoroughly exploited by 1646 after almost two years of rebel occupation.[20]

The decision for abandoning Chengtu raised the problem of what was to be the disposition of the area after it had been left behind. This problem was the chief topic in a series of discussions between Chang and one of his favorite advisers, Wang Chao-ling, the eccentric member of a Nanchihli gentry family who had been captured by the rebels while a young man. In these discussions, Chang at first expressed the view that Szechwan should be maintained as an area which could provide future support, and therefore moderate policies should be adopted to obtain the loyalty of the people. Wang objected to this view and argued that the Szechwanese were untrustworthy and evil. Therefore, a scorched-earth policy should be adopted which would destroy the area so thoroughly that it would have no military value for any subsequent conqueror. Chang apparently eventually accepted Wang's view and the sources all go into considerable detail concerning the succession of gory mass slaughters, burnings, looting, and general destruction prior to the rebel departure from the city. Most attention is given to the alleged campaigns of systematic slaughter conducted by Chang's personal forces and by the military units commanded by his four principal lieutenants, Li Ting-kuo, Sun K'o-wang, Liu Wen-hsiu, and Ai Neng-ch'i. Each force is said to have been assigned a specific area both in Chengtu itself and in the surrounding counties and made responsible for slaughtering all the inhabitants in the assigned area.

Lists were kept of the number of people killed and rewards were given on the basis of such lists. These lists are utterly fantastic and are probably the basis for the 600,000,000 figure in the *Ming shih* for the number of people killed by Chang in Szechwan. The following is a typical example of one of these grossly exaggerated lists:[21]

Officer in charge	Number of people killed	
	Males	Females
Sun K'o-wang	59,880,000	95,000,000
Liu Wen-hsiu	99,600,000	86,600,000
Li Ting-kuo	79,000,000	88,000,000
Ai Neng-ch'i	76,000,000	94,000,000
Total:	314,480,000	363,600,000
Grand Total:	678,080,000	

In addition to the mass slaughters of people, the systematic destruction campaigns are also said to have attempted the annihilation of domestic and wild animals and the wholesale burnings of towns and cities, especially Chengtu. Brush and other inflammable material are said to have been tied to the pillars of large buildings and set afire to make their destruction more certain. Furthermore, there are accounts of last minute efforts to bury vast amounts of looted treasure in the bed of the Mien River after the stream had been temporarily diverted into another channel. All the workmen engaged in the project were slaughtered to insure that the secret of the location of the treasure would not be discovered by outsiders. Finally, there is said to have occurred a wholesale slaughter by the rebel troops of their wives, an action supposedly led by Chang himself.

One can have serious doubts about the basic validity of the systematic destruction accounts contained in the sources. It may be true that the eccentric Wang Chao-ling advocated such thoroughgoing destruction and it is possible that he persuaded Chang to grant at least formal acceptance of such a policy. However, it is known that the four principal lieutenants, Sun, Liu, Li, and Ai, were opposed to such a policy of violence, and there exists a strong statement, said to have been made by Sun to Chang, attacking the proposal that called for systematic destruction. Sun's statement is as follows:

The king [i.e. Chang Hsien-chung] has been moving around and waging war for thirty years. Every place the king went through in the past was slaughtered, with the result that there is not even an inch of land left to depend on for our defense. That is not what the generals and soldiers have aimed at in following the King's command. We struggled to take over this land at the risk of dying ten thousand times, and now we have got it. It is hoped that you will become a king and that the great business of overlordship can be accomplished. If the massacre of the people is attempted again in this area, what, then, is the good for us to continue living? I would like to ask you to let me kill myself before the people with the sword which you are holding in your hand.*

If the four officers charged with carrying out the destruction policy were opposed to it, the likelihood is that they were scarcely serious in implementing their assignments for slaughtering even if such were issued. Consequently, the fantastic figures said to have been kept of the slaughters are obviously inventions either by the four officers themselves to pretend to comply with Chang's wishes or by later historians seeking to discredit the rebel regime.

Other bits of evidence also tend to confirm the view that one can doubt the systematic destruction policy. For one thing, virtually the last act performed by Chang in Chengtu was to hold a solemn service in a local Taoist temple where he kowtowed before the image of Lao-tzu. Furthermore, Chang ordered a commemorative tablet erected in Chengtu. Neither of these acts would have occurred had Chengtu been subjected to the absolutely thorough destruction alleged by the sources.

The above arguments against accepting the systematic destruction of Chengtu do not imply, however, that the rebel departure from the city was not accompanied by a great deal of looting and suffering. Even if there was no systematic slaughtering, there were probably widespread raids to obtain supplies needed by the still large rebel army, and the Jesuits attest to the fact that thousands of local people were killed, including the wives of some rebel soldiers.** Such slaughter of women by the rebels is mentioned so frequently in the sources that it seems to have been one of the stereotyped means employed by the rebels for displaying loyalty and valor, though it undoubtedly had more restricted usage than the sources would indicate. Also, there may have been considerable burn-

---

* *SKCL* 10/20b. The Jesuits had an especially high opinion of Sun K'o-wang. Father de Magalhaens, in his *Nouvelle Relation de la Chine*, 44-45, described him as intelligent, prudent, affable, courageous, and good.

** Martini, 213-217, and Dunin Spot, 108, 117. Mention is made that 600,000 people were killed in Chengtu, a figure which is undoubtedly a variation of the 600,000,000 mentioned in the *MS* and the 678,080,000 mentioned in the lists of people killed said to have been kept by Chang's four principal lieutenants during the systematic slaughtering campaigns. This is not the only instance of evidences of borrowing by the Jesuits from the Chinese sources. For example, the Jesuits also employ such stereotyped phrases as rivers around Chengtu rising visibly because of the vast amount of blood and the large numbers of corpses dumped into them. In addition, the Jesuits report that Chang ordered the slaying of all but twenty of his 300 concubines. At the same time, the fathers were permitted to pick out the Christians from the groups being led to execution, and they were spared.

ing of public buildings in Chengtu. The buildings had been employed by Chang as the centers for his dynastic pretensions, and fanciful though these pretensions were, he would probably be opposed to having them occupied by anyone else.

The exact date of Chang's withdrawal from Chengtu is uncertain, but it probably occurred around mid-autumn of 1646. No attempt whatever was made to hold Chengtu by leaving behind even a modest-sized garrison, and the city was occupied shortly after Chang's departure by Ming loyalist forces under Yang Chan and Ts'ao Hsün.

As for Chang's destination following the abandonment of Chengtu, it does not seem initially to have been absolutely definite. Probably his most likely ultimate goal was Shensi, though he did not take the most direct route from Chengtu north to that province. Instead, he went almost due east and established a camp at Hsi-ch'ung for reasons which are not clear, though probably the dominant motive was the availability of supplies in an area which had been relatively untouched by plundering. There is evidence, directly stated in a few of the sources, which indicates that Chang at least was considering pushing east again into the Hukuang area where he had been active earlier. But whatever his ultimate intended destination was, it was never attained, and fate overtook him in Hsi-ch'ung.[22]

The withdrawal from Chengtu and the establishment of a relatively permanent camp at Mt. Feng-huang in Hsi-ch'ung failed to solve the problems and tensions within Chang's group which had been all too apparent already in Chengtu. Supplies are said to have been deficient and the brutal terroristic policies remained in effect to some degree, being particularly directed toward the remaining Szechwanese troops who were now even more disaffected and whose loyalty was suspect. The sources mention continuing slaughter and violence, and despite what is undoubtedly considerable exaggeration, it is apparent that Chang's army was so riddled by internal strife that it was incapable of resisting effectively a really determined opponent. One source reports Chang in such a pessimistic mood that he told his four principal lieutenants the Ming dynasty had not yet lost the Mandate of Heaven and advised them to surrender to the Ming following his death. And another account depicts the situation at Hsi-ch'ung deteriorating to such an extent that the four principal lieutenants launched a plot to assassinate Chang.

The only real threat posed to Chang at Hsi-ch'ung was from the Manchus who, during the latter part of 1645 and the first half of 1646, had established themselves quite firmly in control of Shensi. This assertion of Manchu authority had been accomplished after remnant forces of Li Tzu-ch'eng had been wiped out and an attempted comeback by diffuse

Ming loyalist groups had been frustrated. Regularized governmental procedures were being restored in Shensi, and Censors were making all of the expected proposals to Peking: agricultural production in the province should be restored, common people who had been forced to join the rebels should be forgiven, and lower officials should be prevented from exploiting the people.

Both Chang and the Manchus were quite aware of one another and realized conflict would likely occur. As early as the spring of 1645, it is recorded that one of Chang's officials had surrendered to the Manchus and that an attempt would be made to bring about the surrender of Chang himself by approaching him through the surrendered official. For his part, Chang is reported by the Jesuits to have made such openly anti-Manchu statements as "I hope by your valour to obtain the empire of the world when I have expelled the Tartars...," and "I already see these foreigners chased out of China" when he addressed his troops just prior to his abandonment of Chengtu.*

The confrontation between Chang and the Manchus, when it finally did occur, took place on terms highly unfavorable to Chang because of the defection of one of his most important generals, Liu Chin-chung. Liu was a native of Szechwan and had long been restive because of the violent policies adopted by Chang's Chengtu regime. Also, he had aroused Chang's ire by an unsuccessful attack on Han-chung, Shensi, a campaign which was apparently undertaken on Liu's own initiative and occurred probably during the summer of 1646. The final event which propelled Liu to defect was Chang's attempt to eliminate large numbers of his Szechwanese troops following the withdrawal from Chengtu to Hsi-ch'ung. Apparently several Szechwanese units fled northward from Hsi-ch'ung to join Liu whom Chang then attempted to destroy by unsuccessfully summoning him to appear in Hsi-ch'ung.

Having determined finally to break with Chang, Liu at first engaged in negotiations with Tseng Ying, the Ming loyalist warlord whose center of power was in Chungking. These negotiations were unsuccessful and Liu determined to come to an agreement with the Manchus. An approach was made via an intermediary to Prince Haoge, the chief Manchu commander in Shensi, and a formula was soon arrived at whereby Liu was permitted to surrender and his army was integrated into the Manchu forces. Liu's first assignment was to accompany and guide a small advance party

---

* The first quotation is from Martini, 117; and the second is from Joseph-Anne-Marie de Moyriac de Mailla, *Histoire générale de la Chine*, XI, 26. The Chinese sources make no mention of Chang's awareness of the Manchus, an omission partly due to the pro-Manchu prejudice of some of the sources.

to move southward and begin operations against Chang Hsien-chung prior to the arrival of the main Manchu force.

The mission assigned Liu and the Manchu advance force was carried out according to plan and they reached Chang's camp at Hsi-ch'ung so rapidly that Chang had not even been informed of Liu's defection to the Manchus. Chang refused to believe the first two reports that the Manchus had arrived, and flew into such a rage that he ordered the messengers executed. The third message convinced him that the report should be investigated and, according to the account of Martini, ". . . he being of a bold and courageous humor, burst out of his tent, and without either head-piece or breast-plate, snatched up a lance, and went out with a few to view the enemy."[23]

From this point on, the details of what transpired at Mt. Feng-huang are unclear, the fog, which is said to have covered the landscape, invading the sources as well. In Martini, the following sentence describes the death of Chang in exaggeratedly dramatic terms which probably exhibit deliberate pro-Manchu prejudice:

The Tartars presently assaulted the tyrant and the first discharged arrow, which was as happy to the Tartars as it was to many others, pierced the heart of that monster of cruelty, killing that man who had the intention to make an end to all men; and who from the base condition of a rascally thief presumed to take the sacred title of king and emperor.[24]

Only one of the Chinese sources maintains that Chang was disposed of by one shot and there is considerable disagreement with the Jesuit sources and among themselves on other points.[25] Some sources affirm that Chang was killed quickly by several arrows and that the Manchus seized his body after his lieutenant, Wang Shang-li, who had tried to carry his dead leader back to the rebel camp, was forced to abandon him and flee for his life. Other sources maintain that Chang was only wounded and depict him attempting to hide under a pile of brush, an effort which was not successful and ended when the Manchus seized him and cut off his head. Finally one source states that the rebels succeeded in escaping with Chang's body and in burying it, dressed in fine silk, before retreating south. However, the Manchus were able to find the grave and dig up the body. Other information about Chang's death exhibits more obvious Manchu prejudices. The most glaring example is contained in the *Shu pi* which states that Chang, only lightly wounded, was captured by the Manchus and brought before Prince Haoge who ordered him executed after facing Heaven and reciting the enormity of his crimes.

Beyond rejecting obviously prejudiced material, it is impossible to sort out the definitely reliable details concerning Chang's death on Mt. Feng-huang. It can only be said with certainty that, after ignoring several warnings, Chang finally left his camp at the head of a small group and encountered an advance party of Prince Haoge's army. In the ensuing clash, Chang was killed.

As for the date on which Chang's death occurred, there is also no general agreement, but probably for this type of information the *Ch'ing Shih-lu* would be the most accurate source, the particular section dealing with Chang's death being based on a memorial submitted by Prince Haoge. In other respects, the *Shih-lu* account is decidedly exaggerated; for example, when it states that Chang attacked in full force, but the Manchus succeeded in killing several tens of thousands of rebels and in capturing 12,200 horses. But there would seem to be no reason for the *Shih-lu* to falsify the date, and thus probably Chang was killed on January 2, 1647.

Following Chang's death, his army almost certainly avoided any decisive defeat at the hands of the Sino-Manchu force, despite the allegations in the *Shih-lu* and elsewhere that large numbers of rebels were killed. On the contrary, Chang's army, prior to the arrival of the main Manchu force, withdrew rapidly southward, defeating and killing the Ming loyalist warlord, Tseng Ying, at Chungking. The retreat was continued into the southwest where Chang's four principal lieutenants eventually surrendered to the Yung-li Pretender. Li Ting-kuo, in particular, was destined to serve the Southern Ming loyally until the bitter end and is one of the few genuine heroes. At the same time, Chang became the focal point for the growth of folk tales in Szechwan. Despite such lingering after-affects, Chang's death may be considered to mark the conclusion of the late Ming peasant rebellions.

Chapter VI

Specialized Aspects of the Rebellions

The Problem of Statistics

Statistics are frequently cited in the sources dealing with the rebellions and have been noted from time to time in the preceding chapters. It is proper now to attempt an overview and possibly add some contribution to assessing the place of statistics in Chinese historiography generally, particularly in relation to the extent to which they can be accepted and utilized for historical purposes.

Some of the statistics given in the sources are patently absurd and do not merit extensive consideration. For example, there is the previously noted *Ming shih* statement that 600,000,000 people were slaughtered during Chang Hsien-chung's occupation of the province of Szechwan. Surely no more fantastic figure ever appeared in any Chinese dynastic history, and it is almost two hundred times the total Szechwanese population as stated in the geographical chapter of the *Ming-shih*!* Also, generally when the sources mention that the rebels on a particular occasion numbered several hundred thousand, such vague figures cannot be accepted as meaning anything more than a large mass which could not be accurately numbered.

Putting aside the obviously absurd figures and those which are too vague, there is still great difficulty in arriving at an estimate of rebel numerical strength which seems reasonably certain. For example, Chang Hsien-chung is said to have had 5,000 men in 1630; 300 in 1631; 500 in 1632; 2,000 in 1633; 5,000 in 1636; 5,000 in 1638; 1,000 in 1640; 30,000 in 1641; 1,000 in 1643; 100,000, or 150,000, or 200,000 in 1644. There are equally varying statements about the strength of Li Tzu-ch'eng's

---

* See my article, "The Culmination of a Chinese Peasant Rebellion: Chang Hsien-chung in Szechwan, 1644-46," *Journal of Asian Studies*, XVI (1957), 393-398 for a discussion of the loss of life in Szechwan during Chang's occupation of the province.

Table I. Total Rebel Battle Fatalities

1629— 700	1637—14,470
1630— 2,880	1638—11,130
1631—21,240	1639—10,100
1632—12,470	1640—32,420
1633—19,695	1641—13,100
1634—35,300	1642—10,320
1635—15,120	1643—18,320
1636—12,450	1644— 4,470

Total: 234,185

Table II. Rebel Battle Fatalities

Given in number of battles; e.g., in 1631, there were twenty-three battles in which rebel fatalities numbered from 200 to 500.

Year	50 or less	50-100	100-200	200-500	500-1,000	1,000-1,500	1,500-2,000	2,000-3,000	3,000-5,000	5,000-10,000	over 10,000
1628											
1629				1	1						
1630	1	2	3	1	3						
1631	1	3	4	23	12	2	1				1
1632		6	9	7	6	2		1			
1633	1	3	11	18	2	5	3		2		
1634		5	16	15	12	4	1		1	2	
1635	5	3	18	19	4	4					
1636	4	3	9	18	4	4					
1637	1	1	5	5	2	2	1	2	1		
1638	2		3	5	1	2			3		
1639					2	2	1	1	1		
1640	2	1	1	5	5	7	2	2	4		
1641				1	1	2	1	4			
1642				2	2	6			1		1
1643		2	1	4	3			4	3		
1644				1	2				1		2

forces even at the time of his occupation of Peking when one would think there would have been the greatest opportunity for an accurate estimate of his numerical strength. The figures in the sources vary all the way from 1,000,000 to 50,000, with 500,000 and 200,000 in between. That the figures cited directly in the sources concerning the size of rebel groups are conflicting and inadequate undoubtedly is due to the quite obvious difficulty official sources would have had in obtaining information about the rebels generally, including their numbers.

The most abundant statistical material concerning the rebellions is the citation of rebel battle fatalities. Probably it was easy to obtain such figures, since they could be taken from what must have been voluminous records of military engagements submitted by officials and military commanders. These rebel battlefield fatalities are outlined above in two tables.

The chief fact which strikes one from Table I is the relatively modest total number of rebel fatalities, 234,185, claimed by the government, and undoubtedly such claims were considerably exaggerated. Thus, it does not seem unreasonable to estimate that the total number of rebels associated with the several score of organized bands throughout the entire course of the rebellions was probably no more than 1,000,000.

Table II demonstrates that rebel fatalities in the average battle tended to be quite small, below 500, a fact which suggests that the rebel bands were of modest size and that the military engagements were typically small-scale affairs. Also, the table shows a decided decline in the number of battles fought after 1636. Such a decline is due to a number of factors: the temporary lull in rebel activity during the latter 1630's, the increasing inability of the government even to attempt to cope with the rebel situation, and the consolidation of the rebel bands into fewer units. Also, it should be noted that rebel fatalities in the average engagement tended to increase during the earlier 1640's, so that though fewer battles were fought, they tended to be on a somewhat larger scale than formerly. However, the military engagements still could not be described as really formidable ones, since the average later battle fatalities were only around 1,000.

Statistics concerning the government forces are extraordinarily limited. In contrast to the wealth of figures on rebel fatalities, government losses are virtually never mentioned. Also, the size of the official forces is relatively rarely cited. However, based on figures cited for government armies in some sixty battles, their average size was definitely below 4,000 men. Other information confirms this picture of rather inadequate official forces. For example, in 1637 the Grand Coordinator of Shansi memorialized that he had only 600 troops under his personal command and that there were only 6,000 professional soldiers in the entire province.* In another instance, the Ministry of War reported in 1644 that the garrison at Pao-ting, Pei-chihli, was supposed to have 30,000 men, but actually consisted of only 3,000 troops who were in possession of a mere 900 horses. Finally, during Li Tzu-ch'eng's attack on Peking, one source maintains that the city was defended by only a few thousand eunuchs and a force of some 10,000 troops, most of whom were superannuated and physically unfit.[1] The capital defense force was supposed to consist of 120,000 troops on the outskirts and 54,000 stationed on the wall itself.

---

* *MMNM* 190-192. This figure of 6,000 troops for all of Shansi did not include those enrolled in the Wei-So or militia systems, but the inference is that these forces were ineffective.

Thus, it seems possible to say that the government was never capable of marshalling really effective armies of adequate size to put in the field against the rebels, indicating a real collapse of Ming military institutions.

Surveying the question of statistics generally in the late Ming rebellions, it can be said that they are definitely inadequate for any precise statistical calculations. They are of some limited value in serving as a basis for three possible conclusions: the rebellions were characterized by small-scale military engagements, the rebel bands were typically of modest size, and the official forces were decidedly undermanned.

Elements of Religion and Superstition in the Late Ming Rebellions

Unlike some of the earlier peasant rebellions in Chinese history and the subsequent Taiping movement, the late Ming uprisings did not manifest any fundamental religious orientation revolving around a popular cult. The White Lotus Society, so prominent in the revolts at the end of the Yüan, still existed in late Ming times and there are scattered references to it in the sources. However, there is no evidence whatsoever to suggest that it played any really important role in the rebellions. Other cultist elements in the revolts were equally insignificant. It is true that one of the early leaders of a rebel band was named "Monk" Wang and may indeed have been a Buddhist monk or ex-monk. Also, the members of a rebel group in Shantung are said to have wrapped their heads in red cloths, and the rebel leader Kao Ying-hsiang at one time wore white clothes and dressed his men in uniforms the colors of which accorded with those associated with the five directions.[2] In none of these cases is there any evidence of general trends. They were all highly individual and temporary.

Despite the lack of any specific and definite religious orientation of the rebellions, they still displayed many features which manifested religious and superstitious overtones. For example, both the rebels and the official forces upon occasion conducted religious ceremonies.[3] General Tso Liang-yü sacrificed a horse to one of his favorite lieutenants who died as a result of wounds received while fighting the rebels. At the conclusion of the great rebel conclave at Jung-yang, Honan, in 1635, there was a sacrifice of both a horse and a cow. Just prior to his abandonment of Chengtu late in 1646, Chang Hsien-chung led his entire retinue to a Taoist temple where he kowtowed three times before a statue of Lao-tzu. In the winter of 1642, an official performed a sacrifice to the god of the Yellow River at the spot where the river's dike had been cut during the disastrous third rebel attack on Kaifeng.

More macabre ceremonies became rather common toward the end of the rebellions when a kind of human sacrifice was indulged in. Li Tzu-ch'eng for example is said to have offered the flesh of the Prince of Fu as a sacrifice to the spirits before he and his men ate it. On the official side, rebels were sacrificed on several occasions, one such ceremony taking place at the Ming tombs to which some private citizens had carried rebel captives. Similar sacrifices occurred in Peking where local Ming zealots seized rebels who had been left behind following Li's flight from the city. Even Li's head is said to have been severed from his body and offered as a sacrifice to the Ch'ung-chen Emperor by Supreme Commander Ho T'eng-chiao, to whom Li's corpse is alleged to have been presented. Also, Wu San-kuei is reported to have planned to sacrifice Li's chief lieutenant, Liu Tsung-min, to the memory of his own father, slain by the rebels. Prince Dodo supposedly forbade the sacrifice, after branding it as illegal, and instead ordered Liu executed by the relatively merciful method of strangling.

Another category of superstitious practices, resorted to by both the rebels and the official side, involved the desecration of tombs. It has already been noted that Chang Hsien-chung despoiled the Yang family graveyard during his occupation of Hukuang as a final stroke of revenge against his hated enemy, Yang Ssu-ch'ang. Li Tzu-ch'eng is also said to have engaged in similar acts. On the official side, the single most famous incident of tomb desecration was carried out by the Ming authorities against the Li family cemetery.[4] The act was initiated by the Grand Coordinator of Shensi, Wang Ch'iao-nien, in 1642 after the start of Li Tzu-ch'eng's rise to power in Honan. A rumor had arisen that the basis of Li's good fortune was a light continually burning in his family tombs, and his success would continue as long as the light was not extinguished. Responding to this tale, Grand Coordinator Wang instructed the magistrate of Li's native Mi-chih County, Pien Ta-shou, to discover the location of the family cemetery. After considerable difficulty, the site was found some sixty-five miles west of the town of Mi-chih. The area bore the marks of a decade and a half of natural and man-made calamities: it was quite overgrown, and the family village nearby was completely deserted.

Following the discovery of the cemetery, the graves of Li's father and grandfather were excavated, but instead of a continually burning light, the first thing the diggers discovered was nothing more unusual than a large mass of ants. Subsequent investigation did turn up two rather curious phenomena: a red horned snake inhabiting the skull of Li's father and a thick growth of yellow hair sprouting from his undecayed corpse. Before departing, the official party cut down the trees growing around the graves and burned the corpses except for the head of Li's father which was dispatched to Peking, together with the red snake.

In 1643, about a year and a half after the desecration, Li's power had expanded over most of Shensi, and during a visit to his native county, he ordered the ancestral tombs repaired following the completion of which one of his officials held a sacrifice there in honor of his ancestors. Also, Li is said to have seized two prominent Mi-chih degree-holders, who had played a role in the desecration, and condemned them to be quartered in the streets of the town.

Other types of superstitious elements in the rebellions were the divinations and magical practices resorted to in order to gain knowledge of the future or to obtain an advantage over an opponent.[5] Most of these activities are ascribed to the rebels, but the official side was responsible for a few. For example, in 1639 the Emperor and a group of officials held a séance in the Imperial City during which a medium contacted the spirit of the Ming founder and posed questions about the future course of events. Apparently the spirit made known its answers to questions by moving a writing brush in the medium's hand to form characters, and certainly the replies painted a grim picture. Continued natural and man-made calamities were predicted, and though the rebellions would be temporarily suppressed, they would break out again and cause great distress to the people. Furthermore, the spirit intimated that the Emperor had been inept in his conduct of affairs. The séance ended with an enigmatic statement, "The generals and ministers of the Han dynasty are before your very eyes," which apparently meant that the Emperor was not making use of the capable talent available to him.

There are several cases of the rebels, particularly Li Tzu-ch'eng, resorting to divination. One such case happened following Li's significant breakthrough to power in Honan and Hukuang. The incident occurred at Hsiang-yang in 1643 and came in response to unfavorable developments: the failure in the attempt to coin money for the new rebel regime and the collapse of one of the palace buildings being constructed at Hsiang-yang. The results of the divination were highly unfavorable for Li, the medium stating outright that "Tzu-ch'eng is not a true Son of Heaven" and going on to suggest that rebel power would soon topple and that the Ming dynasty was still in possession of the Mandate. Li is said to have been so upset at the medium's prediction that he ordered him executed.

A later divination took place a short time prior to Li's attack on Peking and produced the curious response that the rebels would succeed provided they employed children in the vanguard of their forces. Complying with the divination results, Li is said to have raised a band of some 5,000 boys around sixteen years old and used them during the brief fighting around the capital. Finally, a conference attended by all of Li's principal subordinates was held on May 14, 1644 to discuss such pressing matters as dispatching a force against Wu San-kuei, and when they were unable to decide upon a policy to pursue, they resorted to divination. The results are described as so unfavorable that Sung Hsien-ts'e, Li's chief expert in the supernatural, predicted that his chieftain's power could endure for only three more years.

Divination does not seem to have been as important for Chang Hsien-chung as it was for Li Tzu-ch'eng, and there is only one case where it is definitely known that he resorted to it. This case occurred in 1643 when Chang was about to embark on a naval expedition across Tung-t'ing Lake. The resulting prediction was one of faliure for the expedition and Chang's irreverent response was to throw down the lots and curse. A possible second case of divination resorted to by Chang came in Chengtu toward the very end of his rebel career when he is said to have announced that it had been revealed to him that the next three years would be unlucky ones. Therefore, he had decided to retire to a secluded Taoist temple where he would wait out the unlucky period before resuming his career and seizing the empire. There is no evidence that he made any serious attempts to carry out this announced plan.

The most notable attempts of the rebels to employ magic to defeat their official opponents occurred during the attack on Lu-chou in 1635 and Ch'u-chou in 1636 by Chang Hsien-chung and on Kaifeng in 1642 by Li Tzu-ch'eng. All three incidents involved the rebels using nude women, alive in two cases but apparently dead in the Ch'u-chou attack, to exude such an excess of the *yin* principle before the city walls that the firearms of the defending forces would be adversely affected. The rebel attempt at victory through magic failed at Lu-chou, but had initial success at Ch'u-chou and Kaifeng, in the first instance silencing the defending cannon altogether, and in the second instance causing them to fire backward against the official troops. However, at both Ch'u-chou and Kaifeng, the authorities resorted to successful magical countermeasures. At Ch'u-chou, the officials had night soil emptied over the wall, an act which succeeded in negating the power of the nude women, and at Kaifeng, similar results were obtained by placing nude Buddhist monks on top of the city wall.

The most voluminous material concerning the supernatural in the late Ming rebellions is that which deals with portents, prognostications, and dreams that foretell the future.[6] Some of these supernatural manifestations are rather vague, indicating a general disorder in nature to coincide with the disturbances in the world of man produced by the rebellions. Thus, a pole erected on a military training ground in Tientsin emitted a thunderous noise one night; in Shensi the sky upon one occasion turned red as blood and a bright blue fire entered people's houses accompanied by the sound of fighting; in Szechwan the image of the Jade Emperor in a Chengtu temple moved and there were reports of strange lights, beans growing in the shape of knives, peculiarly colored melons, and unusual noises issuing continually from caves and drums; and in Peking, shortly before the city's fall to the rebels, there was yellow dust and black fog.

Other portents and related supernatural occurrences are more specific, and, for example, pointed to the coming collapse of the Ming. One such incident is said to have happened on the very day that the Ch'ung-chen Emperor was enthroned (October 2, 1627) when a blast occurred west of the palace so intense that it startled the imperial party, the assembled officials, and the ceremonial horses. A similar event took place on the first day of the Ch'ung-chen reign period (February 5, 1628) when the new Emperor received his ministers for the celebration of the New Year only to have the festivities disturbed by a great noise coming out of the northwest. And it so happened that at this very same time, Li Tzu-ch'eng was gambling in his native Mi-chih in northern Shensi and made the prediction that if he could get six red pawns at the same time, he would become emperor. He was lucky enough to draw his six red pawns whereupon his companions bowed before him and shouted *wan-sui*. Other portents about the fall of the dynasty tend to be clustered around its end. In 1643, for example, there was discovered a picture scroll in the Imperial Library which told a story in three parts. The first section depicted a military fiasco with routed troops fleeing and civilians milling about in confusion; the second showed harried officials in flight; and the third portrayed a bareheaded man with uncombed hair in the act of hanging himself. The Emperor is said to have been dismayed after viewing the scroll and felt that it portended ill. Again, early in 1644, a heavenly body moved into the center of the moon, an occurrence which was interpreted explicitly as foretelling the collapse of the dynasty and the death of the Emperor. And at about the same time, a beam in one of the palace halls emitted a strange sound when the Emperor was in the midst of performing a ceremony. Finally, only a few weeks prior to Peking's fall, it was reported that weeping had been heard in the tomb of the Hung-wu Emperor at Nanking.

Most of the portents and related phenomena, however, deal with the rebels, and one category seeks to present such rebel leaders as Li Tzu-ch'eng as having intimate connections with strange powers from the very beginning of his life and as being predestined to an evil and violent career, a destiny written into his very physical features. Two such stories deal with Li's conception and birth. In one of them, his father, concerned that he had had no son, went to pray for one at a temple on Mt. Hua.

Answering his prayer, a spirit informed him that he would be given the "Breaking-the-Army-Star" (P'o-chün hsing) as a son. The portent here is that Li would destroy the Ming army. The second story is concerned with Li's mother who is said to have had a vision of gems like those attached to the headdress of an empress when she gave birth to Li. Subsequently, as a youth, Li is said to have joined with his two constant companions, Liu Tsung-min and Li Kuo (his nephew) in taking an oath at a temple dedicated to Kuan-kung, imitating the famous Peach Garden Oath of the Three Kingdoms period. After the oath, Li lifted a brazier weighing about a hundred pounds and walked around the temple carrying it in one hand. When his companions attempted to imitate his performance, they were barely able to lift the brazier with both hands and could walk only a few steps while carrying it. Witnessing the scene, a temple priest remarked that Li's father was indeed fortunate to have such a gifted son, a statement which prompted Li to reply that a great man was noteworthy in his own right and not just as a reflection of his father. He then added that a great man could control the empire.

Other supernatural occurrences involving Li as a youth or young man include a strange encounter with wolves and two significant dreams. The wolf encounter is said to have taken place while he was serving as a post station attendant and became lost one night while relaying a message. He was unable to find his way until he met two wolves that, instead of attacking him, led him back to familiar territory. In one of the dreams, he encountered a great general who called him Tzu-ch'eng, and subsequently Li adopted this as his given name, replacing the earlier Hung-chi. In the second dream, Li saw the exact sequence of future events concerning his wife's infidelity, his murder of her, and the escape of her lover.

Li's physical characteristics are said to include high cheek bones, deep-set owl-like eyes, a pressed-in chest, broad shoulders, a nose like a grub, a wolf's voice, and hair that curled in the back like a scorpion. He is described as resembling a demon as depicted in popular art, and indeed his features are obviously intended to convey something more than merely an impression of physical ugliness.

Following the outbreak of the rebellions, most of the portents and similar phenomena are oriented in the direction of demonstrating that the rebels did not enjoy divine favor and indeed were actually being opposed by supernatural forces. Such occurrences are particularly commonly cited in connection with Chang Hsien-chung and Li Tzu-ch'eng, tending to be concentrated toward the end of their rebel careers. In 1643 when Chang desecrated the Yang family tombs in Hukuang, blood is said to have appeared after the corpse of Yang Ssu-ch'ang was slashed, despite the fact that he had been dead for more than two years. Following the invasion and occupation of Szechwan in 1644, numerous anti-Chang portents appeared. The most ubiquitous of these portents was a strange star which became visible over the province at the outset of Chang's invasion and remained until his death when it disappeared. The other portents were more localized in scope. In Chungking, after Chang's forces had captured the city and were in the act of killing the Prince of Jui and several provincial officials, there was thunder and lightning on a cloudless day which became so violent that several rebels were fatally struck by bolts from the heavens. Chang, far from heeding this display of divine displeasure, ordered cannon discharged in irreverent defiance of Heaven. In Chengtu, after Chang had established his government, he ordered a pagoda outside the city wall destroyed, because it produced unfavorable *Feng-shui* by pointing like an arrow toward the city. In the foundations of the pagoda, there was said to have been discovered a stone tablet on which it was recorded that the structure would be destroyed by Chang who in turn would meet his end at the hands of one named Su. This prediction proved to be completely correct some two years later when Chang was killed by the Manchus under Hoage whose princely title was Su. Also in Chengtu, the Confucian temple was consumed by an unexplained fire. In his palace, Chang saw visions of headless women playing musical instruments and had to endure mysterious hands appearing to snatch food he was about to eat, as well as ghosts who killed palace women in broad daylight. Even Chang was initially somewhat disturbed over the burning of the Confucian temple, for as it happened after a particularly bloody massacre of candidates who had assembled to take the official examinations, it could be taken as indicating disapproval by the spirit of Confucius. However, Chang's renegade gentry adviser, Wang Chao-ling, assured him that the fiery event merely signified that all the literati had been exterminated. In Pao-ning, in north-central Szechwan, there was a famous temple dedicated to the Three Kingdoms hero, Chang Fei, and when Chang Hsien-chung's forces captured the town, the spirit of Chang Fei, in the form of a large black man, appeared on the wall. The town escaped serious harm, although control of it changed hands several times, and this good fortune was attributed to the protection afforded by the spirit of Chang Fei. Finally, following Chang Hsien-chung's death, his heart was pulled from his body and found to be pure black. After the burial of his corpse, a strange pointed grass, poisonous in nature, grew out of his grave which was guarded by a black, tiger-like animal—indications that the evil power associated with Chang was so intense that even his death did not destroy immediately all of its manifestations.

Portents similar to those associated with Chang Hsien-chung are also recounted in connection with Li Tzu-ch'eng, most of them occurring toward the end of his rebellion. Two of the portents took place in 1643 and involved the attempted desecration of the tomb of a Ming district prince and that of Emperor Ming of the Han dynasty. In the first instance, a noise so resounding that it shook the earth, frightened the rebels from their task, and an equally remarkable intervention of the supernatural occurred at the tomb of Emperor Ming—a golden armored man appeared and killed one of the rebel officers in charge of the excavation. Again, early in 1644 when Li proclaimed himself Prince of Shun in Sian, there was a dust storm and yellow fog. Uneasy at this turn of events, Li requested an explanation from his Minister of Rites who placated him by replying that the rebel dynasty was now assured of supplanting the Ming, because when a new ruler arose, the sun and the moon had no light. Several portents occurred following Li's capture of Peking. One involved a ceremonial elephant which was brought before Li in the Imperial City and made to kneel, whereupon the animal looked toward the late Emperor's residence and burst into tears. Other portents have a special connection with Li's plan to proclaim himself Emperor: he became dizzy and sleepy when he sat on the throne for audiences, the carved dragon on the throne moved its claws and bristles, and a giant holding a sword appeared in the palace once when he was seriously considering his elevation to the imperial position. The most violent of all the portents occurred when lightning struck and killed several rebel officials.

The final portent involving Li took place in the autumn of 1644 when he had retreated from Peking to Shensi. A special ceremony to Li's ancestors had been planned and a robe, embroidered with dragons and mountains, had been made for him to wear. When he put on the robe, he felt coldness and pressure so intense that he cancelled the ceremony, accused his Minister of Rites of wanting to crush him underneath the embroidered mountains, and almost had the offending official executed.

It should be noted that there were some rigged portents. For example, following the fall of Peking, the rebels arranged the unearthing of a box which was inscribed with the characters "Yung-ch'ang," the title of Li's reign period. The expected claim was made that the box indicated Heaven's approval of the new regime.

The last of the religious and superstitious elements in the rebellions are rather special and involve Chang Hsien-chung alone: his relations with the Jesuit missionaries in Chengtu and his belief that he had been accorded a divine mission to slaughter. As noted previously, there were two Jesuit missionaries in Szechwan at the time of Chang's invasion,

Fathers Louis Buglio and Gabriel de Magalhaens.* Buglio, a Sicilian, had arrived in China in 1637 and initially worked in the lower Yangtze area before being sent to Szechwan in 1640 as the first missionary ever to proselytize in the province. De Magalhaens, a Portuguese, was a member of the same family as the famous navigator, Magellan. He arrived in China in 1640, was first assigned to Hangchow, and in 1642 was dispatched to Chengtu to assist Father Buglio. The missionary efforts of the fathers had a modest success in Chengtu: a church was erected and attempts by Buddhist elements to drive them out were frustrated partly as a result of support from provincial officials who knew of the prestige enjoyed by the Jesuits in Peking.

When Chang invaded Szechwan, Fathers Buglio and de Magalhaens fled from Chengtu to the northwestern section of the province and even made plans to return to the lower Yangtze. Chang, hearing of the fathers from officials who joined his cause, ordered them captured and brought to his court. They were well received by Chang, were housed as his guests, and were forced to accept formal official status. The close connection then established between the fathers and Chang was to last for more than two years, continuing until the very day of his death. During this time, Chang had numerous meetings with the fathers, discussing such topics as Christianity and European affairs. At one point, Chang expressed praise for Christianity and promised to construct a church, but at the same time he warned that the Chinese were so imbued with old habits of religious thought that it would be difficult to get them to accept a new religion. On another occasion, Chang expressed an interest in invading Europe and asked the fathers about distances. Upon being told that it had taken them a year to reach China from Europe by sea, Chang responded in a very Chinese way by stating that he would move southwestward into Yunnan and proceed on to Europe by land. Other evidence of Chang's regard for Buglio and de Magalhaens is provided by his having presented them with the following poems which he is supposed to have composed and copied out himself:

Heaven takes the ten thousand things to bestow upon man.
Man has not one thing to bestow upon Heaven.
The gods are perspicacious.
Consider yourself and judge yourself.
In the heights of the mountains stand green pines.
At the foot of the mountains, flowers bloom in the valley.

---

* The chief sources for the relationship between Chang and the two Jesuit fathers in Szechwan are the previously cited works by Martini and Dunin Spot. Chang's relations with the fathers are almost entirely ignored in all the Chinese sources.

But one day will come when the hail will fall,
And the pine, to be sure, will keep its green,
But the flowers with all their beauty will wither away.[7]

For their part, the fathers manufactured and presented to Chang a celestial and a terrestial sphere.

In commenting upon Chang's relations with the fathers, Martini states:

> It is true this cruel beast loved these fathers, and would often converse with them whom he experienced wise and learned, and he would often call them to the palace to entertain him in discourse. . . . He would often confer also with the fathers of Christian religion and that so properly as a man would take him for a Christian. He praised and highly extolled the religion of Christians which he well understood, partly by the conferences which he frequently had with the fathers, and partly by reading their books, which for the instructions of Christians they had writ in the China language; and hath often promised to build a church to the God of Christians, worthy of his magnificence, when he once came to be emperor of China.[8]

Toward the end of his life, Chang's relations with the two Jesuits deteriorated for reasons which are not altogether clear, but which undoubtedly stemmed mainly from his disillusionment produced by the increasing evidence of the failure of his Chengtu regime. Furthermore, the fathers were horrified at the bloody measures Chang resorted to in an effort to maintain his control, though they were usually able to save the lives of their Christian converts and were even permitted to baptize dying infants who were killed in the massacres. Finally, Chang's terror policy became so intense that the fathers decided to leave Szechwan and requested permission to return to Macao. Chang refused their request and subsequently held them as virtual prisoners in his entourage. Forced to accompany the rebel forces following the abandonment of Chengtu and the move to north-central Szechwan, the fathers were still in Chang's camp when he was attacked and killed by the Manchus. Wounded in the melée which ensued after Chang's death, the fathers were soon discovered by the Manchus who arranged for their being sent to Peking.

Chang's relationship with the two Jesuit fathers is an interesting footnote to his carrer, but cannot be said to have real significance. His interest in Christianity was definitely superficial and was produced by his partial alienation from traditional Chinese values, his attraction to the exotic, and perhaps his admiration for the courage displayed by the missionaries in coming from the other side of the world to propagate their faith in a distant foreign land. There is not the slightest evidence that Chang even considered employing Christianity as an element for forming a religious basis for his rebellion. It can be said, then, that the Jesuit presence in Szechwan was important chiefly for making possible the only non-Chinese treatment of Chang's rebellion which contains elements not usually found in the Chinese sources. For example, the Jesuits credit Chang with considerably more intelligence and acumen than do their Chinese counterparts.

Chang's divine mission to slaughter is presented in some of the sources as a belief which he apparently sincerely accepted, but in others it is depicted as a deliberately perpetrated fraud.[9] The sources which present the mission as a genuinely held belief state that it was first revealed to Chang on Mt. Wu-tang in Hukuang when he and a few other rebels were looting a Taoist temple. An image in the temple spoke to Chang, stating that he deserved to be slain, but his life had to be spared because he had been ordained by Heaven to conduct a mission of slaughter. In Szechwan, Chang began to take this revelation seriously and to carry it out, claiming that the Jade Emperor had designated him to gather together and punish the wicked of the world by slaughtering them. The sources which brand the mission a deliberate fraud affirm that the entire concept was conceived by Chang and Wang Chao-ling as a means of justifying the terror policy adopted by the rebel Chengtu regime. According to these sources, Chang and Wang formulated the idea of a fake divine mission to slaughter and waited for an auspicious occasion to announce it. Soon afterwards, there was a night during which a heavy rain fell, accompanied by a spectacular display of thunder and lightning. The next day, it was announced that during the storm Heaven had granted Chang an audience, had told him that the people in the world were evil and lacking in filial piety, and had commissioned him to slaughter them. Based on this trumped-up justification, Chang issued orders for the extermination campaigns.

It is impossible to determine which of these two interpretations of the divine-slaughter mission is valid. However, whether the mission was a complete fraud or a genuinely held belief, it is still an interesting prototype of a similar, though much more well developed, concept which was to play a prominent role in the Taiping rebellion, whose leader also claimed to have a divine mission to slaughter those who worshipped demons and opposed the new order.

Summing up the role played by religion and superstition in the late Ming rebellions, it should be emphasized again that they were not of major significance. Some of the supernatural phenomena are, at least in part, stereotypes which the traditional Chinese historian employed partly for literary effect without always believing that they had actually happened. However, it is still true that religious and magical concepts exerted some influence over the actions of both sides in the rebellions.

The Concept of Patriotism as Expressed by Opponents of the Rebels

Sources dealing with the late Ming rebellions contain considerable material treating of the way in which opposition to the rebels was expressed in situations of ultimate extremity, and from such material one can derive some understanding of the era's conception of the patriotic ideal. As one would expect, most of this material deals with officials and military men who were connected, directly or indirectly, with the struggle against the rebels, and when they reached a point of ultimate gravity, there were several types of action by means of which the patriotic ideal could be expressed.[10] One such type of action was a relatively quiet and dignified suicide usually in the privacy of the home where one could perform various ceremonial observances and perhaps be joined in death by wives, children, and concubines.

There are many examples of such suicides, particularly toward the end of the dynasty. For instance, while Peking was being occupied by the rebels, Minister of Revenue Ni Yüan-lu determined to commit suicide. He returned to his home and, after donning his official robes, paid his last respects to the Emperor by kowtowing toward the north, the direction of the Imperial City. Then, removing his formal dress, he kowtowed toward the south to pay tribute to his aged mother who was living at home. Having completed the ceremonial observances, he invited two friends in to drink wine with him, and during the drinking, he spoke of his coming death, instructing his family not to bury his body until the late Emperor had been buried. He then attempted to strangle himself, but having insufficient strength to accomplish the task alone, he had to be aided by his two friends. Another instance of suicide occurring at approximately the same time was that of Wang Wei who held only a minor official post. Wang had refused to eat since the beginning of the siege of Peking, and when the city fell, he determined to kill himself. His wife decided to join him and after he had suspended two ropes from a beam in the house, he started to hang himself from the one on the right. Noting the impropriety of the position he had chosen, his wife reminded him that the proper order of seniority could not be disregarded even in a time of crisis. Thus, Wang switched to the rope on the left, his wife took the one on the right, and they hung themselves simultaneously.

Other suicides were much more spectacular and involved more people. Three examples are particularly striking. One centered around the Earl of Hui-an who, upon hearing that Peking had fallen, gave away all his wealth, and ordered a great feast prepared to which many of his relatives were invited. At the height of the festivities, he instructed that the house be set afire and he and his relatives burned themselves to death. The second case of mass suicide also took place in Peking and involved Kung Yung-ku, an intimate of the Ch'ung-chen Emperor and the husband of a recently deceased imperial princess, the daughter of the T'ai-ch'ang Emperor. After making a vain last-minute effort to get the Emperor out of Peking and to safety in Nanking, Kung returned home where he killed his favorite horse, burned his bow, sword, and armor, and wrote the following inscription on the wall: "Being favored by the court for generations, my body cannot be insulted." The coffin containing his wife's corpse was still in the house, because the recent disturbances had made it impossible to conduct the funeral. He bound his seven children with a yellow rope, tied it to the coffin of their mother, and ordered the house set afire. He and the seven children perished in the flames. The third example of mass suicide occurred at Hanyang in the early summer of 1643. Chang Hsien-chung was attacking the city and it was on the verge of falling. Grand Secretary Ho Feng-sheng happened to be in Hanyang and determined to commit suicide rather than be captured by or surrender to the rebels. He put on his official robes, kowtowed toward the north, and then loaded his entire family into a boat at the bank of the Yangtze. The boat was rowed to the middle of the river and sunk after a hole was knocked in the bottom. The entire family was drowned.

Another accepted means of displaying patriotism was to allow oneself to be captured by the rebels, but then to refuse adamantly all offers to surrender, to scoff at threats, and to curse one's captors vehemently even up to the very point of death. Numerous examples of such cases are depicted in the sources. One occurred at Chia-hsien, Honan, captured by Li Tzu-ch'eng in 1643. The town had fallen only after a vigorous fight and the rebels, upon finally overcoming the defenders, started widespread slaughtering in revenge. The county magistrate shouted at the rebels, demanding that they cease killing innocent people and proclaiming that he alone was responsible for the desperate resistance. The magistrate was seized and brought before Li, who after being cursed roundly, ordered him stripped of his clothes and hung upside down on a tree. Even this treatment did not silence the determined magistrate who continued cursing and threatened to present the case against the rebels before the spirit of the Hung-wu Emperor in Heaven. Finally, the rebels cut out his tongue and chopped him in pieces. Another case occurred early in 1644 when Ta-t'ung fell to Li Tzu-ch'eng and the Grand Coordinator Wei Ching-yüan was taken captive. Li offered Wei a high position in his administration, but Wei refused and burst into tears. Li, apparently feeling that Wei would eventually change his mind, called him a loyal official and ordered that he not be killed. Wei responded to Li's statement by violently hitting his head against the ground, and though seriously wounded, he cursed the rebels so bitterly that they became enraged and killed him. A third example occurred during Chang Hsien-chung's invasion of Szechwan in 1644 when Regional Inspector Liu Chih-po was captured. Since he was a native of Shensi, the rebels were particularly anxious to have him join their administration. He refused their offer and cursed them. They responded by starting to slash at him, and just before he was killed, he screamed at them the following appropriately paternalistic Confucian phrase: "I would have you pierce me one more time than you want to, but in return for this, you should kill one person less than you had originally planned to." The final example occurred in the winter of 1642 when Li Tzu-ch'eng defeated a government force under Yang Wen-yüeh in Honan. Yang was captured and brought before Li who pointed out that even though he was a high Ming official, such a position was of little aid to him in his present hopeless situation. Yang replied, "I regret that I have no more troops to kill the rebels. What I have in mind now is to die. I have nothing else to say." He then started cursing the rebels and was soon killed. The rebels had so much respect for his bravery and loyalty that they erected a tombstone over his grave inscribed with the words "Tomb of Loyal Minister Yang Wen-yüeh."

A third type of action which an official could employ in an extreme situation and be considered patriotic was to respond to rebel capture with dignity and quiet determination, rather than with violence and curses. An example occurred as early as 1634 when the Shensi town of Lin-yu fell to the rebels and the magistrate was taken captive. Refusing a rebel proposal that he surrender, he was imprisoned and proceeded to starve himself to death in only six days time. Another example took place in 1643 when Chang Hsien-chung captured Yung-chou in Hukuang and Censor Liu Hsi-tso was made prisoner. He was detained first in a post station and subsequently in a Confucian temple where he wrote a short essay on the walls of his room. The essay's basic theme was an exhortation to himself to endure even death before betraying his loyalty to the Emperor. Finally, after confronting Chang Hsien-chung himself and refusing to surrender, he was killed. A third example occurred in Szechwan during Chang's invasion when the magistrate of Hua-yang was taken captive and imprisoned in a Buddhist temple. He determined to starve himself to death, but when he was still alive after continuing his fast for two weeks, the rebels attempted to lure him into surrendering by placing food before him and inviting him to eat. Instead of accepting their invitation, he responded with the acid remark, "I eat only the rebels' flesh, never their food." His reply so enraged the rebels that they killed him.

Another acceptably patriotic type of gesture was that made by officials who, while captives of the rebels, performed a service for the imperial cause at the cost of their own lives. For example, in 1635, the rebels seized Ch'in-an, Shensi, and took the magistrate prisoner. They forced him to accompany them to the town of Ning-chiang and demanded that he persuade the garrison troops of the town to surrender. Instead, the magistrate exhorted the soldiers to do their best to defend the town, and was immediately killed by the rebels.

The most obvious and expected manifestation of patriotism by officials and military officers was the display of bravery and courage while fighting the rebels in battles. There are innumerable examples of this type of patriotism, but certainly one of the most striking is recounted in the following passage:

On the 14th [of July, 1643], Rebel Chang Hsien-chung approached Wuchang. Ts'ui Wen-yung attacked him at Hung-shan Temple and some rebels were slain or captured. The rebels arrived in ranks and Wen-yung gathered his forces and entered the city. Together with Ho Feng-sheng, he guarded it. On the 15th, the rebels attacked the city. The Local Commander, Chu Shih-ting, commanded the naval forces and Hsü Hsüeh-yen commanded the new land forces. Wen-yung led them and went out of the city to attack the rebels. He uttered a great shout and killed three rebels. He fought to the death. Hsüeh-yen struggled with the rebels and they cut off his left arm. His right arm grasped a knife and did not falter. The rebels seized and dismembered him. Shih-ting was seized by the rebels and both hands were cut off at the wrist. He ran away to the river bank. Shih-ting tied a writing brush to his arm and wrote a passage for his family's records. When he had finished, he cursed the rebels and died.[11]

Though the majority of the displays of patriotism mentioned in the sources are credited to officials and military officers, they by no means have a monopoly. Many other types of people—common soldiers, palace ladies, degree holders who occupied no office, wives, daughters, sing-song girls, private scholars, eunuchs, actors, beggars, artisans, and even children—are depicted as performing praiseworthy acts of patriotism.[12] Examples in each of the above twelve categories will be cited to illustrate the extent to which the sources present patriotism as a rather broadly based phenomenon.

Common soldiers: When Chang Hsien-chung captured Changsha, he killed the official who had assumed the responsibility for the defense of the city. The unfortunate man had been abandoned by all but nine of his troops, and the rebels killed five of the nine loyal holdouts. However, they consented to allow the surviving four to remain alive and bury their former commander. After the task of burial had been accomplished, all four of the soldiers committed suicide beside the newly constructed tomb.

Palace ladies: Following the capture of Peking by the rebels, some two hundred palace ladies in the Imperial City threw themselves in the moat or in wells. One of them, a sixteen-year-old girl surnamed Fei, was rescued by the rebels before she had succeeded in taking her life. At first, she was mistakenly identified as the daughter of the Emperor, but when it was discovered that she was not, she was given to a rebel officer as a wife. During the celebration of the nuptials, she enticed her husband to become completely intoxicated, killed him, and then cut her own throat.

Degree-holders who occupied no office: Hsü Yen, a *chu-sheng* of Ch'ang-chou, Nan-chihli, had a great reputation for loyalty and filial piety. As a youth, he had cut flesh from his own buttocks and served it to his mother who was suffering from an illness which supposedly could be cured only by her eating human flesh. When the news of the fall of Peking and the suicide of the Emperor arrived in his district, he determined to commit suicide. His first three attempts, twice by hanging and once by drowning, ended in failure, because each time he was forcibly prevented from destroying himself. He then decided to starve himself to death and finally managed to die in this fashion.

Wives: The son of a Grand Secretary, who was a native of Szechwan and was residing at home when Chang Hsien-chung invaded the province, surrendered to the rebels and consented to serve in their administration. His wife was so outraged at him that she hanged herself after shouting, "You can become a rebel official, but I do not think I can become a rebel's wife."

Daughters: When Chang Hsien-chung captured Ch'ien-shan, Nan-chihli in 1637, he seized a local Confucian scholar and his daughter. The daughter managed to persuade the rebels to release her father in exchange for her consenting to remain with them. Then, as soon as her father had mounted his horse and ridden away, she took a dagger out of her sleeve and stabbed herself to death.

Sing-song girls: When Chang Hsien-chung occupied Ching-chou, Hukuang, he ordered a dancing troupe to entertain him and his entourage. One girl in the troupe was especially famous for her singing and dancing, but she adamantly refused to perform for rebels. Threats of death failed to make her retract her refusal and she was finally killed by being cut into pieces.

Private scholars: In 1634, when the rebels captured Ta-ch'ang, Szechwan, virtually everyone had fled from the town except a private scholar who donned his formal robes and calmly sat in his study reading historical works. He did not budge when the rebels burst in upon him, but allowed himself to be killed after cursing the intruders roundly.

Eunuchs: When the Prince of Fu was captured by Li Tzu-ch'eng in 1642, he had been abandoned by everyone except a thirteen-year-old eunuch who refused to desert his master. The eunuch exhorted the Prince to maintain his dignity and not degrade himself by grovelling before the rebels. However, the Prince made himself despicable by his abject pleas to Li Tzu-ch'eng that his life be spared. After all the Prince's supplications were rejected and he was killed, the eunuch still refused to renounce his loyalty to his dead master and was slain himself.

Actors: An actor in Peking had been the catamite of a high Ming official and was taken to serve in the same capacity by the rebel officer, Kuan Fu-min, following the rebel occupation of the capital. The actor hated his new patron, and after unsuccessfully attempting to kill him, cut his own throat.

Beggars: Shih Tien of Ch'ang-chou, Nan-chihli, was from a family which had been beggars for generations, but in spite of his lowly status, he had a passionate interest in military affairs and went to extreme lengths to obtain specialized knowledge and training. In 1635, rebels besieged the city of T'ung-ch'eng and Shih volunteered to accompany the official force dispatched to aid the city. In the ensuing battle, Shih demonstrated great bravery and fought until he was decapitated by the rebels. His valor is said to have been displayed even after death, for although his head had been cut off, his body remained standing.

Artisans: A lacquer-worker in Peking was so disturbed over the rebel capture of the capital that he refused to accept payment for lacquering the coffin of one of the loyal officials who had died defending the city. Subsequently, the artisan became grief-stricken upon hearing the news that the rebels had burned the Ming ancestral tablets, and drowned himself in a well after proclaiming that though he was only a common workman, he was still a citizen of the Great Ming.

Children: A small boy in Peking, after learning of the city's fall and the suicide of the Emperor and Empress, threw away his books and knelt crying at his mother's feet. Refusing to be comforted, he ran away and drowned himself.

It can been seen that the ideal of patriotism was a well-developed concept in late Ming times. However, the ideal was considerably more restricted than its modern counterpart which has derived greater scope and sophistication from the phenomenon of nationalism. Lacking a basis in nationalism, late Ming patriotism upheld a limited number of values and its expression was confined almost entirely to the officials, the gentry, the military, and the urban commoners, the peasants being largely unaffected.

Rebel Leadership and Relations with the Gentry

When the late Ming rebellions broke out in northern Shensi, there was little to distinguish the leaders from the rank and file. Both came from similar backgrounds, having been either simple peasants or soldiers who had mutinied against their officers. The gentry and military commanders of the area were almost unanimously opposed to the uprisings, and though they obviously suffered to some extent from the same conditions, particularly the disastrous drought of the late 1620's, the years of ruinous taxation, and the shortage of military supplies and rations, which had pushed the peasants and soldiers into committing acts of violence, they still remained firmly loyal to the dynasty. Thus, there is not a single name of even moderate prominence among the participants in the rebellions at the time of their outbreak. Two or three of the early rebel leaders were perhaps from the fringes of the gentry or from the lower echelons of the military officers.[13] It is known that the rebel chieftain, Chao Sheng, was an educated man and therefore undoubtedly from a family of at least modest standing. Also, at some point during the first half of the 1630's, Liu Kuo-neng, a native of Yenan Prefecture and the holder of the lowest degree, began participating in the uprisings, apparently at first as a result of having been kidnapped by the rebels. He rose to be one of the moderately important chieftains, formed an intimate friendship with Li Tzu-ch'eng, and gained considerable repute in rebel circles for his intelligence, gallantry, and filial piety. However, neither Chao nor Liu ever emerged as a major rebel figure. Chao's career came to a speedy end when he was killed and Liu surrendered to the authorities in 1638, was appointed to a military post, and subsequently sacrificed his life fighting against his former fellow rebel, Li Tzu-ch'eng.

The main initial fact, then, to be noted about rebel leadership is that it had to be produced within the rebel groups themselves. Established leadership talent was not available, and partly as a consequence of this condition, the early phase of the rebellions was extraordinarily chaotic, with numerous small rebel bands operating almost entirely independently. During this initial period, groups would collect rather haphazardly, usually forming around a figure who typically at first displayed no qualities of leadership other than raw courage and physical prowess. Gradually, a more definite group of rebel leaders emerged, largely as a result of demonstrating their ability to survive government attempts at suppression. Such survival was achieved by a combination of sheer good luck, native ability in military affairs, and sufficient negotiating skill to arrange an occasional surrender agreement with the authorities. By the mid-1630's, a vague rebel hierarchy had developed with about a dozen leaders, still operating almost entirely independently, being accorded some recognition as the top echelon of rebel leadership. And even among this top group, Kao Ying-hsiang was awarded the indefinite status of being first among equals. Finally as has been seen, the climax in the emergence of rebel leadership was achieved in the early 1640's when power was concentrated in the hands of Chang Hsien-chung and Li Tzu-ch'eng both of whom had been associated with the rebel movement almost from its very beginnings. Thus, from the very early period of the rebellions until their collapse, one has an unbroken continuity in leadership development, with Chang and Li representing the ultimate in the process of the rebel movement's producing its own top leaders. Furthermore, Chang and Li were born and grew to manhood within a hundred miles of one another in northern Shensi, a fact which provides one indication that their rugged native area was able to capitalize on its having been the spawning grounds for the rebellions by having its native sons play an important leadership role in them until their final collapse.

Looking at the principal subordinates associated with Chang and Li, one is even more impressed at the tenacity with which natives of Shensi held on to power within the rebel movement. Chang's most important lieutenants were the quartet, Li Ting-kuo, Sun K'o-wang, Liu Wen-hsiu, and Ai Neng-ch'i. All four of these men were probably natives of northern Shensi and, judging from the lack of information concerning their early lives, their backgrounds were probably as modest as that of Chang. They undoubtedly joined his rebellion at a very early stage, became his adopted sons, endured the hardships and dangers of the first decade of rebel activities, and shared the relative success of the last phase prior to the final disaster. It is true that all four of them were in substantial disagreement with Chang's resort to violence during the last months of his occupation of Szechwan, and there may be some truth to reports that they plotted to assassinate him. However, if such a plot did exist, it was never carried out, and as far as is definitely known, they remained loyal to their long-time leader until the end of his life. Furthermore, they honored his memory following his sudden death at the hands of the Sino-Manchu force. Thus, Li, Sun, Liu, and Ai represent a leadership continuity at an upper level paralleling that of Chang himself.

Li Tzu-ch'eng's most trusted and long-continuing lieutenants were his nephew and companion from childhood, Li Kuo (his given name was later changed to Chin), and Liu Tsung-min, a blacksmith and a native of Shensi. Both were associated with Li from the early period of his rebellion and were always allowed to act very informally in his presence, even after Li occupied the Imperial City of Peking. For example, at a wine party in the Imperial City, Li Kuo and Liu sat in the presence of Li while all the other rebel leaders stood, and Liu even referred to Li as "elder brother." Thus Li, like Chang, until the very end, shared power most immediately with fellow-provincials with whom he had had a long-term relationship.

Among the wielders of military power in the rebel ranks, one finds the Shensi monopoly broken only when one comes to what might be termed the second echelon of officers and below. At least one finds it broken beginning in the early 1640's when both Chang and Li found their troop strength greatly increased over what it had been in the past. Unfortunately, though the sources contain lists of names of Li Tzu-ch'eng's officers, little information is given concerning their backgrounds, and we do not even know the native areas of most of them. However, there exists a list of fourteen of Chang's officers who were sentenced to execution during the turbulent final months of his occupation of Szechwan, and this list does mention their native areas. Four of the officers were from Shensi, three from Hukuang, three from Nan-chihli, two from Honan, one from Shantung, and one from Szechwan. This provincial distribution is probably fairly typical for Chang's officer group as a whole and for that of Li Tzu-ch'eng as well, although Honanese officers would probably be considerably more numerous in Li's forces. The most significant fact to be noted from the list is the expected one that the officers came from precisely those areas most affected by the rebellions (Shantung excepted) following 1634. It is obvious that once the rebellions had spread outside of Shensi, the rebel groups compensated for losses and gained added troop strength by recruiting new forces, undoubtedly on a rather haphazard basis, in the widespread regions through which they coursed. And though the top positions of military command remained in the hands of the original Shensi group, some authority at lower levels had to be granted to natives of areas in which later recruits were gained. There simply cannot have been enough Shensi natives surviving to fill all the officer positions made necessary by the great expansion of the rebel forces in the early 1640's. In addition, having the new recruits commanded by officers from their native areas would increase military effectiveness.

The Achilles heel of the late Ming rebel movement was the failure to translate military power into political power in the form of solid administrative structures. To be sure, the military power attained by the rebel leaders never assured them of absolute dominance and always exhibited basic weakness. Yet, they did come to possess real military potential, and they remained almost exclusively militarily oriented until the final catastrophes. With few exceptions, the civilian leaders who ultimately attached themselves to the rebel cause were treated as little more than window-dressing and failed to exercise real influence over the direction of affairs. In essence, rebel failure resulted from the inability of the leaders to share power with the members of the gentry who finally were enlisted in the rebel cause, and to follow policies designed to gain more substantial support from the gentry.

As noted earlier, only two or three of the early rebel leaders could be considered as possibly belonging to at least the fringes of the gentry. Also, members of the gentry showed no interest whatsoever in attaching themselves to the rebel cause even after the uprisings had been in progress for several years, and virtually the only instance of a degree-holder joining the rebels prior to the 1640's occurred in the autumn of 1633 when Liang Ming-lun, a holder of the lowest degree, went over to the rebel side during their occupation of Lin-hsien in central Shansi.[14] Liang became an adviser to the rebels, but obviously had no real opportunity to influence rebel policy, because he was killed only four months later when a government force attacked and defeated the rebel group in which he had taken service. For their part, the rebels showed very little interest in deliberately seeking gentry support, and there are only a few instances known when they attempted to persuade captured members of the gentry to join them. And in virtually all of these few instances, the rebel attempts at persuasion were met with refusals. For example, in the summer of 1632, Kao Ch'i-feng of Shun-hua, Shensi, a holder of the lowest degree, came to a rebel group, which was operating in his locality, and sought to obtain the release of his stepmother and sister who had been kidnapped by the rebels.[15] The rebels demanded a horse as ransom for each of the two women, and since Kao had only one horse, he ransomed his stepmother and instructed his sister to commit suicide. The rebels allowed the stepmother to return home, but detained Kao, attempting to persuade him to remain with them as a keeper of records. He refused the requests with such vigor that the rebels were angered and killed him. Thus, the gulf between the rebels and the gentry was wide and rigidly preserved during the first decade of the rebellions.

The first significant contact, albeit still on a decidedly modest scale, between the gentry and a rebel leader occurred in 1638-39 when Chang Hsien-chung arranged a surrender agreement with the authorities and occupied Ku-ch'eng in northwestern Hukuang.[16] At Ku-ch'eng, Chang was openly joined by three members of the gentry: Wang Ping-chen, who was a *chü-jen*, and Hsü I-hsien and P'an Tu-ao, both of whom were holders of the lower *chu-sheng* degree. They remained with Chang during his occupation of Ku-ch'eng, retreated with him when he abandoned the town and resumed his rebellion in the summer of 1639, were captured by Tso Liang-yü when Chang was defeated disastrously at Mt. Ma-nao in the spring of 1640, and were rescued from prison by Chang when he captured Hsiang-yang on March 14, 1641. Thus, the three had a relationship with Chang which extended over a period of some two and a half years. Precisely what role they played is not really known, though it is said that Hsü I-hsien specialized in providing Chang with technical military advice. Their eventual fate is unknown, and they simply disappear from the records following their rescue by Chang at Hsiang-yang. Probably, they were either killed or deserted the rebel cause during the defeats Chang suffered later in 1641. There is no evidence, then, to suggest that Hsü, Wang or P'an exercised any substantial influence on Chang or wielded any real power in the rebel movement.

Chang's next contact with a member of the gentry began in 1642 when he was operating in Nan-chihli and captured T'ung-ch'eng where Wang Chao-ling fell into his hands.[17] Wang was a member of a prominent family and his elder brother held the coveted *chin-shih* degree. Though he was only eighteen years old when he seized by the rebels, for reasons which are never explained in the sources, he soon became a favorite of Chang's and is said to have been granted Chang's daughter as his wife. Wang's influence was destined to be longstanding and he was the only member of the rebel group who succeeded in competing for power with the tightly knit Shensi coterie that had been associated with Chang virtually from the very beginning of his rebellion.

One would give a great deal to know more about Wang and what had occurred in his personal situation to alienate him so completely from the generally accepted gentry values. Perhaps the alienation can be explained simply by his youth and the delight he felt in being freed from the heavy restrictions of a large, tradition-bound gentry household. Certainly, the life he led with the rebels must have been a complete contrast with anything he had experienced previously. Anyway, for whatever reason, he was definitely not a spokensman for moderation, order, and stability. Instead, he pushed Chang toward violence and was probably the single most important architect of the terroristic methods employed by Chang, particularly during the final months of his occupation of Szechwan.

Wang remained with Chang until the very end and his subsequent fate provided an appropriate climax to a career marked by excess and violence. Following Chang's death at Hsi-ch'ung, his group fled southward to Chungking and, in the flight, Wang became separated from the main rebel units. He did succeed in making his way to Chungking, and after rejoining the rebel group, sought to restore himself to a position of power. A dramatic encounter ensued at Chungking between Wang and Ai Neng-ch'i, Chang's adopted son and longtime subordinate. Ai expressed bitter hatred of Wang, stating that his terroristic methods had destroyed the rebel regime at Chengtu and had reduced the group to its present perilous state. Having worked himself into a state of frenzy during this expression of bitterness, Ai seized a bow and arrow and shot Wang in the eye. He fell to the ground and was hacked to pieces by Ai's companions.

Chang Hsien-chung's next contact with the gentry occurred beginning in the spring of 1643 when he moved out of Nan-chihli and invaded Hukuang.[18] His cause was materially aided by his being joined by the leaders of a local rebellion already underway for some months at Ma-ch'eng. Two of these leaders, T'ang Chih and Chou Wen-chiang, were members of the gentry, the latter being the holder of a *chu-sheng* degree. T'ang's subsequent fate is unknown, but Chou accompanied Chang on his successful campaign to capture Wuchang, after the fall of which, he was named Minister of War during Chang's first, though quite desultory, attempts to establish a regularized administrative structure.

In addition to Chou Wen-chiang, some nineteen persons are mentioned by name as having received official appointments to various levels of government from Chang at Wuchang. Two of these are known to have held degrees, one being a *chu-sheng* and another a *chü-jen*. Probably some of the others also held lower degrees, although the fact is not mentioned specifically in the sources, and it seems definite that none of them was really prominent.

As is known, Chang's hold on Wuchang was short-lived and he soon transferred his power base southward to Changsha where he was joined by Shih K'o-ching who seems to have been the first *chin-shih* attracted to his cause.[19] Shih had capped his official career by serving as a Supervising Secretary, but at the time of Chang's capture of Changsha, he was living in retirement at home. For unexplained reasons, he was on very bad terms with the local people and his home had been burned by a mob shortly before the city's fall to the rebels. Thus, Shih undoubtedly was motivated by purely personal grievances, rather than any genuine attraction to the rebel cause, when he attached himself to Chang. Shih was placed in charge of Ch'ang-te Prefecture where his administration is said to have been marked by particularly flagrant displays of violence, earning him the bitter hatred of the local populace.

Apparently only one or two of Chang's Hukuang gentry supporters accompanied him when he abandoned their province to invade Szechwan. Probably, most of them suffered fates similar to that of Shih K'o-ching who was seized by local citizens at Ch'ang-te and handed over to provincial authorities, presumably eventually being executed. Thus, it seems certain that none of the Hukuang gentry succeeded in attaining a position of real power in Chang's group and the great gulf which separated him from the gentry remained unbridged.

It was in Szechwan that Chang had his most extensive contacts with the gentry and had the final opportunity to attach them to his cause.[20] These contacts became important only after his capture of Chengtu when he launched his most ambitious attempts to establish a formal civilian administrative structure. Four *chin-shih*, Chiang Ting-chen, Wu Chi-shan, Kung Wan-ching, and Yen Hsi-ming, became associated with Chang's Chengtu government, Chiang serving as Minister of Rites (first appointee), Wu as Minister of Rites (second appointee), Kung as Minister of War, and Yen as Prime Minister of the Right and Grand Secretary. Chiang, Yen, and Kung were natives of Szechwan and were living at home without official appointments at the time of Chang's invasion of the province. Chiang and perhaps Kung appear to have had no real desire to serve in the rebel regime and had their offices virtually forced upon them. Wu was a native of T'ai-tsang, Nan-chihli and was serving as magistrate of Chengtu County when the area fell to the rebels. His submission to Chang seems to have been entirely voluntary. Following the appointment of the four to office, there was an initial period during which relatively good relations prevailed between them and Chang. Eventually, however, all four of them met violent fates. Chiang burned himself to death, together with his entire family, after he had deliberately set his home on fire. Kung, Yen, and Wu were executed, Wu meeting his end in a particularly brutal fashion. He was skinned and suffered the posthumous indignity of having his skin stuffed with straw, dressed in his official cap and gown, placed in a cart, and paraded through the streets of Chengtu as a means of striking terror into the populace.

Two other known members of the gentry served in the top echelons of the Chengtu administration: Wang Chao-ling and Hu Mo. Wang served as Prime Minister of the Left, the highest position in the governmental hierarchy, and because of his longstanding relationship with Chang, he exercised real power. Hu is described as a student and presumably was a native of Szechwan. He is little more than a name in the sources and obviously exerted no real influence even though he was named Minister of Personnel.

The Ministry of Revenue at Chengtu was headed by Wang Kuo-ning, the Ministry of Justice by Li Shih-ying, and the Ministry of Works by Wang Ying-lung. Nothing is known about Wang Kuo-ning, but Li Shih-ying is described as being a Taoist priest and Wang Ying-lung as an arrow-maker. Thus, it seems certain that Li and Wang Ying-lung were commoners and probably were natives of Chengtu who performed some service to the rebel cause which was sufficiently impressive to make Chang want to award them special recognition. It is interesting that Li and Wang are the only Ministers who are known to have survived the collapse of the Chengtu administration. They accompanied Chang to central Szechwan and apparently were still with him when he was overtaken by the final disaster at Hsi-ch'ung.

At the local level, Chang's regime undoubtedly attracted the support of a number of gentry members and commoners of some standing who served in the hastily constructed administrations set up in the prefectures, subprefectures, and counties over which the rebels exercised an ephemeral control. However, very little is known about Chang's local adminsistrations beyond the fact that in most areas they were short-lived. Thus, Chang's local civil officials, like those in the central government, remained always on the periphery of authority and were afforded no opportunity to make real contributions to the stability of the Chengtu rebel regime.

Li Tzu-ch'eng's first significant contact with the gentry did not occur until early in 1641 when he was well on his way to a major breakthrough for power in famine-stricken Honan.[21] It must not be supposed, though, that the gentry flocked in large numbers to Li, for the fact is that he was joined by a mere handful, of whom only Li Yen and Niu Chin-hsing ever became really important. The essential facts about Li Yen and Niu Chin-hsing have already been related, and the only point of reminder which needs to be said here is that they represented quite different types of attitude. Li Yen was a dedicated exponent of the Confucian humanistic ideals of moderation, stability, and order, and he joined the rebel cause out of a sincere desire to see these ideals infused into the new dynasty which he hoped Li Tzu-ch'eng would found. Niu Chin-hsing, on the other hand, was a self-server and attached himself to the rebels largely as a means or promoting his own personal interests.

The next period to see a substantial increment to Li's gentry supporters began early in 1643 when the rebel center shifted from Honan to Hukuang[22] and Li established himself at Hsiang-yang from where he sought to expand toward the west, south, and east. In the course of this expansion, at least four members of the gentry attached themselves to his cause: Li Chen-sheng, Yang Yung-yü, Kung Yu, and Chang Kuo-shen. All of these men were probably either *chü-jen* or *chin-shih* and had occupied or were currently occupying official positions: Li as a Censor, Yang as an Erudite in the Directorate of Astronomy, and Kung and Chang as Circuit Intendants. They were all perfectly respectable representatives of the established order, but none of them could be said to have held really prominent positions. All of them were appointed to serve in one or another of the Six Ministries which Li first set up in Hsiang-yang and later reshuffled at Sian.

Throughout the remainder of 1643, when Li returned to Honan, crushed the last major force the dynasty mustered against him, and then marched to victory in Shensi, other members of the gentry joined him.[23] Still, the movement to his cause was a mere trickle, rather than a tidal wave. Furthermore, undoubtedly many of the officials who ostensibly submitted and served in local administrations supposedly loyal to him, were not really committed to the rebel cause. They were chiefly interested in preserving order locally and were waiting to see what the future brought on the national level.

At Sian, Li had the opportunity of solidifying his administrative structure in a situation which saw him freed entirely of military threats and pressures, and he made appointments to all of the Six Ministries as well as to certain other offices. However, though his civil government probably became slightly more functional than that of Chang Hsien-chung at Chengtu, it remained a rather bloodless entity, and there is even some confusion in the sources as to exactly which individuals were appointed to what offices. Thus, Li set out for Peking early in 1644 at the head of a movement which was still almost entirely narrowly military in orientation. A breakthrough to broad political power had not been achieved and authority in his organization was still confined to a well-established and relatively longstanding coterie tied to him in a complicated system of personal relationships.

Following his victory at Peking, Li Tzu-ch'eng had his final chance to broaden his political support, and most of the bureaucracy of the Ming central government was at hand to be used as a quarry for talent.[24] But he made no really effective efforts to enlist supporters and expended a great deal of energy in the rather sterile pursuit of milking the ex-officials of their hoarded gold and silver, most of which was later lost to the Manchus and Wu San-kuei. To be sure, Li was operating under great pressure at Peking, particularly the threat posed from the northeast, and probably he would eventually have been destroyed by the Manchus and Wu San-kuei, no matter what he had done in Peking. Furthermore, occupying the capital only from April 24 to June 4, he did not have sufficient time to make any systematic effort to gain wider support. However, he certainly could have made greater endeavors toward strengthening his administrative structure and his failure to do so definitely hastened the disaster which befell him.

Li fled from Peking without a single new supporter of any stature and with his old organization badly shattered by the defeat at Shanhaikuan. His future, as has been seen, was one of continuous decline, and far from gaining additional support, he lost most of what he had.

A final type of leader that succeeded in exerting some influence in the rebel movement was the shaman[25] who sometimes combined a more routine practice of medicine with a display of magical powers. The shaman in Chang Hsien-chung's group was named Ch'en Shih-ch'ing, a native of Honan, who is alleged to have learned such amazing medical skills from a book obtained from an old man in the mountains that he was able to bring the dead back to life. Such an ability is said to have been highly prized by Chang who was disposed to sudden bursts of anger during which he would kill valuable subordinates, and later when he regretted his actions, he would use Ch'en's skills to restore them to life. Chang greatly honored Ch'en, calling him "Old Divine Immortal," and once in Changsha, he had a high platform erected, placed Ch'en on top of it, and surrounded it with masses of rebel troops who raised a great cheer in recognition of the shaman's special position. Li Tzu-ch'eng's shaman, named Sung Hsien-ts'e, was also a Honanese. He was nicknamed "Dwarf" or "Little Child" because of his crippled body and short stature. He was used upon several occasions to perform divinations, and is said to have predicted correctly the time at which Peking would fall. However, despite the honors bestowed upon the shaman by the rebels and their use of his services, we have seen that the supernatural was not a major force in the late Ming peasant rebellions, and no shaman ever succeeded in occupying a dominant position of power in any of the rebel groups.

Summing up the leadership in the rebel movement, particularly that associated with Chang Hsien-chung and Li Tzu-ch'eng, it is obvious that the rebellions had to fashion their own leaders out of persons from quite lowly backgrounds. Not a single really distinguished Ming official or really prominent military commander ever gave the rebellions his support. Furthermore, the rebel leaders, undoubtedly due in part to the fact that they had been initially only simple peasants or soldiers, always remained committed to narrow military orientations. They could not attract widespread gentry support which would have permitted them to erect really viable administrative structures. It is true that some members of the gentry joined the rebel cause, but they were insignificant numerically (certainly no more than a few hundred even if one includes those who served only on a local level); many gave only half-hearted support at best; and, with a few exceptions, none of them ever attained a position of real power and influence in any of the rebel groups. The exceptions would be Wang Chao-ling with Chang Hsien-chung and Li Yen and Niu Chin-hsing with Li Tzu-ch'eng. However, Wang, although technically a member of the gentry, for unknown personal reasons was completely alienated from the dominant values of the gentry "Great Tradition" and therefore was atypical of his class. Niu Chin-hsing was not a genuine exponent of gentry values either and joined the rebels mainly out of self-interest. Li Yen alone could have bridged the gap between the rebels and the gentry, but he never came close to success in making himself the dominant voice in the inner circle surrounding Li Tzu-ch'eng, and was finally destroyed by his master. Thus, the rebels remained unreconciled with the gentry, and the overwhelmingly dominant gentry attitude is aptly expressed by the magistrate of Li's native Mi-chih County when he said, "If Ch'uang had not been born, the country would not be in disorder; if Ch'uang does not die, the country will not have peace."[26]

In the area of supplying leadership, then, the rebels demonstrated a certain competence only in the military sphere. Otherwise, their leadership displayed obvious and fatal deficiencies.

Relations Between the Rebels and the General Populace

In treating relations between the rebels and the general populace, the sources emphasize violence as a major theme, and atrocities attributed to the rebels appear on every hand. In some instances, the atrocities are presented in a rather unspecific fashion and are depicted as general slaughterings and violent actions. For example, when Chang Hsien-chung captured Wuchang in 1643, he is said to have killed, drowned, or mutilated every inhabitant of the city; and a similar fate befell the citizens of a Shansi town in 1644 when it was seized by Li Tzu-ch'eng.[27] In other instances, the atrocities are described in some detail with what appears to be a deliberate effort to make them seem as bizarre and grisly as possible. The following are some of the more horrible examples:[28] the wombs of pregnant women were cut open after the rebels had made bets among themselves as to the sex of the unborn child; the sons of one rebel leader lived on a diet of human hearts which caused their hair and eyes to turn red; disemboweled corpses were used as troughs for the feeding of horses, and in the winter when fodder was scarce, human intestines were fed to horses; a rebel leader killed one of his lieutenants, cooked his flesh, and served it to his other lieutenants; and children were bound together and set afire, the rebels finding pleasure in listening to their screams.

As for the reasons motivating the atrocities, in most instances they are depicted as resulting from nothing more than a basic rebel need to express irrational cruelty. In a few instances, however, the atrocities do have some rational basis.[29] For example, Li Tzu-ch'eng is said to have adopted the following policy in order to encourage towns and cities to surrender to him: if no resistance was offered, no one would be killed; if there was resistance for one day, thirty percent of the inhabitants would be killed; if there was resistance for two days, seventy percent would be killed; and if there was resistance for three days, everyone would be killed. Undoubtedly the percentages cited here are open to considerable doubt, but probably the general principle, a relationship between the vigor of resistance and subsequent rebel violence, was partially valid. Similarly, Chang Hsien-chung's rapid success during his 1644 invasion of Szechwan is said to have been due to his having proclaimed that any city which surrendered to him without resistance would not suffer the fate of Chungking where he had unleashed a massacre following its fall.

It is clear that many of the atrocities and violent acts attributed to the rebels in the sources are highly exaggerated, and in some instances are nothing more than literary stereotypes which are employed to convey only a general impression of barbarity. The alleged rebel practice of cutting open the wombs of pregnant women is undoubtedly such a stereotype, and this particular atrocity has a venerable ancestry going all the way back to the *Book of History* itself where it is cited as one of the crimes committed by the tyrannical last ruler of the Shang dynasty.[30] Furthermore, there are more practical reasons for believing that the sources exaggerate rebel violence. In the first place, during the beginning decade of the rebellions, very few towns were captured by the rebels and even those which did fall were usually occupied for only a few days. Secondly, the sources specifically state on several occasions that the rebels obeyed what was apparently a folk tradition governing their actions following the capture of a town. This tradition held that looting and violence were permitted for only three days and subsequently order should be restored.[31] Thus, the time available would not have allowed the rebels to be very thorough in committing atrocities. Also, the rebel bands until the early 1640's were typically relatively small, and purely on the basis of numbers, could not have succeeded in carrying out widespread slaughtering. Finally, as will be seen, rebel leaders at times performed deliberate acts of benevolence to gain popular support.

It obviously cannot be maintained that the sources are entirely unjustified in ascribing atrocities and violence to the rebels. Certainly the rebels were brutal and violent upon numerous occasions even if never to the degree they are accused of by the sources. As has been seen, until the early 1640's, all the rebel groups were highly mobile bands, moving rapidly from place to place, living off the areas through which they passed, possessing no real motivation more sophisticated than plundering, and being made up virtually entirely of simple peasants and mutinous soldiers. By their very nature, such groups would be disposed to violence. Furthermore, even after Li Tzu-ch'eng and Chang Hsien-chung began to develop vague aims of founding a dynasty in the early 1640's, they were never able to integrate effectively into their plans the Confucian values of benevolence, moderation, and order. They could not rise above irrational violence. As a matter of fact, it was during the last stage of the rebellions that the greatest loss of life occurred, particularly during Li Tzu-ch'eng's third siege of Kaifeng in 1642 and the final phase of Chang Hsien-chung's occupation of Szechwan in 1645. Thus, though the sources admittedly exaggerate rebel barbarism, violence was definitely a feature of the rebellions from their inception to their conclusion. At the same time, it should be noted that in some instances the official forces were even more violent than the rebels, a situation which produced the late Ming popular proverb, "The rebels comb with a coarse comb, but the official forces comb with a fine-toothed comb."

Rebel attempts to appeal to the general populace with benevolent gestures and propogandistic slogans did not occur until relatively late (beginning in the early 1640's) and were never systematically pursued. One of the first of such bevevolent gestures was performed by Chang Hsien-chung when he captured Pa-chou, Szechwan, early in 1641 and proceeded to release the inmates of the prison and to distribute to the populace the funds seized from the local governmental offices.[32] Two months later, he repeated this gesture on a larger scale when he captured Hsiang-yang, took possession of a large amount of bullion, and gave away 150,000 taels of silver to the city poor. Following the fall of Wuchang in 1643, Chang again distributed a large amount of silver, obtained mostly from the wealthy Prince of Ch'u. There is little evidence of more subtle propaganda efforts made by Chang. As noted above, his attempts to discourage opposition, by promising not to harm towns which did not resist him, met with some success during his 1644 invasion of Szechwan. Also, during his occupation of Szechwan, he did make a few bizarre and heavy-handed efforts to obtain popular support.[33] For example, following his capture of Pao-ning, a Buddhist monk appeared at his headquarters with a request that he not harm the town. Chang responded that he would grant the monk's request provided he violated his religious vows and ate pork and dog meat. The monk did eat the meat and Chang ordered that the city not be harmed, adding that, unlike the Ming rulers, he always kept his word.

Li Tzu-ch'eng's first gesture in the direction of obtaining popular support, like Chang's, was a donation to charity following his capture of Loyang and the looting of its official storehouse and wealthy families early in 1641. At approximately this same time, Li began to employ propaganda appeals more extensive than those ever used by any other rebel leader. Li Yen was mainly responsible for formulating and popularizing these appeals whose chief aim was to present Li Tzu-ch'eng as the reliever of economic burdens, the bringer of order, and the upholder of moral values. The appeals were presented mainly in the form of popular slogans, some of which were set to music to facilitate their rapid spread. There flowed out over the Honan countryside such slogans as "To kill a man is like killing my father; to violate a woman is like violating my mother," and "Provide him with things to wear; provide him with things to eat; open the main gate and welcome Prince Ch'uang; when Prince Ch'uang arrives, you will not pay taxes."[34]

More formal attempts to attract public support were launched by Li Tzu-ch'eng in Hukuang in 1643 when he began his efforts to establish an administrative structure. One of his first official proclamations was issued at Huang-p'o in northeastern Hukuang and presents in more sophisticated terms the image which Li had sought to project of himself earlier in the popular slogans. It read as follows:

The befuddled ruler of the Ming dynasty is not benevolent. He holds the eunuchs in his favor, overemphasizes family background in matters of promotion, is greedy about taxation, and uses penalties overly much as a means of ruling. He is not able to rescue the people. The necessities of life are being daily exhausted. Government troops rob the people of their property, ravish their wives and daughters, sap from them their very sinews, and divest them of their skins. Those in my camp have been farming for ten generations and are altogether good. We have raised an army of benevolence and righteousness in great anxiety to rescue the people from suffering. We have already pacified Ch'eng-t'ien and Te-an, and are coming in person to Huang-chou. A notification board is sent informing you of our arrival. People shall not be frightened. Let them maintain their ordinary way of life. If there are those in any of our groups who arbitrarily kill good and innocent people, the entire group will be executed. You, people, who welcome our royal army with cheering and trumpet-blowing, will be given important employment. The rest of you shall not be in army uniforms, as that would make it difficult for us to distinguish stone from jade.[35]

Li's most extensive surviving proclamation was made public when his armies had pressed to the gates of Peking. It was composed by Niu Chin-hsing, assisted by other gentry subordinates of Li, and was shot into Peking by arrow. It read as follows:

The Divinity-on-High looks down upon the earth with actually only the one purpose of detecting distress among the people. Below, the people go with someone only expecting of him forthcoming relief. Since the Mandate is not permanent, the popular sentiment is even more inclined to change. By investigating into the foregoing dynasties, the origin of a gain or a loss can be ascertained. By looking into the past and meditating on the present, the reasons for a period of peace and prosperity or a period of disturbance will be obtained. Your Ming Dynasty has long been sitting on peace and prosperity, but your grand virtues have been declining. The ruler is not too ignorant, but being isolated as he is, numerous things are constantly hidden from him. The ministers are all pursuing their selfish interests, faction-ridden and rarely public spirited or loyal. There are even those who bribe their way through the Inner Palace. The prestige and blessings of the Imperial Court are daily moving away, while the benefits are being monopolized by the gentry. The wealth of the people has almost been exhausted. Great Heaven is poor in benevolent love. Multitudes of people are thus suffering from calamities. We have risen up from the common folk. We have seen with Our own eyes the actualities of the people's sufferings. We have experienced with Our body the pains of the ailing masses. Thinking of the whole country being afflicted with poverty and suffering, how could We bear to leave the I River and Mt. Yen to themselves without being relieved from the boiling water and fire. We have gone in person to Heng and Chi and pacified a group of leaders. Fearing that you, Sir, and your ministers have not quite penetrated the meaning in Our Imperial heart, and not quite understood Our intentions, We henceforth speak directly to you and officially inform you. If you are capable of perceiving the will of Heaven, thinking of your ancestors, weighing your own virtues, and seeing the times clearly, We will grant favors to your predecessors and will not be parsimonious toward outsiders. Just as in the cases of the states of Ch'i and Sung, the enjoyment of worship by your ancestors will continue forever. Your filial piety is thus made widely known. With family retained and the people pleased, your benevolence is thus made clear to everybody. All the officials, if diligent and obedient, will get new appointments. Let the practice of bestowing abundant emoluments upon the descendants of the Shang dynasty be perpetuated and let the good reputation of the descendants of the Hsia dynasty be continued. And let the ministers' way of serving be unchanged. In order to demonstrate sincerely Our very heart, this Edict is announced. You, Sir, think about it. Do not blame the lower officials. Do not endanger the people at large. Let the ministers be cautious. It is hoped that all of you will be loyal to the ruler-father and extend benefits to yourselves and to your families. Respectfully announced.*

Most of the rebel leaders, other than Chang and Li, made few efforts in the direction of propaganda appeals. However, there was at least one interesting exception, and that was a minor rebel group in Pei-chihli which always displayed a banner on which was inscribed what is probably the most revolutionary slogan appearing during the entire late Ming rebel movement. The slogan read, "To follow the right Way on behalf of Heaven in killing the wealthy and aiding the poor."[36] Undoubtedly the group had close connections with a religiously oriented

---

* *PKC* 9/6a-b. Heng and Chi refer to the north China provinces of Pei-chihli, Honan, and Shansi, or, probably, in the context here, to north China generally. The Ch'i and Sung states existed during the Chou feudal period, the ruling family of Ch'i supposedly being descendants of the Hsia royal house and the ruling family of Sung being descendants of the Shang royal house. Thus, the Ch'i rulers carried on the sacrifices to the Hsia kings and the Sung rulers continued those to the Shang kings. The inference is obviously that Li Tzu-ch'eng will follow this venerable precedent and allow sacrifices to be continued to the Ming emperors.

secret society, because the members are said to have worn red cloths wrapped around their heads and green and red clothes. The group never attained more than local importance.

What success did the rebels have in their efforts, both deliberate and indirect, to evoke a popular response in support of their cause? The evidence quite clearly suggests that until around 1643, there were only sporadic instances of popular support offered to the rebels. For example, in late 1631 the rebels attacked An-ting, Shensi, and the tensions between rich and poor in the town were so acute that the lower classes joined with the rebels and the town was occupied.[37] Similarly, disaffected elements assisted the rebels in capturing Lo-t'ien, Hukuang, and T'ai-ho, Nan-chihli, in the spring of 1635.[38] Generally speaking, however, cooperation between the rebels and the civil population prior to the 1640's was limited and tended to be confined to highly temporary situations when a rebel band and some local group would discover that they had certain interests in common.[39] Thus, upon occasion peasants would supply the rebels with information about the official forces in exchange for a remuneration or they would sell provisions to rebels who had withdrawn into concealment after suffering a particularly devastating defeat. Also, cases are known to have occurred when local groups would join the rebels temporarily in looting neighboring areas. In addition, there were instances when the rebels killed oppressive and unpopular local officials who had been seized by a mob and subsequently handed over to a nearby rebel band for punishment.

It was only in the early 1640's, particularly beginning in 1643, that there were significant indications that the rebels were gaining popular support for reasons other than transitory mutual self-interest. As has been seen, early in 1643, Chang Hsien-chung moved into eastern Hukuang[40] from Nan-chihli, and found his cause considerably aided by being invited to join forces with a rather important local rebellion at Ma-ch'eng, an area where disparities in wealth seem to have been particularly acute. Partly on the basis of the momentum his cause gained from the new forces he obtained at Ma-ch'eng, Chang subsequently established a power base first at Wuchang and later at Changsha. As he expanded from the Changsha base to encompass a rather extended area in central Hukuang and Kiangsi, there occurred several instances of additional local groups showing considerable enthusiasm in submitting to Chang and bringing about the surrender of their areas to him.

Paralleling the experience of Chang Hsien-chung, Li Tzu-ch'eng, beginning in 1642 or 1643, also started to attract a certain amount of popular support.[41] Such support first manifested itself particularly in Honan where several localities accepted his authority in a completely orderly manner and a quite regularized transfer of power was accomplished between the incoming appointees of Li and the outgoing Ming officials. Subsequently, in Shensi, there is evidence of a general initial acceptance of Li and some areas even requested that he dispatch officials to govern them, replacing the Ming authorities. Finally, Li's sweep across Shansi and a portion of Pei-chihli to Peking was virtually a triumphal march with little resistance and indications of considerable popular acceptance.

Assessing the rebel propaganda efforts, it can be said that only those made by Li Tzu-ch'eng ever became significant in degree or enjoyed any marked success. Undoubtedly, Li's popular slogans eschewing violence and promising relief from taxation exerted real appeal in Honan where the peasantry was suffering from famine, onerous tax burdens, and administrative chaos. However, it should be emphasized that none of Li's propaganda called for real departure from established precedents and was all safely within the confines of Confucian benevolence, order, and moderation. His Peking proclamation, drawn up as it was by gentry hangers-on, strikes one as being particularly conservative. Its main appeal is for the Ming Emperor and officials to recognize that the Mandate of Heaven has shifted to Li's Shun dynasty and that there should be as peaceful a transfer of power as possible.

As for popular support accorded the rebels, such support was not significant until the early 1640's when it began to be granted to Chang Hsien-chung in Hukuang and subsequently in Szechwan. Chang's abject failure in utilizing the potentialities of popular support has been made clear in previous sections. Li Tzu-ch'eng's evocation of popular support achieved more success than that enjoyed by any other late Ming rebel leader. Such support was particularly strong in Honan and Shensi and existed to a lesser degree in Shansi and Pei-chihli. However, one senses that Li's popular support was primarily negative in character, being accorded him largely because temporarily there was no other choice available. Furthermore, Li was never able to utilize or channel effectively the popular acceptance he had gained. His support evaporated almost overnight following the decisive defeat he suffered at Shanhaikuan and it was impossible for him even to attempt to employ it in escaping the final disaster which overwhelmed him.

Rebel Organization

Rebel organization is a topic which is relatively neglected in the sources undoubtedly due to the difficulty the officials had in gaining information about what went on inside rebel groups. Reports on rebel organization were probably quite rare, making it difficult for the future compilers of the works dealing with the rebellions to treat the subject with even a fair degree of completeness. It is apparent, though, that officials did make some attempt to inform themselves about the inner workings of rebel groups, employing such means as questioning captured rebels and examining rebel documents that had come into their possession. Thus, some information is available concerning rebel organization.

As would be expected, it is particularly difficult to treat rebel organization during the early years of the rebellions, due both to the lack of information in the sources and to the fact that the organization of the rebel groups was undoubtedly extraordinarily simple, consisting probably of no more than a leader, a handful of lieutenants, and a mass of followers. Virtually the only general organizational terms referred to in the sources during the early years are *chia*, which might be translated as "unit," and *ying* ("camp"). It is said, for example, that the rebels who assembled for the conclave at Jung-yang, Honan, early in 1635 were divided into thirteen "units" which were subdivided into seventy-two "camps."[42] The term "thirteen units" was even used to refer to the rebels in general.

Beginning in the middle of the 1630's, slightly more information about rebel organization is available and probably the organizational structure of the rebel groups became somewhat more elaborate. The term "unit" (*chia*) virtually disappeared and was rarely employed, but "camp" (*ying*) continued to be used and remained the most basic factor in rebel organization until the very end of the movement. Thus, we are told that Li Tzu-ch'eng's forces in 1634 consisted of three camps with the names "Old Camp" (commanded by Li personally), "Outer Camp," and "Inner Camp."[43] Likewise, Chang Hsien-chung's forces when he first occupied Ku-ch'eng, Hukuang, in 1638, consisted of four camps.[44] In 1642 when Chang was operating in Nan-chihli, his forces are still described as being divided into four camps, although given the many defeats he had suffered between 1638 and 1642, there undoubtedly had been many changes in the camps during the four-year period. Other information is available concerning the organization of Chang's camps in 1642.[45] Chang occupied the center camp and in tents most immediately surrounding his own lived the scholars whom he had forced into following him and who presumably were kept for the prestige their presence conferred and for the potentially valuable advice they might offer. The next series of tents were inhabited by women, physicians, secretaries, and personal guards, roughly in that order. Camp life was obviously not entirely grim and military-oriented, for the celebration of Chang's birthday is described as being enlivened with considerable gaiety. The commanders of the other three camps and the subordinate officers in his own camp came to offer their congratulations and a wide variety of entertainment was presented, consisting of dancing, singing, music, and the performance of operas.

Apparently after the decline of "unit" (*chia*) organization in the mid-1630's, there was no element in the rebel organizational structure superior to the camp (*ying*). Thus, Chang himself seems to have been the sole unifying factor in the four-camp structure of his forces in 1638 and 1642. There is fleeting mention in a few sources of the term *shao* ("encampment"), and one work states that in 1642, Chang's forces were divided into an "Old Encampment" and a "Little Encampment," the former consisting of thirty-two camps (*ying*) and the latter of twenty-four.[46] However, another source defines an "encampment" as the most basic rebel division and states that it consisted of from 1,000 to 2,000 men.[47] Probably "encampment" (*shao*) was used by some rebel groups instead of camp (*ying*), and the information that it was an organizational structure superior to the camp is in error.

It was in 1643 that rebel military organization began to attain its highest developmental sophistication. As has been seen, Li Tzu-ch'eng in that year occupied Hsiang-yang, Hukuang, and proceeded to form a more definite military structure. He divided his forces into a "Center Camp," "Left Camp," "Right Camp," "Front Camp," and "Rear Camp."[48] The "Center Camp" was under the personal command of Li and consisted of a hundred "companies" (*tui*). Each company was composed of fifty cavalrymen, from 100 to 150 infantrymen, and thirty to forty "little boys" whose chief duty was to take care of horses and perform other servant work. The four other camps consisted of only about thirty companies each, making the total number of companies in all five camps come to around 220. If all the companies were at full strength, Li's army would have consisted of 11,000 cavalrymen and 33,000 infantrymen. Each camp is described as possessing flags and other insignia of its own and various duties were shared by the five camps on a rotating basis. Presumably, this organizational arrangement remained more or less in effect for Li's forces until their rapid decline following the disaster at Shanhaikuan.

The organization of the forces of Chang Hsien-chung also became more complex beginning in 1643 when he moved into Hukuang and launched his efforts to found a new dynasty. As noted previously, in 1643 Chang's army is said to have been divided into four camps, and shortly after going to Hukuang, his strength was augmented by the addition of five camps of new recruits.[49] Thus, it would seem that the camp organization served as the chief means utilized by the rebel leaders in attaching new elements to their forces. That is, the new elements would not be integrated into the already existing rebel camps, but would form new camps of their own.

Chang's military organization reached its ultimate in development following the 1644 occupation of Szechwan, though few details are available concerning the precise form it took. It is said that his forces were divided into 120 camps, though the names of only some twenty-two of them are known: "The Eight Diagrams," "Enciting to Martial Acts," "Surpassing Prosperity," "The Three Rare Things," "Eternal Stability," "The Three Powers," "Thousand Walled," "Bringing Forth Destruction," "Deciding Victory," "Stabilizer of Distant Places," "Inner Storehouse," "Heroic Courage," "Heavenly Majesty," "Dragon Scabbard," "Determined Righteousness," "Heavenly Punisher," "Golden Spear," "Supernatural Divining-straw," "Tiger-like Majesty," "Tiger-like Energy," "Panther Scabbard," and "Tiger-like Plunderer."[50] The existence of such a large number of camps in Chang's forces suggests that there undoubtedly had been alterations in the composition of the camps, making them considerably smaller than they had been previously. Probably the "camp" in Chang's organization was roughly analogous to Li Tzu-ch'eng's "company." At any rate, the very names of Chang's camps are something of an indication of how much more complex his organizational structure had become over what it had been in former times when such simple terms as "Old Camp," "Left Camp," and "Right Camp" had been employed.

The command structure in the rebel military organizations during the first decade was simple and undoubtedly quite indefinite. There does not seem to have been any title whatever to designate the leader of the various rebel groups. However, there were a few titles which were assigned to those who held subordinate positions of military command: *ling-t'ou-tzu, tsung-kuan, kuan-tui,* and *chang-p'an-tzu*.[51] The relationship of these positions to one another is not known and undoubtedly varied considerably. Probably few of the rebel groups made use of all of the titles. For example, it seems that only Chang Hsien-chung's group had *ling-t'ou-tzu*.

In 1643 from his center at Hsiang-yang, Li Tzu-ch'eng made his command structure considerably more formal, setting up four ranks of categories of upper-level positions: *ch'üan chiang-chün, chih chiang-chün, wei-wu chiang-chün,* and *kuo-i chiang-chün*.[52] Two *ch'üan chiang-chün* served directly under Li himself and their authority extended over all five of the camps. The "Center Camp" was commanded by a *chih chiang-chün* under whom served five *wei-wu chiang-chün* and two *kuo-i chiang-chün*. The other four camps were commanded by a *chih chiang-chün* under whom served two *kuo-i chiang-chün*. Beneath these upper-level command positions was the following hierarchy of lower-level officers: *tu-wei, chang-lü, pu-tsung,* and *shao-tsung*. Thus, it is apparent that, at least on paper, Li's group by 1643 had become quite highly structured, though it is doubtful if the formal structure had much meaning in and of itself, probably serving only to confirm already existing personal relationships within the rebel group.

Specialization within the rebel organization definitely existed, particularly in Li Tzu-ch'eng's group, during the later years.[53] The most significant manifestation of such specialization was the existence of an elite body of troops known as *ch'ing-ping*. These troops comprised the cavalry unit in Li's group and were the key element in military engagements. They were accorded such privileges as being permitted to have their wives accompany them and being provided with servants who cared for their personal needs as well as for their four or five horses. Various types of artisans, such as metalsmiths and tailors, also were organized into special units. In addition, there was a supply unit charged with obtaining provisions for the rebel troops and horses.

One of the greatest weaknesses in rebel organization was the failure to establish effective coordination among the various rebel groups until the enforced concentration of power in the hands of Chang Hsien-chung and particularly Li Tzu-ch'eng beginning in 1642. Before 1642, there was little in rebel organizational structure which encouraged intergroup cooperation. During the very early years of the rebellions, the original leaders were accorded some informal recognition as holders of top positions of prestige, though such recognition meant very little in practical terms. Efforts by the rebels to establish more formal and effective intergroup cooperation were attempted on a few occasions, the most ambitious effort occurring at the great rebel conclave held at Jung-yang, Honan, early in 1635. But none of these efforts proved to be at all successful, and prior to 1642, intergroup contacts among the rebels remained sporadic, temporary, and limited. Alliances were formed solely to meet the needs of the moment and typically were soon dissolved except in cases where a rebel leader had been killed or had died. Under these circumstances, the followers of the dead leader would usually attach themselves permanently to another rebel group.

In 1642, the power of Li Tzu-ch'eng increased to such an extent that he was able to attract or force such formerly independent leaders as Ko-kuo-yen, Tso-chin-wang, Lao-hui-hui, Ho I-lung, Ho Chin, Liu Hsi-yao, Cheng-shih-wang, Chih-shih-wang, Yüan Shih-chung, and Lo Ju-ts'ai to join him. Later, in 1643, as has been seen, Li strengthened his grasp on power by destroying Tso-chin-wang, Ko-kuo-yen, Yüan Shih-chung, and Lo Ju-ts'ai whom he regarded as still able to offer some challenge to his position of dominance. Thus, the concentration of control within the rebel movement was accomplished by the expansion of the power of one rebel group rather than by the development of institutions within the rebel organizational structure which succeeded in promoting intergroup cooperation.

The most ambitious rebel organizational efforts were their attempts to establish civil administrative structures. Many of the circumstances involved in these efforts and the failure which so speedily engulfed them have been discussed already. However, a few additional points might be made concerning the administration set up by Li Tzu-ch'eng at Sian and Peking which represented the only rebel government with even a faint chance of becoming the successor to the Ming.

The most significant impression to be gained from Li's government is that it was totally traditional in character, and no evidence exists to suggest that he considered adopting policies designed to favor the peasantry from which he sprang. Any deviation from Ming institutions and practices were superficial and involved mainly alterations in style of court dress and changes in official nomenclature, usually going back to Han and T'ang precedents.[54] For example, the Ming *chi-shih-chung* (Supervising Secretary) was changed to *chien-i ta-fu*, *yü-shih* (Censor) to *chih-chih-shih*, *hsün-fu* (Grand Coordinator) to *chieh-tu-shih*, *chih-fu* (Prefect) to *fu-yin*, *chih-chou* (Subprefecture Magistrate) to *chou-mu*, and *chih-hsien* (County Magistrate) to *hsien-ling*. Also, Li's governmental structure had a kind of triple prime ministry in three offices known as *tso-fu*, *yu-pi*, and *shang-hsiang-kuo*. The Prime Ministry had been abolished by the Ming in 1380, but it had been a common feature of earlier dynasties, although the three official titles used by Li had not been employed. Finally, court dress styles were altered by Li to accord with those in use during the T'ang dynasty.

Other traditional usage employed by Li included his ascending the imperial throne amid as many of the customary rituals as the disturbed conditions in Peking would allow, his awarding titles of nobility (marquis, earl, viscount, and baron) to his favorite subordinates, and his making use of the official examination system.[55] There was apparently a minor alteration (at least the alteration was proposed) in the examination system whereby the stereotyped eight-legged essay style, employed in writing the answers to examination questions throughout most of the Ming dynasty, was abandoned in favor of the less artificial regular essay style. However, the Confucian Classics remained the foundation of the examination system,* and such excerpts as the following were assigned as topic sentences for the essays to be written by the candidates during the examinations

---

* The Marxist-influenced historian, Fan Wen-lan, in his *Chung-kuo t'ung-shih Chien-pien*, 608, maintains that Li's rebel regime in its official examinations asked questions on contemporary problems, instead of on the Confucian classics. However, no real evidence to support Fan's claim has been found in the sources, and it probably represents an attempt to discover in Li some tendencies which are at least faintly new.

held at Sian and Peking: "Heaven gives the Empire to him" (T'ien yü chih) from *Mencius*, "As if hoping for clouds during great drought" (Ta han chih wang yün kuan yeh) from *Mencius*, "To rule the Middle Kingdom and pacify the barbarians" (Li Chung-kuo erh fu ssu i yeh) from *Mencius*, and "The whole world would submit to benevolent rule" (T'ien-hsia kuei jen yen) from the *Analects*. Even Li's move against the eunuchs, ordering that no more than a thousand of them be employed in Peking's Imperial City, was quite traditional. The Ming dynasty, too, in its early years, had issued regulations designed to keep the eunuchs under strict control.

The other significant observation concerning Li's civil administration has been made previously, but shall be re-emphasized here: the administration never escaped from military dominance. Even after the rebel occupation of Peking, civil officials, when paying calls on military officers, were required to kneel at their feet.[56] Furthermore, all civil officials, with the exception of Niu Chin-hsing and Sung Ch'i-chiao, were explicitly subject to military officers. Thus, Li's civil administration was little more than an extension of his military organization, but this is not to say that it could not have evolved and become a viable entity. However, it endured far too short a period to be allowed such an evolution.

Military Aspects of the Rebellions

One of the frequently mentioned and basic military features of the rebellions was their mobility, the most fundamental means by which they survived throughout the first decade and a half. Officials and military commanders constantly pointed out the peculiar difficulties of crushing the rebels when it was impossible to tie them down in one position long enough for a decisive blow to be rendered. Though the authorities attempted to solve the military problems posed by the hit-and-run tactics of the rebels with various combinations of pursuit forces joined to garrison forces, success proved as elusive as the constantly moving rebels themselves.

Mobility meant that no rebel leader established a real base until 1642 when Li Tzu-ch'eng succeeded in obtaining some degree of unsteady control over a considerable portion of southern Honan. It is true that upon occasion previously, various rebel leaders had settled down in a particular locality for a relatively extended period of time. Already in the summer of 1630, Wang Chia-yün captured Fu-ku, in extreme northeastern Shensi, held the town for three months, and attempted to erect fortifications.[57] However, he was unsuccessful in maintaining any permanent base at Fu-ku, being forced out of the area by government forces and subsequently slain. In later years, other rebel groups are known to have settled down, but the abandonment of mobility was temporary and usually occurred in isolated areas to which the rebel groups had withdrawn to escape from the official forces after a particularly devastating defeat. As observed earlier, the area where the provinces of Honan, Shensi, Hukuang, and Szechwan join was an especially favorite one to which the rebels retreated for recuperation.[58] The area had the twin advantages of isolation and strategic location. The isolation made it difficult for the authorities to pursue the rebels into the area and the strategic location meant that regions in which plundering was lucrative were still relatively nearby and could be returned to without much difficulty following regrouping and recuperation. A second recuperation area, though considerably less significant than the first, was the region around Ying-shan and Huo-shan in west-central Nan-chihli. Neither of the recuperation areas, however, constituted a real base either militarily or ideologically.

Though it is obvious that the rebels acquired temporary military advantages from their mobility, in the long run it did serious damage to the rebel cause, for the relative success which had resulted from it caused the rebel leaders to be disposed toward movement for a considerable period after mobility no longer served a useful purpose either militarily or politically. Furthermore, the psychological outlook of the rebel leaders came to be deeply influenced by mobility. For example, Chang Hsien-chung in 1645, confronted with the increasingly hopeless problem posed by his Chengtu government, is said to have looked back with great nostalgia to the carefree days when he was a mere roving plunderer. Obviously, such an attitude made it even less likely that the defects of his civil administration could be rectified. Undoubtedly, though, the most serious mistake in favor of movement was committed by Li Tzu-ch'eng in 1642 when he abandoned Honan before he had acquired real control in depth over the province.

A final misfortune derived from the mobility of the rebels was the blow to agricultural production which must have resulted from the seizure of horses and other draft animals from the peasantry. During the first decade of the rebellions, the rebel troops were probably mostly mounted and it is apparent that they placed great emphasis on obtaining horses. Even subsequently, when the rebel forces consisted of both cavalry and infantry, the former were accorded the position of greater prestige. Though the disaster to agricultural production from horse-raiding was undoubtedly not as dire as is sometimes depicted in the sources, it was still very real.

How did the rebel leaders obtain recruits for their groups? As noted, in the early period of the rebellions, rebel ranks were filled largely by army deserters and peasants who had been driven to lawlessness by drought, famine, increased taxes, and governmental injustices. Subsequent years saw these two groups, and particularly the disaffected peasantry, continue to serve as the principal sources for rebel troops, since the continuance of famine-producing natural calamities and attempts to collect heavy taxes meant that conditions persisted which made recruitment by the rebel groups quite easy. The mere presence of a rebel group in an area would almost automatically inspire disaffected elements in the locality to join it, and the rebel forces came to be composed of troops from virtually the entire diverse rebel-affected region. The rebels upon occasion did resort to more drastic methods of recruitment and would use force to compel young men to accompany them.[59] At times, the rebels would even brand the enforced recruits on the face with some kind of rebel insignia. This action would make desertion from the rebel ranks fraught with some danger, as the authorities would be able to discern that there had been association with the rebels and would very likely conclude that the association had been voluntary.

Desertion from the government armies as a source of rebel recruits seems to have been especially important only during the initial and final periods of the rebel movement. As has been seen, conditions existed in northern Shensi which encouraged desertion. It was a difficult area of service, there was a chronic shortage of supplies, and the isolation of the region made it a haven where survivors from the disasters suffered by Chinese armies in Manchuria could find refuge. Subsequently, when the rebellions expanded into other areas from northern Shensi, there is no evidence to suggest that desertion from the government forces continued to be significant. It seems clear that sizable numbers of deserters did not join the rebels again until the early 1640's when the tide began to turn against the dynasty. Then, undoubtedly, a considerable number of troops from such disintegrating armies as that of Tso Liang-yü switched loyalties in favor of the rebels.

Another aspect to the rebel recruitment of deserters from the imperial forces is that extremely few officers were persuaded to join the rebel cause prior to 1643. For example, during the successful rebel attack on Tse-chou, Shansi, in 1632, it was something of a sensation when the Local Commander of the town deserted to the rebels.[60] During subsequent years, a handful of officers defected to the rebels, but such an occurrence remained highly unusual until 1643. In that year, several defections to Chang Hsien-chung took place during his push southward into Hukuang and central Kiangsi. Even more significant defections occurred in 1643 in favor of Li Tzu-ch'eng, especially following his defeat of Sun Ch'üan-t'ing and advance into Shensi. However, even at their height, the defections of officers were not impressive numerically when one considers them in relation to the total number of Ming officers. Also, the defections which did occur came too late for the rebel cause to derive substantial benefit from them, and virtually none of the top echelon of the Ming military command joined in the move to defect. Thus, Ming military officers were almost as reluctant as their counterparts in the civil bureaucracy to cast their lots with the rebels.

A final point in regard to rebel recruitment is that there was considerable interchange of personnel among the various rebel groups. As noted, when a rebel leader died his followers would usually attach themselves to another rebel group. In other cases, the rebel rank and file might refuse to accompany their commander in surrendering to the authorities and would join a nearby rebel band. In addition, all the rebel groups suffered numerous defeats during the first decade and a half of the rebellions and after such defeats, the troops would often scatter over a wide area. In the process of regrouping, some of the rebels might prefer to join another rebel group instead of rejoining their former one. Thus, during the last phase of Chang Hsien-chung's rebellion in Szechwan, his army is said to have contained remnants from at least six rebel groups, formerly separate and independent.[61]

In the realm of military strategy, the accomplishments of the rebels are singularly unimpressive. In the entire career of Chang Hsien-chung, there is virtually no evidence of strategy except possibly the 1644 decision to withdraw from Hukuang to Szechwan, a move which was probably the greatest mistake of Chang's career. In Li Tzu-ch'eng's case, real considerations of strategy were involved in the decision to attack Peking via the extended semi-circular route leading across Shensi and Shansi instead of the two alternative possibilities: (1) moving directly across Honan to Peking and (2) first seizing the lower Yangtze area and severing the capital's economic lifeline, the Grand Canal. Of the three plans to attack Peking, probably the one chosen by the rebels was the best, particularly because in approaching the city from the north, the rebels either defeated piecemeal or isolated the frontier armies which might have been summoned to the aid of the capital if the rebel forces had approached from another route.[62] There is virtually no other evidence of considerations of strategy by Li, and certainly he was a miserable failure in meeting the major test in strategy: the confrontation between himself and the Sino-Manchu force in the northeast.

In the realm of tactics, where the demands are more modest than those of strategy, the rebels achieved some success. Generally speaking, rebel tactics increased in complexity throughout the 1630's roughly in proportion to the intensifying sophistication of rebel military organization. In the early years of the rebel movement, about the only tactic employed by the rebels was mobility which is hardly deserving of classification as a tactic, since it was almost entirely a spontaneous rebel reaction to basic facts of the military situation they faced. Gradually, the rebel groups developed a series of true tactics, such as ambush, the forced use of civilians in battles, continuously maintaining pressure during an attack, and the use of fifth columns planted inside towns.[63] The prime example of the success of a rebel ambush occurred in the summer of 1639 when Chang Hsien-chung trapped the army of Tso Liang-yü at Mt. Lo-ying in the Szechwan-Hukuang border area. Tso's force was completely dispersed or slaughtered and Chang gained the most significant rebel victory prior to Li Tzu-ch'eng's successes in 1642. Chang also achieved notable gains in capturing towns by the use of fifth columns. The use of civilians in battles was one of the earlier rebel tactics. It involved mainly the rounding up of a mob of ordinary people in a locality and forcibly detaining them in front of the rebel lines where they would be compelled to bear the initial onslaught of the government troops. The tactic does not impress one as having a great deal of military potential, since the civilian mob would undoubtedly soon be scattered by the attacking troops. Perhaps the mob's presence contributed to the rebel cause by creating confusion on the battlefield. The tactic of maintaining continuous pressure against an objective is exemplified by the practice of Chang Hsien-chung who, prior to an important attack, is said to have divided his army into three groups, each headed by a *ling-t'ou-tzu*. The groups would relieve one another in pressing the assault, but if the third group failed to achieve the objective, the attack would be called off.

It was in the forces of Li Tzu-ch'eng that rebel tactics reached their highest point of development in the early 1640's.[64] One of Li's most notable achievements was the development of what was apparently quite an effective system of patrol and communication. This was based on a special corps of horsemen, known as *t'ang-ma*, who maintained a systematic patrol over an area extending for many miles around the rebel encampment. The patrollers noted the movements of government armies, warned of possible enemy attacks, and apprehended rebel troops who tried to desert. Other rebel security efforts included deliberate attempts to discover the military plans of the government and endeavors to keep their own aims secret. For example, Li is said never to have identified the next objective in a campaign until his army was nearing the destination.

Li's battle tactics included the "three-wall tactic" and the "four-layer tactic." The "three-wall tactic" involved arranging his forces in three overlapping lines with troops in the back lines instructed to kill those in front of them if they attempted to retreat. If the enemy stood firm against the pressure of all three lines, Li's cavalry would feign defeat and their withdrawal would entice the government forces to push forward into the rebel center where they would be closed in upon from both sides. The "four-layer" tactic was essentially a somewhat more complicated version of the "three-layer tactic." The additional element was a front line composed of irregulars, mostly untrained famine victims, who had collected around the rebel encampment. Serving in the front line, the irregulars were expected only to slow down the thrust of an enemy attack. Apparently in the crucial battle between Li Tzu-ch'eng and Sun Ch'üan-t'ing in the autumn of 1643, Li employed the "four-layer tactic" and narrowly escaped disaster. Sun's forces penetrated the first three layers and were stopped only by the most elite of Li's cavalry who made up the fourth layer. Subsequently, the tide turned against Sun and he suffered a crushing defeat.

Another element concerning the tactics employed by the rebels was their failure to develop effective naval strength. This failure reflects particularly the land-oriented attitudes of the rebel leadership, dominated as it was by natives of landlocked northern Shensi. The rebel leaders generally deliberately avoided pushing into areas where naval operations would have been necessary or even feasible. It is true that Li Tzu-ch'eng in his move down the Han Valley from Hsiang-yang in 1643 transported his troops partly by water. Furthermore, Chang Hsien-chung's use of naval forces was essential for the success of his 1643 invasion of Hukuang south of the Yangtze. In fact, as has been seen, Chang was the only rebel leader to launch significant operations beyond the Yangtze. Chang's invasion of Szechwan was also based in part on naval power, and following his initial successes in Szechwan, he continued his naval operations at least to some degree. Although Chang developed naval strength more fully than any other rebel leader, he still did not get beyond the preliminary stage in exploiting its military potential. He did not move in the direction of developing a navy until toward the end of his career, used it effectively only briefly, and never altered his primary reliance upon land forces.

Rebel seizure of walled cities and towns and their methods of attacking them provide a good demonstration of increasing rebel mastery of the more technical aspects of warfare.[65] In the early years of the rebellions, even small towns generally were beyond the capacities of the rebels to capture, armed as they were with only the simplest weapons. Thus, the fall of Fu-ku to Wang Chia-yün in the summer of 1630, although the town was quite isolated and relatively unimportant, represented an exceptional rebel achievement.

In 1631 and 1632, when the rebel groups spilled over the Yellow River from Shensi into Shansi, Pei-chihli, and Honan, they manifested a considerably increased military potential, succeeding in capturing such important towns as Tse-chou, Shansi, and Hsiu-wu, Honan, in 1632. Thus, the rebels were launched on a career of town seizures and numerous urban centers fell to them in the years following 1632. Between 1632 and 1641, though the rebels were perfectly capable upon occasion of capturing quite large towns (such as Feng-yang, Nan-chihli, which fell to them early in 1635), really important cities remained definitely beyond their reach. Such cities within the rebel-afflicted area as Sian, Chengtu, Chungking, Hsiang-yang, Loyang, and Kaifeng, though they saw rebel groups operate nearby upon several occasions, remained in safety behind their walls at least until 1641. Furthermore, during the 1632-41 decade, the towns which the rebels did manage to capture could not be held for more than a short time, usually no more than a few days. The seizure of a town, then, meant little more to the rebels than more lucrative possibilities for plunder.

The methods employed by the rebels in capturing towns during the 1632-41 decade included scaling the walls with ladders, having the gates opened by agents working secretly within the town, piling up lumber or soil to form a ramp alongside the wall, and using some means to achieve a breach in the wall. The last method, breaching the wall, was obviously the most difficult, but the rebels did manage upon occasion to succeed in accomplishing it. For example, early in 1636, Kao Ying-hsiang and Lo Ju-ts'ai used cannons to destroy a section of the Kuang-chou, Honan, wall, and the town subsequently fell. This case is one of the earliest examples of the successful use of cannons by the rebels in attacking a town, though they had attempted the same tactic without success as early as 1632 in Shensi during an assault on Ho-shui.

In 1641, the two dominant rebel leaders, Li Tzu-ch'eng and Chang Hsien-chung began to move toward a new level of competence in seizing urban areas, for in the spring of that year, two important cities, Loyang and Hsiang-yang, previously immune to capture, fell to the rebels. From a technical military standpoint, neither Chang's seizure of Hsiang-yang nor Li's seizure of Loyang was particularly noteworthy. The fall of Hsiang-yang was mainly due to a combination of surprise, good luck, and skillful use of inside agents; and Loyang was overrun largely because of massive unrest in the defending forces. Furthermore, neither city remained in rebel hands for longer than a few days. Still, the rebel capture of Hsiang-yang and Loyang marked the beginning of a series of key urban centers lost to the dynasty.

The classic sieges of the entire period of the rebellions were the three (early 1641, early 1642, and the summer of 1642) that Li Tzu-ch'eng laid against Kaifeng. The first siege was insignificant, lasting only seven days.

The second endured for more than a month and was pressed with great determination, most of the rebel energy being directed toward a rather novel attempt to breach the wall. Rebel soldiers in armor dug holes in the wall, and the sections of the wall between holes would be brought down by having large numbers of rebels pull on ropes which had been fastened to the intact sections. Also, some of the holes were enlarged by exploding gunpowder in them. Another novel technique employed by the rebels during the second siege was the construction of a platform higher than the wall, the advantage of which was that the defenders of the city could be fired upon by cannons placed on top of the structure. This rebel technique was rendered useless when the defending troops constructed a platform of their own on top of the wall which towered over the rebel structure. Thus, the second rebel siege of the city ended in failure.

The third Kaifeng siege was planned as a very simple affair indeed. The rebels would merely surround the city and starve it into submission. Thus, the opposing forces sat facing one another throughout the entire summer of 1642 with relatively little action taking place. The very fact that the rebels could engage in such a long siege is of great significance in and of itself. Even a year earlier, if a rebel group had attempted to remain stationary for any length of time, in all probability it would have been descended upon and destroyed by government forces. Thus, even in his inactivity outside Kaifeng, Li was demonstrating the new stage of military power he had attained. The disastrous conclusion of the third siege, when the Yellow River dike was deliberately broken, introduced a quite unique tactic into the military history of the rebellions.

Li Tzu-ch'eng's seizures of cities and towns, following the conclusion of the third Kaifeng siege, is impressive, at least on the surface. There was an almost unbroken series of successes, leading to Peking itself. However, no new techniques emerged in the attacks on the various urban areas during this long succession of victories, and indeed the entire sequence is rather boring from a military point of view. Little serious opposition was encountered and even important cities like Sian offered no resistance whatever. The undramatic submission of Peking to the rebels was a fitting climax to the lackluster campaign which had brought the rebels to the capital.

Paralleling Li Tzu-ch'eng's successes at a somewhat lower level, Chang Hsien-chung, beginning in 1643, marched through the streets of cities which would have been beyond his fondest dreams of conquest even a year earlier. For example, Wuchang and Changsha fell to him in 1643; Chungking and Chengtu in 1644. His capture of Chungking and Chengtu impress one as exhibiting considerable technical military competence. In both cases, the defenders refused invitations to surrender and gave every indication of resisting as long as they possibly could. Chang responded by having his troops dig holes in softer sections of the walls and fill the holes with gunpowder. The gunpowder was then exploded with fire-arrows and the result was a breach in the walls sufficiently large for the rebels to rush in and overcome the defenders. It is apparent that Chang's military capacity had increased markedly by 1644 over what it had been a decade and a half earlier, though this increase had not been accompanied by a corresponding enhancement of his political acumen.

The final elements which might be discussed in connection with the rebel approach to military questions are discipline and training.[66] As has been seen, most of the rebel recruits were peasants who had had no previous military training. Yet obviously the rebel forces must have become something more than a simple mob of peasants or they could not have defeated Ming armies such as the rather effective one under Sun Ch'üan-t'ing. Undoubtedly, the rebel groups varied considerably in discipline, though it probably improved in later years over what it had been earlier. Certainly the initial primary orientation of the rebels toward mere raiding mitigated against their military effectiveness, for obviously rebel troops were not giving a great deal of thought to becoming better soldiers when their attentions were riveted upon such simple and direct interests as pouring water on the foundations of a burned-out house in the hope of discovering where gold and silver had been buried. (If the soil in a particular spot absorbed water quickly, the deduction to be made was that it had been disturbed recently and was likely to have something valuable buried beneath it.)

By the late 1630's or early 1640's, there are definite indications that both the army of Li Tzu-ch'eng and that of Chang Hsien-chung engaged in some more or less formal training exercises and possessed disciplinary regulations. The approach to training and discipline in Chang's group displayed the rough-and-ready attitudes of Chang himself. For example, one of the chief features in training exercises was to have the infantry attack the cavalry, and if an infantryman was able to triumph over a cavalryman, he would be rewarded by being made the successor of his vanquished foe. In discipline, Chang was quite strict about the appearance of his troops on parade. Also, he permitted them to retain only small amounts of the plundered gold and silver, fearing that desertion would be encouraged if they became too wealthy.

Li Tzu-ch'eng enacted quite elaborate and strict disciplinary regulations: no women except wives could accompany the army; desertion was punished by the death penalty, except that in cases when the deserter possessed a really valuable skill, the punishment would be reduced to tattooing or cutting off an ear; hoarding of gold and silver by individual soldiers was prohibited; troops were usually forbidden to live in civilian homes and were required to have their quarters in the rebel encampment where tents, made of such excellent cloth that they were virtually arrow-proof, were provided; and if a cavalryman even accidentally allowed his horse to trample a planted field, he was executed. As for training exercises, the regimen in Li's army strikes one as being almost spartan. The troops are said to have been required to arise at 3:00 A. M. when they were given a meal and had the orders of the day read to them. If no actual military operations were scheduled, the day would be spent in riding, shooting, and climbing mountains.

It is apparent that the rebel leadership had some success in imposing a degree of discipline and training upon the tens of thousands of peasant recruits who joined or were swept up in the rebellions. Li Tzu-ch'eng, in particular, succeeded in fashioning a force militarily superior to anything the Ming authorities were able finally to put in the field against him. Also, in the quality of discipline, probably Li's troops deserve a higher rating than their counterparts in such government armies as that of Tso Liang-yü. However, that basic defects always remained in rebel discipline and military training is attested to in a dramatic fashion by the sudden collapse of the rebel armies when confronted by the Manchus and their Chinese allies.

Turning to a consideration of the military aspects of the rebellions from the government's point of view, perhaps the most basic impression to be gained is that the military institutions of the dynasty had been allowed to deteriorate to a point where they were beyond repair. The military structure established early in the Ming dynasty was the famous Wei-So system which consisted of special hereditary groups, varying in size. Land was assigned these groups and the enrolled soldiers were supposed to be virtually self-supporting by combining their military duties with farming. The groups were settled at various strategic points throughout the country with the expected concentration along the northern frontier. The Wei-So system seems to have remained reasonably effective throughout the first century of Ming rule, but as a result of its subsequent decline, the military needs of the dynasty had to be supplied by mercenaries, whose services were paid for directly, and by a kind of popular militia, enrollment in which was required as part of the expected corvée service. Though the Wei-So system continued its formal existence until the end of the dynasty, it obviously played a very limited role in the anti-rebel campaigns, and is seldom even mentioned in the sources dealing with the rebellions.

The substitutes for the defunct Wei-So system, mercenaries and militia, did not produce effective strength which was capable of withstanding severe tests. Already before the outbreak of the rebellions, the Ming military record against the Japanese in Korea and against the Manchus was a shabby one. No rational system for the recruitment of mercenaries was ever developed and the military potential of the militia was little more than sheer pretense, a condition quite emphatically attested to by such an astute observer as the Jesuit missionary, Alvare de Semedo, who arrived in China in 1613 and lived there until his death in 1658. Semedo speaks of the "small courage and valor" of the militiamen and compares their training exercises to the antics of actors performing upon a stage.[67] Even in sheer numbers, as suggested earlier in the discussion of statistics, the mercenary forces and militia probably were seriously deficient. The modern scholar, Wu Han, cites figures which claim that the Chinese army numbered 1,120,658 men during the early Wan-li period (1573-1620), and Semedo gives a similar figure for the 1620's and 1630's: 1,276,888 (682,888 stationed on the northern frontier and 594,000 inside the country).[68] Probably a substantial percentage of these numbers existed only as fake names on padded roster lists, a type of graft referred to upon several occasions in the sources. Thus, it seems highly likely that the actual numerical strength of the Chinese army was considerably below 1,000,000. Furthermore, many of the soldiers, who in fact really did exist, were assigned to perform completely nonmilitary tasks.[69] This practice seems to have been particularly prevalent at the capital where the garrison troops were frequently used as common laborers, employed in such work as constructing imperial tombs and palaces. It is recorded upon several occasions that troops from the Peking garrison were rated lowest on the scale of military effectiveness by the rebels.

The authorities could scarcely have been unaware of the increasingly desperate need to recruit more and better troops, and the suggestion probably most often paraded forth in memorials was to establish an effective system of local defense. This really meant, though it is seldom explicitly stated as such, revitalizing the Wei-So system or at least reforming the militia system.[70] The expected arguments were advanced to support the suggestions for emphasizing local defense: local recruits would have real commitment to defending their own areas and forces brought in from outside tended to be on bad terms with native residents as well as being disposed to violence. There were many examples of localities which managed to make effective contributions to their own defense, but, in the long run, whatever appeal the arguments for local defense had in the abstract, the military demands became too great to be satisfied on the local level. Already by the early 1630's, there were too many rebel bands operating and they had attained a numerical strength which enabled them upon occasion to overrun even walled towns of some size. In the final analysis, all the suggestions about local defense did little to help solve the military problems of the dynasty.

In attempting to formulate a viable recruiting policy, the government had some limited success in turning to such groups as salt workers and miners.[71] Also, it is interesting that several officials expressed a high opinion of the military abilities of the southwest aboriginal people, one source elaborating further by stating that the aborigines had a good knowledge of firearms.[72] Probably such knowledge was gained from contact with European-style firearms through Southeast Asian sources at a time when such weapons were relatively unknown in most sections of China. However, although some aboriginal forces were dispatched outside their native southwest for service against the rebels, it was vain to expect them to save the dynasty. In the final analysis, the only real chance that the government had of obtaining any substantial military strength was provided by the recruitment efforts undertaken by provincial officials and military commanders, Sun Ch'üan-t'ing and Tso Liang-yü being particularly good examples.[73] Sun's army, raised and supplied entirely on his own initiative in Shensi, impresses one as possessing real potential and it could undoubtedly have given a good account of itself if challenged in the home area. However, before it could develop solid foundations, it was sacrificed in a futile attempt to crush Li Tzuch'eng in Honan. The army of Tso Liang-yü, in contrast, is hardly deserving of much praise. Raised in a decidedly *ad hoc* fashion which could not have differed substantially from the recruitment methods employed by the rebel leaders, its structure and management undoubtedly reflected the lowly origins and complete lack of formal education of its founder. The discipline of Tso's army, always a problem, virtually disappeared following the defeats at the hands of Li Tzu-ch'eng in the summer of 1642, and Tso's forces had to be recalled from operations against Chang Hsien-chung in central Kiangsi in 1643 when their depradations threatened to spark serious popular reprisals. In short, though Tso was able for some time to achieve success by what amounted to outdoing the rebels at their own game of collecting recruits from uprooted elements, his total impact upon the late Ming military scene produced more misfortunes than benefits. Tso's troops, with their disposition to plundering and other acts of violence, were all too typical of the late Ming forces generally.

Before bestowing a verdict of absolute condemnation upon the wielders of military power in the late Ming dynasty, one should examine somewhat more carefully the extensive problems they faced and the moderate successes they achieved. Perhaps most dangerous of all the problems was the legacy of defeat in Manchuria, extending back to the late Wan-li period, and the consequent necessity of fighting on two fronts: against the Manchus and the peasant rebels. The struggle with the Manchus had initiated a vicious cycle with political, economic, and military ramifications: an increasing need for more tax revenues. The internal rebellions obviously supplied additional pressures which caused the cycle to spin even more dizzily and made efforts to stop it all the more impossible. A somewhat more restricted problem was the frequently-mentioned rebel mobility about which only one additional point needs to be made: there seems to have been an institutional inadequacy which frustrated the effective handling of problems involving several provinces. Reference here is particularly concerned with the office of Supreme Commander. As has been seen, several Supreme Commanders were appointed and at times their authority was supposed to extend over virtually the entire rebel-afflicted area: Nan-chihli, Honan, Hukuang, Szechwan, and Shensi. However, none of the Supreme Commanders achieved really notable successes against the rebels and certainly their accomplishments cannot compare with victories gained upon occasion by professional commanders or officials whose base of power was largely or wholly provincial. Undoubtedly, part of the general ineffectiveness of the Supreme Commanders was due to accidental or personal factors. For example, the Supreme Commander of whom the most spectacular achievements were anticipated, Yang Ssu-ch'ang, proved to be probably the most miserable failure of them all, and his appointment was a drastic mistake, rivaled in its lack of realism only by the later proposal (1643) that the Emperor assume personal command of the dynasty's forces and defend the Yellow River against Li Tzu-ch'eng's advance from Shensi. However, though one recognizes the personal deficiencies of individual Supreme Commanders, probably more basic weaknesses were the cause of their general lack of success, and it seems likely that institutional flaws in the office deprived it of the authority necessary to cope with major interprovincial problems.

The major official military success undoubtedly was the long-maintained defense of the Yellow River.[74] As has been pointed out, the rebels in 1632 and 1633 had pushed east from Shensi across the Yellow River and during those two years operated mainly in Shansi, northern Honan, and western Pei-chihli. By 1634 the government forces had succeeded in pressing the rebels southward across the river, thus relieving the pressure on the capital. And following 1634, there were no really serious rebel operations north of the river until Li Tzu-ch'eng launched the final phase of his drive to Peking early in 1644. The defense of the river was relatively easy throughout most of the year when the volume of water and other physical features made crossings quite difficult for the rebels, though they easily forded such other rivers as the Huai and Wei. The defense picture became much more serious during the depth of winter when the volume of water was low and the ice became thick enough to support troops on horseback. Once the rebels are said even to have erected a rudimentary causeway on top of the ice, consisting of boards covered with soil. Thus, during the winter, officials and military commanders had to give considerable attention to guarding the river and forces were generally dispatched from other areas to serve as temporary garrisons. The success of these efforts meant that the provinces of Shantung, Pei-chihli, and Shansi were kept outside the main current of the rebellions until early 1644.

The government also achieved success in defending another strategic waterway, the Grand Canal. No major rebel group ever succeeded in cutting this vital artery, and, in fact, none managed to approach closer than some sixty miles of it.[75] There was occasional harassment of traffic on the canal by local outlaw bands, but this does not seem to have been serious. The only real opportunity for a rebel group to cut the canal occurred in 1642 when Chang Hsien-chung was operating in Nan-chihli. However, Chang decided to move westward into Hukuang and subsequently rejected a proposal that he return to Nan-chihli.

In a more technical realm, the government military authorities displayed at least some imagination in supplementing traditional Chinese weapons with more effective European-style firearms and cannons.[76] The effectiveness of these new weapons had been demonstrated in fighting against the Manchus and their use against the rebels is occasionally referred to in the sources where the weapons are given such terms as *Hsi-yang ta-p'ao* and *Fo-lang-chi*. Also, as has been noted, the Jesuit missionary, Schall, was appointed technical adviser to the Grand Coordinator of Shansi, though the appointment came too late to be effective. The new-style weapons were hardly available in sufficient numbers to play any really significant role, but old-style Chinese firearms and cannons were used quite extensively, at least in some battles. For example, in a Nan-chihli engagement in 1641, a government force of 10,000 is said to have been armed with 3,000 "long guns" (Ch'ang ch'iang) and 3,000 "bird guns" (Niao ch'ung).[77] During the initial years of the rebellions, the official forces undoubtedly had an overwhelming superiority in firearms, but there is evidence that by the mid-1630's, the rebels were making considerable use of them also.

In other aspects of conducting the hostilities against the rebels, the authorities showed an awareness that the problem had to be approached in a many-sided fashion. There was never any disposition to seek a purely military solution. On the contrary, it has been made clear that the officials charged with the conduct of the anti-rebel campaigns were almost always ready to allow the rebels to surrender and indeed sometimes granted them terms which were much too generous. Furthermore, though most of the rebel surrenders were fraudulent and temporary, some of the surrendered rebel leaders served the cause of the dynasty loyally for several years following their submission. The authorities also had some success, especially in the early years, in playing one rebel group off against another.

The actions of individual commanders and officials in specific cases often displayed both courage and military competence. Particularly striking are the defenses of Yün-yang and Kaifeng. Wang Kuang-en, the defender of Yün-yang, frustrated all of Li Tzu-ch'eng's attempts to capture the city, and what is most significant, he accomplished this feat when Li was approaching the peak of his power. The defenders of Kaifeng, during the terrible third and last siege of the city, probably displayed more raw determination and courage than was ever exhibited by any group of late Ming leaders.

Finally, it must be remembered that the rebel victory was not swift or dramatic. On the contrary, the dynasty maintained opposition against them for some seventeen years and in the late 1630's even achieved a temporary diminution in the intensity and extent of the rebellions. Thus, although bungled campaigns, "official" atrocities, and inadequate institutions obviously occupy the dominant positions in the military record of the late Ming government, that record is still not entirely lacking in commendable achievements.

To sum up the rebellions as military phenomena, one major point which should be emphasized is that there was a relatively steady increase in rebel military potential from the beginnings of the rebellions in 1628 until they attained their apex in 1644 and subsequently suffered a precipitous decline. This increase was produced by and expressed itself in more concentrated leadership; larger, more disciplined, and better trained armies; more complex military organization; more sophisticated tactics; and more effective weapons. The only notable hiatus which occurred in the increase of rebel military potential took place in 1638-39 when some of the major rebel leaders arranged surrender agreements with the authorities and most of the other rebel groups were forced into relative quiescence. However, the events of 1638-39 do not indicate any real decline of rebel power in absolute terms. There was only a temporary marking of time before the process of power escalation was to resume once more, and it undoubtedly came as no surprise to the more astute Ming officials that such a resumption occurred. Some of them had started to point out as early as the mid-1630's that there was real danger the rebels would achieve parity with the government forces in strength. The resumption of the rebel increase in military potential in 1639 continued, arriving at a new stage in 1642 when Li Tzu-ch'eng won a series of major victories in Honan, and, in purely military terms, acquired control over most of the province. Thus, in 1642, the first true rebel breakthrough to power occurred, and Li, unlike any rebel leader previously, found himself occupying such a position of strength that no available Ming army had more than a slim chance of defeating him. Following 1642, the increase in Li's military potential continued during his operations in Hukuang and his invasion of Shensi in 1643. His push across Shansi to Peking early in 1644 undoubtedly brought at least some additional increment to his military power, but a precipitous reduction in his military potential began in late May of 1644 when the Manchu-Chinese forces won a smashing victory over him at Shanhaikuan.

Chang Hsien-chung's military position parallels, at a considerably lower level, that of Li Tzu-ch'eng. Like Li, Chang, during the first decade of his rebellion, followed a career which alternated quite radically between relative success and near-disastrous defeat. Also like Li, there was a general trend toward the gradual enhancement of his military potential until he achieved a modest power breakthrough in 1643, an achievement which was of much less significance than that of Li and occurred a year later. Although Chang's power in 1643 in Hukuang was real, his presence there succeeded in accomplishing little more than a stalemate with the official forces. Chang's subsequent position in Szechwan was somewhat more solidly based, but to a considerable degree, it was founded on the province's isolation rather than on the inherent military potential of his forces. He certainly would have been destroyed much sooner than he was if mere distance and difficult terrain had not offered temporary protection from his Manchu-Chinese enemies.

Although rebel military potential did increase relatively steadily to achieve the power breakthrough of 1642-43 and although the military strength of the rebels greatly exceeded their political power, basic deficiencies in military potential remained, making the final contests between the rebels and their Manchu-Chinese opponents extraordinarily onesided in favor of the latter.

Another major general point concerning the military aspects of the rebellions is that although an enormous area was included within the main current of rebel movements and thus was subjected to military operations of varying intensity, a region of at least equal size remained relatively untouched until the final phase of the rebellions, and some areas were never affected at all. As has been noted, the principal rebel-affected sphere extended in an east-west direction from central Nan-chihli to western Szechwan and in a north-south direction from the Yangtze River to the Yellow River. The government was able to maintain an effective defense of the Grand Canal up until the collapse of the dynasty and although the Yellow River line was breached in 1631-33, the rebels were subsequently forced to move south and west of the river and were held there until 1644. The Yangtze did not require any major defense effort by the government, the difficulties of crossing it being sufficiently formidable of themselves to keep the rebels north of the river until 1643. Even after Chang Hsien-chung pushed south of the river in 1643, engulfing central Hukuang and central Kiangsi for the first time, he was able to maintain himself in these new areas for less than a year. Thus, all of China south of the Yangtze, except for Chang's relatively brief incursion into Hukuang and Kiangsi, remained quite unaffected by the rebellions. Furthermore, there does not seem to have been any significant number of local lawless outbreaks. That the regions south of the Yangtze remained outside of the main rebel sphere is of real significance, because some of these regions played particularly key roles in Ming China. Central Kiangsi, the coastal region of Fukien, and especially the northern Chekiang and southeastern Nan-chihli area were the most vital economic centers in the entire country, important for both agricultural surpluses and handicraft production. These same areas were important culturally and politically, producing a disproportionate number of artists, scholars, and successful officials. As for the northern provinces of Shantung, Peichihli, and Shansi, they were more plagued with local disturbances than the trans-Yangtze provinces, but these disturbances were kept under control and the fundamental stability of the area was not shaken until 1644. It can be observed that, until the very end, the dynasty always had a substantial area which was sound economically and relatively stable politically; yet because of institutional inadequacies and personal incompetence, the officials, who held the fate of the Ming in their hands, were unable to utilize this substantial loyal area as a base from which to bring about a restoration of the dynasty's authority.

The final general point is that within the main rebel-affected area, the portion of the province of Honan lying south of the Yellow River served as the focal region in which the resolution of the struggle between the government and the rebels was achieved in favor of the latter. Northern Shensi was important for initiating the rebellions, giving them a strong beginning momentum, and providing them with leadership. Furthermore, Shensi continued to be the scene of extensive rebel operations throughout most of the 1628-44 period. However, the center of the rebellions shifted to Honan during the latter half of 1633 and in most years of the succeeding decade, the province witnessed more significant rebel activities than any other province. Another indication of Honan's central role is that virtually all of the rebel unification efforts took place at conferences held within the province. Most importantly, though, Honan was the setting for the only really significant rebel breakthrough to power, an event which occurred in stages, extending over a year and a half, and was finally brought to fruition during the late spring and early summer of 1642 in the series of victories Li Tzu-ch'eng achieved over the Ming generals in the area of Kaifeng. From this point on, the rebels had military superiority over the government. Obviously, it would be incorrect to argue that rebel military operations outside of Honan were not important, but the importance of such operations lay mainly in diverting government strength away from Honan where the crucial battles were to take place. For example, in 1640, most of the military efforts of the official forces were directed against Chang Hsien-chung, chasing him from Hukuang to western Szechwan and back again. During this time, Honan appeared to be relatively calm, but underneath the apparent stability, conditions were developing which provided Li with the beginnings of the strength he needed to win the key victories of 1642. These victories in Honan were the major source of the momentum which carried Li all the way to Peking and was not halted until his decisive defeat at Shanhaikuan.

The Rebellions and the Northern Frontier

Since the rebellions began in northern Shensi in the region immediately south of the Great Wall and rather soon extended over a wide area, there existed a definite possibility that the rebels might receive additional strength by being joined by nearby Mongol or other foreign groups whose disposition for raiding the Chinese frontier is well known. Indeed, there were a few incidents during the early years of the rebellions when the rebels allied themselves with mounted raiders from beyond the frontier.[78] For example, in a 1636 memorial presented by the Supervising Secretary of the Ministry of War, Li Tzu-ch'eng is labeled as the most dangerous rebel and his army is said to have contained barbarian troops.[79] Much later, at the end of 1644, one of Li's lieutenants launched an attack against forces of Chang Hsien-chung in northern Szechwan, and his army is said to have numbered 10,000 men of whom 4,000 were Mongols.[80] Thus, it is apparent that some connection between the rebels and groups from beyond the Great Wall existed throughout virtually the entire period of the rebellions, and it is possible that the sources fail to indicate the true extent of the connection. However, it seems unlikely that a really significant rebel-foreign combination would be neglected in the sources, and it is probable that such alliances were relatively unimportant and temporary.

Undoubtedly, the principal explanation of the limited extent of cooperation between the rebels and trans-Great Wall groups is that the rebellions remained concentrated near the border for only a short period. There was insufficient time for a rebel-barbarian combination to form before the rebellions pushed south and east to become a purely internal Chinese phenomenon. In addition, it seems that the government's defense posture along the northern frontier remained reasonably strong until virtually the very end of the dynasty, and, as a result, the border forces not only were able to prevent significant rebel-Mongol contacts, but also succeeded in blocking any Mongol group from taking advantage of the disturbed conditions produced by the rebellions to launch major raids south of the Great Wall.

In great contrast to the relatively peaceful northern and northwestern frontier, the northeastern border harbored pressing dangers, for the Manchu thrust southward had been a dire threat to the Ming for at least a decade prior to the beginning of the internal rebellions in 1628. The chief connection between the rebels and the Manchus was the obvious one of sharing a common opponent. However, the rebel-Manchu connection was almost entirely an indirect one until 1644, for operating as they did south and west of the Yellow River, the rebels were prevented from having close contact with the Manchus. It is definite, though, that both the rebels and the Manchus were aware of one another at least to some degree, and in 1642, the Manchu Emperor issued the following instructions to the commander of the Manchu forces conducting raids south of the Great Wall:

If you meet the rebels, you should tell them, "You have been forced into rebellion by the corruption of the Ming government. The very reason for your rebellion also explains why we launched attacks upon the Ming." You should try to pacify them with kind words and the soldiers should be forbidden to kill the rebels which would cause ill feeling between the rebels and us.[81]

It is doubtful that there were ever many opportunities to put into practice the benevolent sentiments expressed in these instructions, for although the Manchus on two raids penetrated as far south as central Shantung, if they had contact with any rebels at all, it would have been with only unimportant local groups. Subsequently, early in 1644, a general notice was issued in the name of the Manchu Emperor addressed to military commanders throughout north China, inviting their cooperation in assuming control over the area.[82] The theory has been advanced that the invitation extended by this notice was intended to include Li Tzu-ch'eng.[83] It seems doubtful that this theory is valid, as by early 1644, the Manchus must have been well on the way toward basing their appeal for Chinese support on presenting themselves as destroyers of rebels and upholders of order and stability. The invitation extended by the notice was probably meant only for Ming commanders in north China who had been left in considerable doubt about what course they should take during the current chaotic times. Even if the invitation was supposed to include Li Tzu-ch'eng, there is no evidence that he even received it, much less took action upon it. It seems almost certain, then, that the first direct contact of any real significance between the Manchus and the rebels occurred at the fateful battle of Shanhaikuan. In conclusion, it should be emphasized again that the rebel-Manchu connection, though primarily indirect, was of crucial importance, for in posing simultaneous threats and forcing the Ming to fight on two fronts, the rebels and the Manchus made it impossible for the dynasty to save itself.

A Summary Assessment of Li Tzu-ch'eng and Chang Hsien-chung

Though Li Tzu-ch'eng and Chang Hsien-chung have played major roles throughout most of this account, some benefit may be gained from a brief general interpretation of them. At the same time, a few new details, mostly of a personal nature, that were neglected earlier can be added.

Probably the assessment of Li Tzu-ch'eng which would be most fair can be rendered by describing him as being limited, but not really evil. To be sure, he is accused of numerous brutalities in the sources and of being so cruel as to kill his own elder brother. His biography in the *Ming-shih* sums him up as follows:

By nature he was suspicious and repressive. Every day he killed people, severed their feet, and cut out their hearts as a sport. Wherever he went, the people all guarded their embankments and did not descend.[84]

The judgment expressed in this statement is contradicted by other passages in the very same biography, and is little more than one of the most blatant examples of the basic anti-rebel prejudice so frequently encountered in the sources. On the other hand, even though he did not employ cruelty as a policy, obviously it cannot be maintained that he did not commit, or at least condone, numerous brutalities, particularly during the first decade of his rebellion and during the final year when his very existence was often at stake. However, it is still true that, in the context of his time and situation, if one judges him on the basis of moderation and good intentions, his record is not a completely unworthy one.

Probably Li's most admirable trait was the absolute dedication he gave to his cause and the avoidance of being seduced into abandoning himself to a life of luxury after he became powerful.[85] It seems quite clear that he lived an extraordinarily frugal life. One source states that

Li did not maintain a large group of servants and that he had only one wife and one concubine, both of whom were old and ugly. There is also an account of how one of the Ming officials, who had surrendered to him, once sought to curry favor by presenting him with a charming lady, noted for being well versed in the classics and poetry. Li reacted by having the official killed and treating the lady with great consideration until she could be returned to her home. Finally, Li does not seem to have been interested in amassing a personal fortune, and one source states, in one of the few displays of pro-rebel exaggeration, that he would mix gold and silver with lead and employ the resulting ingots for target practice.

Another worthy element in Li's character was his considerable intellectual curiosity.* Though some of the sources maintain or infer that he received quite a thorough education as a child and youth, it is probable that he grew up semi-literate at best, and it is rather extraordinary that during his rebel career, particularly in the latter years when he had achieved a degree of stability, he devoted at least some time to learning to read and write as well as to discussing the classics and historical writings with those few followers who had scholarly backgrounds. He seems to have been especially interested in the *Tz'u chih t'ung chien*, and in offering his personal opinions on the events recorded in this work, his judgements are said to have been quite reasonable. Thus, he was undoubtedly not motivated entirely by considerations of blatant political advantage when, in 1636, he gave funds to the magistrate of his native Mi-chih County for the repair of the local Confucian temple.

Other good traits which Li possessed were relative moderation and general avoidance of succumbing to expressions of narrow personal revenge.[86] There is little evidence that any of the cities he occupied were subjected to wholesale massacres. Peking, for example, was treated quite leniently, and although lootings and other examples of misconduct certainly did occur, the only group in the city to suffer severely were the Ming officials, hundreds of whom were arrested and tortured to make them surrender the fortunes they had accumulated. There is, of course, the case of the terrible fate of Kaifeng at the conclusion of the third siege, but Li could hardly have known that the cutting of the dike would have caused the monumental disaster which actually occurred. As for Li's

---

* *HLLK* 18/20b; *MS* 309/9b; and *MCNL* 23/21a. The last-named work contains a quite complicated poem about a crab which Li composed as a young man and presented to his teacher. The poem is said to reflect Li's ambition, and his teacher predicted that he would become famous, but only after creating disturbances. If Li actually wrote the poem, he was obviously quite literate. However, it is doubtful if the poem is genuine, as the *MCNL* is noted for containing rather fanciful material.

avoiding personal revenge, the evidence is not entirely to his credit, as he did kill some persons who, he felt, had insulted him: the shaman at Hsiang-yang who told him he was not a "true son of Heaven" and two Mi-chih natives who had been involved in the desecration of his family tombs. However, he did overlook other personal affronts. He welcomed the surrender of the Ming general who had been partly responsible for the wound which caused him to lose the sight of one eye; he was amused when one of his subordinates became intoxicated and referred to him as "just a worthless commoner"; and while visiting his native Mi-chih after he became famous, he received one of his old neighbors very kindly even though the man had had him beaten for stealing a sheep when he was a youth.

Turning to another area, Li's control of his army was commendable and in his relations with his subordinates, he did not display an obsession with maintaining his personal authority.[87] As noted, the discipline in Li's army, especially during the years 1642-44, was quite strict, and his forces were probably considerably better behaved than many of those loyal to the dynasty. Furthermore, decisions about the conduct of military operations were not dictated by Li, but were arrived at through discussions in which several of his principal subordinates participated.

Finally, Li probably sincerely believed in the slogans proclaiming tax relief, order, and land equalizaton which Li Yen circulated in his behalf, particularly in Honan. It is true that few practical results were produced from such slogans, but, in the abstract, Li's acceptance of them was undoubtedly genuine.

Since an assessment of Li's character makes it seem possible to state that there is a balance in favor of the positive, why did he suffer such a signal failure in his attempts to obtain the essential gentry support? Part of the answer undoubtedly lies in the nature of rebel organization and in Li's vision being too limited to permit him to see the necessity for breaking out of some of the restrictions it placed upon him. Li's organization centered around men who, in most cases, had been associated with him during at least part of the desperate years when he was forced to wander from place to place. Undoubtedly, Li was emotionally attached to his lieutenants who had shared his initial period of trials, and it is understandable why he continued to depend upon them after he became powerful, instead of actively seeking to broaden his basis of support by deliberately recruiting gentry adherents. Also, it is understandable why Li's long-time lieutenants would have sought to preserve their virtual monopoly on power. In time, a gentry clique would probably have formed around Li, competed with the lieutenants for power, and eventually attained a dominant position. But time was a commodity which Li did not possess in any abundance. He was not in a position to attract gentry support to any significant degree until his breakthrough to power in the late spring of 1642, and he suffered his fatal defeat in May of 1644. Two years was all the time that was available to him and this was too short.

Even more important in explaining Li's lack of success in appealing effectively to the gentry was his failure to recognize the importance of developing a stable base and expanding his power outward from this solid foundation. He simply did not remain in one place long enough to allow gentry support to form around him. Between his breakthrough to power and his defeat by the Manchus, he moved from Honan to Hukuang, back to Honan, to Shensi, and finally, across Shansi to Peking. In none of these places did he remain longer than some nine months, and in one, Peking, for only six weeks. It is interesting and significant to compare Li's method of operations with the far more astute strategy adopted by Chu Yüan-chang which led to the founding of the Ming. Chu, quite early in his career, seized Nanking, remained settled there, and during more than a decade developed it into a stable base from which he expanded his control, first over the surrounding regions of the middle and lower Yangtze, and subsequently over the entire country. He resisted any temptation to push northward against Peking after having achieved some relatively superficial successes and initial, rudimentary territorial control. In contrast, Li, after his power breakthrough, never developed a true base, and made the drastic mistake of abandoning Honan when his real authority over the province was only beginning to be established. He moved from easy victory to easy victory, continuing to be satisfied with only superficial control. When the fatal blow fell at Shanhaikuan, he had no firm base to which he could retreat for protection, and his hastily constructed power structure quickly collapsed.

It is relatively simple to assess the historical significance of Chang Hsien-chung, and such an assessment must be almost entirely negative, as he was even more limited than Li Tzu-ch'eng and possessed few, if any, of Li's virtues. His least objectionable traits would include a rather heavyhanded sense of humor, expressed in such incidents as his "borrowing" the head of the district prince in Hsiang-yang; a certain facility for conducting a highly mobile type of guerilla warfare; at least some intellectual curiosity, as evidenced by his relations with the two Jesuits in Szechwan; and a native craftiness, as shown in his successfully negotiating with the authorities to be allowed to surrender at Ku-ch'eng. However, any positive contributions which these traits and abilities might have made were totally cancelled out by his violence and abject ignorance of political questions. In the earlier years of the rebellions, Chang's violence was probably no worse than that of most of the other rebels, and it was resorted to in a sporadic and quite unsystematic fashion. Even during his invasion of Hukuang in 1643, it does not seem to have reached flagrant proportions. But during the last year and a half of his occupation of Szechwan, violence of such magnitude was unleashed that quite possibly more people lost their lives than had been killed by all the other rebel groups combined. As has been seen, the violence was resorted to as an insane means of striking back at the opponents of the rebel regime in Szechwan, who arose because Chang could not provide the province with even the rudiments of an effective civil administration, and could not control the province militarily. Thus, although Chang remained in Szechwan far longer than any other rebel leader stayed in one location, his sole accomplishment was devastation.

It is apparent, then, that Chang must be judged a total failure as a founder of an administrative structure. Furthermore, even his military successes are unimpressive, and he failed to gain a single victory as significant as any of those Li Tzu-ch'eng achieved during his 1642-44 campaigns. In sum, Chang was probably no more able than any number of his fellow rebel leaders, and it was purely by chance that he survived longer than most of them. Despite his fanciful imperial pretensions, it is inconceivable that he could ever have succeeded in founding a dynasty. He always remained a freebooter at heart and it is no accident that his favorite character from past Chinese history was the dashing, colorful, politically incompetent, and brutal Hsiang Yü.

One final general question might be asked concerning both Li and Chang: did they have any conception of the rebels in earlier periods of Chinese history and look upon themselves as expressions of a rebel tradition? This is a significant question, but unfortunately in answering it, one must rely almost entirely on negative evidence. The sources do occasionally mention earlier rebellions, but in every instance, these passages are contained in comments by the compilers, and usually merely state that the late Ming rebellions were more terrible than any which had occurred in all previous history. Not a single indication has been discovered to suggest that Li, Chang, or any other rebel leader ever even mentioned an earlier rebellion, much less stated that he considered himself the inheritor of the mantle of some rebel chieftain of a previous era. Undoubtedly, some folk traditions concerning past rebellions were extant, but if such traditions were really an important influence on the rebel leaders, the fact would almost certainly have been mentioned in the sources.

There is evidence that the *Shui hu chuan* exerted some influence on the rebellions, and, in 1642, the Emperor ordered the work destroyed.[88]

Plays, based on the novel, were commonly performed in villages and pictures of heroes from the novel were engraved on gambling cards.[89] It seems quite clear, then, that the principal *Shui hu chuan* characters enjoyed considerable popularity, and it is not surprising that some of the nicknames, which they had adopted, were copied (or at least employed) by late Ming rebel leaders. Furthermore, most of the other leaders took similar nicknames. Probably, though, the influence of the *Shui hu chuan* extended little further than popularizing the general idea of opposition to an oppressive and corrupt government, for there is no evidence that it served as a source of late Ming rebel policies or tactics. Certainly the "Robin Hood" activities of the novel's heroes have little relevance for the late Ming leaders. In sum, except for minor influences from a fictionalized rebellion, Li, Chang, and the other late Ming rebels had little conception of or connection with past Chinese rebellions.

Varying Interpretations of the Late Ming Rebellions

Three general categories of interpretations of the late Ming rebellions are: the traditional, the modern non-Communist, and the Communist.* Undoubtedly the most notable characteristic of the traditional view of the rebellions is an overriding concern for factual detail and the presentation of this detail in a highly straightforward, non-analytical fashion. For example, the most extensive of the sources, the *Huai-ling liu-k'ou shih-chung lu*, presents the specific events connected with the rebellions in a completely chronological manner. Only rarely do the compilers intervene to offer some interpretative comment. Quite clearly the work, like all the better sources, is based primarily on archival materials and thus represents what is undoubtedly a drastic condensation of the voluminous official records of the rebellions. The work also, and again like the other sources, gives evidence of having employed, at least to some minor extent, local traditions and popular tales. Given the diffuse origins and highly unsystematic nature of the traditional sources, then, it is not surprising that no monolithic unity in interpretation is produced. There is, of course, a general unity: a prejudice against the rebels as destroyers of such basic Confucian values as moderation, harmony, and order. However, the anti-rebel prejudice is not expressed crudely or in absolute terms. Individual good actions or worthy traits are ascribed to the rebels, and, at the same time, cases of incompetence or brutality, committed by officials or government commanders, are not hidden.

---

* This topic has been treated in my article, "Attitudes toward the Late Ming Rebellions," *Oriens Extremus*, VI (1959), 177-209, and thus only a relatively brief treatment will be given here.

Unsuccessful rebellions have not been a popular topic of research with modern non-Communist historians, and only a handful of articles and one book, the quite good study by Li Wen-chih, have been devoted to the late Ming rebel movement. These historians approach the rebellions from a rather non-doctrinaire point of view and devote most of their attention to a determination of what actually happened. At the same time, attempts are made to impose systematic presentation and interpretation upon the facts. In addition, general trends and background factors, difficult to deal with in the chronology-dominated traditional works, are treated with some use of modern sociological and historical methods. These historians avoid obvious anti-rebel prejudices and occasionally point out their existence in the traditional sources, but none of them show any particular enthusiasm for any aspect (with one exception) of the peasant rebellions. The rebel leaders are depicted as limited men who failed to establish stable regimes or adopt effective policies. There is one element in the rebellions, though, of which the modernists heartily approve, and that is their role as expressions of nationalism. Such expressions are considered to be present because the rebels were opponents of the Manchus, and, in some instances, even ended their anti-dynastic operations and joined with the remnant Southern Ming regime in an attempt to defeat the Manchus and their Chinese allies. Particularly praised is Li Ting-kuo, a lieutenant of Chang Hsien-chung who is indeed an anti-Manchu hero. In assessing the validity of the modernists' praise for the anti-Manchu aspect of the rebellions, it is difficult to escape the conclusion that the enthusiasm for the alleged nationalism is derived more from Sun Yat-sen and the 1911 Revolution than from a proper interpretation of the late Ming rebellions themselves.

The Communists developed an interest in the numerous peasant rebellions throughout Chinese history quite late, and the vast majority of their works dealing with this topic has been written since 1949.* In the earlier period, Communist scholars were too engaged with practical revolutionary tasks or with questions of more immediate relevance to Marxist dialectics. Beginning in the early 1950's, the subject of peasant rebellions rapidly emerged as a favorite topic of Communist historians and several hundred articles and many books have appeared, some of which have elicited considerable debate.

One basis for the Communist interest in the rebellions is the same as

---

* James P. Harrison, "The Communist Treatment of Chinese Peasant Wars, a Case Study in the Reinterpretation and Uses of History" (Unpublished paper presented to the Ditchley Manor Conference on Chinese Communist Historiography, 1964) has been of great aid in considering the Communist attitudes toward the late Ming rebellions.

has been noted for the modernist: nationalism. The Communist historians give even more enthusiastic applause to the late Ming rebellions for their nationalism than the modernists do, and at times express their enthusiasm in highly flamboyant language. Li Wen-chih, for example, states that the Manchus dispatched an embassy to Sian late in 1643 for the purpose of proposing an alliance to Li Tzu-ch'eng, and Li, to his great credit, refused the Manchu offer.* Later, when the rebel armies were besieging Peking, and the eunuch Tu Hsün was dispatched to negotiate with the court, Li Wen-chih maintains that one of the principal proposals Tu made to the Emperor, and rejected by him, was a Ming-rebel alliance against the Manchus.[90] Li Wen-chih, naturally, is highly favorable to a Ming-rebel alliance, and feels that the total troop strength which would have resulted from such an alliance would have come to 1,000,000 men, more than sufficient to have defeated the Manchu army of slightly less than 200,000. There are many other expressions of approval for additional manifestations of nationalistic acts and sacrifices on the part of the rebels who are compared very favorably with the gentry, most of whom surrendered to the Manchus.

The second reason for the Communist interest in and general approval of peasant rebels is based upon a desire to find some evidence of "progressive" forces during the traditional (and in Communist terms "feudal") period of Chinese history. With the lack of a bourgeoisie, what class was in the position of assuming a role which produced change and created pressures that moved historical development to a new stage? There was virtually no other class which could be assigned such a dynamic role in China but the peasantry, and in practical revolutionary terms, Lenin and especially Mao had demonstrated how the peasantry could be employed for purposes of revolution, despite certain attitudes in classical Marxism which looked upon the peasantry as essentially conservative or even reactionary. Thus, in Communist writings, beginning especially in the early 1950's, the peasant rebels started to be accepted as a force for change within Chinese feudal society, and stages in the development of "progressive" ideas in peasant rebellions began to be delineated. For example, it was felt that a new stage in the sophistication of "progressive" ideas in rebellions was introduced with the late Ming rebel movement, since in that movement, the rebels had a more precise realization of such a key element as land equalization than they had ever had previously. Subsequently, the Taiping rebellion represented an advance over the late

---

* Li, "Wan Ming t'ung-chih chieh-chi . . .," 150. The author is the same as the one who wrote *Wan Ming min-pien*. Thus, Li appears first in the modern non-Communist group and subsequently in the Communist group.

Ming period. The periodization of the various stages and such questions as whether the peasant rebels were conscious or spontaneous opponents of the feudal order (i.e., were they a conscious or spontaneous "progressive" force) have occasioned a great deal of discussion and debate, raising issues that have not yet been answered. Furthermore, in all stages of the increasing sophistication of the "progressive" concepts held by the rebels, it has been recognized that the ultimate breakthrough to a true revolutionary stage was impossible. The peasant rebels were severely restricted by the historical limitations of their particular periods. Thus, while claiming the rebels as ancestors for their own movement and accepting the rebels as a force for as much change as conditions permitted, the Communists have been careful to preserve for themselves the unique status of having accomplished the final and true revolution.

To sum up, the traditional historian displays a basic, but not absolute, anti-rebel bias and a particularly keen interest in presenting voluminous factual detail about the rebellions in a highly unsystematic fashion. The modern non-Communist historian subjects factual information to a certain amount of analysis and interpretation, producing conclusions generally unfavorable to the rebellions except in those aspects considered to display nationalism, for which considerable enthusiasm is shown. The Communist historian applauds the nationalistic manifestations of the rebellions even more fervently than his non-Communist predecessor, and also approves of the rebellions as evidence of "progressive" forces operating in traditional China.

Conclusion

The late Ming peasant rebellions began on a small scale in northern Shensi in 1628. They arose as a result of the conjunction of several developments and conditions. Political stability in the area had been undermined by the appointment of officials to provincial, prefectural, and county posts who were of inferior quality, and there was also a decided tendency to leave offices on the prefectural and county levels vacant. Economically and socially, the area suffered from isolation and the limitations imposed by geography. An economic backwater, the region was unaffected by the progress in agriculture and in the handicrafts enjoyed by such more favored areas as the lower Yangtze Valley and the Fukien coast. Furthermore, because of its poverty, northern Shensi undoubtedly suffered especially acutely from the added tax burdens made necessary by the military operations against the Manchus.

Natural calamities and special military conditions exacerbated the political instability and unfortunate socio-economic situation. The drought of 1628, though probably no worse than scores of such calamities earlier in the Ming dynasty, was still a real disaster, and might be said to have provided the final impetus needed to launch the rebellions. The military dangers stemmed primarily from the mutinous mood prevailing among numerous groups of soldiers in the area whose dissatisfaction had been aroused by inadequate rations and other grievances. This disposition to mutiny was increased by the presence in the area of runaway troops many of whom had fled to the isolation of northern Shensi from as far away as Manchuria. On many sides, then, it can be seen that by the late 1620's the foundations for stability in northern Shensi had been badly undermined. The result was peasant rebellion.

The late Ming rebellions can be divided into two main phases: disorganized raiding and dynastic ambitions. The disorganized raiding phase, lasting from the beginning to 1641, was characterized by disunity in rebel leadership, limited goals, and continual mobility in operations. Despite superficial attempts at coordination, reaching a climax in the Jung-yang conclave of 1635, the rebel leaders remained quite independent. They formed only highly temporary alliances dominated by transitory self-interest. Their chief goals were confined to plundering and survival, and even the most ambitious had no more than a vague conception of overthrowing the Ming and establishing a new dynasty. Their operations depended almost entirely on rapid movement, and there was not a single really serious effort to create a permanent base of power.

In geographical spread, the rebellions, during the first part of the disorganized raiding phase, were confined to Shensi. By 1630, they has spilled over into Shansi, and during the next three years, encroached upon Pei-chihli and Honan as well. By 1634, the rebellions had been forced south of the Yellow River, and during the next decade, rebel bands rapidly moved about in an erratic fashion in the huge midsection of China: that area between the Yangtze and the Yellow rivers and between western Szechwan and central Nan-chihli.

The nadir of the disorganized raiding phase of the rebellions occurred during 1638-39 when most of the rebel leaders were forced into inactivity or into arranging surrender agreements with the government. However, the prospects of a real suppression of the rebellions during the 1638-39 period proved to be illusory, and the resumption of activity by the rebel groups in 1639 was accompanied by a gradual escalation of their power. Such escalation is demonstrated by the failure of the government's campaign headed by Yang Ssu-ch'ang, the most ambitious anti-rebel effort. Thus, during the disorganized raiding phase (1628-41), the rebel groups were transformed from hastily organized and weak bands of peasants and renegade soldiers into units which possessed much more formidable military power. The government's attempts at suppression, generally based on a combination of appeasement and military force, though successful in destroying numerous rebels and in forcing all the rebel groups to remain continually on the move, failed to achieve the final goal: the destruction of rebel power.

The dynastic ambitions phase of the rebellions was launched in 1641 when Li Tzu-ch'eng began to move toward a major breakthrough to power in Honan, transforming that province into the key area which made possible the subsequent rebel success. During 1642, Li achieved such a position of strength militarily that no Ming force posed a serious threat to him any longer. What were the reasons behind Li's greatly enhanced power? He was obviously the beneficiary of the gradual increase of rebel military strength which had occurred, in a relatively steady fashion, throughout the 1630's. Also, he was aided by a drought in Honan which greatly enhanced peasant disaffection. More fundamentally, Li's success was based on the general inability of the dynasty to deal effectively with the nexus of challenges which faced it. It is obvious that the position of the Ming government by 1641 was a difficult one, confronted as it was by both internal and external opponents, and supported by political and military institutions which were in some respects inadequate or had been allowed to deteriorate. In particular, the position of Supreme Commander seems to have been so fettered with institutional weaknesses that it was incapable of dealing competently with interprovincial problems. Most immediately important of all, in the area of military affairs, it is apparent that the Ming authorities had erected no viable substitute for the defunct Wei-So system. Even if one admits the seriousness of the threats facing the dynasty in 1641, it still had available to it important sources of strength. Large areas of the country were still completely stable. South of the Yangtze, China had remained almost entirely unaffected by the rebellions, and the rebels had never seriously threatened to disrupt traffic on the vital Grand Canal. The three northern provinces of Shansi, Pei-chihli, and Shantung, following 1634, had witnessed rebel activities conducted by only relatively unimportant local groups. In addition, the dynasty still had the overwhelming support of the gentry, only a handful of whom had shown any disposition to join the peasant rebels. Greater will and more effective leadership might have enabled the Ming authorities to have utilized the real strengths which still remained to them in 1641 as a basis for a resurgence of dynastic power, but no display of greater will and more effective leadership ever came. Instead of attempting basic reforms, the authorities continued with their ineffectual programs to raise military forces and with their futile efforts to collect the increased tax revenues (doubled between 1618 and 1636) the chief results of which were to enhance opportunities for official corruption and to intensify peasant discontent.

Another reason for the successful breakthrough to power by Li Tzu-ch'eng was the absence of a gentry-led rebellion which could compete with him in the exploitation of the dynasty's increasing incompetence and unpopularity. Not a single significant gentry rebellion against the Ming ever occurred, due mainly to the fragmentation of gentry power which had occurred by Ming times. Unlike earlier periods in Chinese history, the Ming did not possess great gentry clans with firmly grounded regional power which could be transformed into national power. Thus, the gentry remained committed to the Ming as long as that was possible.

On the basis of the military power he had achieved by 1642, Li Tzu-ch'eng consolidated his position of leadership within the rebel movement and made manifest his determination to found a dynasty of his own. Li's consolidation of his leadership position reached a climax in 1643 by which time he had destroyed four formerly independent rebel leaders, who had been serving as his lieutenants, and had forced other leaders into a subordinate position. Subsequently, the only major rebel figure who remained independent of Li was Chang Hsien-chung, who was definitely inferior to Li in power and importance. Li's ambitions to found a dynasty were first made apparent in Hukuang in 1643 when he assumed a princely title. Another princely title was proclaimed at the beginning of 1644, and the climax of his dynastic ambitions came some time following his capture of Peking in April, 1644 when he assumed the imperial position. Thus, in both leadership and purpose, the dynastic ambitions phase of the rebellions presents a considerable contrast to the disorganized raiding phase. Chaos in rebel leadership had been replaced by unity, and such simple rebel aims as plunder and survival had given way to the ultimate ambition: the establishment of a new dynasty.

The dynastic ambitions phase of the rebellions continued, for Li Tzu-ch'eng, until his death in the summer of 1645 and, for Chang Hsien-chung, until his death early in January of 1647. Both Li and Chang were destroyed quite soon after they had been confronted with Manchu power, and one might ask why they, and with them the entire late Ming rebel movement, met with such a rapid and inglorious end. Viewed entirely as a phenomenon of peasant unrest, the greatest weakness of the late Ming rebellions was the lack of any esprit-building and charisma-providing factors, such as a messianic belief with roots in a folk religion. Consequently, the late Ming rebellions, possessing relatively unimportant religious overtones, lacked the strength of the peasant movement at the end of the Yuan when the White Lotus doctrine provided a dynamic impetus and a foundation. Viewed more generally, the most fundamental reasons for the defeat of the rebellions were their failure to attract gentry support and, closely related, their neglect to develop secure strength in a base area before attempting to seize national power. The failure to attract gentry support was mainly due to the limited and lowly backgrounds of the rebel leaders, as well as their relative lack of native ability, which made it impossible for them to display the political wisdom necessary to gain a following. The late Ming rebellions had no peasant genius like Chu Yuan-chang. Furthermore, the long-surviving rebel leaders, mostly natives of northern Shensi, who monopolized the top positions of leadership throughout the entire late Ming period, had a vested interest in maintaining a firm grasp on the dominant positions and could not bring themselves to share power with a gentry group. Had rebel leadership been more diverse, it would have been more possible for a gentry faction to have exerted influence. Also, if Li had been able to maintain his position in Peking for a longer period than he did, he would have had more success in building up a gentry following.

It is more difficult to account for the rebel failure to develop firm control over a base area. Between his breakthrough to power in 1641-42 and his disastrous defeat at Shanhaikuan in 1644, Li Tzu-ch'eng established central headquarters in such widely scattered areas as southwestern Honan, northwestern Hukuang, Sian (Shensi), and Peking. In none of these places did he remain long enough to develop secure control, failing to erect a solid political structure to supplement his military strength. Undoubtedly, the previously-mentioned rebel lack of political sophistication was one reason for the failure to develop a secure base. In addition, there were the attractions of easy victories over collapsing Ming armies and influences surviving from the disorganized raiding phase of the rebellions when all the rebel groups had been constantly on the move.

Lacking a solid political structure and possessing no secure base area, the peasant rebels were destroyed swiftly and overwhelmingly by the Manchus. Rebel military power was impressive only in the context of their competition with the Ming forces. The rebels were hopelessly surpassed by the Manchus with their longstanding military tradition and their half century of experience in conducting campaigns against rivals in Manchuria and against the Ming. Equally important, the Manchus, benefitting from the sinification produced by their long exposure to Chinese civilization, had erected an impressive political administration, and could present themselves as upholders of traditional Chinese values more effectively than the rebels. To the gentry, the rebels were more "foreign" than the Manchus. Thus, it was a hardy people from the northeastern frontier rather than a peasant rebel from northern Shensi that succeeded in seizing control of the destinies of China following the collapse of the Ming dynasty in 1644.

Appendixes

Rebel nicknames

Ch'a-chih-hu	插翅虎	Ambitious Tiger
Chan-chih-fei	展翅飛	Spread-winged Flight
Chang-shih-wang	掌世王	Controlling-the-times King
Cheng-ch'i-wang	整奇王	Good-order King
Cheng-shih-wan	整十萬	One-hundred-thousand-only
Cheng-hsi-wang	征西王	Reducing-the-west-to-submission King
Cheng-kuan-wang	争管王	Contending-for-governing King
Cheng-shih-wang	争世王	Contending-for-the-world King
Ch'i-t'ien-wang	奇天王	Heaven-regulating King
Ch'iang-t'ien-wang	强天王	Strong Heavenly King
Chih-shih-wang	治世王	Governing-the-world King
Chin-ch'ih-tiao	金翅雕	Golden-winged Eagle
Chin-lung	金龍	Golden Dragon
Ching-lien-tzu	荊聯子	Thorn-like Union
Ching-shan-wang	静山王	King of Mount Ching
Ch'ing-pei-lang	青背狼	Blue-backed Wolf
Chiu-liang-hsing	九梁星	Nine-ridged Star
Chiu-t'iao-lung	九條龍	Nine Dragons
Ch'u-lieh-yen	出獵雁	Wild-goose Going Hunting
Chua-ti-hu	抓地虎	Land-scratching Tiger
Ch'uan-shan-hu	穿山虎	Boring-through-the-mountains Tiger
Chuang-t'a-t'ien	撞塌天	Striking-down-heaven
Chuang-t'ien-chu	撞天柱	Striking-heaven Pillar
Ch'uang-chiang	闖將	Dashing General
Ch'uang-shan-hu	闖山虎	Dashing-against-the-mountain Tiger
Ch'uang-t'a-t'ien	闖塌天	Pushing-down-heaven
Ch'uang-t'ien-shao	闖天哨	Dashing-against-heaven Whistle
Ch'uang-t'ien-wang	闖天王	Dashing-against-heaven King
Ch'uang-wang	闖王	Dashing King
Chung-tou-hsing	中斗星	Hit-the-Dipper-in-the-center
Erh-t'iao-lung	二條龍	Two Dragons

Erh-tui-pa-ta-wang 二隊八大王	Eight Great Kings of the Two Companies
Fan-shan-hu 翻山虎	Crossing-the-mountain Tiger
Fan-shan-yao 翻山鷂	Soaring-over-the-mountain Hawk
Fan-t'ien-yao 翻天鷂	Soaring-in-heaven Hawk
Fei-hu 飛虎	Flying Tiger
Fei-hu-chiang 飛虎將	Flying-tiger General
Fei-shan-pao 飛山豹	Flying-over-the-mountain Panther
Fei-t'ien-hu 飛天虎	Flying-in-heaven Tiger
Fei-t'ien-yeh-cha 飛天夜叉	Flying-in-heaven Demon
Fu-shou-wang 福壽王	Prosperity and Longevity King
Han-chih-shan 捍至山	Ward-off-those-coming-to-the-mountain
Han-t'ou-lang 憨頭狼	Silly-headed Wolf
Hei-hsieh-tzu 黑蠍子	Black Scorpion
Hei-hsin-hu 黑心虎	Black-hearted Tiger
Hei-sha-shen 黑殺神	Black Slaughtering Deity
Hei-yün-lung 黑雲龍	Black-cloud Dragon
Heng-fei-hu 橫飛虎	Recklessly-flying Tiger
Heng-t'ien-wang 橫天王	Crossing-heaven King
Hsi-ying-pa-ta-wang 西營八大王	Eight Great Kings of the Western Camp
Hsiang-li-jen 鄉里人	Villager
Hsiao-ch'in-wang 小秦王	Little King of Shensi
Hsiao-huang-ying 小黃鶯	Little Oriole
Hsiao-hung-lang 小紅狼	Little Red Wolf
Hsiao-hung-niang 小紅娘	Little Red Amazon
Hsiao-ts'ai-feng 小裁縫	Little Tailor
Hsieh-tzu-k'uai 蠍子塊	Scorpion Lump
Hsien-tao-shen 顯道神	Displaying-the-Way Deity
Hsin-i-tzu-wang 新一字王	New One-character King
Hsin-lai-hu 新來虎	Newly-arrived Tiger
Hsin-li-wang 忻戾王	Delighting-in-violence King
Huang-hu 黃虎	Yellow Tiger
Huang-lung-yen 黃龍眼	Yellow Dragon Eye
Huang-ying-erh 黃鸚兒	Yellow Parrot
Hun-chiang-lung 混江龍	River-disturbing Dragon
Hun-hai-lung 混海龍	Sea-disturbing Dragon
Hun-shih-wan 混十萬	Disturbing-a-hundred-thousand
Hun-shih-wang 混世王	Disturbing-the-times King
Hun-t'ien-hou 混天猴	Heaven-disturbing Monkey
Hun-t'ien-hsing 混天星	Heaven-disturbing Star
Hun-t'ien-lung 混天龍	Heaven-disturbing Dragon

Hun-t'ien-lang	混天狼	Heaven-disturbing Wolf
Hun-t'ien-wang	混天王	Heaven-disturbing King
Hung-chün-yu	紅軍友	Friend of the Red Army
Huo-ti-ts'ao	活地草	Enlivening-earth Grass
Huo-tse-shou	火柞手	One-who-clears-away-bushes-with-fire
I-chan-teng	一盞燈	One Lamp
I-chang-ch'ing	一丈青	Ten-foot Blue
I-chang-hung	一丈紅	Ten-foot Red
I-chen-feng	一陳風	Gust of Wind
I-chih-hu	一隻虎	One Tiger
I-kan-ch'iang	一桿槍	One Gun
I-ken-hsü	一根鬚	One Whisker
I-lien-ying	一連鶯	Joined Orioles
I-t'iao-lung	一條龍	One Dragon
I-t'iao-ts'ung	一條葱	One Onion
I-to-yün	一朵雲	One Cloud
I-tou-ku	一斗穀	One Peck of Grain
I-tou-su	一斗粟	One Peck of Grain
I-tso-ch'eng	一座城	One Town
I-tu-ch'iang	一堵墙	One Wall
I-tzu-wang	一字王	One-character King
Jen-i-wang	仁義王	Humane and Righteous King
K'ai-shan-fu	開山斧	Mountain-splitting Axe
Kang-tuan-mao	剛短毛	Hard Short Hair
Ko-kou-fei	隔溝飛	Separate-from-the-ditch Flight
Ko-kuo-yen	革裹眼	Forcing-people-to-join-the-rebels Eye
Ko-li-yüan	蛤蜊圓	Round-as-a-clam
Ko-liao-yen	格嘹鴈	Honking Wild-goose
K'o-t'ien-fei	可天飛	Able-to-fly-in-heaven
K'uei-huang-hu	魁黃虎	Monstrous Yellow Tiger
Kun-ti-hu	滾地虎	Rolling-on-the-ground Tiger
Kun-ti-lang	滾地狼	Rolling-on-the-ground Wolf
Kuo-chiang-wang	過江王	Passing-across-the-river King
Kuo-shan-lung	過山龍	Passing-by-the-mountain Dragon
Kuo-t'ien-hsing	過天星	Passing-through-heaven Star
Lai-shan-hu	來山虎	Tiger of Mount Lai
Lan-shou-shih	嬾収拾	Lazy-in-tidying-up
Lang-shan-hu	狼山虎	Tiger of Mount Lang
Lao Chang Fei	老張飛	Old Chang Fei*

* Chang Fei is a famous figure of the Three Kingdoms period as well as a prominent character in the *San-kuo-chih yen-i (Romance of the Three Kingdoms)*.

Lao-hsing	老刑	Old Punisher
Lao-hui-hui	老回回	Old Moslem
Ling-hung-ch'i	領紅旗	Commanding-the-red-flag
Ling-ping-wang	領兵王	Troop-leading King
Liu-hsing-chung	流星鍾	Meteor Goblet
Liu-tui	六隊	Six Companies
Lo-shan-hu	樓山虎	Tiger of Mount Lo
Luan-shih-wang	亂世王	Disordering-the-times King
Luan-tien-chün	亂點軍	Disordering-a-little Army
Lüeh-ti-hu	掠地虎	Land-plundering Tiger
Lung-te-shui	龍得水	Dragon-in-the-water
Man-t'ien-hsing	滿天星	Filling-heaven Star
Mang-chia	蟒甲	Python Armor
Meng-hu	猛虎	Fierce Tiger
Mi-ling-wang	密靈王	Mysterious Spirit King
Nan-ying-pa-ta-wang 南營八大王		Eight Great Kings of the Southern Camp
O-hu	惡虎	Vicious Tiger
Pa-chin-kang	八金剛	Eight Vajras
Pa-chua-lung	八爪龍	Eight-clawed Dragon
Pa-tui	八隊	Eight Companies
P'a-shan-hu	扒山虎	Crawling-up-the-mountain Tiger
P'a-t'ien-wang	爬天王	Crawling-up-to-heaven King
Pao-hsien	保險	Proof-against-risk
Pei-ying-pa-ta-wang 北營八大王		Eight Great Kings of the Northern Camp
P'o-chia-chui	破甲錐	Armor-piercing Awl
Pu-chan-ni	不沾泥	Unmuddied
San-ko-wang	三閣王	King of Three Halls
San-t'ai-chi	三臺吉	Ursa Major Good Fortune
Sao-ti-hu	掃地虎	Ground-sweeping Tiger
Sao-ti-wang	掃地王	Ground-sweeping King
Sha-chin-wang	殺盡王	All-slaughtering King
Shang-shan-hu	上山虎	Mountain-ascending Tiger
Shang-t'ien-hou	上天猴	Heaven-ascending Monkey
Shang-t'ien-lung	上天龍	Heaven-ascending Dragon
She-t'a-t'ien	射塌天	Shooting-down-heaven
Shen-i-k'uei	神一魁	Sole Chieftain
Shen-i-yüan	神一元	Sole Head
Shih-fan-wang	十反王	Tenth Rebellious King
Shih-tsao	石竈	Stone Stove
Shun-i-wang	順義王	Submitting-to-righteousness King

APPENDIXES

Shun-t'ien-wang	順天王	Submitting-to-heaven King
Ssu-t'ien wang	四天王	Four Heavenly Kings
Ssu-tui	四隊	Four Companies
Ta-hung-lang	大紅狼	Big Red Wolf
Ta-liang-wang	大梁王	Great Ridge King
Ta-tan-wang	大膽王	Great Courage King
Ta-wang-chu	大王柱	Great Kingly Pillar
T'ai-p'ing-wang	太平王	Great Peace King
Tao-t'ien-wang	道天星	Leading-heaven King
T'ieh-lu-kang	鐵鑪剛	Iron Stove Hardness
Tien-teng-tzu	點燈子	Lighted Lamp
Ting-p'o-t'ien	頂破天	Head-pushing-through-heaven
Ting-t'ien-hung	定天紅	Stabilizing-heaven Red
T'o-t'ien-wang	托天王	Supporting-heaven King
Tsan-t'ien-shao	鑽天哨	Heaven-piercing Whistle
Tsan-t'ien-yao	鑽天鷂	Heaven-piercing Hawk
Ts'ao-shang-fei	草上飛	Flying-over-the-grass
Ts'ao-shang-shuang	草上霜	Frost-on-the-grass
Ts'ao Ts'ao	曹操	Ts'ao Ts'ao*
Tso-chin-wang	左金王	Left Gold King
Tu-hsing-lang	獨行狼	Lone-going Wolf
Tu-hu	獨虎	Solitary Tiger
Tu-t'ou-hu	獨頭虎	Single-headed Tiger
Tzu-chin-liang	紫金梁	Purple Gold Ridge
Tzu-wei-hsing	紫薇星	Tzu-wei Star
Tzu-lai-hu	自來虎	Self-moving Tiger
Wa-kuan-tzu	瓦礶子	Earthenware Pot
Wu-t'iao-lung	五條龍	Five Dragons
Yao-t'ien-tung	搖天動	Heaven-shaking Movement
Yeh-pu-shou	夜不收	Night Unending
Yen-ch'ien-erh	眼錢兒	Eye Money Child
Yen-wang	閻王	King of Hell
Yen-wang-chu-p'o	閻王猪婆	Pig-like Wife of the King of Hell
Ying-wang	英王	Brave King
Yün-chiao-yüeh	雲交月	Cloud-crossing-the-moon
Yün-li-fei	雲裡飛	Flying-in-the-clouds

---

* Ts'ao Ts'ao is a famous figure of the late Han dynasty as well as a prominent character in the *San-kuo-chih yen-i (Romance of the Three Kingdoms)*.

Names of persons

Ai Neng-ch'i 艾能奇
Chang Ch'i-tsai 張其在
Chang Feng-i 張鳳翼
Chang Hsien-chung 張獻忠
Chang Kuo-shen 張國紳
Chang Ling 張令
Chang Sui-jan 張遜然
Chang Ta-shou 張大受
Chao Sheng 趙勝
Ch'en Ch'i-jui 陳奇瑜
Ch'en Hung-fan 陳洪範
Ch'en Pi-ch'ien 陳必謙
Ch'en Sheng 陳生
Ch'en Shih-ch'i 陳士奇
Ch'en Shih-ch'ing 陳士慶
Ch'en Te 陳德
Ch'en Yen 陳演
Ch'en Yüan 陳沅
Ch'en Yung-fu 陳永福
Chiang Ting-chen 江鼎鎮
Ch'iao Ying-chia 喬應甲
Ch'ien Shih-sheng 錢士升
Ch'in Liang-yü 秦良玉
Ch'iu Chih-t'ao 丘之陶
Chou K'uei 周奎
Chou Wen-chiang 周文江
Chou Yen-ju 周延儒
Chou Yü-chi 周遇吉
Chu Hua-lung 朱化龍
Chu Shih-ting 朱大鼎
Chu T'ung-meng 朱童蒙
Fang Kuo-an 方國安
Fu Tsung-lung 傅宗龍
Ho Chin 賀錦
Ho Feng-sheng 賀逢聖
Ho I-lung 賀一龍
Ho Jen-lung 賀人龍
Ho T'eng-chiao 何騰蛟
Hsiung Wen-ts'an 熊文燦
Hsü Hsüeh-yen 徐學顏
Hsü I-hsien 徐以顯
Hsü Kao 徐高
Hsü Ting-ch'en 許鼎臣
Hsü Yen 許琰
Hsüeh Kuo-kuan 薛國觀
Hu Ch'uang-tzu 胡闖子
Hu Mo 胡默
Hu Shou-heng 胡守恒
Huang Ch'ang-chi 黃裳吉
Huang Te-hung 黃得功
Hung Ch'eng-ch'ou 洪承疇
Hung-niang-tzu 紅娘子
Hou Hsün 侯恂
Kao Ch'i-feng 高起鳳
Kao Chieh 高傑
Kao Ming-heng 高名衡
Kao Ying-hsiang 高迎祥
Ku Chün-en 顧君恩
Ku Ta-ch'eng 谷大成
Kuan Fu-min 官撫民
Kung Chi-min 龔濟民
Kung Wan-ching 龔完敬
Kung Yü 鞏焴
Kung Yung-ku 鞏永固
K'ung T'ing-hsün 孔廷訓
Li Chen-sheng 李振聲
Li Chien-t'ai 李建泰
Li Chin 李錦
Li Ch'ing-shan 李青山
Li Hung-chi 李鴻基
Li Jen-hui 李人會
Li Kuo 李過
Li Ming-jui 李明睿
Li Mou 李牟
Li Pang-hua 李邦華
Li Shih-ying 李時英
Li Ting-kuo 李定國
Li Tzu-ch'eng 李自成
Li Yen 李巖
Li Yu 李友
Liang Ming-lun 梁明倫
Liu Chih-po 劉之渤

Liu Chin-chung　劉進忠
Liu Hsi-tso　劉熙祚
Liu Hsi-yao　劉希堯
Liu Kuo-neng　劉國能
Liu Liang-tso　劉良佐
Liu Mao　劉懋
Liu Tao-chiang　劉道江
Liu T'ing-chü　劉廷舉
Liu Tse-ch'ing　劉澤清
Liu Tsung-min　劉宗敏
Liu Wen-hsiu　劉文秀
Lo Ju-ts'ai　羅汝才
Lu Chiu-te　盧九德
Lu Hsiang-sheng　盧象昇
Lü Ta-ch'i　呂大器
Ma K'o　馬科（苛）
Ma Shih-yao　馬世耀
Ma Shou-ying　馬守應
Meng-ju-hu　猛如虎
Miao Mei　苗美
Ni Yüan-lu　倪元璐
Niu Chin-hsing　牛金星
Pai Kuang-en　白廣恩
P'an Tu-ao　潘獨鰲
Pien Ta-shou　邊大受
Shang Chiung　尚絅
Shao Chieh-ch'un　邵捷春
Shao Shih-ch'ang　邵時昌
Shih Ching-ch'un　郝景春
Shih K'o-ching　史可敬
Shih Lin-an　郝臨菴
Shih Tien　石電
Sun Ch'üan-t'ing　孫傳廷
Sun K'o-wang　孫可望
Sung Hsien-ts'e　孫獻策
Sung I-ho　宋一鶴
T'ang Chih　湯志
T'ang Chiu-chou　湯九州
T'ang T'ung　唐通
Teng I　鄧玘
T'ien Chien-hsiu　田見秀
Ting Ch'i-jui　丁啟濬

Ts'ao Hsün　曹勳
Ts'ao Hua-shun　曹化淳
Ts'ao Pien-chiao　曹變蛟
Ts'ao Wen-chao　曹文詔
Tseng Ying　曾英
Tso Kuang-hsien　左光先
Tso Liang-yü　左良玉
Tu Hsün　杜勳
Tu Wen-huan　杜文煥
Wan Yüan-chi　萬元吉
Wang Ch'eng-en　王承恩
Wang Chia-yün　王嘉允
Wang Hsiang　王祥
Wang Hsieh　王燮
Wang Kuang-en　王光恩
Wang Kuo-ning　王國寧
Wang Ping-chen　王秉貞
Wang Shang-li　王尚禮
Wang Ssu　王四
Wang Tso-kua　王左掛
Wang Tzu-yung　王自用
Wang Ying-hsiung　王應熊
Wang Ying-lung　王應龍
Wang Chao-ling　汪兆齡
Wang Ch'iao-nien　汪喬年
Wang Wei　汪偉
Wei Ching-yüan　衛景瑗
Wei Tsao-te　魏藻德
Wen T'i-jen　温體仁
Wu Chi-shan　吳繼善
Wu Hsiang　吳襄
Wu San-kuei　吳三桂
Wu Sheng　吳甡
Wu Ta-wei　吳大威
Yang Chan　楊展
Yang Ho　楊鶴
Yang Ssu-ch'ang　楊嗣昌
Yang Wen-yüeh　楊文岳
Yang Yung-yü　楊永裕
Yen Chi-tsu　顏繼祖
Yen Hsi-ming　嚴錫命
Yü Ying-kuei　余應桂
Yüan Shih-chung　袁時中

APPENDIXES

Names of places

Ang-chou 卬州
Changsha 長沙
Ch'ang-p'ing 昌平
Ch'ang-te 常德
Ch'ao-hsien 巢縣
Che-ch'uan 浙川
Ch'e-hsiang 車箱
Chen-ning 真寧
Chen-ting 真定
Chengtu 成都
Ch'eng-t'ien 承天
Chi-hsien (Honan, Wei-hui Prefecture) 汲縣
Chi-hsien (Honan, Kaifeng Prefecture) 杞縣
Chi-an 吉安
Chi-ning 濟寧
Ch'i-chou 蘄州
Ch'i-shui 蘄水
Chia-hsien 郟縣
Chia-ting 嘉定
Chiang-chin 江津
Chien-chou 劍州
Chien-ch'ang 建昌
Ch'ien-chou 乾州
Ch'ien-shan 潛山
Chin-hsien 金縣
Ch'in-shui 沁水
Ching-chou 荊州
Chiu-chiang 九江
Chiu-kung 九公
Chu-ch'i 竹谿
Ch'u-chou 滁州
Ch'uan-chou 全州
Chung-chou 忠州
Chungking 重慶
Fan-ch'eng 樊城
Fang-hsien 房縣
Feng-tu 酆都
Feng-yang 鳳陽
Fu-chou 撫州
Fu-feng 扶風
Fu-ku 府谷
Fu-ning 撫寧
Fu-shih 膚施
Han-ch'eng 韓城
Han-chung 漢中
Hanyang 漢陽
Heng-chou 衡州
Ho-chou (Nan-chihli) 和州
Ho-chou (Szechwan) 合州
Ho-chin 河津
Ho-shui 合水
Hsi-ch'ung 西充
Hsiang-ch'eng 襄城
Hsiang-yang 襄陽
Hsiang-yin 湘陰
Hsien-ning 咸寧
Hsin-chou 忻州
Hsin-chin 新津
Hsin-fan 新繁
Hsin-ts'ai 新蔡
Hsin-yang 信陽
Hsing-an 興安
Hsing-shan 興山
Hsiu-wu 修武
Hsü-chou (Nan-chihli) 徐州
Hsü-chou (Szechwan) 叙州
Hsü-chou (Honan) 許州
Huai-an 淮安
Huai-ch'ing 懷慶
Huang-chou 黄州
Huang-mei 黄梅
Huo-shan 霍山
I-chün 宜君
I-ling 夷陵
I-yang 宜陽
Ju-chou 汝州
Ju-ning 汝寧
Jung-yang 榮陽
Kaifeng 開封
K'ai-hsien 開縣

Kan-ch'üan 甘泉
Kao-yang 高陽
K'ao-ch'eng 考城
Ku-an 固安
Ku-ch'eng 穀城
Ku-yüan 固原
Kuang-chou 光州
Kuang-chi 廣濟
Kuang-yüan 廣元
Kuei-te 歸德
K'uei-chou 夔州
Kung-ch'ang 鞏昌
Lan-t'ien 藍田
Li-chou-an-fu-ssu 黎州安撫司
Lien-chou 連州
Lin-hsien 臨縣
Lin-t'ao 臨洮
Ling-pao 靈寶
Liu-an 六安
Liu-ho 六合
Lo-nan 雒南
Lo-shan 羅山
Lo-t'ien 羅田
Lo-ying 羅猰
Loyang 洛陽
Lu-chou (Szechwan) 瀘州
Lu-chou (Nan-chihli) 盧州
Lu-chiang 盧江
Lu-shih 盧氏
Lung-an 龍安
Ma-ch'eng 麻城
Ma-nao 瑪瑙
Mei-chou 眉州
Meng-hsien 孟縣
Mi-chih 米脂
Mien-chou 綿州
Mou-chou 茂州
Nan-chao 南召
Nan-li 南豊
Nan-yang 南陽
Nei-hsiang 內鄉
Pa-chou 巴州

Pao-chi 寶雞
Pao-chih 寶坻
Pao-ch'ing 寶慶
Pao-feng 寶豐
Pao-ning 保寧
Pao-ting 保定
P'eng-shui 彭水
Pi-yang 泌陽
P'ing-hsiang 苹鄉
P'ing-li 平利
P'ing-yang 平陽
Po-chou 亳州
P'u-chou 蒲州
P'u-ch'eng 蒲城
Shan-chou 陝州
Shang-chou 商州
Shang-nan 商南
Shanhaikuan 山海関
Shu-ch'eng 舒城
Shun-ch'ing 順慶
Sian 西安
Su-chou 宿州
Sui-chou (Hukuang) 隨州
Sui-chou (Honan) 睢州
Sung-hsien 嵩縣
Ta-chou 達州
Ta-t'ung 大同
Tai-chou 代州
T'ai-hu 太湖
T'ai-ho 泰和
T'ai-yüan 太原
T'ang-hsien 唐縣
Te-an 德州
Teng-chou 鄧州
Ting-chou 定州
Tse-chou 澤州
Tsun-i 遵義
T'ung-ch'eng (Hukuang) 通城
T'ung-ch'eng (Nan-chihli) 桐城
T'ung-ch'uan 潼川
T'ung-po 桐柏
Tzu-t'ung 梓潼

Tzu-yang (Szechwan) 資陽
Tzu-yang (Shensi) 紫陽
Wan-hsien 萬縣
Wan-tsai 萬載
Wei-nan 渭南
Wuchang 武昌
Wu-ling 武隆
Wu-tang 武當
Wu-wei 無為
Wu-yang 舞陽
Ya-chou 雅州
Yangchow 揚州
Yang-ho 陽和
Yeh-hsien 葉縣
Yenan 延安

Yen-chin 延津
Yen-ch'eng 鄢城
Ying-shan 英山
Ying-chou 潁州
Ying-ch'eng 應城
Yo-chou 岳州
Yü-chou 禹州
Yü-lin 榆林
Yü-tz'u 榆次
Yüan-chou 沅州
Yün-yang 鄖陽
Yung-chou 永州
Yung-ning (Honan) 永寧
Yung-ning (Szechwan) 永寧
Yung-p'ing 永平

Miscellaneous Entries

An-hsi chiang-chün 安西將軍
Chang-lü 掌旅
Chang-p'an-tzu 掌盤子
Ch'ang-ch'iang 長鎗
Chi-shih-chung 給事中
Chia 家
Chieh-tu-shih 節度使
Chien-i-ta-fu 諫議大夫
Chih chiang-chün 制將軍
Chih-chih-shih 直指使
Chih-chou 知州
Chih-fu 知府
Chih-hsien 知縣
Ch'ing ping 精兵
Chou-mu 州牧
Ch'üan chiang-chün 權將軍
Fo-lang-chi 佛郎機
Fu-lu-chiu 福祿酒
Fu-nan chiang-chün 撫南將軍
Fu-yin 府尹
Hsi-yang ta p'ao 西洋大炮
Hsien-ling 縣令
Hsin-shun wang 新順王

Hsün-fu 巡撫
Ku yüan chen lung huang-ti
　古元真龍皇帝
Kuan-tui 管隊
Kuo-i chiang-chün 果毅將軍
Lao-fu feng-t'ien ch'ang-i
　ta-chiang-chün
　老府奉天倡義大將軍
Li Chung-kuo erh fu ssu-i yeh
　蒞中國而撫四夷也
Ling-t'ou-tzu 領頭子
Niao-ch'ung 鳥銃
P'ing-tung chiang-chün 平東將軍
P'o-chün hsing 破軍星
Pu-tsung 部總
Shang-hsiang-kuo 上相國
Shao 哨
Shao-tsung 哨總
Shih-pa sun-erh 十八孫兒
Shun wang 順王
Ta han chih wang yün kuan yeh
　大旱之望雲寬也
Ta Shun (dynastic title of Li
　Tzu-ch'eng) 大順
Ta-shun (reign title of Chang

Hsien-chung) 大順
Ta-yüan-shuai 大元帥
T'ang-ma 塘馬
T'ien yü chih 天與之
T'ien-hsia kuei jen yen
 天下歸仁焉
Ting-pei chiang-chün 定北將軍
Tso-fu 左輔

Tsung-kuan 總管
Tu-wei 都尉
Wei-wu chiang-chün 威武將軍
Ying 營
Yu-pi 右弼
Yü-shih 御史
Yung-ch'ang 永昌

Notes

Abbreviations

HCL:	Mao Ch'i-ling, *Hou chien lu*
HLLK:	Tai Li, *Huai-ling liu-k'ou shih-chung lu*
HS:	Fei Mi, *Huang shu*
KTS:	*K'o T'ien shu*
MCNL:	Chi Liu-ch'i, *Ming chi nan lüeh*
MCPL:	Chi Liu-ch'i, *Ming chi pei lüeh*
MMNM:	Cheng T'ien-t'ing, *Ming mo nung-min ch'i-i shih liao*
MS:	*Ming shih*
MSCSPM:	Ku Ying-t'ai, *Ming shih chi-shih pen-mo*
PKC:	P'eng Sun-i, *P'ing k'ou chih*
PWSCL:	Pai Yü, *Pien wei shih chin lu*
SC:	*Shu chi*
SKCL:	Wu Wei-yeh, *Sui k'ou chi lüeh*
SP:	P'eng Tsun-ch'iu, *Shu pi*
YSCC:	T'an Chi-ts'ung, *Yen-sui-chen chih*
YYN:	Li Fu-jung, *Yen yü nang*

Chapter I

1. Hou Jen-chih, "Frontier Horse Markets in the Ming Dynasty" *in* E-tu Zen Sun and John de Francis, *Chinese Social History*, 328.
2. *HLLK* 1/2a.
3. Li Wen-chih, *Wan Ming min-pien*, 8.
4. *MCPL* 5/10b-11b.
5. *HLLK* 4/3b and *MMNM* 9-13.
6. *HLLK* 3/4a-5a.
7. *HLLK* 4/9b.
8. *MCPL* 7/8a-b; *HLLK* 4/14b-16b; and *MMNM* 24-26.
9. William E. Soothill and Lewis Hodous, *A Dictionary of Chinese Buddhist Terms*, 35.

Chapter II

1. *MMNM* 14-18, 30-32.
2. *PKC* 1/8a; *MCPL* 7/6b; *MMNM* 36-38; and *HLLK* 6/2a.
3. *HLLK* 5/14a-b.
4. *HLLK* 5/3b-4a, 9a.
5. *HLLK* 5/7b, 12a, 16a-b.
6. *HLLK* 5/9b-10a, 12b.
7. *HLLK* 5/14b-15a, 6/10a; *MMNM* 59-64; and *PKC* 1/7a-b.
8. *HLLK* 5/17b, 6/5b.
9. *MMNM* 55-59; *HLLK* 5/12a, 15a, 17a; and *MCPL* 9/2b, 6a.
10. *MMNM* 59-64 and *HLLK* 5/11b, 17a.
11. *HLLK* 6/12a-b; *MCPL* 9/2a-b; and *YSCC* 5/13a.

12. *HLLK* 5/13a, 17a, 6/9b; and *PKC* 1/8a-b.
13. *HLLK* 7/1b, 5a and *MMNM* 111-113.
14. *HLLK* 6/9a; *PKC* 1/14a; and *MCPL* 9/9a-b, 10/4a.
15. *MCPL* 10/4a and *PKC* 1/14b.
16. *MCPL* 10/2b, 3a.
17. *MCPL* 10/4a-b; *PKC* 1/15a-18b; *HLLK* 7/17b-19b; and *SP* 1/2b.
18. *HLLK* 7/21a-22b and *MSCSPM* 78/57.
19. *HLLK* 7/18b-19b and *PKC* 1/8a.
20. *MS* 309/7a-b and *SKCL* 2/10b.
21. *YSCC* 5/15a; *SKCL* 9/2b; *MS* 309/7b-8a; and *PKC* 2/2a-b, 3a-b.
22. *YSCC* 5/15a.
23. *PKC* 2/5b-6a; *MCPL* 11/6a-7b; and *HLLK* 8/28b-29a.
24. *HLLK* 8/19b-20a, 34b.
25. *YSCC* 5/15a; *HLLK* 8/6a, 9a-b, 11b, 12a, 15a-b; and *PKC* 2/4a.
26. *HLLK* 8/4a and *PKC* 2/4b.
27. *HLLK* 8/18a, 22a, 23a-b.
28. *HLLK* 8/24a-b.
29. *HLLK* 8/36a-39b; *PKC* 2/6b; and *SKCL* 4/8a-b.
30. *PKC* 2/7b, 8a-b, 10a; *HLLK* 9/3b; and *MCPL* 11/7a-b.
31. *HLLK* 8/28b and *MCPL* 10/7b.
32. *HLLK* 9/24b and *MCPL* 12/12b-13a.
33. *PKC* 1/16a.
34. *PKC* 2/13b.
35. *HLLK* 8/13b, 9/10b and *MMNM* 124-127.

Chapter III

1. *HLLK* 10/20b-21a and *PKC* 3/5a.
2. *MCPL* 12/4a-b and *MMNM* 119-122.
3. *MMNM* 119-122, 147-154.
4. *MCPL* 13/14b, 15a-b, 18b-20b and *HLLK* 10/2a, 6a-b, 10a, 19b-24b.
5. *MCPL* 12/13b-14a; *HLLK* 10/23a, 25a.
6. *HLLK* 11/4b-5a; *SKCL* 4/6a, 7/35b, 10/2a; *PKC* 3/5a-b; and *MCPL* 15/17b-19a.
7. *PKC* 3/7a, 9a; *SKCL* 6/21a, 10/2a-b; and *MCPL* 15/18a.
8. *HLLK* 11/13a-14a; *MS* 309/10b; and *YSCC* 5/17b.
9. *MS* 24/1a-2a and *HLLK* 11/15b-16a.
10. *HLLK* 12/5b-6a; *SKCL* 6/21b-22a, 10/2a-b; and *MCPL* 15/18a-b.
11. *HLLK* 12/6a and *PKC* 3/9b.
12. *HLLK* 12/7b; *MCPL* 15/18b; and *SKCL* 6/26a-b.
13. *HLLK* 11/11a-b; *PKC* 3/9b-10a; and *MS* 272/8a.
14. *HLLK* 12/9b-10a; *PKC* 3/10a-b; and *MS* 272/6a-b, 8a.
15. *MS* 272/6b-8a.
16. *SKCL* 7/14b and *HLLK* 13/3b.
17. *SP* 1/11a; *KTS* 3b; and *SKCL* 7/23a-b.
18. *SKCL* 7/16a-b; *YYN* 1/14a-b, 15a; *PKC* 3/14a-b; and *HLLK* 13/4a-b.
19. *SKCL* 7/26a and *MS* 309/28a.
20. *PKC* 3/15b and *HLLK* 13/14a, 15a, 16b, 19a.
21. *SKCL* 7/21a, 23a, 26a; *HLLK* 13/6a-b, 17b; and *SP* 1/10b.
22. *HLLK* 14/3b; *PKC* 4/3a-b; *MCPL* 17/16b-17a; and *SKCL* 10/4b-5a.
23. *MSCSPM* 77/47.
24. *HLLK* 14/1b-4a; *MCPL* 17/5b-6a; *PKC* 4/1b-2b; and *MS* 309/11b.
25. *HLLK* 14/5a-7a; *PKC* 4/6a; and *SKCL* 7/29a.
26. *MMNM* 236-238, 287-288.

Chapter IV

1. *MS* 309/11a-b; *MCPL* 13/11a-12b; and *HLLK* 13/23a.
2. *HLLK* 14/4b; *PKC* 4/4b; and *PWSCL* 45-50.

3. *PKC* 4/7a; *HLLK* 14/6b; and *MMNM* 332-334.
4. *PKC* 4/11b; *HLLK* 14/15b; and *YSCC* 5/17b.
5. *HLLK* 14/17a-b and *MCPL* 17/9a-10a.
6. *MCPL* 17/10b and *HLLK* 14/19b-20b.
7. *PWSCL* 50-59; *MS* 309/12b; *PKC* 5/1a-b; and *HLLK* 14/21a, 15/1b-2a.
8. *HLLK* 15/5a; *MCPL* 18/14b-15a; *PKC* 5/2a; and *MMNM* 350-352.
9. *YSCC* 5/22b-23a; *PWSCL* 60-72; *PKC* 5/5a-9a; and *HLLK* 15/10b-14a.
10. *HLLK* 15/7a-b, 15b-16a; *PKC* 5/2b; and *MCPL* 18/13b-14a, 21a-b.
11. *HLLK* 15/19b and *MCPL* 18/21b-22a.
12. *HLLK* 15/15b.
13. *HLLK* 15/19b-21a; *PKC* 6/1a-b; and *MCPL* 18/22a-23b.
14. *HLLK* 16/1a-7a; *PKC* 6/1a-7a; and *MCPL* 19/16b-24a.
15. *HLLK* 16/4b-5a; *PKC* 6/7b; and *MCPL* 19/24a-25a.
16. *HLLK* 16/2a-6a; *MCPL* 19/25b-26b; and *YSCC* 5/23a-b.
17. *HLLK* 16/23a and *MCPL* 19/28b-29a.
18. *PKC* 6/4b and *MMNM* 397.
19. *PKC* 6/12b-14b; *HLLK* 16/9b-10a; and *MMNM* 412-415.
20. *PKC* 6/3a-b; *HLLK* 15/22a, 16/1a-2a; *MMNM* 408-409; and *MCPL* 18/24a-b, 19/21b-22a.
21. *HLLK* 16/13b-15b.
22. *HLLK* 16/15b-20b; *PKC* 7/3a-8a; *MCPL* 19/29b-31a; and *YSCC* 5/24b-25b.
23. *HLLK* 16/22b-25b; *PKC* 7/10b; *MCPL* 19/32b-33a; and *YSCC* 5/26a-b.
24. *HLLK* 16/23b-27b; *MCPL* 19/34a-b; *YSCC* 5/26b-27a; and *PKC* 7/13b-14b.
25. *HLLK* 16/26a and *YSCC* 5/27a-28a.
26. *PKC* 8/1a; *MS* 309/18b; and *YSCC* 5/27b.
27. *HLLK* 16/24a, 28b, 17/3a, 5b; *PKC* 7/15b-16a, 8/7b, 10a; and *MCPL* 19/74a.
28. *HLLK* 16/29b, 17/4b, 10a-12a; *PKC* 7/16b, 8/7a-15b; *MCPL* 19/41a-43b, 20/3a-b, 16a-b; and *MMNM* 424-428, 431-432, 449-452.
29. *HLLK* 17/5b.
30. *HLLK* 17/7b-9b and *PKC* 8/4b-5a, 12a, 13a.
31. *PKC* 8/5b, 10a; *MCPL* 20/21a-b; and *YSCC* 5/29a.
32. *HLLK* 17/1a, 7a-b, 10a-b, 17a; *PKC* 8/1a-2a, 4b-5a, 7b, 13b-14a; *MCPL* 20/16b-17a, 41a-b; and *MMNM* 417-419, 435-439.
33. *HLLK* 17/10a; *PKC* 7/16a, 8/10a, 14a-16a; *MCPL* 20/39b-40a; and *MMNM* 429.
34. *PKC* 8/2b, 7a, 11b-12a, 14b-16a; *MMNM* 422, 426, 441-445; and *MCPL* 20/21b-22a.
35. *HLLK* 17/12a, 14a-b; *PKC* 8/15b, 17b-18a; *MCPL* 20/7a-b; and *MMNM* 446-454.
36. *HLLK* 17/11b, 14a and *PKC* 8/18a.
37. *HLLK* 17/15a-16b; *PKC* 8/18a, 9/1a-b; and *MCPL* 20/50a-51b.
38. *HLLK* 17/15a-18a and *PKC* 8/18a.
39. *HLLK* 17/17b-19a and *PKC* 9/2a-b, 6a.
40. *PKC* 9/6b-7a, 13b, 10/8a, 13a-b; *HLLK* 17/22a, 18/4a, 7a-b; and *MCPL* 22/88b.
41. *PKC* 9/13b, 10/10b-11a; *HLLK* 18/4b-5a, 7a; and *MCNL* 20/61b-62b, 77b, 82b.
42. *PKC* 9/14b, 10/4b, 7b, 9b, 12a-b, 14a-b, 15b-16a; *HLLK* 18/5a; and *MCNL* 20/67a, 81b-82a, 89b-90a.
43. *PKC* 9/7a-b, 12b, 14a-b, 10/4b, 12a-b, 14a-b, 15b-16a; *HLLK* 18/5a; and *MCNL* 20/70b-74b.
44. *PKC* 8/15b-16a, 10/12a, 11/2b and *HLLK* 18/1a.
45. *PKC* 10/5b-6a, 7b-8a, 11b, 12b-13a, 14a-b; *HLLK* 18/4a-5b, 7a-8b; and *MMNM* 455, 463-464.
46. *PKC* 10/15a-b; *HLLK* 18/9a-b; and *YSCC* 5/31a.
47. *PKC* 11/2a-3b; *HLLK* 18/9b-10b; and *Ch'ing Shih-lu* (*Shih-tsu Shih-lu*) 4/15-19.
48. *HLLK* 14/16a-b; *PKC* 4/12a; *MSCSPM* 77/48; and *MS* 309/29a-b.
49. *HLLK* 14/5b 12a-13a; *PKC* 4/5a; and *MMNM* 326-330.
50. *HLLK* 15/4a-21a; *PKC* 5/3a-12b; *MCPL* 18/25b-30a; and *MSCSPM* 77/49.
51. *HLLK* 15/21b, 16/2a-3b; *MCPL* 19/44a-49a; and *MS* 309/30a.

52. *HLLK* 16/7a-13a; *PKC* 6/6b-9a; *MSCSPM* 77/50-51; and *MS* 309/30a-b.
53. *HLLK* 16/13a-15b and *PKC* 7/1a-2b.
54. *HLLK* 16/16a-17b and *PKC* 7/3a-4b.
55. *HLLK* 16/18a-25b; *PKC* 7/5b-16a; and *MCPL* 19/66a-70a.
56. *HLLK* 16/26a-30a; *PKC* 7/13b-16b; and *MCNL* 5/11b-12a.
57. *MCNL* 5/10a-b and *MCPL* 19/70a-71a.
58. *HLLK* 17/2b, 4a-b, 8b, 15a; *MCNL* 5/11b-12b; *HS* 1/11a; *KTS* 5a; *SP* 2/1a-2b; and *YYN* 2/51a.
59. *HLLK* 18/15b; *PKC* 11/11a-12a; *HS* 11b-12a; *SC* 1a-b; *YYN* 2/54a-55a; *MCPL* 21/21a-23b; *MCNL* 12/11b, 26a; and *SP* 2/3a-4a.
60. *HLLK* 18/16a-18a; *YYN* 2/55b-58a; *SC* 1b-2a; *KTS* 6b; and *SP* 2/4b-6a.
61. *SC* 2a-b; *HS* 12a; *PKC* 12/8a-b; *MCNL* 12/27a; *SP* 2/10a-26b; and *KTS* 6b.
62. *MCNL* 12/27a and *SP* 2/15a.

Chapter V

1. *PKC* 11/3b, 5a-6b; *HLLK* 18/10a, 12a; and *YSCC* 5/31b.
2. *PKC* 11/11b-12a; *HLLK* 18/12a, 16a-b, 20a; and *MMNM* 475-479.
3. *PKC* 11/12a-b and *HLLK* 18/16b-17a.
4. *HLLK* 18/15a and *MMNM* 456-459, 477.
5. *HLLK* 18/21a, appendix/1b-2a.
6. *HLLK* appendix/2a-b and *PKC* 12/4a-5b.
7. *Ch'ing Shih-lu (Shih-tsu Shih-lu)* 18/4; *HLLK* appendix 2b, 5a-b; *PKC* 12/5b-6b; *HCL* 5/23a-b; and *YSCC* 5/23a.
8. *HLLK* 18/18b, 23b; *SC* 2b, 4b-5a; *SP* 15a-b; and *HS* 12a-b.
9. *HLLK* 18/28b; *PKC* 11/13b; and *SP* 2/16b.
10. Thomas Dunin Spot, "Collectanea Historiae Sinensis," 112.
11. *HLLK* 18/22b-23a; *PKC* 11/15b; *SP* 3/15b-17b; *SC* 2b; *SKCL* 10/21a; and *MCNL* 12/27b, 30a.
12. *MMNM* 6.
13. Dunin Spot, 100.
14. *HLLK* appendix/2b, 6a; *PKC* 11/14a; *HS* 12b-13a; *SC* 3b-4a; *SP* 3/10a-17a; *YYN* 2/52a, 3/1a; and *KTS* 17a-b.
15. *HLLK* appendix/7a; *MCNL* 12/29a, 32b; *KTS* 7b-10a; and *HS* 13a-16b.
16. *HLLK* 18/23b-24a, appendix/6b-7a; *PKC* 11/14b, 12/3b; *YYN* 3/4a, 9b, 12b; *HS* 12b-17a; *KTS* 7b, 8b, 9a-10b; *MCNL* 12/27a, 29a-b, 32b; and *SP* 3/1a-2b, 4a-b, 11a.
17. *HLLK* 18/18b-23a, appendix/7a-b; *PKC* 11/13a-14a, 12/9b; *SP* 2/15a-21a, 3/4a-5b; *MCNL* 12/27a, 30a, 31a; *KTS* 8a, 11a; *SC* 2b-3a, 5a-9a; *HS* 15a-18b; *MS* 309/32a-b; Martini, 201-203, 209; and Dunin Spot, 100.
18. *SP* 3/20b-21a.
19. Martini, 211-212.
20. *HLLK* 18/19a-b; *SC* 5b-12b; *KTS* 8a, 10b, 11a-b; *SP* 3/7a-16b; *PKC* 11/13b, 14b; *MCNL* 12/32a, 33b; *HS* 17a-19b; Martini, 213-217; and Dunin Spot, 108, 117, 121.
21. *SC* 8a.
22. *HLLK* appendix/7a-b; *PKC* 11/15a-b, 12/6b, 8a; *SC* 12b-14b; *MCNL* 12/31b-34b; *KTS* 11b-12a; *HS* 19b-21a; *SP* 3/17a-b; *YYN* 3/13b, 14b, 16b; *HCL* 6/16a; *Ch'ing Shih-lu (Shih-tsu Shih-lu)* 29/8-9; *MMNM* 485-486, 489-490; Teng Chih-ch'eng, *Ming Ch'ing shih*, 213; Dunin Spot, 108, 117, 121, 129; and Martini, 213-217, 220-223.
23. Martini, 222.
24. Martini, 222.
25. *Ch'ing Shih-lu (Shih-tsu Shih-lu)* 29/9; *HLLK* appendix/7b; *SKCL* 10/29a; *MS* 309/33a; *PKC* 12/8a; *SC* 14a; *HS* 20b-21a; and *KTS* 12b.

Chapter VI

1. *HLLK* 17/15a.
2. *MCPL* 5/19b-20a and *YSCC* 5/11a.
3. *PKC* 4/2a-b, 11/2b-5a; 12/5a-b; *SKCL* 2/10b; *MCPL* 12/14a-17a; *HLLK* 18/7a; *HCL* 5/23b; and Dunin Spot, 117.
4. *HLLK* 15/2b, 16/26a; *PKC* 4/13a; *YSCC* 5/27b-28a; and Pien Ta-shou, *Hu k'ou yü sheng chi*, 27-30.
5. *HLLK* 8/6a, 16/13a, 18/7a; *PKC* 2/8b, 5/1a, 7/1a; *MCPL* 14/1a-b; *MCNL* 23/21a-b; *HS* 19b; *SP* 3/18a-b; *MS* 309/10b, 31a; and *MSCSPM* 77/52.
6. *HLLK* 1/1a-b, 18/2a; *PKC* 4/4a, 6/1b, 8/6a, 17a, 9/3a, 12b-13a, 10/1a, 11a, 11/3a; *MCPL* 5/17a-19a; *MCNL* 20/77b; *YSCC* 5/10b-11a, 27a-b; *HS* 17b-18b; *SC* 19b, 5a-b; *YYN* 3/2a; *SP* 1/2a, 18b, 2/1a, 17a, 20a, 3/18b, 23b; and *MS* 309/2b, 11a, 14a, 20b, 21b, 31a.
7. Dunin Spot, 112.
8. Martini, 206-208.
9. *HLLK* 18/19a; *PKC* 12/10a; *MCNL* 12/23b; *SP* 3/9a, 19b-20a; *SC* 12a-14a; and *KTS* 8a.
10. *HLLK* 14/16a, 17/5a, 22a-b; *PKC* 1/17a, 2/2a-b, 5/11a, 6/3b-4a, 8b, 7/5b, 7/15a, 9/9a-b, 11b; and *SP* 1/6a-b, 2/7a, 8a.
11. *HLLK* 16/9a-b.
12. *HLLK* 10/10a, 14/16a, 17/5a; *PKC* 4/2b, 7/4a-b, 9/7b, 11a-b, 10/5a, 11/4a, 11a; *MCPL* 11/19a-b; and *SP* 1/2b, 7a, 2/10a, 3/22b.
13. *HLLK* 8/7a, 11/1a.
14. *HLLK* 5/12b, 6/2a.
15. *HLLK* 5/3a.
16. *PKC* 3/7a, 9a, 14a.
17. *HLLK* appendix/7b and *SC* 5b, 6a, 15a-b.
18. *HLLK* 16/11a-b; *PKC* 6/5a; and *MSCSPM* 77/50.
19. *MCPL* 19/60b-61a.
20. *HLLK* 18/18b-22b; *PKC* 11/13b; *SP* 3/14a-15b; *SC* 2a-b, 4b-5b, 8b-9b, 13b-14b; *HS* 12a-b; and *KTS* 7a-b.
21. *MCPL* 13/11a-12b and *MS* 309/11a-b.
22. *HLLK* 16/2a-b, 6a; *PKC* 6/1a-b; and *MCPL* 19/25a-26b.
23. *HLLK* 16/23b, 25b, 17/1b-2a; *PKC* 8/7b; and *MCPL* 20/2b-3a.
24. *PKC* 9/12b, 14a-b, 10/7a, 10b, 12b.
25. *PKC* 9/5b-6a; *YSCC* 5/20b-21a; and *MCPL* 17/9a-b.
26. Pien, *Hu k'ou yü sheng chi*, 26.
27. *HLLK* 18/16b; *PKC* 6/9a; and *MSCSPM* 77/51.
28. *HLLK* 7/6a-b, 8/15a-b, 16/12a; *PKC* 12/4b; and *SP* 3/11b.
29. *HLLK* 16/12b; *PKC* 11/12a; and *MCNL* 5/11b.
30. James Legge, *The Chinese Classics*, III, pt. 2, 285.
31. *HLLK* 16/23a; *SP* 3/9a; and *SC* 2a.
32. *YYN* 1/26b.
33. *HLLK* 18/19b.
34. *HLLK* 16/28b and *MCPL* 19/21a.
35. *PKC* 6/1b.
36. *MMNM* 303.
37. *HLLK* 4/20a-b.
38. *HLLK* 8/12a.
39. *HLLK* 13/1a, 14/21a, 15/14b; *PKC* 3/4a, 4/14b; and *MMNM* 206-210.
40. *HLLK* 15/21b, 16/24b; *PKC* 7/12a; *MCPL* 19/48a, 49a; *MMNM* 429-430; and *MS* 309/30a.
41. *HLLK* 17/5b, 10b, 12a; *PKC* 6/7a, 7/16b, 8/10a; and *MMNM* 416-417.
42. *MS* 309/7a.
43. *MCPL* 10/6b-7a.

44. *HLLK* 11-4b.
45. *MCPL* 16/12b-13a.
46. *PKC* 5/6b.
47. *HLLK* 12/5a.
48. *HLLK* 16/12a and *MS* 309/14a.
49. *HLLK* 16/25a.
50. *SP* 3/14a-b.
51. *HLLK* 8/39b, 13/11a, 14/11a and *PKC* 6/11b-12a.
52. *HLLK* 16/5b and Li, *Wan Ming min-pien*, 116.
53. *HLLK* 16/12a; *MS* 309/14b; and *PKC* 6/11b.
54. *HLLK* 18/1a-b; *MCNL* 20/68b; and *YSCC* 5/26b-27a.
55. *MCNL* 20/67a, 81b-82a; *YSCC* 5/27b; and *HLLK* 17/1b, 18/10b.
56. Li, *Wan Ming min-pien*, 116.
57. *HLLK* 3/4a-5a.
58. *HLLK* 4/20b, 8/11a-b, 9/7b.
59. *MCPL* 5/21a-b and *KTS* 2a-b.
60. *HLLK* 5/9b.
61. *SC* 9b-10a.
62. Li, *Wan Ming min-pien*, 131.
63. *HLLK* 6/28a-b, 12/7b; *PKC* 1/17a; and *MCPL* 16/12a.
64. *HLLK* 16/12a; *PKC* 6/11a-b; and Li, *Wan Ming min-pien*, 120-121.
65. *HLLK* 5/9a-10a, 12a, 8/41a, 14/1b-2a, 21a, 15/1b-2a, 10b, 16/26b-27b, 17/3a-b; *PKC* 5/5a, 8/7a-b; *MCPL* 8/1a-b, 11/5a-6b, 21/23b; *YYN* 2/55a, 58a; and *PWSCL*, 45-62.
66. *HLLK* 8/35a, 16/12a, 17/1b; *PKC* 6/10a-b; *MS* 309/14a, 19a, and *MCPL* 13/18b-20b, 16/13b-14a.
67. Alvare de Semedo, *History of that Great and Renowned Monarchy of China*, 99.
68. Semedo, 97; and Wu Han, "Ming-tai ti Chün-ping," 159.
69. Meng Sen, *Ming-tai shih*, 350.
70. *HLLK* 6/4b-5a, 8/3b-4a, 21a-b; *PKC* 8/2b; and *MMNM* 133-135.
71. *HLLK* 5/12a.
72. *MCNL* 1/17a.
73. *HLLK* 16/13a; *PKC* 7/5a; and *MMNM* 408-409.
74. *HLLK* 6/23b, 8/37b; *MS* 309/14b; and *MMNM* 177-182, 186-189, 198-200, 210-211, 326-330.
75. *HLLK* 10/19b-20a.
76. *HLLK* 3/6a; and *PKC* 1/7b, 8/7a.
77. *HLLK* 14/13b-14b.
78. *HLLK* 4/4a, 6a and *PKC* 1/3b.
79. *PKC* 2/11a.
80. *SC* 3b.
81. Quoted in Li, *Wan Ming min-pien*, 181-182.
82. *MMNM* 455.
83. Li, *Wan Ming min-pien*, 181-182, and Li Wen-chih, "Wan Ming t'ung-chih chieh-chi ti t'ou-hsiang Ch'ing-ch'ao chi nung-min ch'i-i ti fan Ch'ing tou-cheng," 150.
84. *MS* 309/11a.
85. *HLLK* 16/12b and *PKC* 6/13a.
86. *HLLK* 18/20b.
87. *HLLK* 16/12b.
88. *MMNM* 355.
89. Li, *Wan Ming min-pien*, 196-197.
90. Li Kuang-pi, "Ming-mo nung-min ta ch'i-i," 116.

Bibliography

Sources

Cheng T'ien-t'ing *et al* (eds.) 鄭天挺. *Ming-mo nung-min ch'i-i shih-liao* 明末農民起義史料 (Peking: Chung-hua Shu-chü 中華書局, 1954). A collection of Ming archival materials dealing with the rebellions.

Chi Liu-ch'i 計六奇. *Ming-chi nan lüeh* 明季南畧 (Peking: Liu-li-ch'ang 琉璃廠; probably late Ch'ing; preface dated 1671).

Chi Liu-ch'i 計六奇. *Ming-chi pei lüeh* 明季北畧 (Peking: Liu-li-ch'ang 琉璃廠; probably late Ch'ing; preface dated 1671).

Dunin Spot, Thomas Ignatius. "Collectanea Historiae Sinensis 1641 ad 1700" Microfilm of the unpublished manuscript in the archives of the Society of Jesus in Rome; written in 1710.

Fei Mi 費密. *Huang shu* 荒書 (Chengtu: I-lan-t'ang 怡蘭堂, probably 1860; preface dated 1669.)

Ku Ying-t'ai 谷應泰. *Ming shih chi-shih-pen-mo* 明史紀事本末 (Shanghai: Commercial Press, 1934; first published in 1658).

K'o T'ien shu 客滇述 in *T'ung shih* 痛史 (Shanghai: Commercial Press, 1912; author and date of writing unknown, but probably early Ch'ing).

Li Fu-jung 李馥榮. *Yen yü nang* 灩澦囊 (Place of publication not stated, 1847; preface dated 1723).

Magalhaens, Gabriel de. *Nouvelle Relation de la Chine*. Translated from Portuguese. (Paris: Barbin, 1688).

Mao Ch'i-ling 毛奇齡. *Hou chien lu* 後鑒錄 (Date of writing unknown, but probably early Ch'ing).

Martini, Martin. *Bellum Tartaricum or the Conquest of the Great and Most Renowned Empire of China*. Translated from Latin. (London: Crook, 1654).

Ming shih 明史. (Wu chou t'ung wen 五洲同文 edition).

Pai Yü 白愚. *Pien wei shih chin lu* 汴圍濕襟錄 in *Chung-kuo nei-luan wai-huo li-shih ts'ung-shu* 中国内乱外禍歷史叢書 (Shanghai: Shen-chou kuo-kuang-she 神州国光社, 1946; written in early Ch'ing).

P'eng Sun-i 彭孫貽. *P'ing k'ou chih* 平寇志 (Peking: National Library, 1931; written prior to 1673, date of author's death).

P'eng Tsun-ch'iu 彭遵泗. *Shu pi* 蜀碧 (Place and date of publication not stated, but probably late Ch'ing; preface dated 1742).

Pien Ta-shou 邊大受. *Hu k'ou yü sheng chi* 虎口餘生紀 in *Chung-kuo nei-luan wai-huo li-shih ts'ung-shu* 中国内乱外禍歷史叢書 Shanghai: Shen-chou kuo-kuang-she 神州国光社, 1946; written early Ch'ing).

Schall, Adam. *Relatio Historica*. Translated from Latin by Paul Bornet, S.J. (Tientsin: Hautes Etudes, 1942; written in early Ch'ing).

Shu chi 蜀記 in *T'ung shih* 痛史 (Shanghai: Commercial Press, 1912; author and date of writing unknown, but probably early Ch'ing).

Ta Ch'ing li-ch'ao shih-lu 大清歷朝實錄 (*Ta Ch'ing Shih-tsu chang Huang-ti shih-lu*) 大清世祖章皇帝實錄 (Taipei: Taiwan hua-wen shu-chü, 1963-64).

Tai Li 戴立. *Huai-ling liu-k'ou chih-chung lu* 懷陵流寇始終錄 in *Hsüan-lan-t'ang ts'ung-shu* 玄覽堂叢書 (Nanking: National Central Library, 1947; preface dated 1697).

T'an Chi-ts'ung 譚吉璁. *Yen-sui-chen chih* 延綏鎭志 (Place of publication not stated, 1673).

Wu Wei-yeh 吳偉業. *Sui k'ou chi lüeh* 綏寇紀畧 (Chao-kuang-ko 照曠閣, undated, but probably early Ch'ing; written in 1652).

Secondary Works

Donnithorne, V. H. "The Golden Age and the Dark Age in Szechwan, II Chang Hsien-chung and the Dark Age," *Journal of the West China Border Research Society*, X (1938), 152-157.

Harrison, James P. "The Communist Treatment of Chinese Peasant Wars, a Case Study in the Reinterpretation and Uses of History" (Unpublished paper presented to the Ditchley Manor Conference on Chinese Communist Historiography, 1964).

Ho, Ping-ti. *The Ladder of Success in Imperial China* (New York: Columbia University Press, 1962).

Hucker, Charles O. "Governmental Organization of the Ming Dynasty," *Harvard Journal of Asian Studies*, XXI (1958), 1-66.

Li Kuang-pi 李光璧. "Ming-mo nung-min ta ch'i-i" 明末農民大起義 in *Ming Ch'ing shih lun ts'ung* 明清史論叢 (Wu-han: Hupeh jen-min ch'u-pan-she 湖北人民出版社, 1957), 106-121.

Li Kuang-t'ao 李光濤. "Lun Chien-chou yü liu-k'ou hsiang-yin wang Ming" 論建州與流賊相因亡明, *Bulletin of the Institute of History and Philology, Academia Sinica*, XII (1947), 193-236.

Li Kuang-t'ao. "Chang Hsien-chung shih shih" 張獻忠史事, *Bulletin of the Institute of History and Philology, Academia Sinica*, XV (1954), 21-30.

Li Kuang-t'ao. *Ming-chi liu-k'ou chih yen-chiu* 明季流寇之研究 (Taipei, ca. 1959).

Li Wen-chih 李文治. *Wan Ming mih-pien* 晚明民变 (Shanghai: Chung-hua shu-chü 中華書局, 1948).

Li Wen-chih. "Wan Ming t'ung-chih chieh-chi ti t'ou-hsiang Ch'ing-ch'ao chi nung-min ch'i-i-chün ti fan Ch'ing tou-cheng" 晚明統治階級的投降清朝及農民起義軍的反清斗争 *in* Li Kuang-pi (ed.), 李光璧, *Ming Ch'ing shih lun ts'ung* 明清史論叢 (Wu-han: Hupeh jen-min ch'u-pan-she 湖北人民出版社, 1957).

Meng Sen 孟森. *Ming-tai shih* 明代史 (Taipei: Taiwan shu-tien 1957).

Parsons, James B. "Attitudes toward the Late Ming Rebellions," *Oriens Extremus*, VI (1959), 177-209.

————. "The Culmination of a Chinese Peasant Rebellion: Chang Hsien-chung in Szechwan, 1644-46," *Journal of Asian Studies*, XVI (1957), 387-400.

————. "The Ming Dynasty Bureaucracy: Aspects of Background Forces," *Monumenta Serica*, XXII (1963), 343-406.

Semedo, Alvarez de. *The History of that Great and Renowned Monarchy of China.* Translated from Portuguese. (London: Crook, 1655).

Teng Chih-ch'eng 鄧之誠. *Ming Ch'ing shih* 明清史 (Peking: privately printed, ca. 1947).

Index

Aborigines of southwest China, service as troops against rebels, 51, 239

Ai Neng-ch'i, appointment as general in Chang Hsien-chung's forces at Chengtu, 168; role in expanding Chang Hsien-chung's power in Szechwan, 172; actions during alleged systematic slaughter campaigns, 179-81; retreat after Chang Hsien-chung's death and surrender to Southern Ming, 185; importance in Chang Hsien-chung's rebellion, 207; killing of Wang Chao-ling, 210-11

Atrocities, by official forces, 12, 49-50, 96; by rebels, 151, 176-81, 216-18

Base area, failure of rebels to develop. See military aspects of rebellions

Buglio, Louis. See Jesuits and rebellions

Causes of rebellions, 1-6

Chang Feng-i, service as Minister of War and incompetence against rebels, 28-29; suicide, 48

Chang Hsien-chung, life prior to rebellion, 17-18; beginning of rebellion, 18-19; incursion into Szechwan and surrender at Ch'e-hsiang Gorge, 34; participation in Jung-yang rebel conclave, 36, 38; alliance with Kao Ying-hsiang and invasion of Nan-chihli, 38-39, 41; operations in Honan and Shensi, 41; invasion of Hukuang and Nan-chihli, 58, 60; withdrawal from Nan-chihli and defeats in Honan and Hukuang by Tso Liang-yü, 60, 62; negotiations for surrender, the Ku-ch'eng surrender agreement, and occupation of Ku-ch'eng, 62-64; resumption of rebellion and capture of Fang-hsien, 68-69; defeat of Tso Liang-yü at Mt. Lo-ying, 69; move into Szechwan, 71; defeat by Tso Liang-yü at Mt. Ma-nao, 72, 74; operations against Yang Ssu-ch'ang in Szechwan, 75, 76, 78; move from Szechwan to Hukuang and capture of Hsiang-yang, 79-80; operations in Honan and Hukuang, defeat by Tso Liang-yü, temporary refuge with Li Tzu-ch'eng, and movement to Nan-chihli, 142, 144; operations in Nan-chihli, beginnings of naval power, and commencement of dynastic pretensions, 145-49; move to Hukuang, first major rebel crossing of Yangtze, proclamation of self as Prince of West, brief occupation of Wuchang and establishment of skeleton administration, tensions with Li Tzu-ch'eng, and use of Changsha as base, 149-56; withdrawal from Hukuang, invasion of Szechwan, capture of Chungking and Chengtu, and proclamation of self as Emperor of Great Western State at Chengtu, 156-60; occupation of Chengtu, establishment of unstable administration, measures to strengthen army and regime, expansion of control into other Szechwan areas, development of opposition to, resort to terroristic policies, and abandonment of Chengtu, 167-82; establishment of base at Hsi-ch'ung, attack by Manchus, and death, 182-85; use of divination and magic, 192, 215; portents concerning, 194-95; relations with Jesuit fathers in Szechwan, 170, 196-99; divine mission to slaughter, 199; support from gentry and failure to develop, 64, 150-52, 167, 171, 176-78, 209-13; propaganda efforts by and popular support for, 80, 151, 159, 171, 218, 221; civil administrations of, 151-53, 167-71, 175-78, 211-13; organization of armed forces, 223-25; mobility of pre-1643 operations, 18-19, 62, 80; strategy, tactics, recruitment, and training and discipline in forces of, 229-37; summary assessment of, 250-52

Chang Kuo-shen, joining of Li Tzu-ch'eng and subsequent service to, 111, 121, 213

Changsha, capture and occupation by Chang Hsien-chung, 153-54

Chao Sheng, role as original rebel leader, 8; death, 11

Ch'e-hsiang Gorge, rebel groups surrender at, 34-36

Ch'en Ch'i-yü, service as Supreme Commander and forcing rebels to surrender at Ch'e-hsiang Gorge, 33-34; collapse of Ch'e-hsiang Gorge surrender agreement with rebels and dismissal as Supreme Commander, 35-36

Ch'en Hung-fan, rescue of Chang Hsien-chung from execution, 18; aid to Chang Hsien-chung in arranging Ku-ch'eng surrender, 62

Ch'en Pi-ch'ien, service as Honan Grand Coordinator, 48-49

Ch'en Yen, killing of by Li Tzu-ch'eng in Peking, 137; daughter as Empress of Chang Hsien-chung at Chengtu, 169

Ch'en Yung-fu, operations against Li Tzu-ch'eng in Honan, 94; surrender to Li Tzu-ch'eng, 120

Chengtu, capture and occupation by Chang Hsien-chung, 159-60, 167-82

Chiang Ting-chen, official service for Chang Hsien-chung in Szechwan and suicide, 167, 212

Ch'in Liang-yü, operations against rebels in Szechwan, 34, 76; defense of area against Chang Hsien-chung, 169

Chou K'uei, contribution to Peking defense, 128; death following capture by Li Tzu-ch'eng, 137

Chou Yen-ju, service as Grand Secretary and incompetence against rebels, 28

Chu Yüan-chang, comparison of Li Tzu-ch'eng to, 250

Ch'uang-wang, adoption as nickname by Kao Ying-hsiang and assumption by by Li Tzu-ch'eng following Kao's death, 8, 44

Chungking, capture and occupation by Chang Hsien-chung, 158-59; recapture by Ming loyalist warlord, Tseng Ying, 174

Ch'ung-chen Emperor, attitude toward Yang Ho's policy, 15-16; dedication and good intentions not accompanied by balanced judgment or competence to deal with formulation of anti-rebel plans, 28, 47-48, 83, 85, 113-14; response to rebel capture of Feng-yang, 39; influence of Yang Ssu-ch'ang over, 70-71, 83; consideration of proposal to move court to Nanking, 126-27; appointment of eunuch supervisors, 127; lack of personal funds in Imperial City, 127; appointment of eunuchs in charge of Peking defense against Li Tzu-ch'eng, 130; conference with Li Tzu-ch'eng's negotiator, 131; presence at two final sessions with officials, 131-32; final hours and suicide, 132; burial by Li Tzu-ch'eng, 135; use of divination, 191

Civil administrations founded by rebels. See Chang Hsien-chung and Li Tzu-ch'eng

Desecration of tombs. See religious and superstitious elements in rebellions

Discipline in official forces, lack of in armies of Tso Liang-yü and other commanders, 12, 49-50, 96, 239

Discipline in rebel forces. See military aspects of rebellions

Disorganized-raiding phase of rebellions (1631-1641), 22-89

Disunity of rebels, typical for earlier period, 5-8, 30, 206, 226; instances of friction between rebel leaders, 30, 36, 38-39, 44, 65, 144, 152; attempts to overcome at Jung-yang rebel conclave, 36, 38; substantially ended by consolidation of power of Li Tzu-ch'eng, 95, 106, 108-11, 226; general comment on, 206-07

Divination. See religious and superstitious elements in rebellions

Dynastic-ambitions phase of rebellions, 90-160

Economic aspects of rebellions, economic limitations of northern Shensi as factor in causing rebellions, 1-2; famine as catalyst for rebellions, 5-6, 81, 92-93, 190; restoration of agriculture in rebel-affected areas, 10, 14, 26; damage to agriculture from rebel seizures of draft animals, 46; tax remission for Yenan Prefecture to alleviate affects of drought, 14; relief measures by government in rebel-afflicted areas, 14, 103, 145; reduction of post stations as economy move and resulting augmentation of rebel ranks, 15; suspension of Shansi-to-Shensi grain traffic as anti-rebel measure, 14; suspension of Hukuang-to-Honan grain traffic as anti-rebel measure, 43; collapse of tea-horse trade due to rebel operations, 114; graft, 28, 62-63; proposals for tax increase by Yang Ssu-ch'ang to support anti-rebel plan, 56-57, 71, 88; Ming district princes as possessors of great wealth and as contributors to defense against rebels, 81, 94, 99, 150-51, 159; intensifying financial difficulties of government, 56-57, 71, 88, 114, 127-28; looting as a major rebel goal during disorganized-raiding phase of rebellions and continuing influence, 20, 47, 80-81, 109, 133-34, 234, 236; rebel agreements about division of loot in captured cities, 102, 133-34; partial rebel acceptance of folk tradition limiting looting in captured towns, 217; collection of customs on Han River traffic by Chang Hsien-chung, 63-64; squeezing of ex-officials of Ming by Li Tzu-ch'eng in Sian and Peking, 121, 137

Eunuchs, graft by, 28; appointment as army inspectors, 30; operations of eunuch commander in Honan against Li Tzu-ch'eng, 96; appointment as supervisors by Emperor, 127; contributions of funds for Peking defense, 128; command of Peking defense against Li Tzu-ch'eng, 130, 132; retainer joining Ch'ung-chen Emperor in suicide, 132; attitude of Li Tzu-ch'eng toward, 137-38; expression of patriotism by, 205

Examinations for granting official degrees, holding by Li Tzu-ch'eng in Sian and Peking, 123, 135-36, 227-28; holding by Chang Hsien-chung in Wuchang, Changsha, and Chengtu, 151-53, 169, 177

Feng-yang, capture by rebels, 38-39

Figueredo, Rodregue de. See Jesuits and rebellions

Focal areas for rebellions. See Shensi, Shansi, Hukuang-Honan-Shensi border region, and especially Honan

Fu, Prince of, killing of by Li Tzu-ch'eng, 81-82

Gentry support for rebels, almost non-existent during earlier period, 8, 206, 209; for Chang Hsien-chung, 64, 150-52, 167, 171, 176-78, 209-13; for Li Tzu-ch'eng, 90, 92-93, 121, 136, 213-14; failure of rebels to develop, 208-09, 211-16, 249-51

Geographical implications of rebellions. See spread of rebellions, Yellow River, Yangtze River, Hukuang, Nan-chihli, Pei-chihli, Shansi, Shantung, Szechwan, and especially Honan

Grand Canal, rebel threats to, 58, 60, 145; success of official forces in defending, 145, 241, 244

Historiography. See sources for rebellions and interpretations of rebellions

Ho Jen-lung, role in anti-rebel campaign of Yang Ssu-ch'ang, 72, 74-75; execution by Sun Ch'üan-t'ing, 105

Honan, rebel operations in and role as single most important focal area of rebellions, 26, 32-34, 36, 38-42, 60,

64, 81-82, 90-106, 118-20, 142, 144, 244-45; collapse of Li Tzu-ch'eng's control in, 162

Hsi-ying-pa-ta-wang, adoption as nickname by Chang Hsien-chung, 18

Hsiang-yang, capture by Chang Hsien-chung, 80; base for Li Tzu-ch'eng, 106-13

Hsiung Wen-ts'an, service as Supreme Commander, policies toward rebels, and anti-rebel campaigns, 54, 57-58, 64; dismissal following Mt. Lo-ying rebel victory, 69-70

Hsü I-hsien, joining of Chang Hsien-chung and subsequent career, 64, 209-10

Hukuang, rebel operations in, 32-33, 38, 40-41, 58, 62-65, 68-69, 71, 74, 80, 106, 113, 124, 142, 149-156; collapse of Li Tzu-ch'eng's control in, 162

Hukuang-Honan-Shensi border region. See military aspects of rebellions

Hung Ch'eng-ch'ou, appointment to succeed Yang Ho as Supreme Commander in Shensi, policies toward rebels, and early anti-rebel campaigns, 22-25; subsequent anti-rebel campaigns, 33-34, 40, 43-44, 60, 64-65; transfer to northern frontier, 68

Huo-shan County, importance as base for rebel recuperation, 47

Interpretations of rebellions, by traditional, modern non-Communist, and Communist historians, 252-55

Jesuits and rebellions, de Figueredo at Kaifeng, 104; Schall's appointment as military adviser against rebels, 129; de Magalhaens and Buglio and their relationship with Chang Hsien-chung, 170, 196-99

Jung-yang rebel conclave, 36, 38-39

Kaifeng, first seige by Li Tzu-ch'eng, 94; second seige by Li Tzu-ch'eng, 97-99; third seige by Li Tzu-ch'eng and Yellow River flood disaster, 99-104

Kao Chieh, defection from Li Tzu-ch'eng and surrender to government, 44; service under Sun Ch'üan-t'ing against Li Tzu-ch'eng in Honan, 117-20; retreat before Li Tzu-ch'eng in Shansi, 125

Kao Ying-hsiang, early role in rebellions and subordination of Li Tzu-ch'eng to, 8, 20; participation in Jung-yang rebel conclave, 36, 38; invasion of Nan-chihli with Chang Hsien-chung, 38-39; operations in Shensi, Honan, and Nan-chihli, 41-42; capture in Shensi and dispatch to Peking for execution, 44

Ko-kuo-yen, participation in Jung-yang rebel conclave, 36, 38; operations in Nan-chihli, 86, 144-45; assassination by Li Tzu-ch'eng, 108

Ku-ch'eng, Chang Hsien-chung's surrender at and occupation of, 62-64

Ku Chün-en, submission of proposal that Li Tzu-ch'eng seize Shensi and Shansi as base for attack on Peking, 112

Kung Wan-ching, official service for Chang Hsien-chung in Szechwan and death, 167, 178, 212

Kuo-t'ien-hsing, participation in Jung-yang rebel conclave, 36, 38; incursion into Szechwan and surrender to Yang Ssu-ch'ang, 75-76

Lao-hui-hui, move from Shensi to Shansi, 12; aid to Li Tzu-ch'eng after defeat, 65; submission to Li Tzu-ch'eng, 95

Leadership in rebel groups, earlier diversity of, 5-8, 30, 206, 226; attempts to tighten at Jung-yang rebel conclave, 36, 38; consolidation in hands of Li Tzu-ch'eng, 95, 106, 108-11, 226; general comments on, 206-08, 249-50

Li Chien-t'ai, grandiose offer as Grand Secretary to defend Shansi against Li Tzu-ch'eng, 129; capture by Li Tzu-ch'eng, 130

Li Kuo, efforts to maintain Li Tzu-ch'eng's control over northern Shensi, 163; successor to Li Tzu-ch'eng and surrender to Southern Ming, 166; importance of in Li Tzu-ch'eng's rebellion, 207-08

Li Ting-kuo, appointment as general in

INDEX

forces of Chang Hsien-chung at Chengtu, 168; role in expanding Chang Hsien-chung's power in Szechwan, 172; actions during alleged systematic slaughter campaigns, 179-81; retreat after Chang Hsien-chung's death and surrender to Southern Ming, 185; importance of in Chang Hsien-chung's rebellion, 207

Li Tzu-ch'eng, life prior to rebellions, 19-20; beginning of rebellion, modest early stature, and limited goals, 20; surrender at Ch'e-hsiang Gorge, 34; leading role at Jung-yang rebel conclave, 36, 38; participation in Nan-chihli invasion, 38-39; return to Shensi from Nan-chihli, 41; operations in Shensi, 1635-36, 41-44; 1637 operations in Shensi and invasion of Szechwan, 60; defeats in Shensi and nadir of rebel career, 64, 65; move to Honan, capture of Loyang, and beginnings of breakthrough to power, 81-82; 1641 operations in Honan, first seige of Kaifeng and other campaigns, 90-96; consolidation of dominant position in rebel movement by surrender and assassination of rebel leaders, 95, 106, 108-11; 1642 operations in Honan, second seige of Kaifeng, third seige of Kaifeng and other campaigns, 96-106; move from Honan to Hukuang and attempts to expand control from Hsiang-yang headquarters, 106-13; proclamation of self as Prince of Hsin-shun and establishment of skeleton administrative structure at Hsiang-yang, 111-12; assessment of strengths and weaknesses by Ming official, 114-15; defeat of Sun Ch'üan-t'ing in Honan, the last significant Ming effort against him, 117-20; move into Shensi, seizure of Sian, and expansion of control over province, 120-22; proclamation of self as Prince of Shun at Sian, attempts to strengthen administration, moves toward establishing new dynasty, and efforts to retain control over Honan and Hukuang, 122-24; campaigns across Shansi, 124-26; approach to Peking, arrival, dispatch of negotiators to Ming court, and entrance into city, 130-32; occupation of Peking, relations with Peking populace, moves on behalf of new dynasty, burial of Ch'ung-chen Emperor, contacts with ex-officials of Ming and extortion of funds from them, attempts to expand control in Shantung and Nan-chihli, overtures to Wu San-kuei, and decision for military confrontation with Wu, 132-40; defeat at Shanhaikuan and abandonment of Peking, 140-42; flight from Peking across Shansi, loss of control in Shantung, Honan, and Hukuang, and attempts to make comeback in Shensi, 161-64; abandonment of Shensi, withdrawal down Han Valley, and final months, 165-66; sacrifice of head to spirit of Ch'ung-chen Emperor, 190; desecration of Li family tombs by Shensi officials, 190-91; use of divination and magic, 65, 191-92, 215; portents concerning, 193-94, 196; support from gentry and failure to develop, 90, 92-93, 121, 136, 213-14, 249-50; propaganda efforts by and popular support for, 80-82, 90, 92-93, 106-07, 121, 124-25, 133, 218-22; civil administrations of, 111-12, 121, 132-38, 227-28; organization of armed forces, 224-26; consolidation of rebel leadership in hands of, 95, 106, 108-11, 226; strategy, tactics, recruitment, and training and discipline in forces of, 229-37; summary assessment of, 247-52

Li Yen, background and joining of Li Tzu-ch'eng, 90, 92-93; role during occupation of Peking by Li Tzu-ch'eng, 134-36; killing of by Li Tzu-ch'eng, 163; general comment on, 213-16

Liu Chin-chung, break with Chang Hsien-chung, surrender to Manchus, and aid given to Manchus in destroying Chang Hsien-chung, 183-85

Liu Kuo-neng, aid to official forces in Mt. Ma-nao victory over Chang Hsien-chung, 74; defense of Yeh-hsien, Honan against Li Tzu-ch'eng and death, 96; background and summary of career, 206

Liu Tse-ch'ing, operations against Li Tzu-ch'eng at Kaifeng, 101; failure to defend Peking against Li Tzu-ch'eng, 129; proposals to persuade to defend Peking, 131-32

Liu Tsung-min, divination for Li Tzu-ch'eng, 65; lack of restraint in Peking and extortion of funds from ex-officials of Ming, 134, 137; accompanying of Li Tzu-ch'eng to Shanhaikuan, 140; displeasure over killing of Li Yen, 163; probable capture by Manchus and death, 166, 190; importance of in Li Tzu-ch'eng's rebellion, 207-08

Liu Wen-hsiu, appointment as general in Chang Hsien-chung's forces at Chengtu, 168; role in expanding Chang Hsien-chung's power in Szechwan, 172; efforts to recapture Chungking, 174; actions during alleged systematic slaughter campaigns, 179-81; retreat after Chang Hsien-chung's death and surrender to Southern Ming, 185; importance of in Chang Hsien-chung's rebellion, 207

Lo Ju-ts'ai, invasion of Szechwan with Chang Hsien-chung, 34; surrender at Ch'e-hsiang Gorge, 34; participation in Jung-yang rebel conclave, 36, 38; invasion of Nan-chihli, 58, 60; surrender, 66; joining of Chang Hsien-chung in resuming rebellion, 68-69; operations in Szechwan with Chang Hsien-chung, 71, 75-76, 78; joining of Li Tzu-ch'eng in Honan and role in Kaifeng seige, 95, 102; assassination by Li Tzu-ch'eng, 109-10

Local defense forces, in Shansi during early rebel incursions, 12; proposals for in northern Shensi, 14; success against rebels in early 1630's, 32; general comment on, 51, 238-39

Lu Hsiang-sheng, service as Supreme Commander against rebels, 40; replacement as Supreme Commander and transferral to northern frontier, 54; death in fighting Manchus, 66

Ma K'o, attempts to expand in northern Szechwan against Chang Hsien-chung, 172

Ma-nao, Mt., defeat at of Chang Hsien-chung, 72, 74

Ma Shou-ying, surrender at Ch'e-hsiang Gorge, 34; participation in Jung-yang rebel conclave, 36, 38; invasion of Nan-chihli and probable death there, 58

Magalhaens, Gabriel de. See Jesuits and rebellions

Magic. See religious and superstitious elements in rebellions

Manchurian frontier troops, use of against rebels, 51, 70

Manchus and their relationship to rebellions, flight of defeated Ming troops from Manchuria to northern Shensi and their role in rebellions, 5; indirect aid to rebellions by raids south of Great Wall, 15, 66, 68, 113; role in defeat of Li Tzu-ch'eng at Shanhaikuan, 140-42; expansion of power in China and campaigns against Li Tzu-ch'eng, 162, 164-66; attack on Chang Hsien-chung in Szechwan, 183-85; 1642 pronouncement concerning rebels, 246; 1644 general notice to military commanders in north China, 246-47

Military aspects of rebellions, importance of Hukuang-Honan-Shensi border region for rebel recuperation, 46-47, 229; mobility of rebel forces and failure to develop base area, 11, 18-20, 40-41, 46-47, 52, 62, 80, 106, 112-13, 228-29, 250-51; major campaigns of Chang Hsien-chung, 149-160; major campaigns of Li Tzu-ch'eng, 90-113, 117-22, 124-26, 130-32, 140-42; recruitment by rebel forces, 229-31; strategy and tactics of rebels, 231-36; discipline and training in rebel forces, 236-37; major anti-rebel operations and gradual loss of government's initial superiority, 6, 8-16, 20, 22-25, 41-48, 50-51, 54-57, 70-78, 93-106, 113-20; assessment of Ming military efforts against rebels, 237-45; general

summary of rebellions as military phenomena, 242-45
Miners, recruitment for service against rebels, 29
Mobility of rebel forces. See military aspects of rebellions
Mongols and their relationship to rebellions, 5, 245-46

Nan-chihli, first invasion by rebels and importance of, 38-41; subsequent rebel operations in, 42, 58, 60, 64, 81, 144-49; decision by Chang Hsien-chung not to re-invade, 156-57
Nicknames of rebels, 8, 18, 252, 261-65
Niu Chin-hsing, joining of Li Tzu-ch'eng, 93; appointment as Minister of Left by Li Tzu-ch'eng, 111; proposal for direct attack on Peking by Li Tzu-ch'eng, 112; role in death of Li Yen, 163

Organization of rebel forces, simplicity of and lack of information about during earlier period, 222-23, 225; in forces of Chang Hsien-chung, 223-25; in forces of Li Tzu-ch'eng, 224-26

Pa-ta-wang, adoption as nickname by Chang Hsien-chung and possible origin of, 18
Pai Kuang-en, service under Sun Ch'üan-t'ing against Li Tzu-ch'eng in Honan, 117-20
P'an Tu-ao, joining of Chang Hsien-chung at Ku-ch'eng and subsequent career, 64, 209-10
Patriotism, expression of in opposition to rebels, 200-05
Peaceful settlement policy for ending rebellions, adoption by Yang Ho in Shensi, 8-16; evidence of in policy of Ch'en Ch'i-yü, 34-35; partial acceptance by Yang Ssu-ch'ang and Hsiung Wen-ts'an, 54-55, 57-58
Pei-chihli, activities in by minor local rebel groups, but relative freedom of from major rebel incursions until 1644, 26, 32, 81, 220-21, 240-41, 244; invasion by Li Tzu-ch'eng in 1644, 130-42

Peking, last days prior to seige by Li Tzu-ch'eng, 126-27; seige and capture by Li Tzu-ch'eng, 130-32; occupation by Li Tzu-ch'eng, 132-42
Peking garrison troops, service against rebels, 29, 70; surrender to Li Tzu-ch'eng, 130-31
Popular support for rebels, 81-82, 90, 92-93, 106-07, 113, 121, 124-25, 133, 171, 221-22
Portents. See religious and superstitious elements in rebellions
Post-station system, reduction of. See economic aspects of rebellions
Princes (Ming) caught up in rebellions: Prince of Hsiang, 80; Prince of Fu, 81-82; Prince of Chou, 94, 99, 103; Prince of Ch'in, 120-21; Prince of Chin, 131; Prince of Tai, 131
Propaganda efforts and benevolent gestures by rebels, 80-82, 92-93, 125, 151, 159, 171, 218-22

Recruitment by rebel forces. See military aspects of rebellions
Relief measures by government in rebel-afflicted areas. See economic aspects of rebellions
Religious and superstitious elements in rebellions, insignificance of relative to other rebellions, 189; sacrifices performed by rebels and others, 189-90; desecration of tombs, 154, 190-91, 194-95; divination, 65, 191-92; magic, 192; portents, 97-98, 192-96; relations between Chang Hsien-chung and Jesuit fathers in Szechwan, 196-99; Chang Hsien-chung's divine mission to slaughter, 199

Salt workers, recruited for service against rebels, 29
Schall von Bell, Adam. See Jesuits and rebellions
Shansi, rebels spread into from Shensi, 12; brief period as focal area of rebellions (1632-1633) and subsequent relative freedom from rebel incursions until 1644, 26, 43, 48, 124, 240-41, 244; campaigns across by Li Tzu-

ch'eng enroute to Peking, 124-26; flight of Li Tzu-ch'eng across and subsequent occupation by Manchus, 163-64

Shantung, activities in by minor local rebel groups, but relative freedom from major rebel incursions until 1644, 81, 145, 240-41, 244; expansion of control of Li Tzu-ch'eng into, 138; collapse of Li Tzu-ch'eng's power in, 162

Shao Chieh-ch'un, participation in Yang Ssu-ch'ang's campaign against rebels and execution for incompetence, 72, 75-76

Shensi, importance of northern section as originating area for rebellions, 1, 5-6, 244; subsequent rebel operations in, 32-35, 38, 41-46, 60, 65, 81, 120-23; attempts by Li Tzu-ch'eng to use as base after Shanhaikuan defeat, his failure, and retreat from, 163-65; monopoly of northern Shensi natives on top rebel leadership positions, 207-08

Shui hu chuan and rebellions, 251-52

Sian, capture and occupation by Li Tzu-ch'eng, 120-24; retreat to and abandonment by Li Tzu-ch'eng, 164-65

Sociological implications of rebellions. See gentry support for rebels

Sources for rebellions, confusion about rebel movements, 6; limited information in about pre-rebellion lives of rebels, 17; anti-rebel prejudice in, 147, 151, 170, 176-77, 179-81, 184-85, 191-96, 199-205, 216-18, 247, 252; pro-Manchu prejudice in, 141, 184-85; limited information in about rebel organization, 222-23

Southern Ming, brief restoration of authority in Shantung, Honan, and Hukuang in wake of collapse of Li Tzu-ch'eng's power, 162; surrender to by forces of Li Tzu-ch'eng after Li's death, 166; efforts to restore authority in Szechwan against Chang Hsien-chung, 173-75; surrender to by forces of Chang Hsien-chung after Chang's death and service to by Chang's lieutenants, 185

Spread of rebellions, into Shansi from Shensi (1630-1633), 12, 26; into Pei-chihli and northern Honan (1632-1633), 26; into Honan south of Yellow River (1634), 32-33; into Hukuang (1634), 32-33; into Szechwan (1634), 34; into Nan-chihli (1635), 38-41; rebels having coursed throughout central China (Shensi, Honan, Szechwan, Hukuang, and Nan-chihli) by 1636, 32-34, 38-42, 46, 52; more restricted area affected by rebels in 1638-1639, 64, 66; move south of Yangtze with Chang Hsien-chung's operations in Hukuang and Kiangsi (1643), 149-56; brief expansion of Li Tzu-ch'eng's control into Shansi, Pei-chihli, and Shantung (1644), 124-26, 130-42

Spy and sabotage operations of official forces against rebels, 24, 30

Statistics for rebellions, 180, 186-89

Strategy of rebels. See military aspects of rebellions

Sun Ch'üan-t'ing, campaigns against rebels in Shensi (1636), 11; failure of first campaign against Li Tzu-ch'eng in Honan, 104-05; final campaign against Li Tzu-ch'eng in Honan, 117-20; defeat and death, 120

Sun K'o-wang, battle rescue of Chang Hsien-chung, 60; appointment as general in forces of Chang Hsien-chung in Szechwan, 168; role in expanding Chang Hsien-chung's power in Szechwan, 172, 175; actions during alleged systematic slaughter campaigns, 179-81; retreat after Chang Hsien-chung's death and surrender to Southern Ming, 185; importance of in Chang Hsien-chung's rebellion, 207

Superstition. See religious and superstitious elements in rebellions

Supreme Commander, position of, institutional defects in, 240

Surrender of rebels, 10-12, 19, 24, 34-36, 62-63, 66, 76, 145, 166, 185, 206

Szechwan, rebel operations in, 34, 60, 70-78, 156-60, 167-85

Ta-t'ung, capture by Li Tzu-ch'eng, 125-26

Tactics of rebels. See military aspects of rebellions

Taiping Rebellion, aspects of compared with late Ming rebellions, 189, 199

T'ai-yüan, capture by Li Tzu-ch'eng, 125; retreat to by Li Tzu-ch'eng, 163; fall to Manchus, 165

T'ang T'ung, defense of Chü-yung Pass against Li Tzu-ch'eng, 129; surrender to Li Tzu-ch'eng, 130; service to Li Tzu-ch'eng at Shanhaikuan and defeats, 139-40; surrender to Manchus, 164

Tea-horse trade. See economic aspects of rebellions.

Teng I, humble origins and beginning of service against rebels, 29; killing of by own troops, 41

T'ien Chien-hsiu, conduct of campaigns for Li Tzu-ch'eng in Shensi, 121; orders to by Li Tzu-ch'eng to destroy Sian, 165; surrender to Manchus, 166

Ting Ch'i-jui, operations as Supreme Commander against Li Tzu-ch'eng in Honan and defeat, 95, 97, 100

Training in rebel forces. See military aspects of rebellions

Ts'ao Hua-shun, appointment to command Peking defense against Li Tzu-ch'eng, 130; surrender of Peking gate to Li Tzu-ch'eng, 132

Ts'ao Wen-chao, campaigns against rebels as subordinate of Hung Ch'eng-ch'ou, 23-24, 29; suicide after defeat by Li Tzu-ch'eng, 41-42

Tseng Ying, campaigns against Chang Hsien-chung in Szechwan, 174; defeat and death, 185

Tso-chin-wang, participation in Jung-yang rebel conclave, 36, 38; assassination by Li Tzu-ch'eng, 108, 110

Tso Liang-yü, humble origins and beginning of service against rebels, 29; semi-personal nature of army, lack of discipline among troops, and general attitude of, 48-50; tensions with Hsiung Wen-ts'an and defeats of Chang Hsien-chung, 58, 60, 62; proposal to attack Chang Hsien-chung at Ku-ch'eng, 63; defeat by Chang Hsien-chung at Mt. Lo-ying, 69; defeat of Chang Hsien-chung at Mt. Ma-nao and disagreement with Yang Ssu-ch'ang, 72, 74-75; defeat of Chang Hsien-chung (1641), 144; failure in Honan against Li Tzu-ch'eng and retreat to Hukuang (1642), 96-97, 100-01; flight from Li Tzu-ch'eng in Hukuang (1643), lawlessness of troops, and failure to resume struggle against Li, 115-18; operations against Chang Hsien-chung in Hukuang (1643), 154-55; restoration of Ming control in areas formerly held by Li Tzu-ch'eng in Hukuang (1644), 162

Tu Hsün, surrender to Li Tzu-ch'eng and service as Li's negotiator with Ming court, 131

Wang Chao-ling, unfortunate influence over Chang Hsien-chung at Chengtu, 167, 179-80; connections with Chang Hsien-chung's divine mission to slaughter, 199; general comment on and death, 210-11

Wang Chia-yün, importance of as original rebel leader and vague recognition as leading figure in rebel movement, 6, 8, 18, 20; capture and occupation of Fu-ku and subsequent death, 11

Wang Kuang-en, surrender to Yang Ssu-ch'ang, 76; subsequent loyal service as government commander in defense of Yün-yang against Li Tzu-ch'eng, 108, 124, 242; attack on Hsiang-yang, 113

Wang Ping-chen, joining of Chang Hsien-chung at Ku-ch'eng and subsequent career, 64, 209-10

Wang Tso-kua, role as original rebel leader and assassination, 8, 12

Wang Tzu-yung, succession of to Wang Chia-yün and vague recognition of as leading figure in rebel movement, 11, 30

Wei Tsao-te, participation as Grand

Secretary in conference with Tu Hsün, 131; meeting with Li Tzu-ch'eng, 136

Wen T'i-jen, service as Grand Secretary and incompetence against rebels, 28

Wuchang, capture and occupation by Chang Hsien-chung, 150-53

Wu Chi-shan, official service for Chang Hsien-chung in Szechwan and death, 178, 212

Wu Hsiang, use of by Li Tzu-ch'eng to exert pressure on son, Wu San-kuei, 139-40, 142; killing of by Li Tzu-ch'eng, 142

Wu San-kuei, failure to defend Peking against Li Tzu-ch'eng, 129-30; overtures to by Li Tzu-ch'eng, 138-39; joining with Manchus in defeating Li Tzu-ch'eng at Shanhaikuan and advance to Peking, 140-42; attacks on Li Tzu-ch'eng after flight from Peking, 161-62, 164

Wu Sheng, service as Censor in charge of Shensi relief measures, 14; disagreement with Yang Ho's policies and 1631 report on rebellions, 16; 1632 report on rebellions, 23-24; service as Grand Coordinator of Shansi and success in keeping province free of rebels, 43, 48

Wu Ta-wei, operations against Li Tzu-ch'eng in Honan and defeat, 100, 105

Yang Chan, campaigns against Chang Hsien-chung in Szechwan, 174-75; recovery of Chengtu following withdrawal of Chang Hsien-chung, 182

Yang Ho, service as Supreme Commander for Northern Shensi and policy of peaceful settlement of rebellions, 8-16

Yang Ssu-ch'ang, earlier career and assessment of abilities, 53-55; appointment as Minister of War and rise to dominant position in Peking, 53-55; plans for crushing rebellions, 54-57; assumption of field command as Supreme Commander and campaigns against rebels in Hukuang and Szechwan, 70-78; death after failure of anti-rebel campaign, 82-83; desecration of grave and corpse by Chang Hsien-chung, 83, 194-95; summary assessment of, 85

Yangtze River, rebels generally kept north of except for 1643 operations of Chang Hsien-chung in Hukuang and Kiangsi, 243-44

Yang Wen-yüeh, operations against Li Tzu-ch'eng in Honan and death, 95, 100, 105-06, 200

Yang Yung-yü, joining Li Tzu-ch'eng and subsequent service to, 112, 213

Yellow River, relative success of official forces in defending and in keeping rebels south and west of, 32, 48, 145, 240-41, 244; cutting of dike near Kaifeng during third seige by Li Tzu-ch'eng and resulting disaster, 102-03

Yen Hsi-ming, official service for Chang Hsien-chung in Szechwan and death, 178, 212

Yün-yang, failures of Li Tzu-ch'eng to capture, 108, 124